Church of England Record Society

Volume 9

ALL SAINTS SISTERS OF THE POOR

AN ANGLICAN SISTERHOOD IN
THE NINETEENTH CENTURY

This book introduces readers to the life of a Victorian religious community, both within the privacy of the convent and in its work in the wider world, based on documents preserved by All Saints Sisters of the Poor. It begins by using the memoirs of first-generation members of the community, a colourful and human introduction to the Anglican 're-invention' of monastic life in the second half of the nineteenth century. The section on government includes the power struggles between the sisters and the religious establishment, and the community's determination to retain its identity after the death of the mother foundress. The sisters nursed with the newly formed Red Cross in the Franco-Prussian War, work recorded in a diary which discusses the difficulties and dangers of Victorian front-line nursing. Most of all, the documents reveal the challenges and excitement of the struggle to establish a women's community, to be unfettered in their work with the poor and suffering, and to govern themselves, in a world largely hostile to their aspirations.

SUSAN MUMM is lecturer in religious studies at the Open University, Milton Keynes.

ALL SAINTS SISTERS OF THE POOR

AN ANGLICAN SISTERHOOD IN
THE NINETEENTH CENTURY

EDITED BY

Susan Mumm

THE BOYDELL PRESS

CHURCH OF ENGLAND RECORD SOCIETY

First published 2001

A Church of England Record Society publication
Published by The Boydell Press
an imprint of Boydell & Brewer Ltd
PO Box 9, Woodbridge, Suffolk IP12 3DF, UK
and of Boydell & Brewer Inc.
PO Box 41026, Rochester, NY 14604–4126, USA
website: http://www.boydell.co.uk

ISBN 0 85115 728 9

ISSN 1351–3087

Series information is listed at the back of this volume

A catalogue record for this book is available
from the British Library

This publication is printed on acid-free paper

Printed in Great Britain by
St Edmundsbury Press Ltd, Bury St Edmunds, Suffolk

Contents

Acknowledgements

I must first thank the Mother Superior and Sisters of All Saints Sisters of the Poor, for allowing me access to their rich and varied archival holdings, only a small proportion of which could be included in this volume. A special debt of gratitude is due to the All Saints' archivist, Sister Margaret, who combines enthusiasm with an encyclopaedic knowledge of the history of her community. In addition, she gave so generously of her time and displayed such gracious tolerance of my manifold areas of ignorance that my work became both easier and more pleasant than it otherwise would have been.

Many other archivists and librarians must also be thanked, especially those of Lambeth Palace Library, the Church of England Record Centre, the Wellcome Institute, Lloyd's Register of Shipping, various county and metropolitan record offices, the Society of Genealogists, the British Library and the Open University. The Open University's willingness to supply temporary secretarial assistance to transcribe these records also contributed to the completion of this volume. Wendy Clarke, Miriam Selwyn, Abigail Stephenson and others not only typed manuscripts in various stages of illegibility, but asked questions about the records that proved most helpful.

My research assistant, Mr Paul Short, was largely responsible for the medical and military background that supports the Franco-Prussian war diary. His erudition and diligence were also of great assistance throughout the project more generally. Alison Fincham's careful copyediting and broad knowledge of Roman catholicism was most helpful. Finally, thanks must go to Ian Merrilees, whose good temper never failed on the many evenings when I arrived home hours late, talking of nothing but sisterhoods, and who benignly tolerated the chaos of papers that grew into fossilized layers in the study. His advice with regard to the legal issues touched on in the statutes was also highly valued.

A Note on Editorial Principles

It is my intention to present a text which mirrors as closely as possible (save for page layout) the appearance of the manuscript originals. Thus the original spellings (including the mixture of British and American conventions), crossings out and corrections, and inconsistencies of punctuation have been retained whenever feasible. Capitals have been reproduced as in the original documents; italics replace underlining.

Individuals have been fully footnoted when first mentioned in the texts. This has been done, in preference to the inclusion of a biographical section at the end of the book, for two reasons. First, the Society of All Saints often 'reused' the names bestowed upon sisters: it seemed better to link the sister to the text, rather than ask the reader to sift through perhaps seven or eight community members with very similar names in religion in an alphabetical biographical section. Second, for many sisters the surname of birth has not been preserved, making firm identification impossible from the surviving documents. These sisters would have been omitted from any biographical section for obvious reasons, thus increasing the possibility of confusing or misleading the reader.

Very few abbreviations are used. In the footnotes, the only important one is 'prof.' for date of profession.

Introduction

In 1825 the idea of religious communities for women within the Church of England was almost inconceivable: by 1900, over ninety sisterhoods had been founded and were operating within that church. Although the first community was not founded until 1845, the idea had been under discussion in 'advanced' anglican circles since the late 1830s, but little or nothing was done until a committee agreed to fund the establishment of the Park Village Sisterhood in the slums near King's Cross. This was the only attempt to found a religious community by committee during the Victorian period: the committee of gentlemen, which included Gladstone, E. B. Pusey[1] and Lord John Manners,[2] were unable to find a suitable woman to lead the society. After a few years of floundering half-life, Park Village was absorbed by Ascot Priory, the community founded by the charismatic and controversial Priscilla Sellon.[3]

Later foundations followed an entirely different path. Communities were ordinarily established by individual women of extraordinary character, who felt called to devote their lives to God and to the poor. Some worked closely with a male co-founder; others avoided such associates as much as possible. Only the rare women who were convinced that they had a vocation to found a religious community would be able to withstand the opprobrium and hostility that greeted the early foundations. Victorian sisterhoods were accused of being outposts of Fenianism, of being Roman catholic orders in disguise, of holding women against their will, of financial chicanery, of cruelty to members and to those for whom they cared and of allowing free rein to power-mad and sadistic mothers superior. None of these accusations was true. But the outpouring of paranoia which greeted the early sisterhoods suggests that they pinched a painful nerve in the Victorian psyche. Combining as they did authority and autonomy for women with anglo-catholic theology, there was something in sisterhoods to offend almost all the taboos of this profoundly paternalistic and fiercely protestant culture.

Founders of successful communities were powerful women, whose combination of leadership and charisma meant that they could not only attract, but keep, other

---

[1] Edward Bouverie Pusey (1800–82), ordained 1829. He was regius professor of Hebrew at Oxford and unofficial leader of the Oxford movement after Newman's conversion.

[2] John Manners, seventh duke of Rutland (1818–1906); Young Englander, tory cabinet minister, and anglo-catholic.

[3] Priscilla Lydia Sellon (1821–76), founder of the Society of Sisters of Mercy of the Holy Trinity, Devonport (Ascot Priory).

women as members of the order. In these early days of anglican religious orders there was little of dignity or beauty to appeal to those whose primary interest was aesthetic. Houses were rented, normally in slums, habits were improvised, the offices were recited in basements or attics hastily fitted up as chapels,[4] and the kitchens were infested with blackbeetles, and required incessant scouring to render them useable. Money was always in short supply.

Not only was there little glamour in a fledgling sisterhood, there was a lot of very hard work, both in the convent and among the poor. It was a hard and demanding life. But that it was a satisfying life as well is testified to by the fact that women poured into sisterhoods, and continued to do so throughout the century; more than 10,000 had tried the life by the end of the century. By then, only teaching and nursing were larger professions than being a 'Sister of Mercy', according to the census.[5] Sisters worked as nurses, teachers, district visitors and ran orphanages. They organized some of the first crèches in London, provided midwifery and mortuary services, founded schools,[6] established convalescent, children's and accident hospitals, and sheltered prostitutes and addicted women. In general, they provided an extremely wide range of services, mostly for women and children, and always for the very poorest in their society.

The work of the sisters did not end at the convent door. Their communities became large and complex institutions, with plenty of work for women with talents for management, finance, architecture, music, painting, needlework, gardening, fund-raising, writing and public relations. All of this work was carried out within an all-female structure of authority, which made the sisterhoods prob- ably the largest women's institutions in Victorian Britain.

Who were these women? Most were of the professional and gentry classes: in the profession rolls that most sisterhoods kept, their fathers were overwhelm- ingly described as clergy, gentry, of no profession or as members of the aristoc- racy. In many sisterhoods, these women either donated capital or paid an annual sum toward the community's work; in some communities, their brains and their energy were the only required donation. Working-class women could and did join sisterhoods, but only in relatively small numbers, and mostly from the upper end of the artisan and small shopkeeper scale. In almost all communities, they carried out the domestic tasks associated with a large institution, where upwards of one-hundred sisters might be living under one roof. All Saints and some other communities did allow working-class women of talent to train as teachers or nurses; one or two even rose to the dignity of mother superior, but these were rare exceptions. Most working-class women who joined toiled in kitchen or

---

4 Some sisterhoods in their early years contented themselves with attending the parish church on Sundays.
5 Domestic service is excepted, being unskilled.
6 Schools were the one area where some of their energies were directed toward the middle classes. While the great majority of sisterhood schools were for poor children, some were also established for middle-class girls.

laundry, much as they might have done in domestic service. But there was one important difference: as lay sisters they were full members of the society, with an absolute right to be cared for in sickness and old age, as well as enjoying the dignity of the title 'sister' and the chance to pursue their vocation.[7]

Sisterhoods were founded for work; for many, the growth of the religious life of the House was subordinated to active work for many years. They worked among the poor, mainly in London, but also in other urban and a few rural areas. All Saints, the subject of this volume, is an exception to this general rule: it followed a mixed life, incorporating an emphasis on the development of the interior life with external work, from the very beginning. Virtually all of its fellow societies pursued the active life until the end of Victoria's reign, or thereabouts: the only important exception was the Society of the Sisters of Bethany, whose founder was trained in the All Saints' noviciate.

The founder of All Saints Sisters of the Poor[8] was Harriet Brownlow Byron, the daughter of the deputy lieutenant of Hertfordshire, who had been an M.P. for Hertford until catholic emancipation. Born into wealth and privilege, she deviated from the expected life of a woman of her class and time when she did not marry. In 1845, at the age of twenty-seven, she became involved with the anglo-catholic revival, and through that met William Upton Richards, the curate of the proprietary chapel that was to evolve into the parish of All Saints, Margaret Street, Marylebone.[9] Around the same time she also trained as a nurse at King's College Hospital. Together Upton Richards and Brownlow Byron first discussed the possibility, and later, the practicalities, of founding a new anglican community. Brownlow Byron had travelled much on the continent, and knew several catholic orders for women as intimately as any Protestant could know them. She had friends who were catholic religious, and who seem to have given her a privileged glimpse of their inner life, as well as of their daily routine.[10] She had also visited the embryonic anglican sisterhoods already in existence, but felt that none of them shared her vision of the religious life.

The growth of the community was spectacular. In 1851 Harriet Brownlow Byron spent six months working alone in the slums of Marylebone before anyone else joined her community. She and two other sisters were professed in 1856, and Brownlow Byron was elected superior for life later that year. By 1900, thirteen years after the foundress's death, over 400 women had been professed as All Saints sisters, and the Society was working in Britain, the United States,

---

[7] One community records the story of a former cook, now a lay sister, who still felt it necessary to confess her former occupation to the lady of title who invited her to stay to dinner. It was the custom for anglo-catholic ladies to stand when a sister, of any class, entered a room.

[8] This is the Society's official title: it is usually abbreviated to All Saints.

[9] Upton Richards first went to Margaret Street in 1845; in 1848 he was appointed to the new parish of All Saints, Marylebone, and in the same year Miss Byron made her first confession to him. From 14 April 1850 he instituted the first daily celebration in the Victorian Church of England.

[10] She had also been educated by a French governess, who was a devout catholic. Brownlow Byron retained a strong attachment to her for the remainder of her life.

India and South Africa. Many more women had tried the life and found it was not for them; others had been rejected by the community as unsuited to the life and work. This fast growth was not unique to All Saints: a number of early foundations, including the Society of St John Baptist, Clewer, the Community of St Mary the Virgin, Wantage, the Society of St Margaret, East Grinstead and the Sisters of the Church, Kilburn, grew at a similar rate, suggesting considerable pent-up demand amongst anglo-catholic women for an alternative to marriage that would develop their potential – intellectual, active and religious – to its fullest extent.

The Society opened its first branch house outside London, in Harlow, in 1860. Little is known of the work done by the sisters here: it probably consisted largely of district visiting. In 1862, they took over the nursing at University College Hospital; in 1866, they responded to a request to provide the nursing staff for the workhouse hospital at Chorlton, Manchester. The next year the convalescent hospital at Eastbourne, the first of its kind, was begun; the large hospital which they eventually built there was staffed by All Saints sisters until 1958.

The 1870s was the decade which saw expansion beyond England. In 1870 the Society commenced work in Edinburgh, where they were to stay for more than half a century. In 1871 a branch house was opened at Clifton, and in the following year the Society began work in the United States, where All Saints remains active today. The year 1873 saw the beginning of work in Bradford, and the commencement of the children's hospital there. In 1876 the sisters accepted an invitation to work in South Africa, and they moved into India in 1878. In the meantime, work had also begun in Lewisham, Liverpool and Helmsley, Yorkshire. This was also the decade in which the Society sent nurses to the Franco-Prussian war.

In the 1880s, the Society undertook projects of various types in Westminster, Leeds, St Leonard's-on-Sea and Finsbury. In that decade they took over the nursing at the Metropolitan Hospital and also accepted the gift of the Oxford hospital for incurables which today is the Society's motherhouse.[11] In the following decade they responded to calls to work in Wolverhampton, Beckenham, Hendon and Hammersmith, as well as taking over a hospital in Osnaburgh Street which had once been the responsibility of another anglican sisterhood.

This apparently scatter-shot list of branch houses, hospitals and assorted projects conceals an underlying unity. The Society was set up to serve God through caring for the sick and the poor. How this was to be done was never planned in advance; Brownlow Byron and the women who joined her simply responded to the needs of those around them; the Society's council minutes make it clear how reluctant the sisters were to refuse any call for help. Today, when the Society looks back on its own history, they see it as a pattern of pioneering work

---

[11] The Society retains the entry book of all hospital admissions to St. John's Home, from a date very close to its foundation up to the present day.

in response to invitations from outside. Eventually, within a few years, or many decades later, it became possible to pass the work on to others.

As mentioned earlier, from the very beginning All Saints was different, in one crucial respect, from other anglican communities of its generation. It embraced, quietly and almost invisibly, the mixed life. Virtually all of the other early anglican foundations were active orders, dedicated to charitable work among the poor. As demonstrated above, All Saints also worked among the poor, primarily as a nursing order. The community, along with another anglican nursing sisterhood, St John the Divine, and the Nightingale training school, was considered to provide the very highest standard of nursing available in England. But it would also seek to protect and enhance its members' careers as spiritual *virtuosi* through the pursuit of the life of prayer. Its spiritual models were Roman catholic, and the community borrowed much more directly from catholic teaching than most other early sisterhoods.

Given the anti-catholic animus of the age, the community's mixed life was played down when the group came into the public eye. What it chose to emphasize in its contacts with the outside world was its active work with the poor. As decades passed and the idea of anglican sisterhoods ceased to be shocking, the development of the internal life of the community perhaps became dominant over the active work. This left some senior members, who had joined when the community could only justify its existence by its charitable efforts, feeling patronized by their younger sisters. As one elderly sister wrote in the 1890s, 'we old 1st Sisters were trained for *work* & not for the Religious Life; therefore I think sometimes the Sisters could be a little more charitable to the older few, left'.[12]

Unthinking and virtually automatic anti-catholicism saturated British society down to the very bottom. Even the very poor among whom they worked suspected them of being disguised Roman catholics[13] in the early days. The suspicion of catholic tendencies was also the sisterhoods' most serious obstacle among the middle and upper classes whose charitable support was to become necessary to the communities' financial stability.

The Society must be understood in the context of its emergence during the first wave of women's communities to emanate from the Victorian Church of England. The first sisterhood was established in 1845;[14] All Saints followed in 1851. Like other early foundations, its purpose was to permit anglican women both to work among the poor and also to develop a regular community life for themselves.

Unlike the Roman catholic sisterhoods to which they were so often compared, anglican religious orders were seldom founded with episcopal or structural

---

12 Sister Etheldreda's letter on the vows, 1895, p. 171 below.
13 For an example of the anti-sisterhood genre, see Walter Walsh, *Secret history of the Oxford Movement* (London, 1898), pp. 162–201.
14 This was the Sisterhood of the Holy Cross (Park Village), founded in London in March 1845; the superior was Emma Langston. This group amalgamated with Ascot Priory in 1856.

support from the church. Rather, they were established by individual women of extraordinary character, who felt called to devote their lives to God and to the poor. For decades their anglicanism was largely self-defined, as the church's hierarchy continued to view their communities with outright hostility or, at best, grudging and suspicious tolerance. Like all pioneering sisterhoods, All Saints received its share of this antagonism, but, unlike many of them, they enjoyed the mixed blessing of episcopal oversight from an early date, due to their determination to have a mitred visitor.

The Texts

The size of All Saints' archive meant that including any more than a representative sample of early documents was impracticable. I have selected a range of texts, either produced in the nineteenth century or dealing with the community's nineteenth-century history, in an attempt to illustrate the kinds of documents created and preserved by the Society, as well as producing a snapshot of one of the earliest and most important anglican communities. Anglican religious communities remain neglected in mainstream accounts of Victorian church history, and it is hoped that making some documents from one society more accessible will encourage scholars of both women's and church history to re-examine such groups.

Sisterhoods were at the forefront of a number of movements of increasing interest to historians: the opening of professions to women, the changing status of women within organized religion and the internal growth and development of that typically nineteenth-century innovation, the woman-only philanthropic endeavour. The history of sisterhoods has also much to offer to an enhanced understanding of anglo-catholicism, whose reassessment has been spurred, most recently, by John Shelton Reed's provocative *Glorious Battle*.[15]

It is important to remember that the history of sisterhoods is an ongoing one. Of the ninety-odd religious orders founded by anglican women in the second half of the nineteenth century, most still exist today. All Saints most certainly does: now based in Oxford, the Society continues its tradition of nursing children and the elderly, of care for the poor and homeless, of response to calls for help, and its pursuit of what the 1859 rule called 'the love of Christ, the end and aim of all their works, prayers and words'.

Part I: Recollections of the Society's early years
Some might argue that memoirs have no place in a volume of this kind. However, it is important to remember the conditions under which the community

---

[15] John Shelton Reed, *Glorious battle. The cultural politics of anglo-catholicism* (London, 1996).

was formed. It was founded as a venture, essentially private, with no assurance of long-term success. The early members were quickly overwhelmed with practical work. During the early years of the community, there was such pressure of active work that few records were created, many of which were later lost or discarded,[16] and there was no attempt to record the history of the Society. The documents that make up the Society's archives today survived almost by accident, except for a few treasures of obvious importance.

This meant that the second generation of sisters had only the vaguest ideas about the early days, and knew little of the foundress, whose spirit, it was hoped, would continue to imbue the Society. Elderly sisters were encouraged to write memoirs of the community's early years, both to educate the next generation and to preserve the tradition of the foundress.[17] Such retrospective records have all the faults of their kind. Selective and at times inaccurate, with a tendency to ramble and to digress, they nevertheless give us most of what we know of the interior life and active work of the Society's early years.

Sister Caroline Mary's memoirs, like most All Saints memoirs, were written in extreme old age. Her 'Memories' is an account of her life from the time she first came into contact with the Society, through her early years in the community, and up to a mid-point in her period of superiority, when the narrative breaks off abruptly in mid-sentence. The closing pages of the account appear to have been lost. This document is the source for much of what we know of the community's nineteenth-century history, and gives us a reasonably coherent narrative of the Society's development from the 1850s to the late 1880s.

A second document by Sister Caroline Mary has been included, entitled 'Memories of Church Life'. This account deals with an earlier period of her experience, describing her family life, religious background and first contacts with the community. As such, it gives us a rare glimpse into the cultural and religious *milieu* out of which sisterhoods developed. The glamour and the turbulence of 1840s' and 1850s' anglo-catholicism are vividly evoked.

The final text in this section was written by Sister Catharine in 1907, who had, over thirty years earlier, kept the Franco-Prussian war diary. This memoir ('Memories of an Old Woman') focuses on the life and personality of the mother foundress, as Sister Catharine describes the period from her first meeting with Brownlow Byron in 1842, and ends with the death of the foundress in 1887. Like 'Memories of Church Life' it also places its author, the young Catharine, as an

---

16 Because of the emphasis upon poverty, there was a tendency to reuse paper if at all possible. Sisters were also discouraged from 'hoarding' items. Thus, records that would be of great interest to us now were recycled and then discarded when they ceased to be immediately useful.

17 Aside from reminiscences, the first systematic history of the Society was written by Sister Elspeth (Hodge, 1868–1970), a trained historian and contributor to the *Victoria County Histories*, who was professed in 1896. She seems to have spent much of her time as a young sister pumping the oldest surviving sisters for information (which was, strictly speaking, against the rule) and her unpublished histories of the Society are valuable and entertaining, although not always reliable.

aspiring sister, in a distinctive religious and social context, and demonstrates the reluctance found, even in devout anglo-catholic families, to give their daughters to the religious life. While it lacks the colour and energy of her war diary, Catharine's account gives us the fullest picture of the community's early years of hospital nursing, and of the early, uncertain years of the Society's life.

Part II: Government

Once a sisterhood had been established, its stability and permanence relied, to a great extent, upon good government. The rule was the essential document in the formation of spiritual and community life, as well as providing the religious framework and justification for the community's existence.

The first rule was printed in 1855, four years after the community's foundation. The revised version of this, dated 1859, has a moderated tone that is probably the result of its having been submitted to the visitor for his approval. The primary rule included here is that of 1859, which was to remain in force for over forty years. The 1859 rule is the only one to include a timetable for the allocation of the day of community members. The first (1855) rule is also reprinted in full, and textual changes and additions from the 1859 to the 1890 (revised) rule are indicated in the 1859 version.

The community's tradition is that the rule was drawn up under the inspiration of the Augustinian rule adopted by the Visitation order, founded by St Francis de Sales and St Jane Frances de Chantal, in early seventeenth-century France. The original Visitation sisters took simple vows and lived a contemplative but uncloistered life in a time when enclosure was considered essential to women's orders, nursing the sick poor. They were later forced by episcopal pressure to adopt strict enclosure, but the early history of the Visitation would have had obvious appeal to the founders of All Saints, who contemplated a community observing the mixed life, with nursing as their chief work of mercy.

Augustine's rule was widely available in French in the period while All Saints was forming, although the rule itself tended to be smothered in pious accretions. The text of the Augustinian 'Rule for Nuns' is a very brief one (eight pages in a modern translation), while a typical Victorian commentary on the rule runs to 216 pages.[18] The main precepts of Augustinian rules are charity and discretion, and the spirit can be summarized in Augustine's maxim: *anima una et cor unum in Deo.* Augustinian-influenced rules abound, both in catholicism and anglicanism, and several hundred Roman catholic orders still use versions of it.[19]

---

[18] Perhaps the best recent translation is George Lawless, *Augustine of Hippo and his monastic rule* (Oxford, 1990). Lawless also convincingly summarizes the argument for Augustinian authorship of the rule (pp. 134–5). A popular nineteenth-century edition was that of Frances Xavier Weniger, translated from the German as *The perfect religious. According to the rule of St Augustine* (Dublin, 1888).

[19] This is partly due to papal discouragement of the introduction of new rules, but the short and practical nature of the Augustinian original (*c.* 397) gives communities wide latitude in

While the spirit may be similar, All Saints' rule is in no way a simple copy of that of the Visitation. There is very little textual similarity. A number of other anglican sisterhoods, which did not consider themselves particularly Augustinian, lifted passages verbatim from the Visitation without any modification. There is none of this in the Society's rule. The All Saints' rule is very much a product of mid-Victorian Britain, in its stresses, its reticences and its moderation.

The purpose of the 1890 revision was to bring the rule into agreement with the Society's life as it had developed by that time. It then incorporated many of the traditions of All Saints that had developed over the decades, as well as clarifying a number of points left undeveloped in the 1859 version. One obvious problem was that the Society had no lay sisters in 1859 (the first arrived to begin her noviciate in the following year) and the rule made no provision for their position. The existing rules were kept virtually without modification, and several new rules were added to take account of changes in the structure of the community, largely as a result of its rapid growth. The ecclesiastical lawyer who was employed to make recommendations on the preliminary new version was Sir Walter Phillimore (later Baron Phillimore),[20] the veteran of many a church dispute in the courts, and an authoritative voice in the late-Victorian and Edwardian interpretation of ecclesiastical law.

The statutes were written in 1859. They regularize what had been the practice of the Society to that time, after the early sisters had had several years' experience of living the life. The most striking feature of the statutes is the great authority given to the mother superior in them. Other officers, such as the visitor and the chaplain, are elected by the mother and sisters, and can be changed at will. When the second chaplain, R. M. Benson, S.S.J.E.,[21] attempted to persuade the archbishop of Canterbury that the chaplain was 'the real Head of the Society',[22] he was in clear violation of statute 1, which stated that the Society consists of the mother and sisters; the function of the chaplain, visitor, auditor, and trustees is to 'assist' the Society.

It was the experience of the running battles with R. M. Benson over the role and authority of the chaplain which led to the 1890 revision of the statutes. This revision expresses the Society's increased determination to clarify and protect its autonomy. (The statutes provided the legal framework for the Society, and in that sense were dominant over the Rule: as Phillimore expressed it, 'the Statutes are

---

interpretation and observance. T. J. Van Bavel, *The rule of St Augustine* (London, 1984), p. 6.

[20] Walter George Frank Phillimore (1845–1929), judge, ecclesiastical lawyer, and international jurist. He was active in many ritual cases, admitted to the privy council in 1913 and created Baron Phillimore of Shiplake in 1918.

[21] Richard Meux Benson (1824–1915), vicar of Cowley, Oxford, 1850–70, and founder and first superior of the Society of St John the Evangelist in 1865/6. He was chaplain of All Saints after Upton Richards' death, resigning in 1890. He served as a lay preacher in the diocese of Boston, Massachusetts, 1892–94, and joined S.S.J.E.'s Boston branch in 1896, returning to the U.K. in 1914.

[22] Lambeth Palace Library, Benson papers 42, fos 314–15, Aug. 1887.

Sovereign'. However, they did not have the same immediate relevance to the life of an ordinary sister as did the rule. Each novice was given a copy of the rule to study before making her decision to ask for election to profession; the statutes were available in each branch house for consultation, and seem to have been asked for rarely.)

The 1890 revision of the statutes formalized the various status divisions and roles that had developed in the life of the Society over the previous four decades. A number of offices are described and regulated by it, and the subordinate role of the lay sisters is made explicit. One striking aspect of the revision is the concern to prevent unauthorized change to the Society's traditions: this is probably in part a response to Benson's attempted innovations, and also expresses the establishment of a regular life that is an ordinary part of the development of religious movements, once the charisma of the founder is removed by death.

Government by rule and statutes took a practical form in the meetings of chapter. Chapter minutes are a key document for tracing the internal dynamics of the Society, as well as illustrating the change in the Society's tone with the election of its second mother superior. The chapter minutes reproduced in part here are those that cover the transition: earlier minutes survive, but are much less full. The minutes are given in their entirety for the first six months, in order to give a flavour of the complete document, and after that the excessively repetitive sections are edited out.

All Saints, while run autocratically by its foundress, did use chapter as a place formally to acknowledge and ratify the decisions made by the mother superior, often in consultation with the chaplain and the novice mistress (when the election of novices was the point at issue).[23] But it could never be claimed that in this period chapter was a place for extended discussion and ventilation of issues. It served very much more of an affirming role, reflecting the confidence that the community felt in its mother's judgement.

The chapter minutes included in this volume show the community in a period of transition and crisis. They open in 1885, when the foundress was already very ill with the cancers (breast and spinal) that were to cause her death in 1887. Other sources suggest that her increasing frailty was causing her to loosen her formerly firm grip on the affairs of the Society by this time. In particular, the community's second chaplain, R. M. Benson, is shown seizing a more prominent role as the founder becomes increasingly unwell. When the new mother superior was elected after the foundress's death, Benson continued to assume that his role as chaplain was essentially that of the community's ultimate authority. He was repeatedly disabused of this, as the second mother, Caroline Mary, and the sisters, with support from the archbishop of Canterbury (confusingly, another

---

[23] It was more than a simple formality, however, as shown by the surprise rejection of a novice whom all the authorities of the Society had confidently expected to reach her profession. Chapter minutes, 22 Oct. 1886.

Benson: E. W.), insisted that the real seat of authority in the Society was its rule and statutes. Despite R. M. Benson's semi-beatified status in some anglo-catholic circles, his strengths are not apparent in this document: instead we see the side of his personality that led one former sister of this era to describe him elsewhere as 'rather dense and absolutely without a sense of humour'.[24] One of the few women to leave during the lifetime of mother foundress, an important figure and potential future leader of the community, went because Benson was chosen as chaplain.[25]

The chapter minutes show the influence of E. B. Pusey's ideas on All Saints, as mediated through Benson, who has been called 'the greatest of Pusey's disciples'.[26] The spirituality that Pusey and Benson espoused may strike the modern reader as gloomy, joyless, unhealthily repressed and obsessed with suffering. On this subject I must follow Peter Mayhew's verdict that it was probably ultimately unhelpful to the community, although very typical of a dominant strand in early anglo-catholicism.[27] At the same time, the sisters themselves seem to have resisted or ignored his rather despondent teaching to some extent: again and again the memoirs praise the qualities of 'cheerfulness, happiness, bright humility, holy merriment, and bright sunny selflessness'. In the time of the mother foundress, novices who came to recreation in a 'gloomy' temper were sent to their rooms until they could recover their spirits; so it is clear that Benson's morbid tendencies were not part of the Society's original tradition.

The chapter minutes display the change in tone with the election of Sister Caroline Mary as second mother superior. Loving and devout, her sentimentality and her soft heart made it difficult for her to govern the large and far-flung Society as firmly as her predecessor had done. Neither was she a woman of business. But she held the community together at a very difficult time, despite a number of defections. Like any elected mother superior, she lacked the special authority of the originator of the community. Defections upon the first election of a new mother were normal in most sisterhoods, although few suffered as many as did All Saints. This volume of chapter minutes closes with Caroline Mary's reluctance to take away the habits of two failed novices: an incident that displays her kindheartedness but is otherwise inexplicable, as the habit was the badge of membership in the group, and these women had just had their provisional membership revoked by the Society.

What can we make of all the defections during the period covered by the chapter minutes, and later by sisters professed during this time? Any woman who succeeds a founding mother is going to have a difficult time: everyone can

---

[24] A. H. Bennett, *Through an anglican sisterhood to Rome* (London, 1914), p. 124.

[25] This was Sarah Easton (1831–1914, prof. 1856). Before leaving because of her dislike of Benson's promotion in 1878, she had been novice mistress, assistant superior and had held other high offices in the community.

[26] Peter Mayhew, *All Saints. Birth and growth of a community* (Oxford, 1987), p. 52.

[27] *Ibid.*, pp. 3–6, 72, 185.

remember the foundress, and has an opinion on what 'mother' would have done or said on any occasion. In addition, some sisters found it most difficult to promise to obey a mother who, until her election, had been just one of themselves.

In the case of All Saints, a number of sisters seem to have waited until after the death of the foundress, to whom they were fiercely loyal, to leave a life they no longer found satisfying. This might explain those who left, as Mother Caroline Mary put it, 'for the most trivial reasons'.[28] Others left because they could not come to terms with a new superior. A deeper problem seems to underlie the dismayingly large number of novices professed during the period covered by these minutes (1885–89) who left at a later date, mostly to convert to catholicism. All Saints was to suffer a kind of slow (but ultimately healthy) haemorrhage of members trained by Sister Clementia,[29] the novice mistress during this period. (She herself was later to leave, presumably with All Saints' consent, to join the small Community of the Epiphany at Truro, where she was eventually to be elected mother superior.) It may be that Clementina was deviating too far from anglo-catholic spiritual teaching in the training of the novices, producing sisters whose tendency was to look to another communion for guidance and authority. It may be that the training of the noviciate under her leadership was not searching enough, and that unsuitable women were professed at a higher rate than was the case before or after her term of office, and that these women were to convert to catholicism in part as an 'easy way out' of their vows. We can only speculate, but one thing is certain. This high rate of attrition was a relatively new problem for the community at this time: during the twenty-seven years from 1851 to 1878, only two sisters left for Rome, both before 1860.

It was the status of women who left which raised the question of the vows. The issue of vows, with reference to both their admissibility and permanence, was a central controversy in the development of anglican sisterhoods in the nineteenth century. Could women take vows, and should they do so? Were religious vows equivalent to the vow taken by priests at ordination? What would the spiritual nature and ecclesiastical standing of such vows be, and who could release sisters from their vows? All women's communities, and the Society of All Saints was no exception to this, struggled to establish their right to take life vows.[30]

Did All Saints' sisters take life vows during the period in which they were prohibited? In 1878 Archbishop Tait wrote to the foundress, saying that the bishop of Lincoln had assured him that life vows were taken by the sisters. He was informed that they renewed their 'promises' every year, and that the 1859 service (approved by himself) was still used. It is hard to reconcile this assurance

---

[28] Chapter minutes, 7 Sept. 1888.

[29] Some of the records call her Sister Clementina; it is not clear which name is correct.

[30] This is discussed at more length in Susan Mumm, *Stolen daughters, virgin mothers. Anglican sisterhoods in Victorian Britain* (London, 1999), pp. 33–5, 143–4.

with some of the letters written by sisters on the subject, but I think it is unlikely that extra promises were made in a private, unauthorized capacity.

The letters in this section were elicited by Mother Mary Augustine in the early 1890s, when a conflict arose over the status of a woman who had left the Society. They give some indication of All Saints' struggle to have the binding nature of their vows officially recognized. They also make it clear that the internal teaching of the community differed in some important aspects from the letter of the law expressed in the rule. This conflict between two authorities seem to have created a situation where members decided their own understanding of the nature and significance of their vows.

Part III: Life and training

The rule for the mistress of the novices (*c*. 1870) is short, sensible and self-explanatory. The successful training of an adequate number of novices was necessary for the community's survival and growth. The rule given to the mistress is refreshingly lacking in sentimentality, and gives credence to the claim of one sister that the tone in the noviciate was bracing, and resembled the *esprit de corps* that one might expect to find in the army.[31] It certainly does not encourage the romantic and somewhat lackadaisical atmosphere found in some smaller sisterhoods' noviciates at this time.

This impression is reinforced by the notes on the lay novices' rule, which follow. Virtually all Victorian sisterhoods divided their members into two orders, choir and lay, again following Roman practice.[32] The division was based on social origin. Women who emerged from the small business/skilled-artisan classes and below were considered suitable only for the lay order. However, as All Saints was a nursing sisterhood, many lay sisters were trained as nurses and enjoyed careers of considerable responsibility within the Society. Many others, of course, devoted their lives to doing the community's domestic work, and this was no inconsiderable task, given the Society's size. Lay sisters held lower rank and performed different tasks; this is made clear in the parts of the novices' regulations that deal specifically with their training. They had no voice or vote in chapter; they did not even attend.[33]

The noviciate, for both lay and choir sisters, was hard work, and the training

---

[31] Bennett, *Through an anglican sisterhood*, pp. 20–1.

[32] The Community of St Mary the Virgin, Wantage, was the only important exception to this practice; after its first mother left to join the Church of Rome after the Gorham judgment, the community selected as its new mother the daughter of a local farmer, Harriet Monsell. Considering it inappropriate for a woman from such a background to govern women of a higher social class, it was decided to sink all social distinctions in a single order. Wantage, probably as a result of this, tended to attract a lot of talented women whose roots were in the working class: many had trained as pupil teachers before entering, and teaching became the community's special work. The mother of another teaching sisterhood lamented, with some reason, 'Wantage gets all the sisters with brains.'

[33] Some early lay sisters appear to have been illiterate. For these, having no obligation to recite the full office may have been a boon.

in poverty, order and self-denial was stringent. The formation of character and the importance of discipline were stressed at all points in the education of sisters. Unfortunately what survives is not the novices' rule, but remarks and notes upon it. Parts of the document are specific to the lay novices, while other sections are applicable to both orders of novices. Nevertheless, it gives us a clear picture of a demanding and highly structured life.

The outer sisters, women who wanted to follow a simple rule of life while living in the world, were an important part of community life in the early days. These were women who could not or did not wish to join a sisterhood, but who were willing to put themselves under its discipline to some extent and to contribute to its work. Many were married; many who joined as spinsters did eventually join, or at least test a vocation in, some sisterhood. Some of them spent long periods of time at the Home, assisting with the work of the Society, and participating in its corporate worship.[34] Others worked on as outer sisters for many years, contributing their money, time and often their social influence to the well-being of the Society. Outer sisters were thus an important source of both money and practical assistance for the community whose rule they followed. Perhaps their most important role was that of publicizing a community and its works among circles of like-minded women. The recruitment of Caroline Mary is an example of this; acquaintances who were All Saints' outer sisters seem to have encouraged her interest in the Society.

Two rules for outer sisters are included in this volume: considerable development can be observed by examining the changes, both in regulations and tone, between the two documents. The first is a typical production of the foundress, succinct, terse, practical. It is brief and simple, but quite demanding. The problems that secular women could cause in communities are made explicit by the rule's list of forbidden activities while staying with the Society. Interleaved with the rule is another version, date unknown, which is extremely Roman in its language and assumptions. It may be that this is a later version, or that this was additional material that outer sisters were given informally. This may have been done because such additional regulations would not have to be submitted to the scrutiny of the visitor, as the printed rule was. In any event, it is a good example of how All Saints, like most other Victorian communities, resorted to Roman usage rather than trying to recreate early anglican or even pre-reformation English historical models of devotional practice. The second version, while incorporating part of the first, is far more Roman in terminology and practice, and contains a short spiritual rule as well as rules of conduct. Taken together, they suggest that for the outer sisters as well as the sisters of All Saints, the life of prayer and personal spiritual development was coming to take precedence over active works of charity, although these continued.

---

[34] In the early days they seem to have worn a uniform dress while staying with or working for the Society; a simple grey habit.

Part IV: Work

Several community members travelled to the continent to assist in the nursing work of the Red Cross during the Franco-Prussian war.[35] While this nursing was not exactly representative of the ordinary hospital nursing usually carried out by the community, it has been included for three reasons. First, nursing was the definitive work of this society, although they also carried out a wide range of other philanthropic works, such as running orphanages. No other substantial records of their hospital-based nursing work survive; this is the only document which gives us a systematic picture of their methods of work, attitudes towards their patients and the doctors, and how the nursing work of sisters was received. Second, this experience of nursing was a key experience in the formation of the Society's identity, and is one on which they still look back with pride. Finally, the diary itself is a lively and useful document which deserves a wider audience, including historians of the war and of nursing. In another sense the document is entirely representative of the Society's active work. Part of the community's charisma, from the outset and continuing today, is to respond to requests for help. The Society's work in the Franco-Prussian war is representative of that: while the duties of war nursing may have been unlike the orderly round of a large London institution like University College Hospital, the attitude of the sister-nurses was the same.

Sister Catharine Williams's diary recounts her experience whilst serving as Red Cross nurse in the Franco-Prussian war of 1870–71. Clearly intended to be read by the sisters at home, it covers the day to day details of life in the ambulances, which were mobile field hospitals providing aid to the wounded of both armies. The sisters joined an ambulance at Sedan, and then at Épernay.

The war itself was short. In the summer of 1870, the kingdom of Prussia and her German allies[36] destroyed the military power of Imperial France under Napoleon III. This led to the unification of Germany under Prussian leadership on 28 January 1871, and established Prussia's military and political hegemony in Europe until 1918. The immediate cause of the war was a diplomatic row between France and Prussia over the candidature of Prince Leopold of Hohenzollern-Silmaringen, a member of the junior branch of the Prussian royal family, for the vacant throne of Spain. Although Prussia abandoned the candidature, France demanded a guarantee to the effect that the matter would never be re-opened. Such a guarantee would have been a diplomatic humiliation. Prussia refused, and Bismarck, the Prussian chancellor, released details of the refusal in

---

[35] Again I must thank my research assistant, Mr Paul Short, for his able and expert assistance with the editing of the Franco-Prussian war diary, especially for his lucid explanations of military and medical matters. The description of the war that follows owes much to his assistance.

[36] These included the states in the Prussian-dominated North German Confederation, such as Saxony as well as the southern German states such as Baden, Bavaria and Württemberg.

the now infamous Ems telegram, which aimed to provoke France. France declared war on 15 July 1870.

Both sides had risked this outcome in their diplomatic manoeuvrings in 1870, and both welcomed it. France was a declining great power, with an emperor looking to bolster his position with foreign-policy success. He believed the French army invincible. Prussia was dominant in Germany, having defeated Austria in 1866, and endeavoured to unify Germany under its power. A successful war would further this aim, and the proven efficiency of its armies ensured Prussian confidence.

The war itself comprised four stages. First were the frontier battles. France had expected to invade Germany, but its army, some 224,000 strong, suffered from incompetence in the French high command. The only plan was 'on to Berlin'. Prussia quickly assembled three well-equipped armies numbering 380,000, under the expert control of Field Marshal Helmuth von Moltke. They crossed the border and defeated both Marshal MacMahon's and Marshal Bazaine's armies. The former retreated to Châlons, whilst the latter fell back on Metz.

In the second stage, the Imperial French armies were defeated. Bazaine's army, 173,000 strong, fought off the Prussians in four bloody battles, but ended up trapped in Metz. An example of the ferocity was the charge of the élite Prussian Guard at St Privat on 18 August 1870. It lost 8,000 officers and men in twenty minutes, having advanced against sustained rifle fire. Meanwhile, MacMahon's reformed army of Châlons advanced to relieve Metz. The Prussians outflanked and trapped this army against the Belgian border. It was utterly defeated at the Battle of Sedan on 1 September 1870. Napoleon III abdicated and followed 94,000 men into captivity.

In the third stage, the newly created French Third Republic, under the inspired leadership of Leon Gambetta, minister of interior, called the whole of the French nation to arms. New armies formed in the Loire valley, and bands of *francs-tireurs*, or guerrillas, harassed Prussian supply and communication lines. Von Moltke besieged Paris on 19 September, and, whilst this city held, France would not consider peace talks. Prussia now occupied most of north-eastern France. The surrender of Bazaine's army at Metz on 27 October 1870, seemed an irrelevance.

The final stage revolved around the siege of Paris. The newly raised armies of the Loire attempted to relieve Paris but were defeated around Orléans on 2–4 December 1870, at Le Mans on 10–12 January 1871, and at Belfort on 15–17 January 1871. Paris underwent bombardment from 5 January 1871; its army failed in two breakout attempts, and the starving city capitulated on 28 January 1871. A weary France sought an armistice, and the war was over. France surrendered Alsace-Lorraine, and paid five billion francs indemnity.

But what of the Society of All Saints in all of this? The Geneva Convention of 1864, signed by various nations including France and the German states, enabled the Red Cross societies to operate neutrally among the combatants, providing for the 'amelioration of the condition of the wounded in armies in the field'.[37] The British National Society for Aid to the Sick and Wounded of War, more commonly known as the British Red Cross, was founded on 22 July 1870, under royal patronage. By the end of Franco-Prussian war, the Society had raised £300,000. This supported relief activity to both sides, in the form of ambulances and medical supplies. Once established, the ambulances went where directed, after consultation with either the French or German Red Cross, or the military medical authorities. Countries such as Austria, Belgium, Holland, Italy and Russia also sent medical personnel and supplies via their Red Cross societies.

The Anglo-American ambulance was formed in Paris on 28 August 1870 under Dr Marion Sims, an American, and Dr William MacCormac, of Britain. In all, it comprised a team of eight American surgeons and eight British surgeons. They went to Sedan, following the army of Châlons under Marshal MacMahon. Whilst there, Dr Philip Frank, one of the English surgeons, established a branch of the ambulance at Balan, and then at Bazeilles and Montvillet as well. Sister Catharine and her companions joined the branch ambulance on 19 September 1870. Sister Catharine mainly worked at the Château Poupart, Balan. Overall the Sisters attended to and nursed 119 French and 161 German patients. Their work came in for high praise; Dr Sims noted the 'unremitting vigilance and tender care displayed . . . by the Sisters of All Saints'.[38]

With the war now moving on to Paris, and the efficient patient evacuation system of the Prussian medical services removing their cases, the Anglo-American ambulance decamped on 14 October 1870. The majority went with Dr T. T. Pratt, an American, on to Orléans, whilst Dr Frank and the sisters sought work elsewhere. They faced much confusion and delay before finally being able to establish an ambulance at Épernay, outside Paris, on 13 December 1870.

Dr Frank's ambulance worked in the Prussian-controlled part of France, but the ambulance travelled through French garrisoned towns. In one of these towns French soldiers held up the ambulance and accused them of taking supplies to the Prussians. Dr Frank also faced frustration in getting the Prussian medical authorities to agree on a site for the ambulance.

Whilst at Épernay, the ambulance treated 162 patients, before handing the place over to the Prussians on 15 January 1871. The sisters returned to England, along with Dr Frank, who later went back to France to help with the interned French army in Switzerland.

The All Saints sisterhood received the Diploma and Insignia of the Bavarian Cross of Merit from the royal government of Bavaria for their services to the Bavarian wounded. The Iron Crosses which they were awarded do not seem to

---

[37] Emily Wood, *The Red Cross story* (London, 1995), p. 6.
[38] *Report of the operations of the British National Society for Aid to the Sick and Wounded during the Franco-German War, 1870–1871* (London, 1871), p. 12.

have survived.[39] They also received a personal letter from Augusta, empress of Germany, which thanked them for having 'stood by the combatants, on the battlefield, and in hospital, in distress and death, with help and comfort, care and support in true Christian love and self-sacrificing devotion'.[40]

---

[39] *The Times* reported on the award of the Iron Crosses by the empress of Germany, 30 Mar. 1870, p. 9.

[40] There is a letter (31 Dec. 1871) from the empress in the All Saints archive.

PART I

RECOLLECTIONS OF
THE SOCIETY'S EARLY YEARS

I. 1

Memories of Sister Caroline Mary[1]

I have been told I ought to write records of our Community of All Saints Sisters of the Poor, being one of the very oldest Sisters left on Earth. I do not know how to begin, but think it best, at first, to record all I personally have known and been and done as belonging to the Community for nearly 60 years – that is from 1859 when I was made *an Outer Sister*,[2] till I could obtain my mother's consent to receive the Habit. I was 18 or 19 years old when my dear father died early in 1857. He knew of my vocation and had spoken of it to our *Father Upton Richards*, when I was only 15. But when my mother became a widow, she felt she could not give me up altogether. She wished me to lead a life *'out of the world and devoted to the poor' in her home*. Our Lord had called me, as a child of 12, to give up 'father and mother etc. and take up the Cross and follow HIM'.[3] This could not have been in any other way, but by becoming a Religious, and entering a Religious Community. The Lent after my father's death, I was allowed to spend at the House of Charity,[4] then in Rose Street, Soho – a very bare, ascetic place; under the care of a devout woman, who was then Matron (before the Clewer Sisters took charge of the House). Mr J. C. Chambers[5] of St. Mary's Crown St. was their Chaplain.

I was able to have Devotional times and to take classes and prepare some of the inmates for Confirmation etc. and I was taken to the services at All Saints, Margaret Street *Temporary Chapel – then in Titchfield Street*, when the All Saints Clergy and Choir boys had a house, and also the Schools; for All Saints Church, and Clergy House were not then finished building. In the temporary Chapel, I was greatly impressed and helped by the intense, deep devotion of the

---

[1] Caroline Grace Millicent Short (1839–1922), prof. 1868, second mother superior of All Saints 1887–93. These memories were written about 1920, when Sister Caroline Mary was over eighty.

[2] Outer sisters help the Society in their work and followed a simple rule. See examples elsewhere in this volume.

[3] This is a conflation of several verses in Mark x.

[4] The house of charity provided accommodation for newcomers to London and shelter for servants out of place.

[5] John Charles Chambers (1817–74), ordained 1846. After serving as a missionary and chaplain in Australia, he became warden of the house of charity and perpetual curate of St Mary's Crown St. from 1856. An enthusiastic builder of schools and churches, he founded Sunday schools in Cambridge while still an undergraduate. He and his wife separated, by consent, each to live crypto-monastic lives of celibacy and charity.

congregation, and deep reverence of Choir and Clergy and Father Upton Richards' most beautiful, helpful teaching on the Passion.

I once called at 82 Margaret St., the All Saints Home, with the House of Charity Matron, to take some flowers for a Sister, who was to be '*Clothed*'.[6] I well remember the door being opened by a young and sweet looking Sister, who received the flowers *graciously*, but only spoke in an *undertone*, as it was *Silence Time*. This Sister's name was Sister Sarah.[7]

Later on in that year 1857, it was the year of the Indian Mutiny, for 6 months we heard nothing of or from my Eldest Sister and her husband who we knew were in Lucknow, whether murdered or not, we knew not. This was another reason why my mother could not part with me. But she let me go to St. Michael's School, Bognor, to help with the younger children's lessons and live a regular life away from home.

Whilst at Bognor, I met a devout Outer Sister of All Saints and a spiritual child of Fr. Upton Richards. *She told me so much about the Community and Life and works of the Sisters*, it made me long more than ever to be *there*.

The following Lent, in 1858, I was allowed to pass some time in London with my friend (who was the sister of Mr. Charles Skinner of 57 Eccleston Sq.). We kept a strict Lent and used to go to St. Barnabas Church, Pimlico. Mr. James Skinner[8] was Priest in Charge there, and his teachings were most spiritual and helpful. My friend, being *Outer Sister of All Saints Convent*, took me to the home in Margaret Street on Mid-Lent Sunday and we saw one or two of the Sisters and again the whole atmosphere, so quiet yet so bright, impressed me much. One Sister was with a few Industrial Girls[9] in the yard and they were singing, as they walked up and down, *so happily*. By Lent 1859, I had persuaded my mother to let me be an Outer Sister, and let me pass *Lent at the Home*. Fr. Upton Richards received me, blessed my medal, whereon was the Image of the Crucified Lord, and it was a great step onward, I felt, to the fulfilment of His Will for me.

That Lent *was very ascetic*. The Sisters and all of us were young and were allowed to be stricter as to food etc. than later on. There were only 9 Sisters, including our Mother Foundress.[10] There were old people in one part of the Home, and *very sick and dying people* in another, and *20 or more orphans* on

---

6 Clothing was the point where a postulant became a novice. She then underwent approximately two years of training before going forward for election to profession. In the early years, both postulants and novices were sometimes termed 'probationers'.

7 Sarah Easton (1831/2–1914), prof. 1856. Assistant superior from 1857.

8 James Skinner (1818–81), ordained 1842, was senior curate of St Barnabas from 1851 to 1856, after the resignation of William Bennett following the 'Holy War of Belgravia'. A writer of popular hymns, he became warden of the Beauchamp charity in 1861 and held the post until 1877. The vicar of the parish (St Paul's Knightsbridge with St Barnabas, Pimlico) was the hon. Robert Liddell (1818–81), ordained 1834, and co-founder of the English Church Union in 1859.

9 Industrial girls were in training for domestic service. Most were in their early teens.

10 Harriet Brownlow Byron (1818–87), founded the community of All Saints Sisters of the Poor in 1852 in Marylebone. Professed and appointed mother superior for life in 1856.

another floor of 82, and Industrial girls who slept in the attics and whose work-room was on the ground floor. Our Reverend Mother Foundress had a tiny room (afterwards the Assistant's room). The Community room was St. Vincent, after-ward made into a 'waiting room'. One room in the house nearest Marylebone Passage was used as a creche where babies were left by their mothers all day whilst the mothers were at work. Our Foundress Mother had visited and seen these Creches at Paris, managed by Sisters, and copied them. One of our Sisters – our first Sister Emily[11] – was the heart of the Creche and Outer Sisters and others worked under her. Sister Emily was a sweet looking Sister, rather large and *comfortable looking* and babies always seemed happy in her arms. She organized everything well. The babies were all fed at proper hours and put into cots to sleep certain hours, were nursed in arms or let crawl about other times.

We young Outer Sisters were generally first given '*a trial*' in the Creche. I remember being put to help there with Sister Anne,[12] then a young Lady in a pretty fresh summer dress. She was Anne Wigram and she lived and managed well her father's house in Portland Place. She used to come daily to 7 o'clock Mass and go back to her home to see to her father's breakfast and to the House-keeping, then return to the All Saints Home and work all day till 7 p.m. when she had to return to dress for dinner and be with her father all the evening – not getting to bed till midnight.

We young Outer Sisters, whilst we lived in the Home, were given our Time-tables and Spiritual Rule. Silence Hours were very strictly kept. We had our times for Spiritual Reading and times for Prayer.

When we broke our Rule, we told it to our Sister, who we were under. We attended the Offices, and I was in the *first* Retreat given by Fr. Benson *before he was 'Father'*, or had founded his Community – S.S.J.E.

I was young and strong and healthy in those days, so I was used for many things. At one time I was given the duty of 'Calling the House'. I got up at 5 and had to go down into the area to turn on the gas into the House, and then with bell and light to go around and to open doors of Dormitories, call with the Invocation, 'In the Name, etc.' at 6 o'clock a.m. I had to say prayers for the Industrial girls, and to give them a short meditation or practice for the day. After that we had Prime, Mass etc. – Mass in the temporary Chapel, until the Church was Conse-crated.

The first Lent I was in the Home, we had no butter (dry bread only), not even on Sundays *till Easter* – and 3 days no meat.

In the first very early days the Sisters, and all, lived very much on 'the scraps'. The orphans, with a Sister, used to go to Hotel kitchens and big houses, where

---

[11] Emily Fuller, entered 1856, prof. 1861. She died in 1868.
[12] Elizabeth Anne Wigram (1830–1918), prof. 1864. She was the first to wear a 'white (wedding) dress' at her profession, showing the early adoption of this catholic custom.

they had special permission, and brought back basketsfull of '*scraps*'.[13] Our *Foundress Mother and all* partook of these at certain meals. No meat, except midday meal. Bread and cheese or butter for our supper.

There was a 'Rostrum' in the Industrial girls' Refectory, where the Sister sat, who took their meals, and at dinner she *read to them*. Once, during my first visit and stay in the home, our Sister Harriet (the first one) who then had charge of the Industrials, told me to 'take' their dinner. I was seized with a shy fit and felt I could not say the Grace and so left the girls and came and told Sister Harriet.[14] She gave a *quiet bright* smile and took me back into the Refectory and said, or sang, the Grace and then left me and said, 'Now you must do it next time', so I was cured of my shyness. Then I was used to help with the old women and with the sick and dying. One night I was put to watch by an old woman who was dying. I had never 'sat up' at night before – or been with anyone in a dying state. I was told to call the Sister who slept near if I saw she was very near death. I did not feel so frightened over that as having to sing Grace and 'take' the Girls'[15] dinner. Another night I sat by a poor woman in the Infirmary who was dying of phthisis. Sister Eliza[16] had been up with her several nights and was exhausted. Sr. Eliza laid down in her Habit on a bed near and I was to call her if I thought death was near.

Our Mother Foundress used to undertake the cases, *when there were bad wounds*. There was one poor woman, Harriet Mailes by name, whose face and hands and feet had terrible wounds and disfigurement from some kind of disease. Our Mother used to let me be her Assistant and hand her the things, *lint* and *ointment*, used to dress the poor woman, and to take away the dressings taken off her. Our Mother did all so beautifully with real skill and gentleness. She used her forceps and never her fingers. It took a long time in the morning to do this work of mercy. Then Mother let me lift this poor 'Harriet' whilst she made her bed and I helped Mother to put her into it again, in an easy position. Then Mother would look around to see any others who were specially bad, and she taught me how to bandage some swollen legs with hot wrung-out flannels – also to cut a large blister, which I had never done before. There was something so *quiet* and *so strong*, so *gentle* in *our dear Mother Foundress*, it inspired confidence.

The other young Outer Sisters, who came daily to the Home to help, were Elizabeth and Louise Stewart[17] who lived with their mother in Cambridge

---

[13] Mother foundress, who described herself as 'a flirting little thing' before her call to the religious life, used to confess to a slight fear of meeting her former dancing partners while begging at grand houses.

[14] Harriet Brewer (b. 1826, d. 1876 in U.S.A.), prof. 1857.

[15] These were industrial girls, who received training in domestic work and their keep in return for their labour. Most sisterhoods had training schools (often small and informal) for these.

[16] Eliza Crofts (1830–1906), prof. 1859, assistant superior from 1862.

[17] These are the 'ponies' referred to in 'Memories of Church Life'.

Terrace near Paddington, *but came every morning down to 7 o'clock Mass at All Saints.*

Elizabeth was a beautiful needlewoman and was given the charge of needlework orders – one of the means of support of the Home. Certain Industrial girls who had aptitude were under her, and Sister Anne, then Anne Wigram, and I used to do, also, some sewing in the afternoon. Elizabeth Stewart taught me to 'stitch', and improved my needlework greatly.

There was an 'Evening School' for the Industrial Girls. Before our Laundry and Chapel were built, the Day Schools for the parish were in a large Building on that site, and in the Evening, the Industrial Girls went across there for secular teaching and also a certain number of girls from the 'District'[18] were admitted. I and 2 other young Outer Sisters helped there, to teach. Sometimes a girl who came from the District was taken into the Home and placed amongst the Industrial girls.

When the girls went up to bed, the Sister in charge of them, who slept in a little room near their dormitories, used often to see them individually in her own room for *private spiritual talks* – and I was often used as a help, to sit near, and see that half of them went to their baths and the other half were at their prayers. *Each had a small prayer table near her bed.*

When they were ready and got into bed, each girl might sit up and read her Bible, till all were ready. Then their Sister said Goodnight to them and lights were put out. On Sundays (at that time), our Foundress Mother always heard the orphans say their Collects and Gospels and gave them an Instruction herself. The children were present at Early Mass, but there was no room for them in the Temporary Chapel at 11 so Mother had them in the morning. I was often told to go and sit with them, until Mother came in, then she would go into the Rostrum with the little ones all in front of her and around the room, and I retired whilst Mother taught them. Of course she did these things all *at the beginning when the Community was small and the weight of numbers and business had not begun.*

I think, now, I had better write down all that I was told at that time and afterwards as to how the Community was brought gradually into existence and form; according to the Will and Inspiration of the Holy Spirit, who led our Foundress, Harriet Brownlow Byron and Fr. Upton Richards *step by step* until the Rule and Constitution was drawn up, written and signed by the Mother, Sisters and Chaplain; and the Foundress Mother elected as Mother for life, blessed and installed by the Bishop of Oxford[19] acting as Visitor for the Bishop of London.[20] This was

---

[18] The 'District' was the area where the sisters visited the poor on a systematic basis. Many charitable ladies did district visiting as well.

[19] Samuel Wilberforce (1805–73), ordained 1829, consecrated bishop of Oxford 1845, translated to Winchester 1869. He was a son of William Wilberforce and a great reforming bishop, with considerable sympathy for the religious life.

[20] Archibald Campbell Tait (1811–82), bishop of London from 1856, archbishop of Canterbury 1869–82.

early in 1859, I think. I must have been received as 'Outer Sister' soon after. The Rules for Outer Sisters and service of admission were in print, and the medals, in silver, were in use.

The first step in the life of the Community was the choice made by Fr. Upton Richards amongst his spiritual children of Harriet Brownlow Byron, as one who was chosen of God to found a Religious Sisterhood in the Church of England. *This was in 1851.*

The Revival of the Religious Life in the English branch of the Church was then beginning, and special priests were called of God to guide and help on this Great Movement.

Dr. Pusey had led the way and the 1st Mother of Holy Trinity Convent, Oxford,[21] had made her Religious Vows and been consecrated by him. He then took the Wardenship as Spiritual Director of 5 or 6 Ladies who were anxious to devote themselves, their lives and fortunes to a Life under Religious Rule. Dr. Pusey drew up their Rule and they lived in a House in Albany Street[22] and visited the sick and poor and taught them to prepare for the Sacraments. They kept the Day Hours of the Church and spent part of their days in prayer.

This was *before our Foundress Mother had left her home*, but she was beginning to withdraw from the world and spent much of her day in visiting poor and sick in the All Saints District and at the Schools.

Her two great friends were Ethel Benett[23] *afterwards Foundress of the Community of Bethany* and Georgie Hoare, afterward *Sister Georgina Mary of S.J.B., Clewer.*[24] These 3 girls, each lived strict lives, privately devoted to religious faith in their own homes. Ethel Benett could not leave her invalid father, but was most anxious to help her friend, Harriet Brownlow Byron, to begin her Life and there is recorded in one of our Foundress Mother's Diaries, that 'Ethel' took her to visit the Sisters' Home in Albany St. However, it was not quite according to her ideal, besides, she did not wish to put herself under Dr. Pusey, as Fr. Upton Richards was her own Spiritual Director. I have lately found a note from Fr. Upton Richards addressed to Miss Brownlow Byron, in which he tells her as his spiritual child that he had taken the lease of a house in Mortimer Street, where she could begin her life of separation from home and the world. That must have been either in 1851 or 52. It was on St. Luke's Day, our Foundress left her

---

[21] Marian Rebecca Hughes (1817–1912), took a vow of celibacy in 1841, four years before the first anglican sisterhood was formed. Her community (the Society of the Holy and Undivided Trinity) was founded around 1851, and its rule was based on that of the Ursulines whom she had visited in France in 1841.

[22] This was the Park Village Sisterhood (Sisterhood of the Holy Cross), later absorbed by the Devonport Society.

[23] Etheldreda Bennett (sometimes spelled Bennet or Benett), founder of the Society of the Sisters of Bethany, Clerkenwell. The community originally attracted women whose health was not robust enough to stand the life of the other anglican sisterhoods: their main function was the giving of retreats for laywomen.

[24] She was professed at Clewer in 1865, and died in 1905.

home and came to this house and took in 2 or 3 aged and infirm women and 3 or 4 little orphans from the District. I think she also took some women to help her. But she herself used to clean the lamps (there was no gas in those days) and scrub the floors. The children got Scarlet Fever and she nursed them entirely by herself. She had the superintendence of the day schools, not then under Government, but supported by the Church people. Very soon a young girl came from Plymouth to help her and also to dedicate her life to God – Miss Sarah Easton[25] – and almost at the same time came our *first* Sister Harriet and then Sister Eliza – all 3 very young. There was also a Miss Ellen Wilson,[26] who became '*a thorn*' and although she continued for a time, she departed as soon as it was decided that Mother Foundress should be Mother Superior for life. When there were 4 or 5 aspirants, including the Foundress Mother, a Religious Rule was drawn up; it was *upon the Constitution of St. Augustine*;[27] there was to be a Novitiate of one year and one day before they took the Religious Vows. By degrees, their Life and work developed and whilst the 3 houses in Margaret St., 82, 83, and 84 were being made into *one Religious House*, our Foundress Mother lived at No. 8 Margaret St. with some of their work, and other Sisters and work went on in Mortimer St. *where also was their Chapel or Oratory.*[28]

In 1858, as far as I know, they were *all in the All Saints Home* in Margaret St., and the *Mortimer Street House*, with some incurables, was *managed by an Outer Sister – for a while*.

Before or by 1859 our Rule and Constitution was drawn up and made a *legal* document, because Dr. Pusey had been subject to great persecution and worry on account of some Lady who had become a fully Professed Sister in Miss Sellon's Community under Dr. Pusey and who had given her whole fortune to the Sisterhood and turned Roman and left the Community and tried to claim back all the money she had given.[29] There was no legal right to keep it, yet as it had been mostly spent, it was not possible to return it. Therefore, it was thought safer in *those days* to make *our Constitution legal* and *our signatures at our Profession* were *legal*.

As these first early years went on, our Foundress Mother, more and more, brought the Community into greater Religious Order and *strictness of Rule*, so that I, who then first became in close touch with it, so very often passed *long*

---

[25] Sarah J. Easton (1831–1914), prof. 1856, assistant superior, novice mistress, and first superior at the Cape. She left the community in 1877 or 1878.

[26] Ellen Wilson entered in 1856 and was professed the same year. She left in 1857.

[27] As mentioned in the introduction, the Augustinian influence may be there, but it is not overt.

[28] The Society did not have a purpose built convent for a mother house until the twentieth century, when they moved to London Colney. These houses were joined by interior doors.

[29] The Devonport rule (published in 1849) begins: 'Rule 1. A legal instrument has been prepared, by which certain of the Sisters have agreed to live together . . . but with free liberty to any sister to withdraw if it shall so seem good to her. Rule 2. Any Sister so withdrawing, or in any way ceasing to be a member of the Society, shall be entitled to her own personal property; but neither she nor her heirs shall be entitled to any share of the common property of the Society.'

visits and *lived* and *worked* for *weeks together* at *All Saints Home* just at that time of our history, can indeed *testify* to the *beautiful, impressive,* true *Order and Strictness of Life and Rule* in *which the Sisters lived and worked.* I remember, for instance, how at 11 a.m. one saw the Sisters in the Chapel at their Spiritual Reading – How silent and quiet all were during Silence Hours – even the Portress Sister, speaking when necessary to those she let in, *in an undertone or whisper.* The orphans and the girls kept strict silence on the *stairs.* The peace and *quietness* of the House was very impressive.

There were illuminated texts over various doors which impressed one, such as 'For your sakes He became *Poor*', etc. and 'Here we have no continuing City' and over the door going out 'The Lord is with thy going out and coming in', etc.

Before our Chapel and Refectory were built – (I think they were built before the Church was Consecrated),[30] the Oratory was a large room in no. 84. We went up to it by the stairs close to the Dispensary, and the Chancel of the Oratory was over the Dispensary and close to what is called *Marylebone Passage* and the poor people used to come to a *door* that side, for medicines and to have 'sores' dressed in the Dispensary. The door opened into a yard where was the *Mortuary Chapel. From the very beginning* there was always the *Mortuary Chapel* where poor or rich could bring the bodies of their dear ones to wait for Burial – and the poor of the District came to that yard door for medicine, or anything they wanted.[31] The Sister in the Dispensary attended to them.

Our Sister Eliza was professed in the *old Oratory* on *August 4th*, St. Dominic's Day 1859. It was the first Profession I had ever seen. The Profession Office was in manuscript – it had not then been printed – but she made her vows as we did afterward when the Office was printed. The address was given by Mr. George Yard[32] who was then *sub Chaplain* and a very holy spiritual priest. It was on St. James leaving his father and all that he had and following JESUS without delay – he made a great point of its being without delay. Sister Anne and I being then only *longing aspirants* wished greatly we could follow on 'without delay'. But we had to wait till the way was possible.

I was summoned to the Home for the Consecration of the Chapel (*when it was built*) – it was in the summer, but I forget the exact date. I did not wear my black dress but had a simple grey one. When Mother Foundress saw me, she said, '*Now what a pity the child is in grey*!! I meant you to go into one of the *stalls*, now you *can't.*' Of course that was a disappointment for me! At that time the Community

---

[30] All Saints, Margaret Street was consecrated in 1859.

[31] Mortuary chapels were very popular, as in the days before commercial funeral parlours were established, the poor had nowhere except their cramped living quarters in which to keep their dead, which often meant that the corpse was laid out on the kitchen table.

[32] George Beckwith Yard (1835–73), a friend of Keble and other Oxford movement leaders. He was rector of Wragby, Lincs., 1842–59; became curate of All Saints, Margaret Street, and converted to catholicism in 1863. He was afterwards a Roman catholic priest in Bayswater.

did not number Sisters enough to fill all the stalls in Chapel. *They are the same stalls as are in our Chapel now in Margaret St.*

What became afterwards our Refectory underneath the Chapel, was at first used as the Orphans' Dormitory. Before I was Clothed I sometimes had to sleep in the little room off the Dormitory and take charge of the children by night. I remember one child being ill with earache and I took her into my bed to soothe and comfort her up. Some of the orphans were very tiny children. As soon as they were 14 – sometimes 13 – they passed from the Orphanage to the Industrial girls who were also under a Sister's care – but did their work under whichever Sister was over that work. In the kitchen *under Sister Eliza,*[33] *Housework under another, Needlework under another.* Needlework was a great feature of the Industrial School, for Needlework orders were taken as part of the support of the Home. Sister Sarah, and Elizabeth Stewart – Outer Sister – were the great teachers and Superintendents of the Needlework (in the *early days before there were any Lay Sisters*).

The next step as I remember was the *1st Lay Sister's Reception.* Our *1st*, Sister *Martha*[34] – who was indeed a Saint and finally died for Our Lord from Typhus Fever when nursing at Chorlton Union Infirmary,[35] where we were called to nurse at a terrible outbreak of this fever in *Manchester.* Sister Martha was a bright, cheerful little Sister. She was the *first* Lay Sister, so it seemed a little lonely – but very soon others came in and were clothed and their Rule settled. Soon after this (again I forget the year) we took up the nursing of *University College Hospital*, but there were steps toward this. First, I remember, when I was still an Outside Aspirant, I was told off to accompany a Sister when she went to U.C.H. *merely as a 'looker on'* to learn how wounds were dressed. We went in the morning and from bed to bed I stood and 'looked on' while the 'Dresser' and nurse attended to the wounds. In those days wounds were kept open and dressed and redressed, causing much agony to the sufferers. It made me feel very bad and one day, when a child's ankle was being dressed, *roughly*, I thought, for excision of the ankle bone, I went off into a dead faint. After I got back to the Convent, to my sorrow, Mother Foundress would not *let me go any more!* So I did not go *until we had taken up the Nursing ourselves.*

About this time, *Sister Elizabeth*[36] *entered the community* and soon after was sent to take up *two* wards (5 and 6) at U.C.H.[37] The Committee wished to see how we Sisters could work them. Very soon the two wards were in such order

---

[33] Sister Eliza was housekeeping sister as well as assistant superior in the early days. When the lay order was established, she became their mistress.

[34] Christian Mann, entered 1859, clothed in 1860, professed 1863. (Lay sisters generally had a longer noviciate than choir sisters). She died in 1868, in Chorlton, Manchester.

[35] Chorlton Union was in Salford. The parish church was St Clements.

[36] Elizabeth Simcox (1830–1919), prof. 1863. She was made sister superior of the nursing at University College hospital while still a novice.

[37] All Saints provided the nursing for University College hospital from 1860 to 1899.

and comfort and refinement that the Committee begged Mother Foundress to take up the *whole nursing of the hospital.*

One day in the summer of 1860(?)[38] I was summoned from my home to come up and help the Sisters take over the U.C. Hospital. *Well* do I remember it! The mess and confusion of the wards which had been in the hands of the Gamps – bad nurses – women who used to drink the patients' stimulant ordered by the doctors and have up the porters and men of the Hospital to *carouse* in the night. Sir Wm. Jenner[39] told our F. Mother he had come upon one of their 'night porters' cooking a chicken before the Ward fire, drinking hot brandy and water and the patients utterly neglected and everything most dirty and untidy. No work-house nowadays could be so *shockingly* attended.

All these women were cleared off that day. Our Sisters took up the charge. But they had *hard* work to get it into decent order. *Sister Jane*[40] (afterwards sent to America) had charge of two wards and I was told off to be her 'scrub' and assistant and I had to keep up the fires and clean all the crockery and the medical glasses and to make poultices and attend on special helpless patients.

In a very few days Everything *improved* and our M. Foundress and Sister Elizabeth, who was made S. Superior, soon transformed the whole Hospital, much to the satisfaction of the head Physicians and Surgeons.

After this, any Outer Sisters waiting to enter the Novitiate and having special drawings to nursing were sent to U.C.H. to help and to learn. So it came to pass I often was sent. I had to be at U.C.H. by 9 a.m. and stayed all day, returning for Supper and Compline to the Home. The Lesser Hours and Vespers I was allowed to say with the Sisters in their Oratory on the Top floor of the Hospital which was given up to them for Cells, Community Room, Refectory and Oratory. My dinner and tea were sent to me down in a private ward adjoining the big ward where I worked. I was used mostly in the Medical Ward as I shrank from surgical operations in those days *and the Hospital Theatre.* I went on learning and helping at U.C.H. until 1866, Feb. When at last my mother's consent was procured, and I entered as Postulant into the Novitiate on the Vigil of St. Matthew, I was given by the Mistress a meditation on the fall of Judas, *Be not high minded but fear*, and sent to Chapel for rest of the Evening.

During the years between 1860 and 66, my memory is not so clear as to events and progress of the Community. There was the Consecration of the Church and the Community grew in numbers. The Sisters Jane and Constance and Helen and

---

[38] Caroline Mary's memory is correct.

[39] William Jenner (1815–98), the son of an innkeeper, qualified as a surgeon in 1837, and became an M.D. in 1844. He published important works on a number of medical subjects, and was physician at University College hospital, the hospital for Sick Children, and London Fever hospital. In 1861 he was appointed physician to the royal family.

[40] Jane Cowing (b. 1807, d. 1892 or 1898 in U.S.A.), prof. 1862. She had previously been a sister at Highgate, an irregular and unsuccessful attempt to found a sisterhood to work with 'fallen women' at the Highgate House of Mercy. The Highgate work was eventually taken over by the community of St John Baptist, Clewer.

Anne and Margaret and Etheldreda and Elizabeth and Emily Mary and others entered the Community about this time, also our Sister Rosamund.

Soon after the Hospital work began, the necessity for a Convalescent Hospital became very pressing. It was then our Foundress Mother began a Home at Eastbourne[41] for about 30 Convalescent patients and then she conceived and brought about the Building of our All Saints Hospital. She did not only conceive the plan for Convalescents alone, but also that it *should be worked by Religious* as she had seen and known in Hospitals abroad – also in Building a separate wing for Sisters[42] and ordering a proper Community Room, Refectory and Tribune for the Offices and Hours, where the Novices and young Professed could come and find all Regular and in order for their lives as Religious. The building of the Hospital was a stupendous work and only begun and carried out and completed by the power of prayer and Perseverance. It was the first Seaside Convalescent Hospital in England and it was the first Hospital founded and worked by Religious of the Church of England, therefore the Clergy and leaders of the Catholic Revival took great interest in the work.

It is well at this part of our Community History to tell something of the holy lives of some of our *Earliest* Sisters and I can specially recall two or three who particularly impressed me, when first I worked and stayed at All Ss. Home.

1st. Our Sister Harriet,[43] her bright spiritual and highly intellectual sacrificial every day life, was an inspiration to me from the first. She taught me spiritual meanings to *flowers*. The single eye toward God of the Daisy, the Presence of God in the turning of the sunflower always to the Sun, etc. She took the Industrial girls' secular night school at one time and always in her lessons drew out spiritual meaning. She was always ready and cheerfully obedient in passing from one work to another, never a shade over her bright face. Very ascetic herself, very tender and lenient to others. She it was who drew up and started all our Confraternities under our F. Mother with Fr. Upton Richards' approval. She had just started the one for young women when she was called off at a day's notice to go with F. Mother and Sisters to nurse the sick and wounded in the Franco-Prussian war. She went as brightly obedient as an angel would have done, and when out there took the hardest part, the night nursing. On her return, she was sent off to begin our school at Clifton under Mr. Randall of All Ss. Clifton so never returned to her Confraternity girls in London – and from Clifton, just as she had got the school and other things started, she was sent to be Superior of our newly taken up work at Baltimore.[44] There she died, as she had lived, wholly devoted in love and obedience.

2nd. Our first Sister Charlotte. She was not strong and was deaf but she was

---

[41] This was in the late 1860s; the hospital was opened in 1869.
[42] Twelve lay sisters and a few choir sisters regularly staffed this hospital.
[43] Harriet Brewer (b. 1826, d. 1876, in U.S.A.), prof. 1857. Novice mistress from 1860.
[44] Sister Harriet arrived in the U.S.A. around 1874, a little over a year since the establishment of the first All Saints sisters there.

Church Sacristan[45] and used, with two orphans to help her, to wash and scrub the Sanctuary and keep all the Holy Vessels and Linen in order and wash and iron the Palls and Chalice Veils – of exquisite texture and Embroidery. She used with 2 orphans to go out scrapping, a daily calling on the kitchens and waiting till the scraps were put into the baskets by the cooks. Sister Charlotte was deaf – she always sat next to Mother Foundress at Recreation and Every now and again Mother would turn to her and tell her of the subject of conversation. Sister Charlotte would give a smile that brightened her whole face and make some remark which always edified as she had beautiful thoughts about the commonest things. She spent long times in Prayer in the Chapel. I often saw her kneeling turned toward one of the Stations of the Cross we then had in Chapel, absorbed in Prayer. She used often to tell me she *prayed* that my mother would soon be able to give me up, and I verily believe that after her death her prayer prevailed. She died December 1865 and in February 1866 I obtained my mother's consent and entered the Novitiate as Postulant.

3rd. Sister Mary Elizabeth[46] – the first – and our first Sister Margaret[47] also were *both wonderful* in their Vow of Poverty. Not only by the complete abnegation of all possession they practised, but their untiring and holy devotion to the very *Poor*. S. Mary Elizabeth never worked amongst the Poor, except in All Saints District which in those days was closely *packed* with poor. There were no Fever Hospitals, etc. in those days, and Scarlet Fever and small pox often broke out. Sister Mary Elizabeth caught small pox visiting a family, and died of it 2 days before S. Charlotte – they were buried together at Brompton. Sister Margaret was sent to our Edinburgh Mission later on and lived and worked there for some years. Her *bright* Humility was a beautiful example of poverty. She had no 'possessions' except a *small* little old basket for her needlework and her Bible and Prayer Book. Once when she broke her spectacles, she uncomplainingly went without – though short sighted, and blind as a bat till the Assistant Superior paid a visit to the poor (very poor, then) Mission House at Edinburgh and got some new spectacles for Sister Margaret. In the world, M. Foundress told us, she *had had possessions* which she *gave up* to Enter Religion, as a Sister of the Poor of All Saints.[48]

4th. Sister *Rosamund*[49] is another of our Saintly early Sisters. She was trained for Nursing at U.C.H. She was artistic and painted flowers from nature. She painted all the first big texts put up over the doors of the Wards at the Eastbourne Hospital – also the iron bannisters of the great staircase. Then she was sent to head the Nursing of the *Typhus* and *smallpox* epidemic at Chorlton Union Infirmary near Manchester. It ended in her remaining in charge of the Infirmary there with one Sister as her companion. This 2nd Sister was often changed, but Sister

---

45 The sacristan's duties were to keep the chapel in proper order.
46 Mary Elizabeth Kergwin, prof. 1861, died 1865. She was a cousin of Upton Richards.
47 Margaret Wilkinson (1823–83), prof. 1863.
48 Her family was extremely wealthy; she brought a small fortune in diamonds into the Society.
49 Rosamund Buckley (b. 1824, d. 1879 in India), prof. 1865.

Rosamund was left year after year[50] – for her saintliness never diminished but grew and her faithfulness to our Rule and Spirit *never* languished. Whenever she was at the Mother House for a short visit and refreshment, she was as simple and regular as the latest Professed.

I once spent the night with her at Chorlton Union. She had to ask the Master of the Union for my rations. The cells we slept in were quite workhouse cells, etc. Sister Rosamund's one little sitting room with its poor furniture served as Refectory and Oratory, the big Crucifix was the only one thing which belonged to us there.

We had to walk about 1½ miles to a Church in Manchester for our Early Communion.

Sister Rosamund, when she got the Protestant Chaplain to give the poor infirm people Communion, it was always fixed *late*, but she *fasted* in order to receive Communion with her sick people. No wonder they loved her as a Mother; and for 13 years she persevered in her wonderful life then she failed in health and as things did not improve with regard to Catholic Chaplain or doctor or Guardians – the Foundress Mother withdrew from the work.

In 1877, Fr. Page[51] pleaded for some of the Sisters for Bombay. Sister Rosamund, Sister Gladys[52] and Sister Vincent[53] were chosen and sent out to India,[54] but not for long for Sr. Rosamund, as before one month had passed she was called to her LORD. Fr. Page wrote a full and beautiful account of her saintly death to Mother Foundress.

I had been sent to our Capetown Mission the end of 1877.[55]

Others of our Early Sisters were notable for their saintliness. Sister Emily Mary, Sister Maria Francesca,[56] S. Harriet Mary and others. Each one, a great example of a true holy Religious of All Saints – and for whose holy lives and

---

50 She spent thirteen years in Edinburgh.

51 Robert Lay Page (1839–1912), ordained 1863, vicar of Coatham, Yorks, 1866–70. He joined S.S.J.E. in 1870, went to India in charge of the S.S.J.E. mission in 1873, and was appointed incumbent of St Peter's Mazagon, Bombay in 1875. He was the S.S.J.E.'s second superior (1890–07), and returned to India in 1908. At some point he also became the spiritual advisor to the community of the Holy Rood in Yorkshire.

52 Secular name unknown, prof. 1877, died 1899, in India. She was the first mother superior of the Indian affiliate.

53 Secular name unknown, prof. 1874, died 1881, in India.

54 All Saints arrived in India in December 1878. They worked in the Cottage hospital in Bombay, and ran the very large Jamshijdjc native hospital from 1882. They had a home for unwanted children at Unarkhadi, and in 1884 opened Bombay cathedral high school for girls, with its boarding house, and in the same year took charge of the nursing at St George's European hospital. In 1897 they took over the diocesan high school for girls in Naini Tal, and nursed in the cholera epidemics of 1896 and subsequently.

55 The first sisters went out in 1876; they ran an orphanage, a boarding school, a penitentiary for fallen women, and nursed lepers.

56 Maria Francesca Rosetti (1827–76), associate from 1860, prof. 1875. Sister of the poet Christina Rosetti, she entered All Saints after her brother William's marriage. She translated the day hours from Latin for the use of the community.

deaths we do indeed give *thanks* – and look upon them as foundation stones of our Community and be glad that they belong to us and we belong to them.

Here, I think it well to tell of our Foundress Mother's frequent visits to France – *Paris*, and Belgium, Bruges and Ghent and later on in her life to Italy, Florence and Rome! Paris was like a home to her, as she had lived there with her parents as a child and under her French governess, who she loved very much, she was Educated till her Early 'teens'. She knew the Churches well and was in touch with Religious Orders. Later on in life, when preparing for her Life-work of founding – or beginning a Religious Order in our English Branch of the Church – she stayed in one of the Convents of the Visitation – and was on cordial terms with the St.Vincent de Paul Sisters and with a Religious Community of 'Mt. Sion'[57] who had Houses in Palestine. She knew one of the Nuns intimately and from *her* our Mother Foundress gathered many 'customs' such as wearing a bride's dress when received as a Novice, the mode of giving the 'Kiss of Peace', Monotoning our Psalms at Lesser Hours, etc. At Paris and Bruges, she also got in touch with holy Ecclesiastics – one especially at Bruges Who evidently hoped to get her as a Convert, and on one occasion Mother's *Obedience* saved her, as Father Upton Richards thought good that she should leave Bruges and return at once to England and go to Dundee for a visit to the great saint and learned doctor of the Church, Alexander Forbes,[58] Bishop of Brechin. He was always a great friend to All Saints and used to visit All Saints Home when in London and give us all his Blessing, as he met any of us.

The visits to Florence and Rome were much later on in our Foundress' life. The Community had grown and become well established, so that these visits were purely for *rest* and climate. All these yearly visits abroad were *ordered* by her physician and with direct permission from the Chaplain and Director of our Community, Fr. Upton Richards, whilst he lived and Fr. Benson, after his death. Fr. Upton Richards' health and strength was declining for a year or more before his death and he had passed us on spiritually to the guidance of Fr. Benson, before he was Fr. Benson – that is, before he had founded his own Order of S.J.E.;[59] and after he *had* founded his Society, and Father Grafton,[60] Fr. Prescott and Fr. O'Neil[61] joined the S.J.E. we had regular Retreats, generally about All

---

[57] The Daughters of Sion were founded in 1843 in Paris. Their object was the conversion of the Jews, and their rule was Augustinian.

[58] Alexander Penrose Forbes (1817–75), ordained 1844; spent three years with the East India company in Madras; vicar of St Saviour, Leeds, 1847; bishop of Brechin, 1848. Censured for promulgating the doctrine of the real presence in 1860. An intimate of friend of E. B. Pusey and member of the Scots noble house of Forbes.

[59] Caroline Mary drops the initial 'S' in S.S.J.E.

[60] Charles Chapman Grafton (1830–1912), ordained 1865, went to England in 1865 to join S.S.J.E., left S.S.J.E. in 1875 or 1882 (sources disagree), consecrated bishop of Fond du Lac 1889.

[61] Simon Wilberforce O'Neil (1837–82), ordained 1863, and served as a curate at Clewer (1861–3) and Wantage (1863–4); joined S.S.J.E. in 1865, went to India 1874, established a mission in the Calcutta diocese in 1875, and worked among the poor rather than attempting conversion.

Saints-tide, before or after the Festival, Retreats of four days conducted by Fathers, Fr. Benson, or one of their Fathers.

When Fr. Upton Richards died on June 16th, 1873, it became, as it were, natural that we should pray Fr. Benson to become our Chaplain and Spiritual Director and he consenting, remained so, until he resigned his own Superior-ship in 1890 and went to America. Fr. Page became Superior of S.S.J.E. and at our earnest request consented to be the Chaplain General and Director of our All Saints Community.

To go back a little in these annals, in 1866, the desire of my heart was granted and years of waiting over, so I was 'Clothed' as a Novice on October 13th, 1866. I remember I was not told the name I should bear in Religion until I heard it in Chapel as I knelt before the Altar and Father Richards said 'We receive you Sister Caroline Mary as a Novice, etc.' I was clothed in our Chapel as it is now, also I was professed there two years afterwards. I had been working under Sisters, up to the time I entered the Novitiate, and the day after my Clothing I was put in Charge of our Infirmary in the Home, with other Novices and Postulants under me. I was under the Mistress, who frequently visited the work and corrected what was amiss or gave directions. To my joy, also our Mother Foundress often came round to visit the old and sick people. She too would point out any thing she thought untidy, or not well done, just as she did when she came round the wards at U.C. Hospital with Sister Elizabeth. She was most particular that the patients' quilts should hang straight and all be alike and that *baskets* under the beds containing patients' clothing should be *straight* and tidy. She would stand at the door of a Ward with Sister Elizabeth and glance round and *quickly* point out anything she thought needed correction, and then give the brightest smile of encouragement and sympathy.

When I entered the Novitiate, Sister Anne was a young Professed and used to *Dispense*,[62] with a Novice under her, and was also Sacristan of the Chapel and very often I saw her carrying up two buckets of water, one in each hand, up the crooked steps (then) to the Chapel. She would wash the whole Chapel herself. Though always the same slight figure, she had great muscular strength. As soon as Convalescent work was begun at Eastbourne, Mother Foundress had her down there – and prepared her to become the first Sister Superior as soon as the large Hospital building was completed and opened.

In 1869 this great day came. Bishop Samuel Wilberforce, the only Bishop in those Protestant days who would do anything for the Religious Communities springing up, fixed July 19th (St. Vincent de Paul's day; not that he knew that) as the only day he could spare to come to bless and open our Hospital. It was on a Monday. The Convalescent Home our Foundress had begun and carried on for 2 years before this was at Compton Lodge, not far from St. Saviour's Church – the

---

[62] She gave out medicine to the poor, and to hospital patients and outpatients.

only Church then in Eastbourne where there was an Early Mass. Mother Foundress sent for Sister Elizabeth from U.C. Hospital to help put the new Hospital into
order and readiness for the opening. She sent for me too, I was then in charge, as a
young Professed Sister, of Sir Wm. Jenner's Ward at U.C.H. It was a great joy
and surprise to me when I was told I was to go down to Eastbourne with S. Elizabeth for the Opening. We went on the Saturday, June 17th. On Sunday we all,
about 20 Sisters with F. Mother made our Communion at St. Saviour's Church,
and later on I went with Sister Elizabeth up to the new Hospital, with many things
that were wanted, and we were hard at work, making up beds and putting the
Wards that were ready into order etc., but the Sisters' Wing and the Men's Wing
were not completed, that is, not inside, though the *Building* was completed.

The large, long Ward at the top of the Women's Wing was made into a
Chapel, for the beautiful, proper Chapel was not built for some time afterwards.

On Monday, July 19th, 1869, the Bishop Samuel Wilberforce, then Bp. of
Winchester and a large concourse of *leading* Cathedral clergy and laymen and
Outer Sisters and friends came from London and all parts to be present at the
Opening. The Foundress Mother of Clewer,[63] Harriet Monsell was there. The
Hospital then stood in the middle of cornfields – no trees or garden or wall
around – so much exposed to the public and I remember after the function was
over and we Sisters had collected round our Mother Foundress in the Community
Room, we had to pull down *blinds* as the people from the town came and looked
through the windows *at the Sisters* who were then 'a *wonder*'! and a *sight* quite
out of the way in those days! – but it was a never to be forgotten day for us, as we
returned to our duties at University C. Hospital full of joy. Sister Anne was then
made Sister Superior, our Founder Upton Richards was there, and then by
degrees, she, with our F. Mother and other Sisters got all into order and Convalescents were received. In the Men's Wing, our F. Mother had an *incurable* boy
and one or two men *incurables* moved there from St. Elizabeth's Home,
Mortimer St. where at one time we had a Ward for incurable boys and men.

Now I must pass on to tell of our *first Mission Branch Houses*.[64]

Our first *Mission* and Branch House was at Edinburgh. 'All Saints' Church
Edinburgh, was then a *very* poor unfinished building. Mr. Murdoch,[65] afterwards
Canon Murdoch and Mr. Chinnery[66] afterwards Bishop Haldane Chinnery of
Argyle and the Isles, were poor, hardworking Mission priests and had one of the
poorest parishes in Edinburgh under their care – *NO schools* – *no* Clergy house,

[63] Clewer is the name by which the community of St John Baptist is often known.
[64] Branch or mission houses were small outposts of the community, where charitable work was done
   among the poor, often involving children.
[65] Alexander Drimmie Murdoch (d. 1907), ordained 1867; became the incumbent of All Saints,
   Edinburgh 1867; canon, 1883.
[66] James Robert Alexander Chinnery-Haldane (1842–1906), ordained 1867, served as a curate at All
   Saints, 1869–1876. Canon of Argyll and the Isles, 1879; bishop of Argyll and the Isles 1883. He
   added Chinnery to his name in 1864, and changed the name in 1878.

no Sisters' house. Miss Robertson, afterwards our *Sister Jane Mary* and two other young ladies kept a rough Day School in one of the sort of cellar rooms in West Canongate. Mr. Murdoch wrote to beg for All Saints Sisters to come and help – his three ladies wished to enter our Novitiate – so they came in as soon after as it could be arranged. The Early part of 1870 Sister Caroline Mary[67] was recalled from U.C. Hospital where she was in charge of Sir Wm. Jenner's Medical Wards, and was made Novice Mistress and the late Mistress with 3 Sisters were sent to Edinburgh – a small and very poor house where *very* bare furniture was provided for them. Mr. Chinnery, then Assistant priest with Mr. Murdoch at All SS. Edinburgh, met the Sisters and took them to their house. Mr. Chinnery and members of the Mission Congregation, who had means, helped to support the Sisters, but real *Poverty* was the portion of our Sisters in Edinburgh for *many* years, and very great and laborious work amongst the very poor. All was carried on as much as possible on the pattern of the Mother House and as the work grew and the Sisters made way with the people, Confraternities of the Holy Family for the young and unmarried women and the Holy Childhood for little girls[68] were all begun besides Bible classes and Sunday Schools. A larger house was then provided for the Sisters, which I remember visiting when I was Novice Mistress. A large room at the top of the house was the Oratory and there, on a *poor* Altar and its *poor* Tabernacle, Our Dear LORD deigned to rest. There was no restriction in the Scottish Church; but in those days, *no* English Bishop would permit Reservation at *all*.[69]

Often, as Novice Mistress, I used to direct the Novices to turn in spirit and adore Our LORD on the *only* poor Altar in our Country where HE was continually. *Poverty* and *Our LORD* seemed the special Blessings vouchsafed to our first Branch House.

I should like to tell you of some of our Sisters, who were there in those early days. Sister Adelaide[70] and S. Ellen Mary[71] were full of Prayer. They were not gifted with powers to do *great* work. The work went on, in a quiet sort of way without change. They lived poorly and their work seemed poor. But no doubt the after development – the Building of the Mission House and beautiful Chapel and increase of means of support for the Sisters and their works was the fruit of the Prayers and Patience of those holy Sisters.

I remember being sent by our Mother Foundress to visit our Edinburgh House, in fact to take charge of it for 3 months when Sister Adelaide was ill. We

---

67 It is unclear why Caroline Mary refers to herself in the third person here. It may be that parts of this account were dictated to another sister; Caroline Mary was eighty-one when she wrote these memoirs.

68 Most sisterhoods established a wide range of confraternities and guilds.

69 The first anglican community to practice reservation in England was the Society of St Margaret, East Grinstead, which began the practice in 1857. This was in the sisters' chapel, and presumably the bishop was not informed of this illegal practice. Certainly Caroline Mary seems to have been unaware of S.S.M.'s privilege.

70 Adelaide Formby, prof. 1871, died 1886.

71 Secular name unknown, prof. 1872, died 1919 in South Africa.

were so poor that our Lay Sister, Mary Winifred,[72] had to weigh our bread and portion it out and measure our butter and milk for each of us. One day we had not a penny in the house to go on with. All the Sisters were out visiting their people and I was alone. The door bell rang and a lady came to pay me a visit. After a few minutes she got up to go and I went with her to the door and she put an envelope in my hand, and when I opened it, I found a cheque for £20 which helped us over till other money came in. It did, indeed, seem a gift from Heaven.

In the first beginning of the house at Edinburgh for about 18 months they had a young Scotch girl to help in the housework, 'Jeannie'.[73] She was one of Bp. Allen Forbes' of Brechin's Orphans, at Dundee. He founded an Orphanage there after the pattern of St. Vincent de Paul and visited it daily. 'Jeannie' was a child without natural relations. She was a baby when he took her there himself, and the child loved him with all her heart. She used to scramble up on his knee when he came to visit them. Then he became her spiritual Father and Director. As she grew older he decided that she had a Religious Vocation and sent her to our Novitiate in Margaret St. when she was 18 – but she was not ready. She fretted at being away from Scotland and the Bishop, so instead of taking the Habit, she went to work for the Sisters in Edinburgh. By degrees her Vocation ripened and she came back to the Novitiate in 1870 and received the Habit and her Life deepened and grew into a near saint. She *suffered* and worked on in patience and fortitude for several months till it was discovered she had the disease of which she died. She died in 1877 after I had gone to the Cape, a holy blessed death. She is buried at Brompton, Sister Martha Jean, perfected in faith and hope and love – our brave little Scotch Lay Sister.

The other Lay Sister, who worked so long at Edinburgh during the time of great poverty, was Sister Winifred Mary. She was much older than 'Jeannie'. She had been maid attendant for some time to Miss Ethel Benett and her aged, invalid father. Miss Ethel Benett was the intimate friend of our Mother Foundress, and a deeply spiritual soul, from her Early youth. She was under the direction of Dr. Pusey, and so was her maid; and they led very *ascetic* lives. Then when Mr. Bennett[74] died, Ethel Benett came at one into our Novitiate in order to *prepare* to found the Community of Religious, after the pattern which the Holy Spirit revealed to her, as her work for the Church. Her maid passed her Novitiate here with us and remained, and was professed as our Lay Sister Mary Winifred. She was a pattern of regularity and faithfulness amongst our Lay Sisters till her death. She was a person of intellect and had read a great deal and read deep spiritual books but she also did all her household duties carefully and well and never shrank from anything because it was 'menial'.

---

72 Secular name unknown, prof. 1875, died 1900. She had been maid to the Suckling sisters and entered with them. It is not clear whether Caroline Mary is conflating two lay sisters in this account. Several were former maidservants who entered with their erstwhile employers.
73 Secular name unknown, clothed in 1870 and died in 1876.
74 These inconsistencies of spelling are in the original text.

I have been asked, as I have written these notes, to say what 'dress' the Sisters wore in those first, early days when the Community was just formally begun – The Foundress Mother and her then *eight* Sisters. They wore a black Habit, such as we wear now, the Foundress Mother and those who had taken their vows wore a scapular and the same girdle and Cross we wear now, but the scapular was, I think, worn under the girdle. They wore white collars, more like what our Novices wear now, and a close muslin cap with beautifully gophered[75] frills. The Professed had 3 frills. They were caught by a thread, through each gopher, so that they laid close on the head, and the cap was tied with black ribbon strings. The Novices had *no scapular* – a *leather* girdle and one (or two, I forget which) frills on their caps. Out of doors the Mother and Professed wore long veils and underneath a sort of black straw bonnet. All this, however, was altered by the *time I entered the Community (1866) as a Postulant and Novice*. By *that* time, our Habits and Scapulars were *just as they are* now and we had begun the large white Hoods and Collars. Then the Novices, too, were *just as they are now* in every particular – that was in 1866 – 53 or 54 years ago. But when I was a Novice, there was a difference in our *out of door* dress. We wore no veils, only an ugly black straw bonnet with just a *cloth* curtain to it and strings to tie underneath our Novices' caps starched flaps, and our cloaks had *hoods*. The short veils for Novices were begun just after I was Professed.

I have been asked about the Novitiate; as it was when I was a Novice – from 1866 to 1868. My novitiate was very strict, but full of deep happiness, as I was taught and trained day by day to grasp, and to live the life of a true Religious. I forget the exact number of Novices we were, when I was first clothed, but I can remember two or three 'bits of discipline'. One was that my best Habit was taken from me and given to a Senior Novice who wanted a new one and I had but *One* Habit for almost the rest of my Novitiate. Another discipline was losing my Communion, on confessing I had drunk some water between meals – *a self-indulgence*.

We assembled in the Novitiate after Terce for Instruction and Chapter of Faults. We had a narrow long room then for Instruction, with one bench the length of the room; and the Mistress in her chair opposite, about the middle of the room, the little table with triptych and Crucifix by her and opposite us. A window at the end of the room, with some plant growing, which had many green leaves and was called *Brother Lawrence*, I do not know why exactly.

Another time I got a big severe reproof once for being careless and putting on the cloak and bonnet of another Novice without noticing it had not my number (26).[76]

---

[75] She presumably means 'goffered'. Goffering was done with a narrow crimping iron, and produced fine pleating.

[76] All novices were given a number on entering: their clothes, office books, etc., were marked with this number. When the sister was professed, the number would revert to the newest novice.

I had the great privilege of being for 3 months in the same Novitiate as '*Sister Ethel*', afterwards *Mother Etheldreda*, and Foundress of the Community of the Sisters of Bethany. She made her vows and was consecrated as Mother Foundress of Bethany in *our* All SS. Chapel, Margaret St. Then went up to Lloyd Sq. to the first House of her Foundation. I was privileged to accompany our Mistress when she paid one or two visits to Mother Etheldreda of Bethany to help her get first Chapel in order. She had to begin with only one Novice.

Mother Etheldreda of Bethany was, as I have before recorded, the *very closest, and most intimate girlfriend* of our Foundress Mother from the time they were both about 18 or 20 years old.

The principal work given me as a Novice was the care and nursing of our aged and infirm and incurable patients. The Infirmary was then on a floor in 82 Margaret St. 3 rooms with beds, and a sitting and meal room between, and my cell was off one of the wards, so I could be called up at night and very often I was up at night with some patient. Some of them were *very* ill and suffering. I had one or two Novices and a postulant or two to help me. I took their dinner always and on Sundays I took a service for them and gave a little instruction to those well enough to attend.

In the afternoons, there was the Time in Chapel for Devotion, and sometimes I had a class of poor women for Confirmation, and on Mondays I was sent to help 'cut bread and butter and mind babies' at St. Elizabeth's Home, Mortimer St., where the Confraternity of the Holy Family met under their Sister Superior.

The Novices not otherwise engaged were bound to go to Evensong daily at the Church at 5, and when we returned we had Evening Instruction and Preparation for Meditation and Chapel – till Supper at 7. In Lent, Novices and Professed all went to the course of Sermons at 11 o'clock on Thursdays – Canon Carter[77] gave these Lent lectures the two Lents I was Novice. Fr. Upton Richards gave a short but most helpful address on some point in the Passion the last two weeks in Lent.

During quite the last 2 months, or 3, of my Novitiate, my little *co-Novice*, Sister Lucy,[78] developed rapid consumption and I was told off to nurse her for the last month of her life. It was a very Hot August. I rested on a couch at night, towards the end, in the Sisters' Infirmary where she died. She got to cling so to me, she could not bear me to be away. She was always a gentle, retiring, silent little Sister, and she never had been ill before it was discovered. She died in my arms August 30th, 1868. This was a solemn ending of my Novitiate and preparation for my coming Profession.

During my Novitiate, our Instructions given by the Mistress were mostly on 'The Divine Art of Systematic Meditation'. She submitted them to the direction

---

[77] Thomas Thellusson Carter (1801–1901), an eminent high churchman, and co-founder of the community of St John Baptist, Clewer. He was ordained in 1833, and served as rector of Clewer 1844–80.

[78] Secular name unknown, clothed 1866, died 1868, of tuberculosis.

of the Rev. Fr. Benson, who, after revising them, published them, with a preface of his own. The little book was printed by the Church Press Company in 1867.[79]

At Recreation we were taught to be bright and cheerful. If any Novice was observed to be gloomy or grumpy, the Mistress would tell her to go to her Cell. Also we had to be very punctual, and if late for Recreation, a Novice was not allowed to come in, but sent to Chapel.

Before Fr. Upton Richards was ill, he used to come daily to the Home, and every Friday heard Confessions. He used to walk up through the Chapel to the Sacristy punctually at 2 p.m. As the Lay Sisters increased in number, an Assistant Chaplain was appointed – Mr. Brinckman[80] and afterwards Fr. Dulby[81] filled the part. After his stroke of paralysis, Fr. Upton Richards passed us on for Confession and direction to Father Benson, who also began to take the Clothings and Professions. This was about 1871–2. Fr. Richards died on June 16, 1873. The Community then unanimously begged Fr. Benson to be our Chaplain General Director. The Rev. Arthur Brinckman was also Sub–Chaplain for a time.

I must now return to the beginning of our Branch Houses, Edinburgh being the *first*. The next was *Bradford*, in St. Jude's Parish, where there had been a Mission which stirred up the Vicar of the Parish, Mr. Eddowes[82] and his people and which then caused them to beg for Sisters to help them. Like Edinburgh we began *very* poor. A house was provided for us in Hanover Sq., Bradford, a quiet corner. Three Sisters were sent and found much work awaiting them – very large Sunday Schools – a young women's Bible Class, large districts and streets upon streets of poor to visit – all very much out of hand and untaught as to Church doctrine or practice. St. Mary Magdalene Parish was then in St. Jude's and Mr. Redhead[83] was Mr. Eddowes' curate. There was only a small iron Chapel there, where Mr. Redhead had Mission Services.[84] The very poor women with shawls on their heads and clogs on their feet came to be taught. One of our Sisters had special charge of that district and Chapel. As time went on, the Church of St. Mary Magdalene was built, Mr. Redhead was appointed as first Vicar. It took

---

[79] I cannot find a copy of this work. It was advertised as already published in the end papers of the *Evangelist Library* (edited by the Cowley Fathers). The Church Press was closely linked to the English Church Union.

[80] Arthur Brinkman, ordained 1864, and curate at All Saints, Margaret Street 1870–7. Formerly in the army (94th Regiment), he served as a missionary in Cashmere, and as mission priest at St Andrew's home, Edinburgh, a penitentiary and sisterhood, dying in 1911.

[81] I can find no trace of a Father Dulby. Perhaps this is a misremembering of Dulley. Benjamin Dulley (1846–80) entered Oxford as a mature student and was priested in 1875. He served as a curate at Saint Saviour's, Hoxton, 1874–80, an anglo-catholic parish with links to sisterhoods.

[82] John Eddowes (1826–1905), ordained 1850, vicar of St Jude's Bradford 1857–86, and 1893–1902; vicar of Eastgate-in-Weardale, Durham, 1886–93, hon. canon of Ripon, 1895–1905.

[83] George Edward Redhead (1845–1920), ordained 1869, vicar of St Mary Magdalene, Manningham, Bradford, in 1878, and retired in 1905.

[84] The mission was described by a contemporary source as 'prosperous'. It was centred on Golden Square; the complex of church buildings constructed for St Mary Magdalene cost over £13,000, including a school.

some months before the Sisters got the Schools and Classes into order, and they were taught *Reverence* in Church and for holy things. But Yorkshire people, when they once grasp the truth, become most loyal and stedfast in their Faith. The people became very devoted to the Sisters. We worked there for some years, and the Sisters were changed, but each made their *mark*. When Mr. Eddowes resigned St. Jude's and another Vicar was appointed, our Sisters were moved from St. Jude's parish to St. *James* parish which was *poorer* even than St. Jude's.

Our Sister Anne Teresa[85] worked at Bradford till she got ill, her lungs gave way. She was very saintly. She was at Eastbourne for a time before her death. She died whilst I was away at the Cape. Mother Foundress used to tell me of her when she wrote to me at the Cape. Sister Gertrude Anna[86] did a great work at Bradford when she was there, during the years I was at Capetown. She started a Hospital for children which was taken up by the Bradford people and *still* continues in existence.[87] The first few months the Sisters were at Bradford, they were so poor, they had barely enough food. Bradford people supplied them with *dinner on Sundays – once* the dinner was forgotten, and there were only 4 eggs and bread and butter in the house, so after waiting a bit for the dinner which did not come, the eggs were boiled and eaten. The poor people often gave the Sisters a dried fish or some scones and would have been greatly hurt and offended if their gifts had been refused.

Confraternities and Guilds were started and flourished on the same patterns as All SS. London and All SS. Edinburgh. Sister Edith Mary[88] managed for a time a Hostel for young women employed in the factories.

Our community was withdrawn from the work at Bradford some few years after our Foundress Mother's death. Sister Maria had worked at Bradford for a time, before she was deputed by our Mother Foundress to begin the Mission in Westminster. She had a very large number of C.H.F. Mothers at Bradford and some of them used to come and see her at Westminster if anything brought them to London. They told her how much they missed the Sisters, but continued loyal to their Church.

During the 2 years after my Profession I did not know much of what went on in our Community, *except as to Eastbourne*, being taken up with the nursing and charge of Sir Wm. Jenner's Medical Wards, one for men and one for women, and the Eye patients' wards. Our life was very regular at UCH. We went to the Home for Recreation in turns, two or three times in the week, where it was a joy to see and be near our Mother Foundress; also we went for our Confessions and I

[85] Secular name unknown, prof. 1872, died 1880, of tuberculosis. (Anna Theresa in some records.)
[86] Secular name unknown, prof. 1873, died 1904, in India.
[87] This was the Bradford hospital for the Sick Children of the Poor, founded in 1883. At first it only had beds for twelve children; in 1887 the sisters turned the hospital over to a local board of management, who renamed it the Bradford Children's hospital. It celebrated its centenary in 1983.
[88] Annie Edith Robinson (1858–1937), prof. 1885.

sometimes was summoned to some particular Address or Function in Chapel. Once I remember, I and others were told to come to receive an *interpreted* address from some Archimandrite or Bishop from Greece and receive his bene-diction. He addressed us through an interpreter and told us that in the Eastern Church there were Monasteries for women, but they did no works of mercy, or for the poor. We all knelt for a long Blessing. He was dressed in flowing black robes and wore a very tall sort of hat and had a magnificent Cross on his breast, sparkling with jewels.[89]

Towards the end of my 2 years at UCH, Mother Foundress told me I was to be made Novice Mistress and to take up the Novitiate when my old Mistress[90] would be sent to begin the Edinburgh House.

I was to prepare myself with prayer and special Confession, which Fr. Benson heard, and gave me some beautiful, helpful thoughts. He also (for Fr. Upton Richards) took the service, and blessed me for the Office which I entered upon at Whitsuntide 1870. Our Mother Foundress helped me again and again with her wise counsel in my duties, and in individual cases. It was so ordered that I had a large and important Novitiate. So many Novices, who were trained during the 6 years I was Mistress, became afterwards S. Superiors or heads of work. Some Novices also were Elderly and some very young. *One* dear saintly Sister, Aimee Mary,[91] was in Consumption. Fr. Page sent her in from a small, irregular Community. She was very delicate and when Foundress Mother sent her to a physician to examine her chest, it was found she had disease incipient in her lung. But she was such a beautiful, holy soul, it was decided she should remain. She was 2nd Sacristan in our Chapel all the time of her Novitiate. She had very few dispensations, and her Devotion and Earnestness were most edifying. She lived to be Professed and was sent to Eastbourne, but gradually became worse – *never giving in, till the last few weeks*. She died soon after I had come to the Cape.

Another of my Novices, Sister Maria Francesca (Rosetti) was not only deeply spiritual, but also highly educated and a thorough Italian. She used to make her Confession weekly, and had a great gift of *'tears'*. She often wept in Prayer when in Chapel. Being very learned in Scripture, I deputed her to give Bible Lessons to some of the very young Novices. Sister Katharine Mary[92] was one. She found these Scripture Instructions helped her very much. Our Mother Foundress often saw Sister Maria Francesca, as she knew and understood her soul well and could help her in her scruples and difficulties more than I could. Mother Foundress also

---

[89] Archimandrite Stratuli visited England in 1865 and was present at the laying of the foundation stone of the Society of St Margaret's convent. I can find no record of a subsequent visit, but it may have been a private one. A. G. Lough, *The influence of John Mason Neale* (London, 1962), pp. 127–8.

[90] This was Sister Sarah (Easton).

[91] Secular name unknown, prof. 1876, died 1878.

[92] Secular name unknown, prof. 1874, died 1926, in South Africa.

gave her the work of translating a Latin Breviary; and our Office book, as it is printed now, was the result.[93] This work took up her time till she was Professed in 1875–6. It was put before our Chapter, whether we would adopt this Office Book; hitherto we had used the 'Day hours' as first published and several *additional* Offices translated and *in manuscript* Foundress Mother had collected, such as the Office for Corpus Christi and for The Holy Name, etc.

The Chapter unanimously adopted the translated Latin Offices, and the book was printed. In 1875–6, the first Sisters were to go out to the Cape – our Office book had to be submitted to Bishop West Jones[94] by Fr. Benson, who was then our Chaplain General and Director. Fr. Benson did not approve of our Office for Our Lady's Assumption and also he struck out of our Kalendar certain Saints: St. Francis de Sales, St. Aloysius and St. John of the Cross. Mother Foundress felt it very much, but in her great Humility, she bade us accept Fr. Benson's decision in all meekness and Childlike humility – but *we knew* she *ever hoped* the Offices for the Feast of the Assumption and those Saints might be restored.[95]

The next thing I had better record with regard to Eastbourne is the purchase of the beautiful old Walled-in Garden Foundress Mother was able to purchase and add to our Community portion of the Hospital. This garden had been made and lived in by an eccentric old man who lived on its fruits and vegetables. He planted many rare trees and when he died, it was to be put up for sale by auction, but our F. Mother was able to purchase it privately and she made it into a thorough Religious Garden, with a Calvary and Shrines for Our Lady and St. Aloysius and there was *then* a beautiful cloistered walk of trees meeting overhead and the stillness and quiet beauty was most helpful to any Novices or visiting Sisters for reading or meditations. On Sundays, F. Mother often took Recreation there – both for Choir and Lay Sisters and Novices. We used to sit on the grass all around her seat. On Festivals we had lovely Processions of Sisters before Vespers, simply right up the spacious Chapel and round by the little Cloister to the stairs leading to the Tribune which was where we Sisters sang or recited our Offices.

The S.S.J.E. Fathers – Fr. Prescott, Fr. Hall[96] and others from time to time

---

[93] *The day hours and other offices as used by the Sisters of All Saints* (privately printed, c. 1876).

[94] William West Jones (1838–1908), vicar, Summertown, Oxford, 1864–74, rural dean, Oxford, 1871–4. Oxford preacher, Whitehall chapel, 1870–2; bishop of Capetown and metropolitan of South Africa, 1894, archbishop of Capetown, 1897. Despite a reputation for being sympathetic to the high church, the sisters of All Saints seem to have found it difficult to work in his diocese.

[95] This is a very curious episode, and does not seem to have been quite as described here. Benson's objection seems to have been not that Aloysius was a Jesuit, but that he was canonized after the Church of England severed its ties with Rome. Although Benson made his objections known to Chapter while the book was still in manuscript, it was printed with the list of saints and festivals (such as the assumption of the B.V.M.) intact, thus including those of which he disapproved. Chapter appears to have agreed to his demands for changes, and then simply ignored him. It is also interesting that Benson was unaware that the community had been celebrating these days, apparently for at least six years.

[96] Probably Arthur Crawshay Alliston Hall (1847–1930). He joined S.S.J.E. in 1870, and became bishop of Vermont in 1894, after serving in Boston from 1874.

were sent by Fr. Benson to 'rest' at our Eastbourne Hospital, or to act as Chaplain, whilst the Resident Chaplain was away for *his* 'rest'. The Fathers used to use our Cloistered Garden at times when the Sisters were not likely to be there. Fr. Prescott specially was fond of walking up and down the walk with trees meeting overhead, reading his Breviary.

As I am writing of Eastbourne, it is as well to mention that later on, whilst I was at the Cape, the Prince of Wales, afterward King Edward, and the Princess Christian[97] took great interest in the Hospital and visited with M. Foundress there. The Prince, with his great foresight told her that she should buy the piece of land stretching down towards the sea, or we should have *houses* built there which would block out the view from the women's wing. This was done and the ground was rented out as playground for boys' and girls' high class schools, so no houses could be built there and the rent is a source of income.

In the year 1870, the year I was made Novice Mistress, the great Franco-Prussian War began and ended with the Battle of Sedan and the complete overthrow of the Emperor Louis Napoleon and Victory of Germany over France. In August and September of that year, the 1st British Red Cross Society was begun. It was organized under British-Royal Government. There were scarcely any trained nurses or *Educated* nurses at that date, but in our All Saints Community, our Foundress Mother and several Sisters had been well-trained and had a great deal of experience in Nursing, so it was thought *right*, and sanctioned by our Father Chaplain – Father Upton Richards – that our Rev. Mother should take with her seven Sisters picked out specially and go out to nurse the sick and wounded, whether French or Prussian or Bavarians; under the direction of the Society of the Red Cross.[98]

They started from home on September 18th, 1870 and were out there in France until February 1871. They did not know *where* they would be sent or under whom they would work till they got over to France – then Col. Brackenbury, who was at the heart of the British Red Cross sent them to Bazeilles and Balan, two Chateaux very near *Sedan* where the last real battle had taken place. They were attached to Dr. *Frank*'s ambulance and after nursing wounded and typhus cases for about a month, some of their patients recovering and some dying, Dr. Frank took them on to Chalons and then to Epernay to nurse the poor sufferers who were sent to them from the fighting around Paris. It needs a separate account to be written of that wonderful time and there are letters from Sister Catharine, Sister Cecilia and Sister Harriet and some from our Mother Foundress which record much of what they went through and the sufferings they witnessed.

During the 4 months they were away, including as it did, Advent and

---

97 Princess Christian was the fifth child of Queen Victoria. All Saints seems to have come into contact with her because of her interest in nursing reform.

98 See the Franco-Prussian war diary, below pp. 207–269.

Christmas, the charge of the All Saints House was committed to Sister Caroline Mary – Mistress of the Novices and Sister Isabella[99] who had charge of the Industrial Girls and filled the place of House-keeper in Sister Eliza's absence. We had our Rev. Father Chaplain, Upton Richards, who came *daily* to the House to whom we could turn for direction and advice if any difficulties occurred. *One* difficulty was a 'rebellion' in the Orphanage caused by one very naughty orphan who stirred up a rebellious spirit. But Fr. Richards soon got it all right; he went in and spoke to the children and then called on their *loyalty* to Rev. Mother and said now, let all the children who want to be on Rev. Mother's side come over to me – at which they *all* came over to him except the 'rebel' and she was sent away. It was a very very cold winter and there was much suffering for the *poor*. There were a great many poor all round Margaret St., in the District, Castle St., Castle St. East, Titchfield St., what used to be called 'Oxford Market'.[100] So Fr. Richards let me start a soup-kitchen and I, with some of my Novices, used to go daily for an hour to give out the soup, which was very *good*. We had a big boiler and employed one or two women to prepare and make it.

Our Rev. Mother wrote to me that she wished me and S. Isabella to get all the Xmas Treat over before their return, as they would be too worn out and also were needing new clothes before anything else could be done. She sent home Sister Harriet to prepare at once to go to Clifton to begin the work there, under Mr. Randall of All Saints Church. Sister Rosamund was sent back to Chorlton Union Infirmary and the others to UC Hospital. Sister Eliza had to take up her post as Housekeeper over the Industrial Girls in the Orphanage. Whilst our Rev. F. Mother was out nursing at the Franco-Prussian War, Sister Anne had to superintend and carry on the Hospital at Eastbourne. This was an anxious and responsible work, but Sister Anne did it in the *quiet, firm* way, as was her characteristic throughout her long life and charge.

It was a trial to me to be left so early in my post as Novice Mistress without the support of our Rev. Mother and especially as it was ordered that I was not to delay clothing 6 Novices, three Choir and three Lay, who had been postulants for some months, but *Obedience* gives one strength and power not one's own. So with our Rev. Fr. Upton Richards to encourage me, I was able to lead their Retreat and help and present them at the Altar, to enter on their Novitiate. Sister, afterwards Mother!, Frances Helen was one of them.[101]

I find I have omitted to talk of one of our dear Sister's illness and death, our *first* Sister who died at University Coll. Hospital, having taken a virulent typhoid fever from a patient she was nursing. This was Sister Mary Christina, a Sister of

---

[99] Isabella Scott Beach (1840–1913), prof. 1870.

[100] In 1889, the area around Castle Street was still impoverished: on Charles Booth's poverty maps, it is dark blue, meaning 'very poor, casual [employment], chronic want'.

[101] Frances Bruce (1831–97), prof. 1872. Irish by birth, she became the first mother superior of the American affiliate in 1890.

Mr. Luke Rivington's.[102] She and her sister Harriet lived with their brother at Oxford when he was quite a young priest. Then he came as the Curate at All SS. Church, and Mary followed her vocation and entered as a Postulant in our Novitiate just before I was professed. She was sent to work in our Infirmary under me the last few weeks of my Novitiate. Such a dear, bright, lovable being. There was a holy merriment about her, a bright *sunny* selflessness. She was professed just before I was recalled from U.C.H. to be Novice Mistress and as soon as Professed, she was sent to U.C.H. We used to nurse fever cases there, in those days. S. Mary Christina never spared herself and did her utmost to recover this patient, who, I think, did recover, but our Sister was called to her Rest. Mr. Luke Rivington, her brother, was in great grief. He used to Celebrate and reserve the Blessed Sacrament[103] in her sick room day by day, ready to give her the Viaticum[104] if she became conscious. I do not think she regained consciousness the last week of her life. But our LORD took her to Himself for she was His true and faithful Bride. Her body was brought to our Mortuary Chapel and Mr. Luke Rivington brought the Reserved Sacrament from her room at U.C.H. to the Mortuary, and It remained there till the day of her burial. I, and my Novices, took watches there day and night till she was buried, and never in my life have I seen such a lovely corpse. She was not at all what is called 'pretty' in feature, but her face was bright with childlike merriment, but as she lay dead in her coffin, a wonderful beauty came on her perfectly reposeful face, and day by day seemed to increase, so that we could not but be sorry when after 4 days and nights, the time came for her to be carried to her grave in Brompton Cemetery.

It is well for us to remember that in those earlier days of our Community, *five* of our Sisters were called to give their lives for the sufferers they nursed or tended. They were: Sister Mary Elizabeth, visiting *smallpox* amongst the poor in the District. Sister Martha, nursing *Typhus* at Chorlton Union Infirmary. Sister Mary Christina, *Typhoid* fever at U.C.H. Sister Rose,[105] *Typhus* at New Somerset Hospital, Capetown. Sister Monica,[106] *Diphtheria* at U.C.H.

It was ordered by God's Holy Will that these dear Sisters should go to HIM by the way of 'giving their life' for others, but we must not think they were exposed to danger more than many others of our Sisters who have nursed virulent diseases, and yet never taken the infection.

Our Foundress Mother nursed young officers and soldiers during the times they were nursing in the Red Cross Ambulance in the Franco-Prussian War. She always took the cases of poisonous fever herself. She was with a young Prussian

102 Luke Rivington (1838–99). Ordained 1863, he was a curate in Oxford 1861–7, and then at Margaret Street (1867–70); he went to Bombay with S.S.J.E. in 1870. He converted to Roman catholicism in 1888 and served as a catholic priest in London.
103 Reservation was legal under these circumstances, as the sister was near death.
104 The eucharist when administered to one who is dying.
105 Secular name unknown, prof. 1877, died 1880, in South Africa.
106 Secular name unknown, prof. 1876, died 1880.

Officer and closed his eyes in death and went to his mother and sister to comfort them, and a little French Trumpeter was another of her special patients. She never shrank from Infection, nor did any of the Sisters with her. Sister Rosamund and other Sisters nursed the Typhus stricken patients at Chorlton Union, Manchester, but only Sister Martha *died* of it. Sister Frances Christina used to go about freely to the small-pox people during the 6 months when it raged at Cape-town in 1882, but she never caught infection. I, myself, used to visit a smallpox tent Hospital on the Veldt to see and encourage one of our Matrons who had charge of it, but kept perfectly well myself. Also, when I was at U.C. Hospital I nursed scarlet fever and Typhoid but kept perfectly well and also Sister Eliza-beth, Sister Sophia Elizabeth[107] and Sister Sophia[108] were for some weeks called to nurse amongst virulent poisonous fever in a country village where there were many deaths, and *a nurse* died of it, but our 3 Sisters in spite of being in it night and day, kept perfectly well.

In later years, and not so long ago, our Sisters at Bombay nursed Plague stricken people during a severe epidemic of that terrible disease, and Sister Beatrice[109] especially was exposed to great risks as she managed and was Head nurse at one of the plague Hospitals. Again our Sisters passed through this danger unhurt.

I must now resume the story of what may interest our Sisters, as to events *after* the return of our Foundress Mother and Sisters from the Red Cross Nursing in France and we all got settled again in our various posts. Sister Isabella was Chief Sacristan Sister with others under her at the Church, also Organist and trainer of the Community Choir. I, as Novice Mistress, used to be with all the Novices who could sing, and we had some good voices then; at the Choir prac-tice every Saturday Evening in Chapel, conducted by S. Isabella. Mother Found-ress was very fond of French rendering of Hymn tunes and brought tunes she had heard in Convent Chapels in Paris, especially for the Salutaris, which we learnt both in our Home Chapel and at Eastbourne.

About this time the first Tenebrae Office book came into print.[110] Then we practised a great deal for the singing of Tenebrae and Mother Foundress sent me to some big Church Furniture shop to choose and order our first Tenebrae Candlestick. I cannot remember which year it was, but it was whilst I was Novice Mistress that we also began having the Creche at Christmas. At first we had no crib or stable, only the Holy Child and His Mother and Joseph and Angels and an ox and ass arrayed on the steps of the Sanctuary. This our F. Mother had also brought from Paris.

---

[107] Ellen Sophia Hughes, became an associate sister in 1860, prof. 1869, died 1893.
[108] Harriet Sophia Robinson (1836/7–1904), prof. 1868.
[109] Secular name unknown, prof. 1891, died 1937, in India.
[110] In actual fact, Frederick Oakeley published the first 'anglican' office of tenebrae in 1842, adopted from the Roman breviary. Tenebrae is the special form of matins and lauds for Thursday to Saturday in holy week.

During the 7 years I was Novice Mistress, I knew literally very little of what passed in the world without, even in Religious things, but had enough to do with 'Retreats', our Community Retreats and Novices' Retreats, etc. I went, as Mother Foundress wished me, to the Professed Recreation once or twice in the week. I did not hear much of the trials of good priests and others who were striving faithfully to teach and carry out the Catholic Faith and practice in their Churches, and the people under their care.

In those days every Postulant that came in to our Novitiate had to come through great opposition from parents and much loved relations. Even *good* people – good Catholic Church people did not understand and fought shy of the Religious Life and Religious Communities. But this trial of 'not being understood' by their nearest and dearest in their own families helped to deepen the reality of their Vocation and their life of Sacrifice.

By this time Retreats for Outer Sisters and others were begun and very often a vocation was settled in a Retreat and such a one became a Postulant.

Early in the year 1875 our first Sisters started for the Cape to take up the works founded by Bishop Gray,[111] 1st Bishop of Capetown and almost founder of our Branch of the Church out there. He had begged for All Saints Sisters to come out there, as far back as 1870. When our Sisters and M. Foundress were out Nursing at the End of the Franco-Prussian War, it was quite *impossible* to send Sisters to a foreign Mission then, so he got Miss Fair and a few ladies to form a kind of Community – one of these was Miss Katharine Buller – Sister Louisa Katharine's aunt. She gave up her School-teaching in England and at Capetown she founded, under Bishop Gray, St. Cyprian's School, and carried it on till she became ill and gave it over to All Saints Sisters as soon as possible. All Miss Fair's Compassion ladies did good work – St. Michael's Home for Destitute Children, the Nursery at New Somerset Hospital, the *visiting* in the parishes that formed in Capetown, etc. etc. were all in their hands. But when Bp. Gray died, a Bishop West Jones came. Many Ladies gave up and returned to England. Miss Fair herself only stayed on to pass the works into our Sisters' hands. But it was all *very* difficult, very much more so than beginning work ourselves and the first two years were years of great trial and our first Sisters were not very happy at the Cape.

But I must return to our Community events at this time in England, for early in that year 1875, two of our Sisters died at All SS. Home Margaret St, and Sister Harriet died after a few days' illness at Baltimore and Sister Harriet Mary[112] was very very ill at Reigate. She had gone there to take charge of one of her own sisters who was mentally ill. Sister Harriet Mary was with her whilst her attendant nurse and companion had a holiday. But she had to return, for Sister Harriet

---

111 Robert Gray (1809–72), first bishop of Capetown, 1847–72. He added five sees to the South African church.
112 Harriet Mary Pleydell Bouverie, prof. 1869, died 1890.

Mary fell ill with fever and lung inflammation and was not expected to live. Our dear Mother Foundress was in much distress. She could not leave S. Emily Mary[113] and S. Maria Francesca and the Assistant Superior had been sent to the Cape, so I was sent to S. Harriet Mary and was with her till she was recovering, and then I returned to help a little in the care of S. Maria Francesca. S. Emily Mary had died – *faithful* unto death.

Our Foundress Mother must have suffered greatly at that time. She was still feeling the great loss to her of her first Spiritual Father and Co-founder, Fr. Upton Richards – he died in 1873 – and she began to suffer the excruciating headaches which so often came upon her. Sister Maria Francesca was nursed by a 'little young Nurse Annie', known to us *now* as Mrs. Gerard, the wife and widow of good Mr. Gerard, so long our Steward at All SS. Hospital, Eastbourne. Nurse Annie was, in those days, a young, slim girl of a Nurse, trained entirely at U.C. Hospital under Sister Helen. She was clever and trustworthy and devoted, so was a great help in Nursing our sick and dying Sisters at All SS. Home. Sister Maria Francesca was always calling her to her bedside in her Italian ecstatic way, 'Oh, Annie, my Annie, come to me!'

Mrs. Rosetti,[114] an old lady then, used to sit for hours one side of her daughter's bed and Christina Rosetti,[115] her sister, the other side, till the end drew near. Hers was a very suffering death.

I have written these Memories at such odd and end times, I am afraid they are not *in order*. I find I have not told of the last illness and death of our much loved Father and Co-Founder, Rev. Fr. Richards. His health began to decline gradually, soon after the return of our Mother and Sisters from the Franco-Prussian War Nursing, and he passed us on chiefly for Confession and Spiritual Direction to Fr. Benson. In 1873, on June 16th, his holy soul passed to GOD after a final stroke. He had had two or three slight strokes before. I was away at the time of his last illness and death. Our F. Mother had sent me for a quiet time and rest to our *first Mission House at Bradford*. This was *then* in a quiet, quaint square, very *small* and *poor*, but all most regular – a tiny Oratory, tiny Refectory and cells, but the Sisters were within easy reach of their work amongst the poor of the large Parish of St. Jude's and the Church. Three Choir Sisters and, I think, one Lay Sister were there as at our Edinburgh 1st Mission House.

I know at that time it was not thought right to begin any Branch Mission house without this number of Sisters, and possibilities in however a condensed fashion, of leading the regular Religious Life. I loved the little Oratory at our 1st Bradford House, but was there only a week when summoned back to our dear Father's and 1st Chaplain's Burial. He was also the 1st Vicar and faithful priest of All Saints Margaret St., having calmly and bravely battled through all the

---

113 Emily Mary Howe, prof. 1863, died 1876.
114 Frances Mary Lavinia Polidori Rosetti (1800–86).
115 Christina Rosetti (1830–94), poet and church worker.

great trials our Church experienced in those early days of Catholic Revival. Numbers of the more leading priests were his personal friends. Canons Carter, Liddon,[116] Dr. Pusey and many others, they came to his Burial and the Requiem at All SS. His *grave* is close to our Foundress and Sisters' graves in Brompton Cemetery.

As soon as possible after his death, our votes were taken for Fr. Benson to become our second Fr. Chaplain and director of the Community, and on his consent, he was appointed by the Bishop of London (our Visitor). Fr. Benson took charge of us in 1873, and *continued* in his Office until 1890 when he resigned his Superiority over the S.S.J.E. and went to America. Then *Fr. Page*, being elected Superior of S.S.J.E., also consented to become our All SS Chaplain-General. Fr. Page had known us as a Community for many years. He had entered the Society of S.S.J.E. Fathers about the time I was made Novice Mistress, and he sent in his own faithful Housekeeper (*our first Sister Ruth*)[117] and two of the York Hospital Nurses to our Lay Novitiate. They were among my *first* Novices when I was made Mistress.

All 3 became *truly* saints. They had strong and beautiful characters and most true Religious Vocations. All 3 were very *different* in temperament. One, dear Sister Elizabeth Mary,[118] died of lung disease, endured with love and simplicity. Sister Ruth was employed a good deal at St. Agnes House, Mr. Brinckman's Home for dying girls rescued from sad lives.[119] He started it after the 1st London Mission. Sister Eliza organized it, and the Lay Sisters under her, Sister Mary Amelia,[120] S. Ruth, S. Veronica,[121] nursed and worked there with great devotion. Sister Ruth's Yorkshire character was determined and not always *easy*, but she conquered herself over and over again with the Grace of God, which she faithfully used.

She worked latterly at our small Orphanage at Whiterock St. Leonards under our Sister Helen Agnes[122] and was a great help there. She *died* there.

Sister Mary Jane, the 3rd of Fr. Page's spiritual children, who received the Lay Sister's Habit when first I was Mistress, had a very deep interior spiritual life. She was drawn to much asceticism. She worked a long time at St. John's

---

116 Henry Parry Liddon (1829–90), ordained 1853, was Butler's curate at Wantage, where his fellow curate was Alexander Heriot Mackonochie, later of St Alban's Holborn. Liddon was vice-principal of Cuddeson college, 1854–59, and canon of St Paul's cathedral from 1870. He is best remembered as the friend and biographer of Pusey, and for his agitation against allowing women to take university degrees.

117 Secular name unknown, professed 1873, died 1893.

118 Secular name unknown, clothed 1870, died 1877.

119 The Rev. Arthur Brinkman established St Agnes home in 1874, at 3 Margaret Street. It held about thirty 'fallen' women at a time, and the All Saints sisters were responsible for its day-to-day management.

120 Secular name unknown, died 1897.

121 Eliza Keene (1826–1905), prof. 1876.

122 Joanna Mary DeVilliers, prof. 1889, died 1906.

Hospital, Cowley.[123] Then she became very ill with cancer and suffered very greatly and for long, till she died a holy, blessed death.

In 1876 it was thought well to make a change of Novice Mistress. Our Mother and Fr. Benson appointed Sister Mary Augustine Mistress, and I was made Assistant Superior. Our Mother sent me *early* in the year of 1877 to take over St. Margaret's Orphanage at Liverpool from the Sisters of St. Thomas (Oxford).[124] There had been a trouble in that Community which resulted in several St. Thomas' Sisters leaving their Community and several came into our Novitiate *by Fr. Benson's ordering*. Sister Elizabeth Margaret[125] (Fr. Black's sister) and Sister Lucy Mary[126] were then in charge of St. Margaret's Orphanage, waiting till relieved by All SS Sisters. I was sent to re-organize the work and settle the Sisters into it. Sister Sophia Elizabeth, Sister Gladys and Afterward Sister Mary Ursula[127] helped me. The children and girls were upset by the changes and had got very rebellious and out of hand and it was hard work to win them and make them into good children and girls. However, we succeeded in winning their affections and loyalty in about 3 months.

Whilst I was there, Mother Foundress wrote to tell me I was to be sent to the Cape to be Superior there, but not till the end of the year. Meanwhile, she wished me to go to our Edinburgh House Mission to relieve Sister Adelaide who was ill. I was to take the place of Superior there for 3 months.

We were very very poor in those days in Edinburgh. Sister Mary Winifred, our Lay Sister housekeeper, had to *measure* our milk and butter and bread in portions for each Sister. No one could have as much as she wanted. We lived chiefly on alms. One day the Sisters were all out visiting their people and I was keeping house alone. A lady, 'Mrs. Drummond Hay',[128] visited me. She sat and talked a little while and then departed. As I let her out at the front door she gave me an envelope. I opened it after she was gone and found a cheque for £20. When I let her in, we had not a *penny* to go on with.

Sister Ellen Mary[129] and Sister Adelaide[130] led most devoted lives of *prayer*. When after their time, and Sister Mary Teresa[131] and then Sister Mary Augustine developed the work and attracted helpers who provided funds and built the beautiful Sisters' Chapel etc., it was surely the outcome of those two very humble,

---

[123] The hospital was officially called St John the Evangelist Hospital for Incurables. All Saints took it over when its founders found it too expensive to run. The community expanded it at a cost of £25,000, enabling it to hold fifty patients, as well as sisters who needed nursing.

[124] The community of St Thomas the Martyr was founded in 1851. The trouble referred to here was the expulsion of the mother superior by vote of the sisters, for breaking the rule.

[125] Elizabeth Black, prof. 1878, left 1893. Her profession with St Thomas Martyr had been in 1871.

[126] Lucy Warren (1841–1929), prof. 1878. Her profession with St Thomas Martyr had been in 1873.

[127] Mary Jane Ward (1843–1930), prof. 1877.

[128] I cannot identify this individual; however, she was probably a member of the earl of Kinnoul's family, based in Edinburgh and broadly sympathetic to the high church.

[129] Secular name unknown, prof. 1872, died 1919, in South Africa.

[130] Adelaide Formby, prof. 1871, died 1886.

[131] Mary Teresa Suckling, prof. 1875, died 1910. She was a sister of the third mother superior.

patient, enduring, prayer lives of S. Adelaide and S. Ellen Mary, known so to GOD, more than to men. Dear Sister Mary Teresa did so *much* for the Chapel and *worship* and devotion to the B. Sacrament as well as other things besides, one felt greatly uplifted into an *atmosphere* of Adoration when I visited the House later on.

In October 1877 I returned to All SS. Home, Margaret Street, to prepare for the Cape. We had our Retreat early in Nov. It was my last in the dear Home Chapel for 10 years. On Nov. 26, 1877 we started for the Cape. Three Choir Sisters, viz: Sister Ellen Mary, Sister Rose[132] and myself and 3 Ladies to help work in the Mission. Miss Catharine Carter, an Outer Sister, Miss Mary Frere, who was consumptive but they hoped Cape climate wd. cure her, and a young cousin of my own. We shared *one* cabin. It was a squeeze. The Donald Carrie Steamboats were *so small* in those days. This one was the first, 'Edinburgh Castle'.[133] It was afterwards made into a coasting vessel. In the tropics, our Sister Rose fell *very* ill of fever, and I was so Bad I could not nurse her. A third Lady going out with a sick husband nursed her. The Captain[134] kindly gave up his own deck cabin that she might have more air, but we quite feared she wd. not live to reach Capetown. However she did, but when we arrived she had to be carried from the Steamer into a carriage and taken to St. Cyprian's School and deposited in *bed*. This was on *Christmas Day* 1877. She gradually recovered and came in to St. George's House and helped in the Refectory work-room, and by degrees taught a few poor ignorant girls who needed to learn the rudiments of the Christian Faith. Sister Ellen Mary became our Chapel Sacristan and took some charges in the Refectory for individual religious instructions. When I arrived at the Cape, our Poverty was *extreme*. It was quite dismaying, for children, girls, workers and Sisters were nearly half starved. My first business was to stir up friends in England to help us, and my appeal met with such kind, effective response, money flowed in before long and proper *clothes* for the destitute children of St. Michael's Home and for the Refuge girls were made and sent. Working parties for our Cape Mission began to help us considerably and have never since ceased.

The first year I was at Capetown was one of great trial however, both spiritually and temporally, for we were very bereft as to our spiritual needs. Everything was so behind-hand as to Catholic practice. We had a bad fever in the Boys' part of the House and Miss Augusta Bridges, a most *devoted* worker, nursed them day and night, fell ill herself, and then I nursed her day and night, for regular nurses did not exist in those days. At the end of a month, just as we hoped she was going to recover, I fell ill and had regular typhoid fever and was in bed nearly 30 days. Then our Sister Charlotte died, just as I was up and about again. I'm afraid I was very naughty and wished *I* might have *gone too*. Then in GOD'S great love, HE

---

132 Secular name unknown, prof. 1877, died 1880, in South Africa.
133 The Edinburgh Castle was classified as a barque; it was built by Napier of Glasgow in 1872.
134 Captain Penfold.

sent us to be our Chaplain the Rev. E. E. Holmes[135] and his spiritual help and his wisdom in helping and dealing with our numberless difficulties, his wonderful influence with every single individual, and his *perseverance* in gaining the Bishop's consent and the concurrence of Archdeacons, the Dean and Canons to invite the S.S.J.E. Fathers to Capetown, changed the whole atmosphere from deadly dryness into life and vigour and revival of Catholic life.

Mr. Holmes was our Chaplain for 4 years. He often had *lung haemorrhage* but he would not leave us until he had succeeded in sending a cable from the Bishop to Fr. Benson to ask for one of the Fathers. Fr. Benson replied by sending out Fr. Puller[136] who arrived in May 1883 and then Mr. Holmes departed.

Fr. Puller was joined by Fr. Shepherd[137] and a Lay Brother and they began their work at St. Philip's about October 1883.

I must not, however, plunge into the history of our Capetown Mission as I believe there are plenty of records of our Early beginnings and developments there.

I was re-called from the Cape in August 1886. Our Mother Foundress was ill and needed me. Events came on rapidly then. Our beloved Mother Foundress was *very* suffering and early in 1887, she was told she had cancer of the breast. An operation was decided upon about the end of June 1887.

Mother was full of hopes. The great doctors and physicians who attended her thought and told her an operation would possibly give her 2 more years on Earth, and I know she thought that would give her time to help to direct and strengthen me to take the charge of the Community for a time, at least, after her death. But it was not to be. She did not rally after the operation. She sent for some of the very young Sisters before she died, for whom she was anxious. She sent for Sister Anne from Eastbourne, and after she had seen them, she sent them back to their posts. Each morning she lived she had her Communion, as for her Viaticum. Early the first hour of August 3rd, we Sisters knelt around her bed. I was privileged to be near her dear head. The prayers for the Departing spirit were said, whether by Fr. Benson or who I cannot remember, and her dear and holy spirit departed and went to GOD.

Later on we brought her dear body and laid it in her sitting room which we made into a Mortuary Chapel till the day of her burial. Over her door she had the Motto, in Latin: '*Humility – Humility – Humility*', and most earnestly had she

---

[135] Ernest Edward Holmes (1854–1931), priested 1877, chaplain, All Saints, Eastbourne convalescent home, 1878–9; commissary of Cape Town, 1879–84 and of St Helena 1899–1905; domestic chaplain to the bishop of Cape Town, 1879–84, and to the bishop of Oxford, 1884–1901; archdeacon of London and canon residentiary, St Paul's, 1911–30; hon. domestic chaplain to Queen Alexandra, 1911 and chaplain to the Order of St John of Jerusalem from 1913.

[136] Frederick William Puller (1843–1938), ordained 1867, a member of S.S.J.E. from 1880. Served in Cape Town 1883–91, and was superior of S.S.J.E.'s London house 1909–19, as well as serving as chaplain to the community of the Holy Family.

[137] Perhaps George Edmund Sheppard, ordained 1865, and a missionary in Cape Town by the mid-1880s. He was from Frome, Somerset, where W. J. E. Bennet was vicar.

made it *the rock* of her life and life work. It was *child-like* Humility, so simple, so bright, so true. Again, I have run on, and my 'history' is, I fear sadly disjointed.

The 9 years I was at the Cape our dearest M. Foundress wrote to me *every week* and told me many interesting Community events. She told me when she made a change of Mistresses. She sent S. Mary Augustine to Bradford and made S. Clementine[138] Mistress.[139] She told me about the Sisters going to Bombay and later on of the death of S. Rosamund and about the Baltimore and Philadelphia Community Houses and of American postulants coming over to our Novitiate and then of the *enlargement* and partly rebuilding of our St. Elizabeth's Home, Mortimer St. She wrote *most* happily of that. It had been possible, through the gift of Sister Frances Gabriel's[140] own sister's money, who had died just before S. Frances Gabriel entered our Novitiate. I was also told of our taking up the charge of St. John Home for Nurses in Norfolk Street and a Maternity Home at Baltimore. I think, too, Wolverhampton and our Helmsley Branches were started whilst I was at the Cape. Sister Mary Louise[141] and S. Annabelle Mary[142] were at the head of very good and large works at Christ Church and St. Andrew, Wolverhampton, the result of a Mission Canon Body[143] took at *CHRIST-Church.*

Mr. Charles Gray[144] begged for Sisters for Helmsley. He was very devoted to our M. Foundress and she liked him very much but was amused at his unique and masterful ways.

Then our Cowley St. John Hospital was developed. The Building was continued and Sister Mary Teresa was made S. Superior, and S. Mary Augustine transferred from Bradford to Edinburgh. I forget who was sent to Bradford. I *think* it was S. Gertrude Anna first, and that she then started a Hospital for Sick children.

I do not think I have said much about the beginning of the Hospital of Cowley St. John. I am not clear as to which year it was. A devout lady[145] built a part of it and then could not go on and handed it on to Fr. Benson and he asked our Mother Foundress to take it. She sent Sister Elizabeth as head to organize and develop the work. I remember paying a visit there, I think, when I was Mistress in *quite*

---

[138] Emily Clementina Williams, prof. 1874, left to join the community of the Epiphany, Truro, in 1894, according to All Saints. However, in the Epiphany records she is recorded (as Sister Clementia) as being professed in 1883. She became Epiphany's mother superior in 1901.

[139] Mistress means novice mistress. After the mother superior, this was the most important role in the Society, given the mistress's role in forming the character of the new generation of sisters; future mothers often served terms as novice mistress, as indeed Caroline Mary had done.

[140] Honora Frances Cadogan, prof. 1885, died 1917, in India.

[141] Louise Blackman (1838–1908), prof. 1876.

[142] Annabella Williams (1854–1928), prof. 1881.

[143] George Body (1840–1911), ordained 1864; rector of Kirby, Yorks, 1870–84; canon missioner, Durham, 1883–1911, warden of the community of the Epiphany, Truro, 1891–1905. He played an active part in the parochial mission movement, and was described as combining evangelical fervour with tractarian principles.

[144] Charles Norris Gray (b. 1841), son of Bishop Gray of Capetown, and his biographer. Ordained 1866, vicar of Helmsley, Yorks., 1870–1913. The community archives hold a number of his letters.

[145] A Miss Sandford.

the early days. The part of the Building was incomplete. There was no Garden, or wall and there was a field where a *cow* was tethered which Fr. Benson gave us to supply us with milk. There was just the *Chancel* of St. John and St. Mary's Church built, but no nave, and ground around rough grass, the Churchyard had not been made. Mass was said daily in the unfinished Chancel. Brother Gardiner[146] used to come and ring the bell and prepare the Vestments for the Father who came to Celebrate. It was all very primitive, but in great odour of sanctity. Fr. Benson used to tuck up his cassock and be seen coming over the rails through the field to the Hospital to see S. Elizabeth and enquire how all were going on. There were a few incurable Lady patients. I do not remember if it was then or later on there was a poor Lady who had been a Missionary in China and had contracted Leprosy. She was in a small room apart from others. Fr. Benson visited her assiduously and when she became more ill and helpless, he used to lift her in bed and arrange her pillows. He was *wonderful* with the sick. I have seen him when he brought the Holy Communion to a sick Sister, put his left arm under her pillow and raise her gently but firmly whilst he communicated her from the Chalice. As years went on and S. Elizabeth got money, the Hospital Building was enlarged and St. Mary and St. John Church and Churchyard were finished and a wall built around our Hospital grounds. Then Mother Foundress made S. Mary Teresa Superior and she and Sister Elizabeth worked away till they got everything *perfect* and the Chapel was built and the Nuns' garden made, and oh! what a great and blessed work for souls as well as bodies she carried on till her own suffering and saintly life on Earth closed and Our Dear LORD called her to HIMSELF. HIS own most true Bride.

After our beloved Foundress Mother's death on August 3rd, 1887, I was left in charge of the Community. There was so much to do for the Sisters in all our many branches. Fr. Benson, being our Chaplain General and Spiritual director, corresponded with Archbishop Benson,[147] our Visitor, and the votes were gathered from all parts of our Community to decide the election of a Mother Superior. Fr. Benson gave us one day's Retreat on Sept. 28th in our All SS Home Chapel, and on 29th, St. Michael and All Angels, he counted the votes and told me I had been chosen to the Office. I was again elected in 1890. The six years I was M. Superior, after the *Foundress'* death, were years of strain and anxiety beyond

---

[146] Charles Edwyn Gardner (sic), curate of St James the Less, Liverpool, 1868, then Llanmadoc, 1869–70; joined S.S.J.E. 1870. Missionary in U.S.A. 1872–78, and 1884–5. In India from 1886, died 1908.

[147] Edward White Benson (1829–96), ordained 1857, first headmaster of Wellington College 1858–72 chaplain in ordinary to Queen Victoria 1875–7, bishop of Truro 1877–83, where he was responsible for the building of Truro cathedral, archbishop of Canterbury 1883. Opposed the disestablishment of the Church in Wales; secured the appointment of a royal commission into education 1886, and introduced the Clergy Discipline Bill, passed in 1892.

words to describe. Fr. Benson resigned his Superiorship in 1890 (I think) and went to America for some few years and Fr. Page, who became Fr. General at Cowley, consented to become our Chaplain General. He was very good to us, devoting much of his time to the Community as also to individual Sisters who needed any special help. He had for some few years watched over and directed our Sisters in India.

The first 3 years I was Mother Superior, some of our elder Sisters died; first dear S. Louisa Mary,[148] sweet and holy soul. She was a sister of Mrs de la Bere's and her home was at Prestbury. She was a Novice when I was made Novice Mistress and was a joy to me, for she was so pure and holy and her vocation so clear. She had that spiritual joyousness about her which was truly a gift from Heaven. After her Profession, she was sent to Clifton to take up the School which Sister Harriet began before she was sent to America. Sister Louisa Mary carried it on happily and imparted a religious tone. Our dear and holy *Sister Mary Beatrix*[149] was one of her pupils. Sister Mary Beatrix worked at Eastbourne and afterwards at St. Saviour's Hospital, where she died.

Sister Louisa Mary, whilst I was at the Cape, was sent to Philadelphia as S. Superior, then had charge of St. Margaret's Home, Liverpool, then was Assistant Superior for a year. But when I returned to England in 1886, she was very ill with lung disease. I had the privilege of caring for her during the last weeks of her Earthly life. She died on Nov. 3rd, 1888.

During our beloved Foundress' last months of suffering on Earth, our *Sister Mildred*[150] (S. Elizabeth Maud's sister) became rapidly[151] worse. She had been Sacristan Sister and sub-organist at All SS Church from 1886 (when I came home from the Cape and was made 'Assistant'). I felt anxious over her. I knew she was suffering, but it was not thought she had any serious illness. She never gave in, and worked so hard. She was a *real* musician and her playing on the organ and her voice when singing was most delightful. There was a Profession (I think) in *June* that year, 1887. It was the last time our Mother was in Chapel for a Function. She had a Chair close up to the Altar Steps. It was also the *last* time Sister Mildred played on our Organ. She was very exhausted afterwards and I was told to take her to a physician to examine her chest. He was very grave and saw me alone after the examination and told me she had scarcely any lungs left. She had only had a little breathy cough, which was thought to be a *nervous* cough, and no one had dreamt she had lung disease. Rapidly she grew worse. I took her to St. John's, Cowley first. Dearest S. M. Teresa was most tender in caring for her, and Father Congreve[152] helped and lifted her soul into great peace. Then it was thought Bournemouth might do her good, so she was sent there under the care of her

[148]   Caroline Mary must mean sister-in-law. Louise de la Bere, prof. 1872, died 1888.
[149]   Secular name unknown, prof. 1891, died 1897.
[150]   Mildred Airey, prof. 1882, died 1887.
[151]   Maud Airey, prof. 1878, died 1931, in South Africa.
[152]   Not identified.

sister, Miss Sybil Airey, who was a trained nurse. Very soon I was sent for. Dear
S. Mildred seemed dying and was most unhappily dying out of her Community.

We were indeed helped by Angels. I never can forget the anxious journey to
Oxford. The Railway officials were most kind. Our carriage from Bournemouth
was shunted at Basingstoke on to another line. S. Mary Teresa met us at Oxford
in a fly, with a bed of cushions into which S. Mildred was placed tenderly by a
good Porter. Her face was *radiant* with holy joy when she was placed in the bed
prepared for her at our Cowley Hospital. She lived just for one fortnight, ministered to and comforted by the holy Father Congreve. She fell asleep at 1st
Vespers of *Holy Cross*, Sept 13th, 1887, the first of our Sisters to join our Mother
in Paradise.

The churchyard of S. John and S. Mary, Cowley, was only just made and
consecrated, and our Sister Mildred was the first Religious buried there. The
S.S.J.E. Fathers have since been buried there and others of our Community who
have died at St. John's Hospital and Home, Cowley.

Sister Mary Gertrude,[153] who was so clever in taking down Retreat and other
Addresses in 'shorthand', and copying them out in a clear, easy-to-be-read writing
to give and send to the Sisters at Branch Houses, suddenly collapsed in health. She
developed rapid consumption. She had worked at Eastbourne for some time before
her Mother, Mrs. Knapping, would consent to her entering the Novitiate. Sister
Anne was very very fond of her and S. Mary Gertrude was devoted to Sister Anne,
so when she was so ill, we took her to Eastbourne where she died, August 11th,
1889. Her room, where she died, was afterward made into the Oratory, where later
on we received Episcopal permission to have the Great Blessing of the Reserved
Sacrament. Dear Sister Mary Gertrude was carried out every day over to the
Balcony of the Sisters' Wing, until the last day or two of her life.

That same year, dear Sister Georgina Frances[154] was sent home from the Cape
in the last stage of consumption – to die. She had worked so faithfully, lovingly
and devoted for *10* years, after a first attack of haemorrhage from the lungs
which she had *soon* after she was sent out in 1887. She was only in her 2nd year
there. She had a great gift for children and her two *Great Loves* were 'Our
LORD' and 'HIS children'. This Love it was that carried her on through the
suffering years of her life. St. Michael's Home for Destitute children was a
miserable 'bear garden' before our Foundress Mother sent out Sister Georgina
Frances. She had great gifts of organization and government and untiring watch-
fulness. At pain and cost to her delicate constitution, she worked night and day
for those poor children, and, by degrees, brought about a wonderful transforma-
tion in the children. Better food and better clothing and, above all, *motherly* love
from their Sister changed them from wild 'impossible' beings into real Christian
children. They were taught to pray and examine their consciences and make their

---

153 Mary Gertrude Knapping, prof. 1886, died 1889.
154 Georgina Frances Somerset (1850–89), prof. 1878.

Confessions and were prepared for Confirmation and their First Communion. Sister Georgina Frances also thought *Preparation for death* one of the most important duties of the Christian Life, and taught the children to prepare for a 'Good Death', as part of their daily lives.

As soon as possible, Sung Masses in the Home Chapel were instituted for the Greater Festivals and the 1st Midnight CHRIST-Mass *was a joy*. S. Georgina Frances, after washing and bathing the little ones thoroughly, put them to bed in the afternoon, then woke them up at 10 p.m. and clothed them in nice new frocks and white 'cappies', and they came softly into Chapel with Banners she had made for them, singing a Christmas Carol. After the Consecration, they sang Faber's Hymn, 'At Last Thou hast come Little Saviour' with the refrain 'Hail Mary's Little FLOWERS', etc. When I left Sister Georgina Frances at Cape-town, on my return to England August 1887, I did not expect to see her again on Earth. But she continued in her work till the following year and was then sent home to die. But she lingered on till June 17th, 1889.

Very soon, after our Mother Foundress' death, the desire to erect a Memorial worthy of her, began to take shape, and after great meetings of influential and old friends of the Community, it was decided to build the Children's Hospital at Eastbourne on the site of the Coast Guard Cottages which had been bought and used for little girls' Convalescence. Convalescent boys, at that time, were in St. Stanislaus Ward in the Adult Hospital.

Much time had to be given with S. Anne, over the plans for the Memorial and the Architect, Mowbray of Oxford, carried out Sister Anne's desires and suggestions very thoroughly. The first stone of the Memorial was laid by the Duchess of Albany on July 19th, 1888. It was a beautiful day and the choir boys from All Saints came down under their priest in charge, Mr. Ward. Their blue cassocks and white cottas and the processional cross glimmering in the sun looked a bright picture as they led the procession from the Hospital to the platform for the laying of the 1st stone. *Numbers* of old friends and All Saints people were there. Afterwards, there was a luncheon for the Princess-Duchess, and Dr. Frank[155] who had known her when she was a child sat beside her. She told us that her little son, the Duke of Albany – born after his father Prince Leopold's death was *four* years old that day.[156]

Those first 6 years after our Foundress' death were indeed full of every kind of event and trials – difficult to relate in order. Poor Sister Helen,[157] who was the S. Sup. of St. Elizabeth's Home, Mortimer Street, went out of her mind and had to be placed in an Asylum. Then the poor little Lay Sister Emily Dorcas[158] who was Kitchen Sister in Mortimer St. *also* became insane, but it was not necessary

---

[155] This is the Dr Frank who features so largely in the Franco-Prussian war diary.

[156] Prince Leopold (1853–84), duke of Albany and fourth son of Victoria.

[157] Helen Bowden (1827–96), prof. 1864. Nursed in Franco-Prussian war, at U.C.H., Chorlton workhouse, and in the U.S.A. and South Africa.

[158] Secular name unknown, sister of Rosa Mary, died 1893. Their father was the Sucklings' gardener.

to place her in an Asylum. We sent her to a quiet seaside place with a trustworthy woman to care for her. There she seemed to recover to a certain degree, but had a sudden chill and died of pneumonia. I was summoned to her one Sunday morning and travelled down in time to be with her a few hours before she died and to get a priest to anoint her. She could not speak, but he asked her certain questions and she was able to move her head in answer. Then he absolved her and her spirit departed as he committed her to God.

Then I had to make arrangements for her body to be removed home to our Mortuary and her Burial at Brompton.

I cannot recall the order of events, but other last illnesses and deaths of Sisters occurred during those crucial years. Sister Sophia Elizabeth had a *most* painful last illness. She bore her suffering heroically, but one could but weep to see and know it. Sister Georgina Mary[159] was another and hers was more prolonged. I was thankful to be allowed to help and comfort them spiritually, but naturally it was a great physical strain. Also we had Mrs Kempe, an elder, widowed sister of our Foundress Mother, staying at All Saints Home and she, too, was taken with her last illness and died there. It seemed as though one great strain after another came in quick succession.

Sister *Georgina Maria* had been put in charge of the little Home at Hastings, called White Rock, where we placed our baby orphans and delicate ones; our Orphanage then being in Margaret St. Sister Georgina Maria was not strong, but we were not prepared for her rapid lung trouble and death. I was called down to White Rock and her mother, Mrs. Golding, and one of her married sisters, also Jeannie, for the end. Then there was her funeral. She is buried in the Churchyard of an old church, the Goldings used to attend – a little way out of St. Leonards. After her death, Sister Helen Agnes was put in Charge.

As soon as events permitted, it was of necessity that I should visit all the Branch Houses: Liverpool, Wolverhampton, Bradford, Edinburgh, Helmsley, Leeds, and then there was Westminster to *begin*, and *Northampton* and *Hammersmith* also – *3 fresh works*. Meanwhile our dear Sister Harriet Mary failed, and after extreme *suffering, died*, Nov. 7th, 1890.

Directly after this, it was necessary for me to go to America to visit our Branches there. It had been settled that Sister Frances Helen should be made 1st Mother Superior and that the American Branch should be affiliated and have a Novitiate and Constitution of its own.[160] They were *building* their 1st House at Baltimore and all was waiting for a formal visit from the Mother General to set going our first Affiliation. I started from Liverpool with Sister Eleanor Mary[161]

159 This sister is listed in other records as Sr Georgina Maria, who was born Georgina Golding, prof. 1882, died 1889 of consumption. In the next paragraph Sr Caroline Mary refers to her as G. Maria.

160 All Saints had started work in the U.S.A. in 1872, associated with Mount Calvary Church, Baltimore.

161 Secular name unknown, professed 1889, died 1938, in India.

as my companion in November 1890 and arrived at New York in 7 days. We went first to Hoboken, as there was then a Branch Mission House there belonging to Holy Innocents Church. Sister Petronilla[162] was in charge. After seeing all these, after one night, we went on to Philadelphia where we then had important works under the S.S.J.E. Fathers who were in charge of S. Clement's Church. Fr. Maturin[163] had done a great work there, but he had just returned to England. Father Field[164] was in charge. There were large Confraternities of the Holy Family for married women; and of St. Mary for girls and unmarried women. They had their service and procession in Church. All wore veils, the Conf. of the H. Family, blue veils and the girls all White, edged with blue. They afterwards assembled for a Festival tea for my benefit. Fr. Field was there and was very kind in giving me welcome. Next day, S. Mary Cecily[165] gathered together the Outer Sisters, a goodly number, all most warm and affectionate in their greetings, as Americans always are. I forgot to say that during the day's visit at Hoboken, I was taken to call on the St. John Baptist (Clewer Affiliation) House in New York,[166] which was very interesting. They had spacious rooms for all their different Guilds and Embroidery and other works and a small but beautifully arranged Hospital for children.

The Foundress, Mother Harriet, was then alive and her Assistant was the Sister Sarah who had come over to our All Saints Novitiate for 3 months when I was Novice Mistress, to learn the rules and spirit of our Novitiate, as she was to be appointed 1st Mistress of St. Mary's Community in America, then being founded. This *Foundress Harriet of St. Mary's* had visited Clewer, East Grinstead,[167] Wantage[168] and All Saints before forming her own American Order, and she decided that All Saints Novitiate was the most Religious and Regular; she therefore asked and obtained permission for her 1st Novice Mistress to learn, by practice, what the life of a Novice should be. This Sister came and was placed as the *Last* Novice, and most edifying she was to all the Novices then under my care. Her simple obedience and Humility and her Devotion and Prayerfulness helped them all, and there was no restraint or difficulty felt by her presence.

Naturally she became a real friend to me. She was 20 years Novice Mistress in her own Community, and after Mother Harriet's death she was elected Mother

162 Ellen Kennett (1847–1904), prof. 1876.
163 Basil William Maturin (1847–1915). Ordained in 1871, he joined S.S.J.E. in 1873. Son of the persecuted tractarian William Maturin, rector of All Saints, Grangegorman, Ireland, B. W. Maturin converted to Catholicism in 1897, and died heroically in the sinking of the Lusitania.
164 Charles Neale Field, ordained 1873. By 1876 he had joined S.S.J.E., and served at St Clement's, Philadelphia, 1876–92. In 1892 he became provincial superior of S.S.J.E.
165 Mary Cecily Stephens, prof. 1883, died 1904.
166 Clewer began their New York branch in 1874, and it became an affiliated house in 1881, with Sr Frances Constance as mother superior until 1882, followed by Gertrude Verena to 1902.
167 Society of St Margaret, founded 1855.
168 Community of St Mary the Virgin, Wantage, founded 1848.

for a time till her health gave way. Fr. Benson thought much of her and she thought no one like him as a spiritual guide.

All Saints and St. Margaret's Communities[169] in America were on most sisterly and affectionate terms, and our Sisters from Baltimore used to attend the Retreats and take rest time at St. Mary's Convent at Peekskill, which was their Mother House in the country. I record these things because it is well for us to remember how our Community was founded and grew up and took all these important steps at the beginning of the Great Revival of Religious Orders in our Branch of the Catholic Church. GOD, in His Great Love, provided the *Foundress* and gave our Mother F. and our Spiritual Fathers and Directors wisdom and knowledge, not only to bring into birth and form our own All Saints Community into a true and faithful Religious Order, for the well-being of the souls HE called in to our Society, but HE also used us in a marked, special way, to teach, direct, and help our *other* Religious Societies. During my own Novitiate, and when I was Novice Mistress, we trained and prepared 3 Foundress Mother Superiors and the American 1st Novice Mistress of S. Mary's:

1   Mother Etheldreda, Foundress of the *Bethany* Sisterhood.
2   Mother Elizabeth Mary Jane, Foundress of St. Mary and St. John, Aberdeen.[170]
3   Mother Frances – of Dundee (now extinct).[171]
4   Sister Sarah of St. Mary's, America.

All these learned to train by being trained themselves in All Saints Novitiate.

I have made, I fear, a long interlude in my story of the first visit of the Mother Superior General to America. The Principal object of that visit being to inaugurate the first Affiliated Branch of our All Saints Community. To continue that account: After the short visit to Philadelphia, I went on to the Mother House at Baltimore where I stayed 10 days and had much business to go through with M. Frances Helen (not yet the 'Mother'). I went for an interview with the Bishop of Maryland,[172] their Diocesan, and after going thoroughly into the matter, he consented and fixed a day for coming to visit their All Saints Home and bless the

---

169 The Society of St Margaret (also known as St Mary's, and not to be confused with the British community of St Mary, Wantage) established an affiliated house in Boston in 1873, later expanding to Newark, Philadelphia, and elsewhere. Their rule at this time displayed Benedictine influences.
170 Mrs Elizabeth Ann Macdowell White was a novice at All Saints 1869–70. This community was also known as the Scottish Society of Reparation, and was founded in 1870. Established at Perth, the community later moved to Aberdeen and became known as the Community of St Mary and St John. The foundress died in 1893.
171 Mrs Frances Elizabeth Barnard Bolland co-founded the community with Bishop Forbes in 1871. This community was first known as the Sisters of the Poor of St Mary the Virgin, and was later styled the community of St Mary the Virgin and St Modwenna. Another member, Margaret Neish, also trained in the All Saints noviciate 1870–1. The community had essentially been absorbed by the Scottish branch of the Society of St Margaret by 1900.
172 William Paret (1826–1911), sixth bishop of Maryland, ordained 1853, consecrated 1885.

Sisters and *install* and consecrate Mother Frances Helen as first Mother of the Affiliation.

After this, I visited our Coloured Sisterhood[173] and coloured Boys Orphanage. Sister Mary Ursula was Sister Superior. There were, I think, then 3 *coloured* Professed Sisters and one or two Novices. They had charge and worked for the Church of St. Mary, set apart entirely for the *coloured* people.[174] There were other interesting works and houses I was taken to see at Baltimore. One was a large, good House where people of gentle birth, but poor, could be given apartments to themselves; sort of almshouses for gentry. The Americans seemed to do their Charities in a Lavish way, regardless of expense. We, All Saints Sisters at Baltimore, then had a small School of better class children, Orphans, or whose parents were poor.[175] The children were on the same par as our Orphans at home, only they were not orphans generally. The Sisters also took charge of Sacristan's work at the Church of Mt. Calvary and worked also under the Rector.[176]

I was there mostly during my 3 weeks' American Visitation. We kept, of course, our Advent Fast days and generally had *oysters*, raw, or boiled or cooked in some way. We never had *fish*, so probably that was too expensive.

After my visit to Baltimore, Mother Frances Helen came with me to Hoboken and New York again on my way back home to England, and I visited and dined in Community with the Mother Superior 'Harriet', Foundress of S. Mary's Sisterhood, New York, and I was placed at table next to the Assistant Superior, Sister Sarah, who had been in our Novitiate under me, while I was *Mistress*. She was very devoted to All Saints and to Fr. Benson. I remember, it being a fast day, we had *oyster soup*, about a doz. *big* oysters floating about in one's plate. I felt they were beyond me to swallow, so I was glad to see Sister Sarah put some of hers aside and I followed her example. I visited a delightful Children's Hospital, nursed and managed by St. Mary Sisters, also a big Mission House where they carried on numbers of works.

Then we went on to our steamer, hoping to reach home safely by Christmas Eve, but when we got close to Liverpool, a *dense* fog set in. . . .

---

[173] Sisters of St Mary and All Saints, Baltimore, was founded in 1880. It became extinct in 1917, when the last remaining sister, Babetta Frances (secular name unknown), with the consent of All Saints, joined the community of St John the Divine, Toronto, Canada.

[174] Many black parishes were established in the American south by the Episcopal church in the period 1865–75, in a largely unsuccessful attempt to win back blacks, who after liberation often left episcopalianism for nonconformity. The oldest black congregation in the southern U.S.A. was St James African church, Baltimore, founded 1824, predominantly for free blacks. St Mary the Virgin church arose out of St Philip's Mission, largely under the leadership of two black lay readers, James Thompson and Cassius Mason, both of whom were later ordained in the diocese of Missouri. All Saints ran day and night schools for black children.

[175] This was the School for Young Ladies, established in 1874 and never able to attract enough students, as fees were charged. It was closed in 1888.

[176] This was the Rev. Joseph Richey.

I. 2

Memories of Church Life

Memories of Church Life[1]

As long as I can remember from babyhood, my parents were heart-&-soul *one* with the Catholic Revival. – In *Nursery* days: we lived in Westminster, not far from the Abbey. – My father[2] went to 'Mattins' at 7 o'ck at the Abbey daily – my nurse dressed me to go with him – as being the only child available, the elder ones were at lessons in the Schoolroom. – It was before I could read, but it began in me the habit of 'Daily service' which was the practice of the family – 'Mattins & Evensong' long before the return of 'Daily Mass'. If we were anywhere out of reach of daily Church service. my parents read with us the Pss & Lessons for the day.

Family Prayers morning & night with the servants, was also the custom – and our Church Catechism repeated on Sunday, to father or mother along with the "paper-boy" & younger servants.

My father's influence extended to my aunts & uncles for they too adopted some of his customs. I have heard, but do not remember, that when he stayed with his brother[3] – a rector of a parish in Northamptonshire, he used to walk 3 miles for *Mattins* before breakfast to a neighbouring Church. Whereupon his brother began & continued daily Mattins in his own Church – though he had to ring his own Church-bell & had only his wife & little children, for congregation. During these very early Nursery days I can remember, a priest – one of the curates of S. Margarets' Church, Westminster, who was a great friend of my father's & must have been thoroughly Catholic in his teaching & life, his name was Mr Cook[4] – under his direction I know my father used to visit amongst the *dens* of poverty & vice in Westminster, & used to set my mother & our Nurse to work to make garments for the poor. Whilst still in the nursery we all went to Boulogne for a time I do not know, how long, but I was only learning to read &

---

[1] Written by Sister Caroline Mary, the author of 'Memories', and second mother superior of the Society.

[2] Charles William Short (1799–1857). He joined the army in 1816, and was promoted to captain and lieutenant-colonel in the Coldstream regiment of footguards in 1830, retiring in 1838. Officers held a rank in the guards, as well as an equivalent higher rank in the regular army.

[3] This was Augustus Short (1802–83), vicar of Ravensthorpe, Northamptonshire, and bishop of Adelaide 1874–81. He wrote a defence of Tract XC.

[4] John Aubone Cook (1811–59), ordained 1839, curate of St Margaret's, Westminster, 1844–50; vicar of South Benfleet, Essex, 1850–9.

was sent to the Ursuline Convent by day to pick up French. The Nuns made a great pet of me, but one day the French girls teazed me & called me a 'petite Protestante' & on the strength of my home teaching I answered 'Non, je suis Catholique' then on telling this episode 'at home' I remember Mr Cook, who was there, patting me & saying – 'quite right' 'so you are a *Catholic*'

A little later on when we were still in Westminster, we used to be sent up with our nursery governess, on Sunday afternoons to St Paul's Church, Knightsbridge to hear 'the clergymen with the kind face, catechize, the children' –

Afterwards, one knew he was *the* Mr Bennett – of S. Paul's and St Barnabas & then of Froome[5] – During this Westminster period which I believe was some time between 1844 to 1848-9 my father was deeply engaged in getting a new Church built for the poor – a Church with *free* seats & *open* – no doors to 'pews', & quite low – seats, instead of the usual 'high-pews' – he & Mr. Talbot – father of the present Bishop of Southwark[6] worked together & the result was, 'Christchurch – Broadway Westminster', then in the heart of slums – *now* 'Christ Church – Victoria St.' with hotels & mansions around it. Great care was taken that the Altar should be *raised*, and approached, with a flight of steps. Mr Cyril Page,[7] another priest friend of my parents, was the first 'Curate in Charge' & I *think* the preacher wore his surplice – but am not quite sure – as the surplice was I know later on, considered as a thing 'bordering on Rome', if seen in a pulpit.

But, I know, as far as they could go then, the Prayer-book's rubrics were followed out at Christ-church.

During this period, of earliest recollection, there was an incident which impressed on me (perhaps afterwards when I was a little older) the *sorrow* of religious or rather Church separation it was when we were at Boulogne. A kind, grave, gentleman friend & relation of my mother's used to visit us – always good to us, children – afterwards I gathered that it was 'poor Robert C. who was a good priest at Oxford but *had gone after Newman*'[8]– to the *sorrow* of his English Catholic friends, but not to the breaking of friendship with him.

At this period of my life, all Church things were as natural to me as my daily surroundings. But since then, one has learnt somewhat of the influences that

5 W. J. E. Bennett, vicar of the wealthy St. Paul's, Knightsbridge, became notorious for the ritual of his services, leading to the St Barnabas riots of 1850. He then accepted a living in Frome, always spelled with two 'o's by Bennett.

6 Mr Talbot senior was the hon. John Chetwynd Talbot (1806–52), a barrister. He was a life-long friend of Pusey, one of the founders of the English Church Union and a signatory to its resolution denouncing the Gorham judgment. His son, Edward Stuart Talbot (1844–1934, was the first anglican bishop of Southwark (1905–11) and bishop of Winchester (1911–23). He had earlier been the first warden of Keble College, vicar of Leeds and bishop of Rochester (1895–1905).

7 Cyril William Page (1806–73), perpetual curate, Christ Church, Westminster, 1843–73. He established daily morning and evening prayers in Westminster, as well as services for holy days.

8 This was probably Robert Aston Coffin (1819–85), vicar of St Mary Magdalen, Oxford, who converted to catholicism in 1845. He became a Redemptorist in 1852 and in 1883 the third Roman catholic bishop of Southwark. (This is not be confused with the anglican diocese of Southwark, founded in 1905.)

affected my parents & how they were drawn as Lay-people into the Catholic 'Revival'– we, their children knew nothing of a 'Revival' but were taught & trained to live & fight for the Truth – the Church of our fathers – & bit by bit, step by step to regain her Rights as a True Branch of the Catholic Church *the* Branch planted by Divine & apostolic Authority in our native land.

As far as I know, from the time my parents married they were personal friends of *Keble* and of *his* friends. As time went on there was scarcely (I believe) a priest or layman who were known leaders in the 'Movement', with whom my father was not in touch – & who did not value him as a personal friend & defender of the Faith. I mean of the older set of men – Dr Pusey – Mr I. Williams[9] – Mr C. Marriot[10] – Mr Upton Richards,[11] Mr Bennett – 'Archdeacon Manning' – & the Talbots & Pagets[12] & Palmers[13] & Munros & Haddan[14] – Lord Blatchford, when he was Sir Fred^rk Rogers[15] & Sir W. Cope[16] &c.

Mr Sidney Herbert[17] – Mr Suckling of Bussage (*father* of F^r Suckling).[18] Bishop Robert Gray of Capetown, Mr Carter of Clewer[19] – Mr Butler of Wantage – all these & many others. My father had to do with the beginning of the Guardian newspaper – & the first little Church Magazine, '*the Penny Post*'.[20] In *that* little paper he once wrote on the necessity of reviving in our Branch of the Church 'Sisterhoods' – and that there should be 'Sisters' with lives given up to GOD & for service of GOD amongst the poor the sick & the fallen – he gave an account of the S. Vincent Sisters & their houses & work in Paris.

[9]   Isaac Williams (1803–65), fellow of Trinity College, Oxford, 1831–40. He wrote numbers 80, 86 and 87 of *Tracts for the Times*. Sister Catharine was his niece.

[10] Charles Marriot (1811–1858), fellow of Oriel 1833–58, subdean of Oriel from 1841, vicar of St Mary the Virgin, Oxford, 1850–8; chief editor of the series *Lives of the Fathers*.

[11] William Upton Richards (1811–73), perpetual curate of All Saints, Margaret St., Marylebone, 1849–73. Co-founder of the All Saints community, he also provided premises for the sisterhood.

[12] Sir James Paget (1814–99) was an ecclesiastical lawyer; his son Francis Paget (1851–1911) was dean of Christ Church, Oxford, and later bishop of Oxford.

[13] The family knew Sir Roundell Palmer (1812–95), later the earl of Selborne, a celebrated ecclesiastical lawyer and Liberal M.P., as well as his brother, the Rev. William Palmer (1811–97), a liturgical scholar, who was anglo–catholic but vehemently anti-Roman. He became a catholic in 1855. Both were associates of Pusey.

[14] Arthur West Haddan (1816–73), ecclesiastical historian, and Thomas Henry Haddan (1814–73), originator of the *Guradian*, the most important high church newspaper of the period.

[15] Sir Frederick Rogers (1811–89), later Lord Blatchford. A close friend of Cardinal Newman, he was influential in anglo-catholic circles, founding the *Church Guardian* newspaper in 1846. He was permanent under secretary of state for the colonies, 1860–71.

[16] Sir William Henry Cope (1821–91), minor canon and librarian, St Peter's Westminster 1842–53; chaplain at Westminster hospital 1843–51.

[17] Sidney Herbert (1810–61), M.P., secretary of state for war, became Lord Herbert of Lea in 1861.

[18] Alfred Sucking (1818–51). 'Sucking of Bussage', where he was perpetual curate 1846–51. Twenty disciples of Keble and Pusey built his church, St Michael and All Angels. He oversaw the founding of the Community of St Michael's and All Angels, 1851. Robert Sucking (1842–1917), rector of Barsham, Suffolk 1868–80, vicar of St Peter London Docks 1880–2, and St Albans, Holborn, 1882–1916.

[19] Thomas Thellusson Carter (1808–1901), rector of Piddlehinton, Dorset, from 1838. He was rector of Clewer (1844–80), co-founder of the Community of St John the Baptist, 1851, and became hon. canon of Christ Church, Oxford, in 1870.

[20] Published 1851–79.

After this Westminster period of family life – we came to live very near St Paul's Church Wilton Place then, we children were enrolled as 'Catecheumens' & our names registered by Mr Bennett & we attended the Sunday Catechism as well as daily Mattins & Evensong. It was a two years Instruction before Confirmation – he took us through the Church Catechism in the year very fully, carefully & thoroughly we were grounded in the Faith by Mr Bennett, and as I believe, 'Baptismal Regeneration' was the doctrine attacked in those days, we were specially taught on that subject & the Sacrament of Holy Baptism always took place, after the 2nd Lesson: with great impressiveness after we had received a lesson upon its meaning –

It was during those two years or so, that we lived close to St Pauls' that one remembers clearly 'the struggle for the Faith' and the enthusiasm it inspired. Heart & mind were *intent*, as one grew to know that the Catholic Cause, was the persecuted cause – that even a little cross on one's prayer book, or having a 'Christian Year' in one's possession brought about Protestant sneers & the nick name of Puseyite.

Then came the St Barnabas riots[21] & my dear father was one of those laymen sworn in as 'Special Constables', who stood at the rood screen guarding the Chancel from any attack by the mob.

During this period I remember that my father always often brought in two or three friends after 8 o'ck Mattins at St Paul's, to breakfast – & that they discussed earnestly. Church matters all the time. Also I remember certain evening gatherings, when *many* clergy & laity met in our house – to consult on Church matters. We children, were banished & I do not think my mother was present, it was a grave consultation of men – probably it was the beginning & before the birth of the '*London* Church Union'[22] to which my father belonged as soon as it was formed.

Churchmen met also to discuss & organize *Church* Penitentiary work[23] – Suckling of Bussage,[24] Carter of Clewer – Scudamore[25] & Armstrong[26] – after-

---

[21] Like the better-known riots at St George's-in-the-Fields in 1859, the parishioners of St. Barnabas utilized a bodyguard of gentlemen to defend the church in the early fifties. According to John Shelton Reed, the bodyguards and defence associations founded 'soon coalesced into the English Church Union, an institutional development of great importance'. Reed, *Glorious battle. The cultural politics of anglo-catholicism* (London, 1996), p. 59.

[22] Despite controversy and some splits, the London Church Union merged in 1859 with a number of other unions to form the English Church Union, which had over 20,000 members by 1882, of which almost 3,000 were clerical, and over 420 branches.

[23] The Church Penitentiary Association, which funded institutions for the reformation of fallen women, staffed by 'dedicated women' (mostly sisterhoods) was founded in 1860.

[24] Two of Suckling's daughters were to join All Saints: Sister Mary Augustine, the Society's third mother superior, and Sister Mary Teresa. The family was notable for its wealth.

[25] W. Edward Scudamore, rector of Ditchingham, Bungay, 1839–71, and warden of the community of All Hallows, Ditchingham.

[26] John Armstrong (1813–56), first bishop of Grahamstown, Cape of Good Hope 1853. He was an advocate of female penitentiaries, and one of the founders of the Church Penitentiary Association.

wards Bishop Armstrong in S. Africa were the leaders of this movement.[27] M[r] Brett, of Stoke Newington[28] was also one whose great spiritual influence was felt in a wide circle – his manuals of Prayer, were full of Catholic teaching & spiritual training for children, as well as for their elders. There were not many Church story-books in those days, but we were sufficient with such books as Gresley's Siege of Lichfield[29] – Paget's Village Stories[30] – Miss Sewell's[31] stories, such as 'Amy Herbert' & 'Margaret Percival – Monro's Allegories[32] – and a Magazine called the Churchmans' Companion wherein was a story called 'the Prisoners of Hope'[33] which instructed one about Confession, & the Church described in it was 'S[t] Thomas' Oxford' & the 'priest' was a description of M[r] Chamberlain[34] – who I suppose had much to do in founding S[t] Thomas' Sisterhood at Osney.

About 1852 was the date when first I knew of the 'Woodward Schools' & my father at once threw himself into the plan of founding *Church* Schools for the middle classes (boys & girls). A spiritual daughter of M[r] Woodwards[35] *began* S[t] *Michaels School* for girls, at Brighton, which has now developed in to S[t] *Michaels' School – Bognor.*[36] Miss Rooper who *began* the School, was the daughter of a clergyman who lived on his own means, in a large house at Brighton – he was very Protestant & would not consent to his daughter dedicating her life to GOD, & the Church – so all she could do was to visit her little school daily & impart to the children, the Church's Truth & very deep spirituality, and rules of self-discipline and mortification. My sister & I were placed under her care for a year, & she did much for our inner life & helped us greatly. She afterwards died when the School was in its infancy – Lady Caroline Eliot came forward to take up this work as a *Church* work & carried it to Bognor –

It is during the year 1853 whilst we were at Brighton, I can recall, the great

---

27 As well as founding the Church Penitentiary Association, all of the men in this list, with the exception of Bishop Gray, co-founded or were closely involved with the establishment of a sisterhood in their parish.

28 Robert Brett was popularly known as 'the pope of Stoke Newington'. A surgeon, he funded the building of a number of anglo-catholic churches in north and east London.

29 William Gresley (1801–76), ordained 1825, incumbent of St Paul's, Brighton, and later prebendary of Lichfield. He advocated the confessional and wrote prolifically on this and other subjects. He wrote a series of didactic historical novels aimed at younger readers.

30 Francis Edward Paget began the series *Tales of the village children* in 1845; the last was published in 1860.

31 Elizabeth Missing Sewell's (1815–1906) first and most popular novel, *Amy Herbert*, was published anonymously in 1844. She was a regular contributor to Charlotte Mary Yonge's *Monthly Packet*, a keen and constant advocate of sisterhoods.

32 Edward Monro (1815–66), perpetual curate of Harrow Weald 1842–60, vicar of St John's Leeds 1860–6. His *Allegories* were published in 1849.

33 This story began serialization in January 1852, and concluded in the following year.

34 Thomas Chamberlain (1810–92), vicar of St Thomas Osney, and co-founder of the Community of St Thomas the Martyr, Oxford.

35 Nathaniel Woodward (1811–91), who established affordable schools for the middle classes, and a friend of Oakeley.

36 The school was founded in 1856 and moved to Petworth when the second world war broke out, where it remained.

work then being carried on by Mr Arthur Wagner[37] at St Paul's the teachings & practice about *Lent* – the Intercessions – and the constant prayers for the *Unity of Christendom*. Also the *persecutions* of the Protestants upon Mr Wagner, chiefly about 'Confession'. Protestants were then still in fury over 'the Papal Aggression' when the Pope divided England into Bishoprics of the Church of Rome – and all our good Catholic Clergy were supposed to be playing into the hands of Rome. As far as I knew, & can remember, it seemed as if *all* the Bishops were against their best & most faithful Clergy – except, I used to hear my father say, Bishop Phillpots of Exeter[38] – was good to his faithful Clergy.

I can remember my parents kept *Lent* strictly, we none of us had butter on week days – father & mother & children all eat dry bread – & gave up sweets & c – and in the evening after 5 o'ck Evensong at S. Pauls', Wilton Place – we, children worked making garments for the poor, whilst our Mother read to us 'Law's serious Call' or other books of the kind – we had no 'parties' in Lent & my parents never dined out, nor did they on Fridays at any time. These customs were not, I think, peculiar to our family. Other families, we knew as children of "good Churchpeople" kept the same rules – Col: Morison in the Guards[39] & the 'Henry Bowdens', intimate friends of my father's in close Church sympathies lived the same kind of lives.

The last four years of my father's life, we left London – and lived in a village in Hampshire[40] – but he used to go constantly to London to attend Church meetings & work for the House of Charity Soho[41] – he threw himself into the Village Church life & backed up & helped his Vicar, as his Church warden and began improving the Church by introducing some open seats – putting up alms boxes & other things – till health & strength failed.

He was 57 when he died.

After his Last Communion, when we were all kneeling round, he exhorted us to be faithful to the Church – and to English Branch of the Catholic Church, which he likened to a vessel in a storm and the sailors must cling to her & not

37 Arthur Douglas Wagner (1825–1902), curate, St Paul's, Brighton, 1848–52; perpetual curate there 1850–1902. Chancellor, Chichester cathedral, 1871–7. He was a devoted parish priest, who adopted very advanced ritual. He was co-founder and patron of the community of St Mary the Virgin, Brighton.
38 Henry Phillpotts (1778–1869), bishop of Exeter from 1830. An extreme tory, he defended the government after the Peterloo massacre, and opposed catholic emancipation. A high churchman, while disapproving of ritualism, he vigorously attacked ultra-protestantism and broad tendencies in his clergy. He presided at an informal inquiry into the conduct of the Devonport Sisterhood in 1849 and, clearly predisposed in their favour, vindicated their conduct.
39 The only identifiable Col. Morison in the army in this period is William Mansfield Morrisson (enlisted 1804, died 1850). He was lt.-col. 23rd Reg. Light Dragoons from 1830, and colonel from 1846.
40 Odiham, Hants.
41 The house of Charity was founded in 1847, providing short-term accommodation for 'distressed persons in London. Lt. colonel Short was one of the founders and first warden. It moved from Rose Street to Greek Street in 1862, and the Clewer sisters began working there the same year.

forsake her, so long as GOD in his Mercy let a plank remain. This was in January 1857 – & that year, my mother permitted me to spend a strict Lent at the Home of Charity – then in Rose Street, Soho, under the care of the Matron, a devout woman – who took me to the services at the *Temporary* 'All Saints Church' – held in a Chapel in Titchfield Street – such reverent, devout services & congregation, which greatly impressed me. Mr Upton Richards gave a short Meditation on the Passion every evening in Passion-tide –

I was also taken to 'All Saints Home' 82 Margaret St – but only on a message. The Home & Sisterhood had only been established there a year – i.e. from August 4th 1856 – and in numbers consisted only of 'the Mother Sup^t. Brownlow Byron' & 4 or 5 Sisters. They had been living by Rule, apart from the world & *preparing* for their life-dedication since 1851 – at least Mother & two or three with her – and until the All Saints Home, Margaret St was ready for them, they had lived at the House in Mortimer St, which is now S^t. Elizabeth's House –

My mother did not consent to my coming to dwell at All Saints House until 1859 & then would not allow me to 'take the Habit' & insisted on my returning home between whiles, for 7 years, so there was a long time of discipline & probation – which in those days was often the ordering of life, for those called to the 'Consecrated Life'.

During those waiting years Mr Upton Richards often told me of others who like myself had to wait 'GOD'S Time' – and have an 'outside' Noviciate, before passing into the actual Noviciate.

It was not an easy thing to enter a Religious Com^{ty} in those days – Much suspicion & 'ill' was thought of them & the *dress* of 'a Sister' disliked & scoffed at. When at length I received 'the Habit' I remember as we walked in the street, passers by often scoffed or showed positive hatred of our outside dress – 'made faces' at us & called us 'Sisters of Misery' (sic) and one's own relations even 'pitied us'.

I put these things down to shew how slowly & with what painful but earnest, faithful, determined steps the Church Revival made its way.

Bit by bit, step by step so far, it has broken down protestant predjudice and in those early days, it used to seem to me something like the early Christian times – not so much outward show or talk, but a deep down life & steadfastness of purpose and holding fast to Catholic Truth.

To go back to the year 1851. At that time, I clearly remember, there were only *two* Daily Eucharists offered in London – viz. (1.) at the Temporary Chapel of All Saints – (the *Church* in Margaret S., was not finished & consecrated till 1859.) and (2.) at St Barnabas Church Pimlico. Mr Bennett began the Daily Eucharist there as soon as the Church was consecrated in 1850.

I. 3

Memories of an Old Woman

The Recollections of an Old Woman. Novr. 1907

I first went to Margaret Chapel[1] in the Spring of 1842 – Mr. Upton Richards[2] was then Curate to Mr. Oakley[3] (sic) the Incumbent. My Father was acquainted with both. Mr. Redhead[4] was Organist & gave me lessons in chaunting.

We used to go to Town[5] from time to time & almost always had lodgings within reach of Margaret Chl. & attended the Services both in the old Chapel, & in Titchfield Street, & 77 Margaret Street before All Saints Church was built.

My Father introduced me to Mr Richards in 1849.

We often saw Mrs. Stewart & her three daughters on their way to Church in the dark mornings, trotting along like so many little ponies. In these years many great & holy men were to be seen in Margaret St. on their way to & from the Chapel & Church to worship or preach. I remember, especially dear Bishop Forbes' of Brechin[6] spare & tall form, standing frequently at the door of the Clergy House waiting for admission.

We all spent the Easter of 1856 in Margaret St.

Mr. Upton Richards took me over the new houses, 80, 81, 2, 3 which were built for the Sisters, & explained that they had to be built like ordinary houses in case they had to be given up at the end of the Lease. The Sisters & Mother were then living in S. Elizabeth's H & they had also No. 8 Margaret St.[7] I made my first Confession in the Oratory there.

1 These recollections were written by Sister Catharine Williams (prof. 1870, died 1917), the sister who wrote the Franco-Prussian war diary. She was in her eighties when she wrote these memoirs.
2 Upton Richards had been perpetual curate of what was to become All Saints, Margaret Street since 1849.
3 Frederic Oakeley (1802–80) was the son of Sir Charles Oakeley, governor of Madras. He was the incumbent of St Margaret's Chapel, Marylebone, and prebendary of Lichfield. He converted to Roman catholicism in 1845, was ordained priest, and served as a canon of Westminster.
4 R. Redhead (1820–1901) was organist at Margaret Street, and was a well-known and prolific composer of religious music of all types. He was among the earliest to set anglican offices to gregorian chant, and his most celebrated hymn tune is probably 'Petra' (Rock of Ages).
5 Sister Catharine was from Aberystwyth.
6 Alexander Penrose Forbes, ordained 1844, consecrated 1847. He was admonished and censured by the college of bishops in 1860 for his views on the real presence, and was co-founder of the sisterhood of St Mary and St Modwenna. He died in 1875.
7 The original home of the community was a series of houses in and around Margaret Street, Marylebone, at that time a place of great poverty.

I first saw Mother at S. Elizabeth's Home in /55 or /56. She & S. Sarah were in a small room there with one or two little girls.

Mr. U. R. showed me the Rules for the Outer Sisters, which were just begun & asked if I would like to join; but I must consult my Father: he would not give his consent as he feared it might take my interests away from home. The Sisters then wore a plain black dress & small white collar – a close fitting cap with black strings like those worn by postulants.

It was in the following year /57 or /58 that I spent some months with a brother who was living in Pimlico, as he was out all day I had a great deal of time to myself & M[r]. U. Richards gave me an introduction to M[r]. Cosby White[8] who gave me a District. It was the year that Mr Poole[9] one of the Curates of S. Barnabas went to Rome.

I first went to stay at All SS Home in 1861 or 2. I was feeling very unwell at the time & soon developed Typhoid fever. Mother took lodgings for me at 74 Margaret St. I had a nurse from U.C.H., S. Martha, who died at Chorlton Un: & S. Helen,[10] who was a Novice, used to come relieve the Nurse.

The Common Room was the room now occupied by S. Isabella:[11] we had no Com: Room Sister but applied to S. Eliza for what we wanted. I think there were only 2 or 3 ladies staying in the house at that time; but Anne Wigram (S. Anne) & Elizabeth Louisa Stewart[12] came in for dinner – it was Lent.

I was allowed to help at the decorations for the Church – I suppose for Easter. We prepared them in the little Waiting Room-Mother, S. Eliza, S. Mary[13] (who left us) & Fr. W. U. R. came in to see how we were getting on, he had a latch key & used to come in every afternoon, I remember he objected to S. Mary making designs with the petals of geraniums stuck on with gum, said it was not real, but sham.[14]

8   George Cosby White (1825–1918), priested 1849, curate and then vicar of St Barnabas, Pimlico 1856–76; and by 1865 a member of St Barnabas college, Pimlico (a hybrid brotherhood/ anglo-catholic clergy house). Became vicar of Malvern Links, 1876–7 and then Newland, Worcs., 1877–97.

9   Alfred Poole (1826–1904) did not go to Rome. Ordained in 1850, he was a curate at St Barnabas, Pimlico when Tait revoked his licence in 1858 due to a scandal over allegations of improper questioning of women in the confessional. Poole appealed to the privy council in 1859 and lost in 1861. It may be this scandal that Sister Catharine is recollecting; it would be easy to confuse who left for Rome, as the curates of this parish fled hence in some profusion: curates converted in 1847, 1849, and three in 1850. Poole later was nominated to a curacy in Purbrook and the bishop of Winchester licensed him to it without objection. He became vicar (1861–86), and was rector of Laindon Hills, Essex from 1886.

10 Helen Bowden (1827–1896), prof. 1864. She was a good medical nurse and worked in many hospitals in Britain, America and South Africa during her religious life, as well as establishing the nurses' training school at Bellevue hospital, New York.

11 Isabella Scott Beach (d. 1913), prof. 1870. She was sister superior at Margaret Street.

12 She may have made an unsuccessful attempt to found a sisterhood, which I cannot identify, in Scotland.

13 Mary Gream, prof. 1859, left 1860 to convert to catholicism.

14 Sister Catharine is suggesting a metaphorical link between Sister Mary's decorations and her anglicanism.

After the Services were transferred from 10 Titchfield St to 77 Margaret St, the old Chapel in Titchfield St was used for an Infant School. Mrs Oldsworthy[15] was the Mistress – I sometimes helped her. When the Clock struck all the children stood up & repeated a verse.

Mrs. Oldsworthy was for years one of the guests at our Xmas dinner & sat next to Mother in Refectory.

I think it was in 1863 that I again stayed at the Home – the Visitors were then in S. Raphael. Annie Baty (S.Gertrude)[16] was then on a visit: she seemed to be always making children's frocks & pinafores

Annie Gutch[17] (S. Anna Maria) & Phoebe Walker[18] (S. Phoebe) were then working in the Orphanage & used to come into the Common Room for some of their meals. The Orphans used then to attend the Parish School – I helped there sometimes, I also used to go the Creche which S. Emily[19] had. She was naturally unpunctual so had to ring the Chapel Bell for Offices: she had a beautiful voice, & was a very simple childlike soul. S. Harriet[20] had the girls & I assisted her at the Night School.

Harriet Bouverie used to come to the House for part of the day sometimes: she was a nominal postulant; but c^d not leave her sister. S. Vincent was then the Community Room.[21]

One or two of the visitors were invited occasionally to join the Sisters at Recreation: it was thought a great honor; but one I did not covet. It was stiff & formal. We sat on the ground as near as possible to Mother, who made a remark to one from time to time. Sometimes a Cat & kittens were brought in. I was surprised to see the Sisters so taken up with them.

In 1865 I went to All SS Home & did not leave the Community again. S. Emily had died that spring. S. Harriet had gone to take charge of S. Elizabeth's Home. S. Mary Elizabeth, a Cousin of Mr Richards's, was Common Room Sister. She was very kind to me & I used to help her with the lending Library &c. In the Autumn I was allowed, to my great joy to go to University College <Hospital> to be trained & I worked on there the following year, both before & after I became a postulant. S. Elizabeth was Sister Superior, S. Emily Mary had 1 & 2 Wards, & I think S. Helen had 3 & 4. S. Charlotte,[22] who was deaf & delicate died on 14th Dec^r & S. Mary Elizabeth died 3 days later of small pox caught

---

15 This was almost certainly Mrs Jane Elsworthy, described in the 1860 *London directory* as mistress at the infant school, 10 Great Titchfield St.
16 Anne Baty, prof. 1865, left 1895.
17 Anna Maria Gutch, an Australian, prof. 1868, died 1906, U.S.A.
18 Phoebe Walker, a lay sister, died 1895 in India.
19 Emily Fuller, prof. 1861, as an elderly woman, died 1868.
20 Harriet Brewer (b. 1826, d. 1876 in U.S.A.), prof. 1857.
21 All the rooms in the sisterhood seem to have had saints' names.
22 Charlotte Smith (1833–65), prof. 1859.

in the District. She was devoted to the poor & they to her. The two Sisters were buried at Brompton on the same day. Mother sent to U.C.H to ask me to go the Funeral as S. M. E was very fond of me. The Cholera raged fearfully in 1866.[23] Some of the Night Nurses at the London Hospital had died of it, & there was a regular panic & no one was willing to take their place. The Night Nurses there at that time were quite a different class to the day-nurses – simply poor women who came from their own homes to take the night duty. They were living in the District where the Cholera was so bad & so became victims themselves. Our Sisters were asked to help[24] – I was a postulant[25] then & went with them for some nights. We took it in turn to go & Mr Christie[26] went with us.

It was a fearful sight-people writhing in pain & so little to be done for souls or bodies. Several Priests came and did what they could.

At the London Hospital[27] there were special wards & arrangements for Hebrew patients;[28] but it was impossible to keep them separate. The jews had their watchers, who stood by them repeating the psalter so long as they breathed. All through the night there was the tramp of men carrying out the dead, & then bringing others to fill the beds they had just gone from.[29]

When we reached Home in the morning we had to have baths & change all our clothes for fear of infection before breakfast & then we went back to our work at U.C.H. & rested that night. But after a short time certain Sisters were told off for the night work, & so were able to go to bed in the day. We had only a poor little room at the top of the Hospital (UCH) for an Oratory; but the rules were very strict: if we wanted to get a book or any-thing we had to take off our apron & leave it on the floor outside. To go into the Chapel, Oratory or Community Room in our apron or veil was a thing unheard of. We walked to All SS Church every morning for the Cele: The Hospital Chaplain was very protestant

---

23 The asiatic cholera struck east London in mid-summer; the first case came into the London hospital (now the Royal London hospital) on July 13. There were 67 cases in ten days, and 230 (with 110 deaths) in two weeks. Pickford's vans came every morning to take away the dead; at the cholera's peak, forty people were dying every night in this one hospital, with similar stories in many others.

24 Mrs Gladstone seems to have taken the initiative in inviting the sisters to step in (she was a regular visitor to the hospital and had close ties with a number of communities). They were at work in July and had withdrawn by mid-September, as the outbreak subsided.

25 In other words she was waiting for her clothing, which would mark her entrance into the noviciate.

26 Not identified.

27 The hospital (now the Royal London hospital) sent a letter of thanks to the community after the outbreak subsided. It is reprinted in E. W. Morris, *A history of the London hospital* (London, 1910), p. 207.

28 In 1860 wards were set aside for Jewish patients, from 1866 in the newly-built Alexandra wing, although during the cholera the pressure on beds meant that such arrangements temporarily broke down.

29 Because east London was still waiting for its new drainage system while the rest of London's was already built, the bulk of the cases were in this area. Three-quarters of the deaths took place in what is now Tower Hamlets.

he walked about the Hospital in his Gown, & had Matins on one of the long Wards on Sunday. He often came into one of the Wards as dinner was placed on the table, & when asked to say Grace repeated a long prayer.[30]

The Noviciate was then in 82. S. Francis Xavier was the Instruction Room. S. Sarah was Mistress. The Choir Novices were S. Ethel[31] (afterwards the Mother of Bethany), S. Emily Catherine,[32] S. Sophia,[33] S. Anna Maria, & a Novice, who left us, & was afterwards professed at Wantage, where she died. S. Caroline Mary & I were postulants, & after a time we were joined by Lucy. S. Phoebe[34] & S. Frances[35] were Lay Novices & Alice[36] (S. Alice) a Postulant.

S. Harriet was in Charge of S. Elizabeth's Home, & when she went away for a short time, I was sent there to take her place. S. Margaret,[37] who worked in the District lived there, & had to come back to change her clothes before going to the Home for Recreation as the Sisters complained of her bringing vermin from the District. She was wonderfully humble & wanted me, a postulant, to say the Offices in Chapel. She always looked like a poor old woman, yet she was of a good old family & brought her diamonds to the Home.

S. Elizabeth's Ward was then occupied by incurable men & boys; but after the Hospital at Eastbourne was opened, they were given up & a man named Carr & Tourncy a crippled boy were sent there. It was intended to have Incurables, as well as Convalescents at the Hospital; but it did not answer.

On Sunday 12th August 1866, S. Lucy & I were Clothed. Carrie Short[38] could not leave her Mother.

The Cholera was still at its height like a plague, & Mother did not think it right to have anything festive during the visitation, so the Reception was quite quiet & on a Sunday.

One night when we were in Retreat a frightful fire broke out in Well Street.[39] The Mistress came & called and told us to get up & dress, so as to be ready to leave the Home if necessary. Mr. Hoskins came backwards & forwards to the House to report the progress of the fire, which was at last extinguished before reaching Margaret St. S. Lucy spent most of her time in writing, copying

---

[30] His black Geneva gown was a marker of low church sympathies, as was his use of matins rather than the eucharist. Anglo-catholics did not approve of long (probably extempore) prayers.

[31] Etheldreda Benett (b. 1824), prof. 1866, after a two years' noviciate; left the day after her profession. She was a friend of the mother foundress who entered the All Saints noviciate in order to prepare herself to found her own community, the Society of the Sisters of Bethany.

[32] Secular name unknown, prof. 1868, dismissed under statute XV, 1897 or 1899.

[33] Harriet Sophia Robinson (1836/7–1904), prof. 1868.

[34] Secular name unknown. Died 1895, in India.

[35] Sarah Farmer (1844–97), prof. 1866.

[36] Alice Tucker (1848–1925), prof. 1868. She had been an orphan in All Saints' home from the age of six.

[37] Margaret Wilkinson (1823–83), prof. 1863.

[38] Sister Caroline Mary.

[39] The *Evening standard* of 13 Aug. 1866 describes the fire as extensive, estimating the damage at several thousand pounds.

Meditations &c & died of Phthysis at the end of 2 years. I was sent to Eastbourne
very soon after I was clothed to help S. Constance[40] at the little Convalescent
Home in Compton St, & after a time went to help S. Philippa,[41] who had Charge
of a small Orphanage at Eastbourne.

Mother was very particular in those days in reserving *the* Sister for the Choir
addressing Lays as simply Sister —.[42]

After leaving Eastbourne, I again returned to U.C.H & worked there on & off
for two years or more.

When at the Home I was sometimes sent to help S. Anne to wash the tiles in
Chapel. She was Sacristan & Dispenser & did all the work alone, & when the
Mistress was away took the Novices' Recreation.

I also did the Chancel of the Church, with one or two other Novices, under the
direction of Mr Hoskins & S. Sarah. They were both very particular & taught so
thoroughly that in after years I was able to be Sister Sacristan at the Church & S.
Isabella thought it a privilege to help me. We had always to take our Bibles to
Church for Matins & Evensong, as we were told that Mr Richards wished us to
follow the Lessons in our books; but one day it was announced to us that he
desired we should follow the Epistles & Gospels in our prayer books also. The
next morning it was perfectly dark, where the Novices knelt, & the Mistress said
it was very edifying to see each Novice with her prayer book in hand though she
could not read a word!

It was also a strict rule that those who were to make their Communion should
say the Confession aloud, & all present must say 'Amen' after the Consecration
Prayer.

[1866 or 7][43] We heard that the authorities of Chorlton Un:[44] had sent to ask
Mother to send Sisters to assist in the nursing at the Infirmary in that place. There
had been a terrible outbreak of Typhus in a low part of Manchester from which
patients were sent to Chorlton Union, some of the Nurses took it, & there had
been such a panic, that it had been impossible to get Nurses to undertake the
numerous cases, which were daily being brought in. S. Elizabeth & another
Sister[45] were sent off at once, & when S. Elizabeth had to return to U.C. H. S.
Rosamund & S. Martha went to Chorlton. S. Martha died of Typhus in 1868, &
was buried in the Workhouse Cemetery. She was much beloved & respected, &
the Guardians put up a stone to her memory. Different Sisters one after another
were sent to take her place: some had the fever & S. Phoebe nearly died of it. S.
Rosamund, however continued to work on, until the Sisters were withdrawn

---

40 Constance Warren (1825–90), prof. 1863.
41 Phillipa Nichols (b. 1833), prof. 1864, left 1869.
42 Lay sisters were referred to as (for example) 'Sister Martha'; a choir sister would be addressed as
    'The Sister Mary'.
43 Written in another hand.
44 Workhouse nursing was one of the last areas of nursing to see reform.
45 'S. Helen' is written over 'another' in the same hand.

about 1877 or 8. Sister Agatha[46] took S. R's place when she went to the German Franco War[47] in 1870. S. Rosamund used to go Home once a year for the Retreat & generally stayed away 2 or 3 months & S. Helen came to the Union during S. Rosamund's absence, until S. H went to America.

S. Rosamund went to India soon after the work in Chorlton was given up & died in India in 1879.

The Refectory was then where it is now – the high table across the window by the yard.

The present Confraternity Chapel was the girls Dormitory. The Orphans were in 77.

The Incurables & aged & infirm women in 83. Those that were able went to Chapel for mid-day Prayer. One old woman had to be carried down in a chair. When the Confraternity of the Holy Family[48] was started S. Sarah was made the Sister Superior – Mr. Richards thought she wanted some outside work in addition to the Noviciate, as he was afraid she was getting too much into a groove. Mr. Luke Rivington[49] was Chaplain. Some of the Novices were jealous of the C.H.F taking the Mistress's time from them.

When there was a Function we had a general Recreation[50] generally in S. Raphael, where we sat on the ground. When the first Mission[51] was held at All SS we went to the Services in Church & as it was very crowded we remained after the afternoon 'Bible Class' on for 5 o'clock Evensong, losing our tea!

About this time S. Cecilia & I were sent to take charge of the Orphans at 77 – They were in wild Confusion – After Susan Woodgate[52] had given them up, & they lost her strict discipline, they had got into disorder under Novices who had no controul over them. Different ladies came for an hour or two in the morning to take a Class & they petted & spoilt the children, allowing them to talk in School & ask all kind of impertinent questions.[53] Some of the children went out scrapping of an afternoon. They had bread & milk for breakfast, & meat 3 or 4 times a week for dinner.

---

46 Agatha Honor Christmas (1840–1913), prof. 1864. The community's third lay sister, she worked in hospitals in Britain and South Africa. In the 1891 census her name is recorded as 'Honor Harriet'.

47 See the Franco-Prussian war diary.

48 It was for married women, and its aim was to 'help wives and mothers to persevere in leading a Christian life, and to train up their children in the love and fear of God'.

49 Luke Rivington was the son of Francis Rivington (b. 1805), of the publishing firm that brought out the *Tracts for the times*. He was ordained in 1863, and was curate of All Saints, Margaret Street 1867–70, before joining S.S.J.E. at Cowley. He later converted to catholicism.

50 A general recreation was attended by both choir sisters and novices, and may have included the lay order as well.

51 This would be a mission held by the church; it is not a reference to the London diocesan mission, which began in 1859.

52 Not identified.

53 Ladies and sisters always had an uneasy relationship. Sisters appreciated their financial support, but thought many of them undisciplined and amateurish in their approach to charitable work.

1870. I was working at U.C. H. It was the year of the German Franco War, & Committees of relief were formed in London under the Princess Christian & others. Mother was at the Hospital at Eastbourne, which had been opened the previous year. We were told that Mother had been applied to for Sisters to go out to help & nurse the sick & wounded. After she came home she arranged to go out herself, taking S. Helen a good medical nurse & firstrate linguist S. Rosamund an excellent surgical Nurse – S. Eliza, S. Harriet, S. Cecilia, a Lay Sister, myself. S. Harriet was no nurse, but she was anxious to go, & as she spoke French Mother thought she might be of use. We started Septr. 1870.[54]

We went under the red + flag & were to join Dr. Frank's Ambulance, under Colonel Brakenbury's direction. Mr. Porter[55] went with us as Chaplain; but as there was no provision for Chaplains he had to be entered as Storekeeper.

At Atlou we presented ourselves to the Hon. Regin^d Capel acting for Colonel B. Mr. Capel said we were to go to Balou & Bazuilles, & that his Wife (one of our Outer S^{rs}) was attending to the wounded in a Chateau there, which had been converted into an Ambulance. We had the wounded in different Chateaux belonging to the German Army – the French were nursed by their own people in some of the cottages.

S. Cecilia & I were sent to Sedan. (see letters)[56]

After a time it was decided we should move on & probably be attached to Prince Charles's Army; but first we must go to Brussels for stores &c.

In the meanwhile the Princess Christian had had such a good report of us that she said she must have one of our Sisters to go to her sister's Hospital at ~~Herre~~ Darmesstadt so S. Caroline Mary, who was in Charge at All SS Home sent S. Charlotte who joined us at Brussels on her way. At last it was decided that S. Harriet, S. Helen, & S. Rosamund should go to the Hospital at Saarbrück, & Mother & the rest to Epernay. We had a School, which was turned into an Ambulance & we worked there until we returned home in Feb. 1871. (see letters & diary[57] written at the time). When Mr. Richards found that S. Charlotte was alone, not with Mother, as he had understood: he insisted on having S. Charlotte recalled, which was difficult when acting with Royalty; but he had to be obeyed. He had a very high ideal of a Sister's life, & was very particular with regard to their outward demeanour. Mr. Randal[58] wished our Sisters to have a high Class School at All SS Clifton & at the same time a nursing Sister to take cases among the upper class – S Charlotte had been sent to undertake this & was taken by her employers for drives either with or without her patients, when Mr Richards heard

54 See the Franco-Prussian war diary, also written by Sister Catharine, for a full account.
55 Reginald Porter (1833–95), ordained 1857. A former curate at Wantage under Butler, he was rector of Kenn, Exeter, 1858–94.
56 The Society has preserved some of the letters sent from the front.
57 This is the Franco-Prussian war diary.
58 Richard William Randall (1844–1906), vicar of All Saints, Clifton, 1868–92, dean of Chichester 1892–1902.

she had been seen out in this way he required for her to be sent for immediately: he would not have his Sisters drive out in an open carriage under a fur rug!

The Emperor of Germany sent an iron Cross for the Mother & Sisters of All SS as an acknowledgement of our services.

1871.

I went back to U.C.H. for a bit after our return, & was then sent to Eastbourne. I had the entire charge of the boys, took the men's meals, dressed their wounds & did what nursing was required.

S. Constance saw them when they arrived, lent them books, &c.

Mr. Cave[59] was Chaplain & lived at the Lodge with his sister. We often had to go without Service when he was away, & those of us that were able walked across corn fields to S. Saviour's, which I think was the only Church in Eastbourne where there were early Celebrations & I believe there only on Sundays & holidays.

We had pigeons & rabbits in the old garden, which I looked after with the Server's (Fred Rupp) help. The boys were in S. Stanislas & the girls in S. Ursula. S. Rose Ward & the men's library were not built. The Chapel was at the top of the Hospital & there was no lift, so the infirm could not get to Chapel. Brother Hall[60] (Bishop of Vermont) often stayed at the Hospital & would carry Tommy & other crippled boys on his back up stairs to Chapel. Several of the Cowley Fathers also came occasionally especially F^r Grafton & F^r Prescott.

Mother frequently stayed at the Hospital & never seemed so happy as when there.

Herbert & Helen Brinckman[61] when small children often came on a visit & ran in & out of Mother's room & over the whole place as they liked. We had a private Omnibus with one horse to take patients to & from the Station & Hospital, & an old Coachman of the Cave's to drive it followed by a splendid S. Bernard's dog 'Chad' a great pet.

I think it was in 1872 that I was sent to join S. Rosamund at Chorlton Union. The Sisters superintended the whole of the Infirmary, which was built in 5 blocks united by open Corridors each block containing 100 beds: they had also to look after the small pox patients in another building; but the Lunatic Asylum was distinct.

When the Sisters first went to Chorleton, I believe there was not a single Church in Manchester where there was an early Eucharist. They had to make their Communion in the plain white washed Chapel of the Union at Mid-day

59 Verney Cave-Browne-Cave (1833–90), chaplain, All Saints Convalescent Home, 1871. Son of John Robert C. B. Cave, 10th baronet, he seceded to Rome in 1875.
60 A native of Berkshire, Arthur Crawshay Alliston Hall (1847–1930) was ordained in 1871, as a member of S.S.J.E. He emigrated to the U.S.A. in 1873, took out American citizenship and was consecrated bishop of Vermont in 1894, after his release from S.S.J.E.
61 These were the children of the Rev. Arthur Brinkman. Herbert joined the army and became a priest.

once a month & the Workhouse Chaplain arranged to Celebrate early in one of the Wards for the aged & infirm on Thursdays, & the Sisters had to drive to S. Albans Ch:[62] several miles distant to make their Confessions. When I went to Chorlton however S. Mary's Church Hulme had been opened, & there were early Celebrations[63] on Sundays & Holidays, which we were able sometimes to get to by walking about 2 miles.

We also went to Mr. Woodhouse[64] the Vicar for Confession.

On 16th June 1873, The Reverend W. Upton Richards our Co. Founder & Chaplain died: he had been failing for 2 or 3 years, & Father Benson had helped him much in the work of the Community taking Receptions & Professions as well as hearing the Sisters Confessions when Mr. R was unequal to do so. In fact Fr. Benson gave up his time as freely as if he had no Society of his own to attend to: it was therefore natural there he should be chosen as Mr. R's successor as Chaplain.

Fr. Grafton & Fr. Prescott often assisted at the Functions & took Retreats.

Father Benson used to go about the House in his short Surplice up & down to Chapel, or at the call bell to ask if any one wanted him, or again knocking at Mother's door, & waiting like a little boy until she said 'come in'. The humility of our Superiors & the deference they paid each other was quite beautiful. Anything Fr. B wished, or objected to was quite enough for Mother.

Mr. Body[65] was much at the Home in those days, when he preached in Church or Conducted the Sisters' Retreats. Mother was devoted to him & went to hear him preach when she could. She once said to me 'I should so like to make my Confession to Canon Body,' I replied why not? & she said 'Fr. Benson would not like it.' Fr. Benson could not understand how Mother was so taken with one who was only 'a popular preacher.'

I left Chorlton Union in 1873 or 4 to go to S. Jude's Bradford. S. Sarah, who had begun the work there had been sent to Edinborough [sic] & left S. Anna Maria in charge at Bradford. Mother thought her too young & sent me to replace her. The other Sisters there were S. Anne Teresa & S. Frances Helen. We lived in a small house in Hanover Sqr. We had a small room for our Oratory upstairs where we made our Confessions – Outside there was a dark Cupboard, which we used for a Cloak Room, & where we knelt when waiting for our Confessions. In about a year & a half I once more returned to Eastbourne. In the meantime

---

62 St Alban's, Cheetwood, Manchester, had daily early celebrations by 1874 and an elaborate ceremonial.

63 St Mary Hulme had communion four days a week by 1874; it was less ritualistic than St Alban's.

64 Frederick Charles Woodhouse, ordained 1851, rector of St Mary's Church, Hulme, Manchester from 1858, vicar of Holy Trinity, Folkestone, 1885, rural dean of Elham 1895, hon. canon of Canterbury 1900. He was the popular author of several devotional works.

65 George Body (1840–1911), ordained 1864. He became canon residentiary of Durham and canon missioner of Durham diocese in 1883, and was warden of the Community of the Epiphany, Truro, 1891–1905.

S. Harriet had gone to Baltimore to take S. Helen's place & carry on the work with S. Serena & S. Winifred who had gone out with S. Helen.

In 1876 Mother determined to send Sisters to Capetown. Bishop Gray[66] had asked for them in 1870 when she was at the War & Bishop Jones[67] had renewed the request after his Consecration & again later. But until now Mother had not a sufficient staff of Sisters to spare to take up the work of 8 or 10 ladies.

S. Sarah, S. Frances Hilary,[68] Sister Jane Mary, & I were chosen with two Lay Sisters, S. Agatha, & S. Martha.

Before starting we went to say good bye to S. Emily Mary who was dying in the Sisters' Infirmary, the back room of the present Community room. S. Harriet was also dying in America.

We sailed from the London Docks in the Courland[69] in the beginning of Feb: 1876 & did not reach Capetown until 30 days later. It was a very small Steamer & some German jews were the only other 1st Class pas[rs]. We reached Darmouth [Dartmouth] early on Sunday morning and the Lay Sisters landed & went to Church; but the rest of us were so unwell after what we had gone through by the chopping in the Channel that we remained quiet. The following Sunday we got to Madeira & remained there to coal: several of us went ashore & found a Church where we were in time for a 10 o'clock Celebration. Mr Burningham[70] being the Priest. We suffered a good deal in the Tropics from the heat particularly as we wore the same clothing as we had in England, & we made no change until the medical men at Capetown represented that we were injuring our health by doing so.

We were detained sometime in Table Bay on account of the tide, so Miss Farr[71] kindly came in a boat to welcome us. She was dressed in their uniform, grey dress & cloak, white cappie & blue veil. White umbrella & green lining. I bid adieu to the Cape in the Autumn of 1885, & returned to All SS Home.

A little while after Mr. Holmes asked for me to work in his brother's Parish[72] S. Philip's Sydenham. S. Isabella Agnes[73] accompanied me.

---

66 Robert Gray (1809–72), priested 1837, consecrated bishop of Capetown and metropolitan of Africa in 1847.

67 William West Jones (1838–1908), ordained 1862, consecrated bishop of Capetown in 1872; a friend of Samuel Wilberforce and a member of the English Church Union.

68 Secular name unknown, prof. 1873, left 1894.

69 The *Courland* was classified as a screw steamer; it was built by Napier of Glasgow in 1872, and was owned by the Leith, Hull and Hamburg co. The master at this date was a Mr Winchester.

70 This was Thomas Burningham (b. 1808), ordained 1832, rector of Charlwood, Sussex, 1855–83. The chaplain of Madeira (diocese of Gibraltar) from 1877 was Richard Addison. From 1862 to 1875 the licence-holder was J. J. Hewitt. There were a number of temporary and seasonal chaplaincies in this diocese, under the jurisdiction of the bishops of Gibraltar and London, and it may be that Mr Burningham was assisting while on holiday or travelling in Madeira in 1876.

71 Not identified.

72 John Garraway Holmes (1840–1904), ordained 1865; vicar of St Philip's Sydenham 1883–9, archdeacon of Grahamstown 1895–9, dean of Maritzburg 1889–99, bishop of St Helena 1899–1904.

73 Isabella Chapman (1838–1917), prof. 1878.

We had a small house of four rooms & a kitchen. The front room we used as a sitting-room & a place to see people in – the small back-room was where we had our meals and said the Offices: the room above was the servants bedroom & the other was divided by a curtain for two Sisters.

I was District Nurse – there were several ladies who were District Visitors & took classes &c, so S I A felt she was not wanted & soon left. She was replaced by S. Helena. I worked on for more than a year, & when I left S. Mary Ruth came.

I was sent to Cowley to recruit & when there Mother desired me to meet her at Eastbourne. Nurse Hogarth was then in charge of the men, & it was proposed I should take her work; but afterwards decided I should take charge of S. Elizabeth's Home, while S. Helen went to Africa to fetch the baby of her niece, who had died there. As things turned out I was glad, as I was thus able to see a good deal of Mother at the last. I travelled to London with her she was in much pain & suffering & hardly spoke on the journey.

At first Mother had to be kept quiet; but when there was no hope of recovery the Sisters were allowed to go to her. She was much gratified by a visit from Archbishop Benson,[74] who gave her his blessing. The last day we went into her room whenever we could & knelt by her bedside. S. Eliza stood at the foot like a Statue & put eau de Cologne on Mother's feet sometimes. Fr. Benson was in a corner of the room & came out to say a prayer or psalm from time to time.

Those of us who not living in the Home went to our various houses, we hoped Mother would live to the next day, the Anniversary of her Consecration; but she passed away on the night of 3rd Aug 1887. She was laid in her Coffin, covered with the choisest (sic) flowers the loving offering of many, & brought down to her room (the present Refectory) where all old friends both the rich & poor were allowed to come for a last look of her they had so loved & revered.

---

74 Edward White Benson (1829–96), ordained 1857, consecrated bishop of Truro in 1877, translated to Canterbury in 1883. He had some high church sympathies, and was visitor to several sisterhoods, despite presiding at the ritual trial of Edward King (bishop of Lincoln) in 1889.

PART II

GOVERNMENT

II. 1

The Rules of 1855 and 1859

(i) THE RULE OF 1855

In the Name of the Father, and of the Son, and of the Holy Ghost. Amen

---

The primary object of this Society is to provide a *religious* Asylum for incurables, aged and infirm persons in destitute circumstances, and to train up Orphan children to useful employments; and although other works of mercy may from time to time be added at the discretion of the Superiors, these shall always have the first consideration and hold the principal place in the work of the Sisters.

It is also another object of this Institution to afford opportunities for persons apart from the world and its distractions to 'perfect Holiness in the fear of the LORD', to grow in the love of our HOLY SAVIOUR, and to show forth love to Him by acts of love to His poor and afflicted.

To this end the Sisters are exhorted to lay aside all secondary motives, together with all love of self and of their own carnal wills, and to study in singleness of heart, and of purpose to make the love of CHRIST the end and aim of all their works, prayers and words – offering up each and every one of them to Him Whose they are, and Whom alone they should desire to serve.

67, Mortimer Street,[1]
Feast of the Ascension, 1855.[2]

---

[1] The first house of the sisterhood was at this address in Marylebone.
[2] 20 May 1855.

GENERAL RULES AND ADMONITIONS

I   Any person desirous of joining this community shall be received as a Probationer[3] upon the recommendation of a clergyman, if confirmed by the Incumbent of All Saints', who has consented to act as the spiritual director of the Sisterhood,[4] but she shall not be admitted as a Sister until she shall have passed a certain time of probation, the length of which shall be decided by the Director and Mother Superior of the House conjointly – who alone shall have power to judge of her fitness for the religious life, and either to reject her if they consider her vocation doubtful, or to subject her to a longer probation, as they may judge expedient. The shortest period of probation shall be one year and one day.[5] If admitted to be a Sister she shall be required to give a promise of obedience to the Rules and Regulations of the Institute.

II   Each Sister according to her ability will be expected to contribute a certain sum annually out of her Income, if she possess any, towards the maintenance of the House as long as she shall remain a member of the Community.

III   No Sister can retain any money in her own possession, or call anything her own so long as she is a member of this Institute.

IV   No Books may be brought into, or used in the House without the approval of the Director or the Mother Superior of the Society.[6]

V   Both the Sisters and the Probationers will attend the daily Celebration of Holy Communion and the other Services in the Church of All Saints, as far as the work of the House will permit, and according to the discretion of the Mother Superior.[7]

Although, however, they shall be expected to be present daily at the Celebration of the Holy Eucharist, when the state of their health and the work of the House will allow of their enjoying this Holy Privilege, yet shall they only receive the Blessed Sacrament at such times as their own spiritual guide shall direct.[8]

---

[3] Probationers (later called postulants) were women interested in joining a sisterhood. They spent a period of time, which could vary considerably, living and working with the community.

[4] This specific reference to Father Upton Richards was omitted from later versions of the rule.

[5] This section was changed significantly for the 1859 rule. In later versions of the rule, the ordinary length of the noviciate is two years; there is no mention of this minimum period.

[6] This was to prevent the introduction of Roman catholic manuals of devotion.

[7] In 1855, this is clearly a parish sisterhood; by 1859 it was necessary to ease the requirements to attend services at All Saints.

[8] This tone of this last sentence is moderated in later rules, to give more autonomy to the sister and less authority to the clergyman.

No Sister shall absent herself either from the Services of the Church, or from the Prayers in the Oratory without leave from the Mother Superior, unless they shall be engaged in some special act of Mercy at the time which cannot be left.

When prevented from being present at the Services, or Offices, the sisters are exhorted to observe the Hour of Prayer by uniting themselves in spirit with those who are engaged in the direct worship of GOD.

VI   The Sisters shall be allowed one day in every three months for a Spiritual Retreat, which shall be spent either in the Oratory, or in their own Rooms in self-examination and meditation according to the counsel of their spiritual guide.[9]

VII   The day shall begin and close with prayer; after Compline, i.e., at nine P.M, the Sisters shall retire to their several rooms at once and in silence, except it be otherwise ordered by the Mother Superior, and they shall be in bed before ten P.M.

VIII   In case of sickness, or for any other cause, but then *only* at the *discretion* of the Mother Superior, the rule for rising in the morning may be relaxed.

IX   None may leave the House but at such times and in such companionship as the Superior shall approve, and must return home at the hour specified.

X   The Sisters shall not go into each other's Bed-room at *any* time without special leave.

XI   It is strictly forbidden to laugh or talk on the stairs, and the Sisters are enjoined to move about quietly and to avoid all unnecessary noises, such as slamming doors, &c.

XII   Personal neatness, punctuality, a due regard to the interests of the House, general order, a gentle and recollected manner, modesty and humility, coupled with *habitual courtesy both among themselves* and towards strangers, shall be regarded by the Sisters a religious duties.

XIII   A Sister shall be at liberty to visit a parent, when necessity or sickness require it, but when absent from the Community, she is enjoined to lead a life becoming one who is engaged in a work of Holy Charity.

---

[9]   Later entirely omitted, probably due to the pressure of active work. All Saints quite early on adopted the practice of having a regular group retreat for all sisters.

XIV The Sisters shall have free intercourse with their *near* relations, who may
     visit them on the days and at the hours which shall hereinafter be specified.
     They may also *occasionally* see such other Friends as may be approved of
     by the Mother Superior. But in such interviews they are recommended to
     avoid all frivolous conversation and to seek to edify by modesty of behav-
     iour.

XV   The correspondence of the Sisters with their relations or with such friends
     as may be sanctioned by the Superior shall be free and unconstrained; but
     all letters shall pass through the Superior's hand, both before they are
     delivered to the Sisters, and before they are sent from the house, that any
     unnecessary correspondence may be checked. The Sisters will of course on
     all ordinary occasions confine their correspondence to the time of recre-
     ation, so as not to let it interfere with their work. Both in writing and speak-
     ing to others the Sisters are exhorted not to disparage another Sister either
     directly, or indirectly, still less the Superior. They should avoid all remarks
     on what passes within the Community, and use all due reserve, remember-
     ing with how close a bond they and their spiritual companions are bound
     together in the LORD.

XVI The Sisters and Probationers will be allowed to see their relations and such
     friends as may visit them, on all Festivals, and also on Thursdays and Sat-
     urdays from half-past three to a quarter before five.

FASTING[10]

The Fast Days appointed by the Church shall be observed by abstinence from
meat, as far as may be consistent with health; any Sister desiring to practise
greater abstinence, or to shorten the regular period of rest for purposes of devotion must first obtain the consent of the Superior and the Spiritual Director, who
if necessary shall consult the Physician of the Institute. When those who are
weak are treated differently as to food, this should not seem unjust to those who
are stronger, but each should take her food as coming from the Hand of her
Heavenly FATHER, Who is thus strengthening her to serve Him in holy works of
Charity. The Sisters shall bear, without a word or look of displeasure, whatever
inconvenience or unpleasantness may be any chance occur in the food or in other
things, as will sometimes be the case, remembering that our LORD Himself often
hungered and suffered privations. The body however is not to be indiscreetly

---

[10] This section on fasting is more detailed than in later rules, and gives some impression of the
     poverty of the early community, in its anticipation that the food provided may quite regularly be
     unpalatable.

fatigued or weakened with watching, abstinence, or other outward acts so as to hinder the performance of greater good, for this would be directly at variance with the spirit of a Sister of Charity.

No food shall be provided out of the ordinary meal times, except with the permission of the Superior. No Sister should be deterred by any false shame from asking for as much as she thinks she requires; and all should remember, that to submit meekly to the mortification and crosses, which arise day by day in the Providence of GOD, is far more needful and is a greater mark of true Christian humility than the bearing of any amount of self-imposed austerities.

When the soul is not faithful in the endurance of daily crosses which are from the Hand of GOD, there is reason to fear lest there be no real submission or humiliation of soul in any voluntary afflicting of oneself.

To overcome self, in its various forms, should be your main and constant effort; whilst self prevails we are exposed on every side, and are continually liable to fall. The more perfect this abandonment of self, the more perfect will be your peace, for as long as we retain inordinate attachment and desires, our peace will never be sure and lasting.

SILENCE[11]

The Sisters shall observe the rule of Silence, both in going to and in coming from Church, and whenever else it may be appointed, unless Charity should require it otherwise. The Superior shall be empowered to appoint other times, e.g., Lent, or Advent, when silence shall be observed, besides those noted in the rule for Distribution of Time,[12] with the concurrence of the majority of the confirmed Sisters. Whilst observing silence outwardly endeavour to keep your minds recollected, and fixed on what may tend to your advancement in the love and fear of GOD.

Whenever it may be necessary to speak in hours of silence, do so in a low voice and as briefly as possible.

In walking to and from Church be careful to remember the greatness of His Majesty, in Whose Presence you are about to appear, or have appeared, and cherish any holy thought you may have received.

---

[11] Later versions of the rule are less specific about the seasons of silence, again probably a response to the pressures of work.

[12] See the timetable attached to the 1859 version of the rule. The earlier timetables were probably very similar.

OBEDIENCE

To the Superior as to a Mother, and still more to the Priest, as one who has charge of your soul, you must be truly obedient, showing all respect and honour, lest by despising such authority you despise GOD.[13]

Comply unhesitatingly and cheerfully with all directions given, whether in matters of greater or less moment, in things agreeable or disagreeable, remembering that 'GOD loveth a cheerful giver'.[14] Perform them with alacrity and spiritual zeal. At the Superior's call, or the sound of the bell, be ready to leave whatever you may be about, e.g., a letter you have begun, or a conversation you have just entered into.

Look on all works as the same, for in all you may equally serve CHRIST, and it is the appointment of GOD only that makes one work to differ from another. Be not therefore particular in keeping your own allotted work, if required to give assistance to another Sister. Rather be ready to accommodate a Sister by passing from one employment to another, or by joining with another Sister in her work, in a loving humble spirit, remembering that 'Love is the fulfilling of the Law'.[15]

Do not allow yourselves to complain of one another, and beware how you judge your Superiors, even if their directions may seem to *you* to be unwise; study to cherish the belief that they may have motives which you know not of, and which would if known, satisfactorily account for any seeming inconsistencies. Remember that they are accountable to GOD, before Whom we all stand, and by Whom we shall all be judged, and be thankful that to you is committed the easier and safer duty of submission and obedience.

HUMILITY

Is the foundation of the spiritual life, and the true characteristic and infallible mark of the children of JESUS CHRIST. It consists first in being content with less than we esteem our due, and in being willing to embrace contempt and reproach in the place of honour and consideration. Secondly, in thinking others always more deserving of honour than ourselves, and never scrupling to pay respect even to the least in the community.

Endeavour to keep yourself little and low in your own eyes, and whenever you are over-looked or slighted, or another is preferred before you, or your feelings are seemingly not considered, or you are (as you fancy) in any way slightingly used, receive the humiliation as coming from the Hand of GOD, and as a

---

[13] This instruction is moderated in later versions of the rule, and tellingly, chaplain is substituted for priest, probably to avoid conflicting advice from spiritual advisors of individual sisters.

[14] 2 Corinthians ix. 7.

[15] Romans xiii. 10.

precious token of His love towards you, for men through whom good or evil comes to us are but His instruments; and He favourably regards what the world despises, and is pleased with the lowliness of those who wish to be low.

Whatever slight may be offered you, endeavour to receive it thankfully, as a wholesome discipline for your soul, remembering the words of S. Peter, – 'For what glory is it if when ye be buffeted for your faults, ye shall take it patiently; but if when ye do well and suffer for it, ye take it patiently, this is acceptable with GOD'.[16]

Accustom yourself not to expect any favour or distinction in the community, and to pay cordially to all others courtesy and respect, not merely in gesture, countenance, and word, but in deed and in truth. Do not allow yourself to wish for any particular work or special office, but leave all to the judgement of the Superior, and do not permit any feeling of disappointment, anger, or jealousy to arise towards any one on account of it. Always set about your work in prayer, beseeching GOD to bless you in it; if you fail, be not disheartened, but think that it is nothing more than what one so imperfect must expect, and only endeavour for the future to fulfil your duty with the deeper humility and more entire love and devotedness; if you prosper in your work, give GOD the entire glory.

Whenever you receive any admonition or reproof, never seek to excuse yourself, but bear it with submission and thankfulness, and let it only incite you to more earnest self-examination.

If however on being reproved, it seem absolutely needful to say something in explanation, in order to avoid scandal, and you can so command your temper as not to offend against charity, do so in as few words and as modestly as possible.

Be careful never to speak hastily, especially when under irritation, but offer up to CHRIST as a sacrifice the wounded spirit which may be within you.

The Superior shall have the first place in the house; the Sisters shall hold no rank amongst themselves; all should seek only to be distinguished by their modesty and recollectedness, remembering the words of our LORD, how He said, 'he that is greatest among you, let him be your minister, and he that is chief as he that doth serve'.[17]

The younger shall nevertheless honour those that are more advanced in age, though newly come to the Sisterhood.

UNION AND CHARITY

Your very profession is to dwell together in unity, i.e., with one heart and one soul in GOD. Let there be no contention then among you, and if any should spring up in the community, let it be the object of the Sisters by a kind word to end it as

[16] 1 Peter ii. 20.
[17] Matthew xx. 26.

quickly as possible, lest a little anger grow into hatred, and there be divisions among you. 'Blessed are the peacemakers, for they shall be called the children of GOD'.[18]

When there happens to be a difference of opinion, and it seems needful to speak your thoughts, let your reasons be given with modesty and charity, and with a view to truth and edification, not to get the better in the argument. True love requires us to labour for the happiness of all. Watch therefore carefully, and strive against your own faults, and be prepared to expect in others the like or similar infirmities, bearing one another's burdens, and so fulfilling the law of CHRIST.

Practise the rule of loving all, even the least loveable, for CHRIST'S sake, notwithstanding her imperfections. The love and union of religious persons should be founded not on flesh and blood, or any human motive, but solely on GOD, seeking to have their hearts united together in JESUS CHRIST. Beware therefore of special and particular friendships and intimacies, lest they lessen the supreme love of GOD, and be the cause of jealousies and divisions. If e.g. your sympathies are drawn more towards one Sister than another by reason of her greater devotedness, or any other good cause, take heed lest it make you unmindful of or uncourteous to others, and so you become partial among yourselves. Avoid partizanships or secret coteries, as such are prejudicial to purity of heart and charity, and are sure sources of jealousies and divisions.

The Superior must be especially careful to put aside all distinctions, and to treat all the sisters alike, with equal love and charity, avoiding all harsh expressions, and striving to overcome impatience and hastiness of speech. If any Sister offend another by injurious words, let her hasten to make all due satisfaction, by unsaying the harsh speech in a spirit of loving humility, and begging the other's forgiveness; and let the injured party be ready to pardon the offence; or in case both have offended, let both be ready cheerfully to pardon one another.

One Sister must not interfere in another Sister's work, or make unkind remarks on her way of doing it. If there seem to be any grave fault, let her speak of it privately to the superior, who by her office is bound to rectify everything that is amiss.

In one word, you shall constantly endeavour to prefer others before yourselves, and to be diligent to give way to one another in all things lawful in a spirit of love and charity.

POVERTY OF SPIRIT

In order to become more comfortable to your LORD and Master JESUS CHRIST, ponder frequently in your heart how tenderly He cherished holy poverty; how He was born in a stable and laid in a manger – how He suffered from cold,

---

[18] Matthew v. 9.

hunger, and thirst, and during His mortal life had not where to lay His Head; how He died, stripped of everything upon the Cross, and having consecrated this grace in His own Person, bequeathed it as a valuable legacy to His children.[19]

Endeavour to keep your heart therefore thoroughly disentangled from the things of this world, such as the love of riches, honours, pleasures, human esteem; and be content to be thought little of, or even despised for CHRIST'S sake. Be content to see others noticed and yourself passed over; and whenever it is left to your own choice, prefer the lowest place and choose the poorest things; count it indifferent what office you may be called to fill, so long as the glory of GOD is furthered; and be willing with a cheerful mind to hold a place of honour to-day and one of humiliation to-morrow, if your Superiors see fit so to appoint it. Do not regard anything you have your own, but let all things be in common.

INQUISITIVENESS

Since in every way the world endeavours to steal in on those who have outwardly quitted it, in all your communications avoid curiosity, and seek to discourage it in others. As you would wish to be dead to the world and live wholly unto GOD, do not curiously pry into the affairs of others, or needlessly talk of them, but let each attend to her own duty, avoiding all unnecessary communications relative to past life or private affairs.

Be not anxious to learn or to communicate what passes in the world without, even as regards religious things, but feel thankful that to you it is given to serve GOD in quietness and without distraction; nevertheless be courteous to all, and refuse not sympathy with what another may say, which though an infringement of this rule, may yet have been innocently intended, and in all you say and do beware of selfishness which requires the utmost vigilance to detect.

RECREATION

In going to recreation, ask grace of GOD that you may neither do nor say anything in it, but what is according to His Will. Do not bring to recreation a sad and uneasy, but rather a cheerful and loving countenance; let your conversation never degenerate into gossip, and let it be on such subjects as may tend to some improvement of mind or heart.

Avoid egotism in speaking, loud talk, boisterous laughter, or the like incongruities, and if the conversation should become unedifying, try to shorten or change it.

---

[19] Much of this sentence is later omitted. Some other phrases in this section are moderated in the 1859 and 1890 versions of the rule.

Speak not of anything that you may have done, or which happened to you in the world, unless some positive duty or charity require it, and then be careful to avoid everything that may foster vanity. If any one be ever drawn to speak of the good she may have derived from any religious exercise, let her always speak of herself in the third person, and so avoid anything like self-laudation.[20]

Laus Deo.

(ii) THE RULE OF 1859

ALL SAINTS' HOME

AND

SISTERHOOD OF CHARITY[21]

✠

Distribution of Time
5.30 Rise. each one making her bed
6.40 Lauds.
7. Daily celebration of Holy Communion.
7.45 Prayers, with aged women, in Their Rooms, by some one appointed
for ye Week.
8. Family Prayers
8.15 Breakfast
Teach Orphans, help aged women to rise, read to them
8.45 Terce. Do Needlework. Attend to out door poor. School, or
District. Fetch Scraps.
12. Sext. Rest until,
12.30 Dinner. *Recreation* until,
2. Orphans walk until,
3. None. after which read to aged women, Orphans
Work School, or District work until
4.15 Recreation.

---

[20] This final paragraph does not appear in later versions of the rule.
[21] This is the 1859 rule, which remained in force until 1890: it is the only one to contain a timetable, and instructions for reading the rule aloud in the refectory, as instructed by the statutes. The manuscript which has survived, and which is held by the community, was thus probably the one reserved for the reader. Significant textual changes from the 1859 rule are indicated as follows: the 1890 version is in bold. Small verbal changes and alterations such as the re-numbering of the rules have not been included.

5. Church. Evensong.

5.45 Vespers

6. Supper. Recreation until,

7. Read to Aged Women. Teach Children of District.

Orphans say Prayers, Needlework.

8. Prayers with Aged Women

8.15 Spiritual Reading, or Private devotion.

9. Compline.

10. In Bed

+ Laus Tibi, Christe. +

†

RULES AND ADMONITIONS FOR THE SISTERS OF THE POOR

[MB[22]]

In the Name of the FATHER, and of the SON, and of the HOLY GHOST.

The primary object of this Society is to provide a religious[23] Asylum for Incurables, and for aged and infirm persons in destitute circumstances, and to train up Orphan Children to useful employments. And although other works of mercy may from time to time be added at the discretion of the Superiors, these shall always have the first consideration and hold the principal place in the work of the Sisters: It is also another object of this Society to afford opportunities for persons apart from the world and its distractions to 'perfect Holiness in the fear of the LORD', to grow in the love of our Holy Saviour, and to show forth love to Him, by acts of love to His poor and afflicted. To this end the Sisters are exhorted to lay aside all secondary motives, together with all love of self and of their own carnal wills, and to study in singleness of heart, and of purpose to make the love of Christ, the end and aim of all their works, prayers and words – offering up each and every one of them to Him whose they are and Whom alone they should desire to serve.

For the better guidance of the Society, the following rules have been established –

---

[22] A portion of the rule was read at meal times; the reader has indicated when each section should be read by pencilling 'MB', 'MD' (Monday breakfast, Monday dinner, and so on) into the manuscript at the appropriate points. These pencil annotations are printed in square brackets at the beginning of each section.

[23] 'Religious' is italicised in the 1891 version, as in 1855.

[pass onto rule *VI*][24]

any person desirous of joining this Community may be received as a Probationer[25] upon the recommendation of a Clergyman, if she be approved by the
Superior and the Chaplain.

I   She must produce a certificate of her Baptism and Confirmation and she
      must obtain the consent of both or either of her parents who may be living,
      or of her Guardian if she be under the age of 21 years. After that age the
      consent of relations more distant than a father or mother will not be
      required of necessity, but each case will be judged of by the superior and
      the Chaplain according to the circumstances who will report to the Visitor
      and be guided entirely by his decision.
      Any Probationer or confirmed Sister may quit the Sisterhood whensoever
      she pleases and as her own conscience before GOD is the guide she ought
      to follow in this matter no one can have any right to blame her for so
      leaving.

II   None shall be admitted as a confirmed Sister until she shall have passed a
      certain time of probation, the ordinary length of which shall be two years,
      after which every probationer who shall desire to be received must be
      elected by the Superior and Sisters, at a meeting to be held by them for that
      purpose and be approved by the chaplain, and being so elected and
      approved she must be presented to the Visitor for his confirmation. She
      shall then make a promise of obedience to the Statutes and Rules of the
      Community and sign the same and be received in the Chapel of the House
      in the forms-approved by the Visitor, and at the same time, or as soon after
      as possible receive the Benediction of the Visitor.

III   Each Sister according to her ability will be expected to contribute a certain
      sum annually out of her income, if she possess any towards the mainten-
      ance of the House so long as she shall remains a member of the Commu-
      nity. She will be provided with clothes, money for **all necessary purposes
      and** all other requisites out of the common fund. The sum to be settled
      between herself and the Superior and Chaplain. No Sister can retain in her
      possession, in the house, any money or other property, or call anything

24 It was decided in chapter in 1874 (at this time chapters were annual) that the sister reading in
    refectory should stop after the prologue to the rule, and then go on to rule IV, 'for the sake of
    those who find the letter of rule I "every Probationer or Confirmed Sister may quit the Sisterhood
    whenever she pleases" a stumbling block – and as rules II, III, IV and V have nothing to do with
    life & manners, but are mere business details, they are also omitted. The mistress will give the
    novices the rule in its completeness' (14 Nov. 1874). This instruction for the reader was added in
    pencil.
25 'Probation' was equivalent to the noviciate. Presumably Tait objected to the Roman term, but it
    was the one used habitually by the Society, regardless of the Rule's terminology.

there her own but anything brought into the House must be considered the common property of the community.

IV   Each Sister will be at the liberty to dispose of her own private property in any way she may see fit, without any interference either as to the Capital or the income. And it is desired that those arrangements should be made if possible, by the Sisters with the advice of their own friends, before they enter the Community. But inasmuch as it is necessary that all the Sisters should, as far as may be, be upon an equality, and that none should engage in any work by any private means apart from the others. No Sister can retain in her possession in the House, any money or other property nor call anything there her own, but everything brought into the House must be considered the common property of the Community.

V   The Sisters shall be addressed by their Christian names and not by their surnames. And the Baptismal Name of each Sister shall always be retained by her unless for the sake of distinction between Sisters having the same name, some change shall be thought convenient.

VI   No books may be brought into, or used in the House without the approval of the Chaplain or the Mother Superior, unless by the express sanction of the Visitor.

VII   Both the Sisters and the Probationers will attend the Services in the Church of All Saints as far as the work of the House will permit and according to the direction of the Mother Superior.

VIII   No Sister shall absent herself either from the Services of the Church, or from the Prayers in the chapel without leave from the Mother Superior, unless she shall be engaged in some special act of mercy at the time which cannot be left. Each Sister or Probationer must determine for herself and with the advice and assistance of the Chaplain how often she will receive the Holy Communion. When prevented from being present at the Services, the Sisters are exhorted to observe the hour of prayer by uniting themselves in spirit with those who are engaged in the direct worship of GOD.

[MD]

IX   The day shall begin and close with prayer. The hour for rising shall be halfpast 5 'O' clk. At nine p.m the Sisters shall retire to their several rooms at once and in silence except it be otherwise ordered by the Mother Superior, and they shall be in bed before 10 p.m.

X   In case of sickness, or any other cause, approved by the Mother Superior, the rule for rising in the morning may be relaxed.

[TB]

XI   None may leave the house but at such times and in such companionship as
      the Superior shall approve and must return home at the hour specified.

XII   The Sisters shall not go into each other's Bed-room at any time without
      special leave.

XIII It is strictly forbidden to laugh or talk on the stairs and the Sisters are
      enjoined to move about quietly and to avoid all unnecessary noise, such as
      slamming the doors, &c.

XIV   Personal neatness, punctuality, a due regard to the interests of the House,
      general order, a gentle manner, modesty and humility, coupled with habit-
      ual courtesy both among themselves and towards strangers, shall be
      regarded by the Sisters as religious duties.

[TD]

XV   Sister shall be at liberty to visit a Parent, when necessity or sickness require
      it, or on any other occasion approved of by the Superior, but when absent
      from the Community, she is enjoined to lead a life becoming one who is
      engaged in a work of Holy Charity.

XVI   The Sisters shall have free intercourse with their near relations who may
      visit them on the days, and at the hours which shall herein after be speci-
      fied. They may also occasionally see such friends as may be approved of
      by the Mother Superior. But in such interviews they are recommended to
      avoid all frivolous conversation and to seek to edify by modesty of behav-
      iour.

[wed B]

XVII The correspondence of the Sisters with their relations or with such friends
      as may be sanctioned by the Superior shall be free and unrestrained: but all
      letters shall pass **unopened** through the Superior's hands, both before they
      are delivered to the Sisters, and before they are sent from the House, that
      any unnecessary correspondence may be checked. The Sisters will of
      course on all ordinary occasions confine their correspondence to the time
      of recreation, so as not to let it interfere with their work. Both in writing
      and speaking to others the Sisters are exhorted not to disparage another
      Sister either directly, or indirectly, still less the Superior. They should
      avoid all remarks on what passes within the Community and use all due
      reserve, remembering with how close a Bond they and their spiritual com-
      panions are bound together in the LORD.

XVIII The Sisters and Probationers will be allowed to see their relations and such friends as may visit them, on all Festivals, and also on Thursdays and Saturdays from half-past three to a quarter before five. During Lent these visits shall be restricted to ~~Thursdays and~~ Festivals. ~~and in advent~~ and in Advent to Thursdays and Festivals.[26]

FASTING [wed. D]

XIX The Fast days appointed by the Church shall be observed in such manner as seems good to the Superior and the Chaplain, subject to the control of the Visitor. When those who are weak are treated differently as to food this should not seem unjust to those who are stronger, but each should take her food as coming from the Hand of her Heavenly Father, Who is thus strengthening her to serve Him in holy works of Charity.

No food shall be provided out of the ordinary meal – times, except with the permission of the Superior. No Sister should be deterred by any false shame from asking for as much as she thinks she requires and all should remember, that to submit meekly to the mortifications and crosses, which arise day by day in the Providence of God, is far more needful and is a greater mark of Christian humility than the bearing of any amount of self-imposed austerities. When the soul is not faithful in the endurance of daily crosses which are from the Hand of God, there is reason to fear lest there be no real submission or humiliation of soul in any voluntary afflicting of oneself. To overcome self, in its various forms should be your main and constant effort; whilst self prevails you are exposed on every side, and are continually liable to fall. The more perfect this abandonment of self, the more perfect will be your peace, for as long as you retain inordinate attachment and desires, your peace will never be sure and lasting.

SILENCE [TH B]

XX The Sisters shall observe silence both in going to and coming from Church and whenever else it may be appointed by the Superior and Chaplain with the concurrence of the majority of the confirmed Sisters. Whilst observing silence outwardly endeavour to keep your minds recollected and fixed on what may tend to your advancement in the love and fear of God. Whenever it may be necessary to speak in hours of silence, do so in a low voice, and as briefly as possible. In walking to and from Church be

---

[26] Altered thus in the manuscript.

careful to remember the greatness of His Majesty, in Whose Presence you are about to appear or have appeared, and cherish any holy thought you may have received.

OBEDIENCE [Th D]

XXI   All members of the Society shall in their several stations yield due and hearty obedience to the Visitor. To the Superior as to a Mother: and still more to the Chaplain, *Priest* as one who has the charge of your soul, all must be truly obedient. Comply unhesitatingly and cheerfully with all directions given, whether in matters of greater or less moment, in things agreeable or disagreeable remembering that 'God loveth a cheerful giver'.[27] Perform them with alacrity and spiritual zeal. At the Superior's call, or the sound of the bell, be ready to leave whatever you may be about, e.g., a letter you have begun, or a conversation you have just entered into. Look on all works as the same, for in all you may equally serve Christ, and it is the appointment of God only that makes one work to differ from another. Be not therefore particular in keeping your own allotted work, if required to give assistance to another Sister. Rather be ready to accommodate a Sister by passing from one employment to another, in a loving humble spirit, remembering that 'Love is the fulfilling of the Law'.[28] Do not allow yourselves to complain of one another, and beware how you judge your Superiors, even if their directions may seem to you to be unwise. Study to cherish the belief that they may have motives which you know not of, and which would if known, satisfactorily account for any seeming inconsistencies. Remember that they are accountable to God, before Whom we all stand, and by Whom we shall all be judged and be thankful that to you is committed the easier and safer duty of submission and obedience.

HUMILITY [Fr B]

XXII   Is the foundation of the spiritual life, and the true characteristic and infallible mark of the children of Jesus Christ. It consists first in being content with less than we esteem our due and in being willing to embrace contempt and reproach in the place of honor and consideration. Secondly, in thinking others always more deserving of honor than ourselves, and never scrupling to pay respect even to the least in the community Endeavour to

---

[27] 2 Corinthians ix. 7.
[28] Romans xiii. 10.

keep yourself little and low in your own eyes, and whenever you are overlooked or slighted, or another is preferred before you, or your feelings are seemingly not considered, or you are (as you fancy) in any way slightingly used, receive the humiliation as coming from the Hand of GOD, and as a precious token of His Love towards you, for they through whom good or evil comes to us are but His instruments; and he favourably regards what the world despises, and is pleased with the lowliness of those who wish to be low. Whatever slight may be offered you, endeavour to receive it thankfully, as a wholesome discipline for your soul, remembering the words of St. Peter 'For what glory is it, if when ye be buffeted for your faults ye shall take it patiently, but if when ye do well and suffer for it, ye take it patiently, this is acceptable with God'.[29] Accustom yourself not to expect any favour or distinction in the Community, and to pay cordially to all others courtesy and respect, not merely in gesture countenance and word, but in deed and in truth. Do not allow yourself to wish for any particular work or special office, but leave all to the judgment of those above you, and do not permit any feeling of disappointment anger or jealousy to arise towards any one on account of it. Always set about your work in prayer beseeching God to bless you in it. If you fail be not disheartened, but think that it is nothing more that what one so imperfect must expect, and only endeavour for the future to fulfil your duty with deeper humility and more entire love and devotedness. If you prosper in your work, give God the entire glory. Whenever you receive any admonition or reproof, never seek to excuse yourself, but bear it with submission and thankfulness, and let it only incite you to more earnest self examination. If however, on being reproved, it seems absolutely needful to say something in explanation, in order to avoid scandal, and you can so command your temper as not to offend against charity do so in as few words and as modestly as possible. Be careful never to speak hastily, especially when under irritation, but offer up to Christ as a sacrifice the wounded spirit which may be within you.

The Superior shall have the first place in the house. The Sisters shall hold no rank amongst themselves, all should seek only to be distinguished by their modesty and recollectedness, remembering the words of our LORD, how, He said, 'he that is greatest among you, let him be your minister, and he that is chief as he that doth serve'.[30]

The younger shall nevertheless honor those that are more advanced in age, though newly come to the Sisterhood.

29 1 Peter ii. 20.
30 Matthew xx. 26.

UNION AND CHARITY [F.D]

XXIII Your very profession is to dwell together in unity, i.e., with one heart and one soul in God. Let there be no contention then among you, and if any should spring up in the Community, let it be the object of the Sisters by a kind word to end it as quickly as possible, lest a little anger grow into hatred, and there be divisions among you. 'Blessed are the peacemakers, for they shall be called the children of God'.[31] When there happens to be a difference of opinion, and it seems needful to speak your thoughts, let your reasons be given with modesty and charity, and with a view to truth and edification, not to get the better in the argument. True love requires us to labour for the happiness of all. Watch therefore carefully, and strive against your own faults, and be prepared to expect in others the like or similar infirmities, bearing one another's burdens, and so fulfilling the law of Christ.[32]

Endeavour to love all, even the least loveable, for Christ's sake, notwithstanding her imperfections. The love and union of religious persons should be founded, solely on God, all seeking to have their hearts united together in Jesus Christ. If your sympathies are drawn more towards one Sister than another by reason of her greater devotedness, or any other good cause, take heed lest it make you unmindful of or uncourteous to others and so you become partial among yourselves. Avoid partizanships or secret coteries, as such are prejudicial to charity, and are sure sources of jealousies and divisions. The Superior must be especially careful to put aside all distinctions, and to treat all the Sisters alike with equal love and charity, avoiding all harsh expressions, and striving to overcome impatience and hastiness of speech. Let the Superior ever remember the difficult and responsible situation in which she is placed and let her be always watchful against the temptations that will be set her from the power placed in her hands.[33] If any Sister offend another by injurious words, let her hasten to make all due satisfaction by unsaying the harsh speech in a spirit of loving humility, and begging the other's forgiveness; and let the injured party be ready to pardon the offence; or in case both have offended, let both be ready cheerfully to pardon one another.

One Sister must not interfere in another Sister's work, nor make unkind remarks on her way of doing it. If there seem to be any grave fault, let her speak of it privately to the Superior who by her Office is bound to rectify everything that is amiss.

In one word you shall constantly endeavour to prefer others before

---

[31] Matthew v. 9.
[32] Galatians vi. 2.
[33] This sentence is omitted from the 1891 version.

yourselves and to be diligent to give way to one another in all things lawful in a spirit of love and charity.

POVERTY OF SPIRIT [S.B]

XXIV   In order to become more comformable to your Lord and Master Jesus Christ, ponder frequently in your heart how tenderly He cherished the poor. How He was born in a stable and laid .ı a Manger; how He suffered from cold, hunger, and thirst, and during His mortal life had not where to lay His Head; how He died stripped of everything upon the Cross. Endeavour to keep your heart therefore thoroughly disentangled from the things of this world, such as the love of riches, honors, pleasures, human esteem; and be content to be thought little of, or even despised for Christ's sake. Be content to see others noticed and yourself passed over. Count it indifferent what office you may be called to fill, so long as the glory of God is furthered and be willing with a cheerful mind to hold a place of honor to-day and to-day one of humiliation to-morrow. Do not regard anything you have as your own, but let all things be in common.

INQUISITIVENESS [SD]

XXV   Since in every way the world endeavours to steal in on those who have outwardly quitted it, in all your communications avoid curiosity, and seek to discourage it in others. As you would wish to be dead to the world and live wholly unto GOD, do not curiously pry into the affairs of others, or needlessly talk of them, but let each attend to her own duty avoiding all unnecessary communications relative to private affairs.
Be not anxious to learn, or to communicate what passes in the world without even as regards religious things but feel thankful that to you it is given to serve GOD in quietness and without distraction. Nevertheless be courteous to all, and refuse not sympathy with what another may say, which though an infringement of this rule, may yet have been innocently intended, and in all you say and do beware of selfishness which requires the utmost vigilance to detect.

RECREATION

XXVI   In going to recreation ask grace of GOD that you may neither do nor say anything in it but what is according to His Will. Do not bring to recreation a sad and uneasy but rather a cheerful and loving countenance; let

your conversation never degenerate into gossip, and let it be on such subjects as may tend to some improvement of mind or heart. Avoid egotism
in speaking, loud talk boisterous laughter, or the like incongruities, and if
the conversation should become unedifying, try to shorten or change it.

ADDITIONAL RULES *agreed to by the unanimous consent of the Sisters,
Chaplain, and Visitor, Oct. 18th, 1890.*[34]

OF THE CHOIR SISTERS

XXVII   The Sisters whose duty it is to recite the seven Canonical hours[35] are for
distinction called Choir Sisters. They are exhorted to fulfil their obligation with all due care and reverence, remembering that the sacred office
of the Choir is one of the most solemn duties appertaining to the Religious Life.

When the bell summons them, they shall walk to Chapel with gravity
and reverence, and shall take their places quietly. They must be careful
to say the Offices as they are appointed, pronouncing the words clearly,
distinctly, and reverently, observing the stops, mediations, and accents,
moderating and adjusting their voices to each other; and composing
their whole deportment as devoutly as possible. The Sisters should
realise that the union with which their Office is said is a great stay to
their own individual life, and therefore they must be careful never to
absent themselves without real necessity. When obliged to say their
Office in private, they should say it as part of their responsibility with
reverence and care.

OF THE LAY SISTERS[36]

XXVIII The Lay Sisters should rejoice that they are counted worthy to serve
their God and King in the more lowly grade of the Religious Life, that
so they may the more resemble Him who was the servant of all men. By

---

[34] While the visitor may have approved these additional rules, they are not included in the document
which he signed in 1890. The signed document, despite being entitled 'Additional Rules and
Statutes', contains only the additional statutes. There is no evidence that the archbishop ever
formally consented to these additional rules, although he very probably gave them his informal
sanction.

[35] The canonical hours are: matins and lauds, prime, terce, sext, nones, vespers and compline.

[36] Lay sisters were ordinarily of working-class background. They brought no money into the
community: their labour was their contribution.

thus accepting their position thankfully, and praying God for grace to discern the privileges and honourable nature thereof, shall the Lay Sisters wait upon God and be blessed of Him, and receive the fulness of His Holy Spirit, and thus striving to bring every affection together with their own carnal wills under the yoke of Christ, shall they find everlasting joy and peace both here and hereafter. They should ever bear in mind the nature and the spirit of their Holy Vocation, which is to serve God in lowliness, humility, obedience, and self-sacrifice, offering up the works of their hands in union with the adoration of their hearts to Christ our Saviour, Who for our sakes gave Himself up to poverty and humiliation, and became obedient unto death, even the death of the Cross. To this end they should contemplate Jesus Christ continually in every occupation, doing all *to* Him, suffering all *for* Him, seeing Him in all. They must study to make Him their sole aim and object in this life, that so He may be their eternal crown and reward in the life to come.

They should cherish holy obedience, cultivate humility and self-abasement, welcome poverty and hardness, and strive to live in all purity and singleness of heart, remembering these are the graces which most adorn the Religious Life. They shall attend Prime, Midday Prayer, or Sext and Compline daily; Vespers on Sundays and greater Festivals, and such other days as the Superior shall appoint.

OF SISTER SUPERIORS

XIX   The Sister Superior must be specially watchful in the exercise of humility, remembering that her duty is to serve others in love. Let her shew herself a pattern of good works to the Sisters placed under her. Let her admonish the wavering, comfort the weak-hearted, assist the afflicted, and be patient towards all. Let her be exact and severe towards herself in observing the discipline and Rules of the House, and prudent in enforcing them on her Sisters. Let her be more careful to be loved than feared, remembering that she must give account of her charge to God.

Laus Deo

II. 2

The Statutes

THE STATUTES OF THE SISTERS OF THE POOR[1]

DRAWN UP AND SIGNED
THE 18TH JANUARY, 1859

Nihil habentes, Omnia possidentes
✟
In the Name of the Holy and Undivided Trinity

The following Statutes have been agreed upon and adopted for the due order and government of the House of the Sisters of the Poor, which has been established for the purposes hereinafter set forth, and these Statutes have been adopted with the desire and intent that through the Blessing of God, the *principles* on which the said House has been founded may be always preserved unchanged and inviolate and that it may be conducted and carried on in accordance with the true Christian Faith as it is set forth in the Doctrine and Discipline of the Church of England to the glory of Almighty God and the Eternal Salvation of souls for whom Christ died. Therefore these presents witness and it is hereby agreed and declared as follows, that is to say –

I

The object of the Said Society called 'The Sisters of the Poor' is the reception and maintenance of Incurables, of aged and infirm persons in destitute circumstances, and Orphans: – the visiting and nursing of the Poor and Sick, and the relief of their spiritual and temporal wants; the burial of the dead and the exercise of other works of mercy and the said society shall consist of a Superior and Sisters and

---

[1] The celebrated ecclesiastical lawyer, Sir (later Baron) Walter Phillimore, made some marginal comments and underlined the key points in this document when he was consulted over the validity of the statutes in the 1890s. His comments and emendations are indicated by italics.

shall be assisted by Trustees, an Auditor, and a Chaplain and such other Officers as the Superior and Sisters shall hereafter think fit to appoint.

II.

The Superior and Sisters shall elect such person as they shall think fit to be their Visitor for the time being. And the person so elected by the Superior and Sisters as aforesaid shall be the Visitor for the time being. And such Visitor shall have full power and authority as well upon his own mere motion as upon appeal lodged or complaint made at *all times to visit the House and every Member, Inmate, or Officer of the same, and to do and, order all things necessary to enforce obedience to the Rules and Statutes for the time being binding on the Members of the said Society, and to enforce therein in all respects the order and discipline of the Church of England, and also to repress and punish all things contrary to the same Rules, order and discipline and also generally to do and order all those things which appertain by Law to the Office of Visitor or which shall be hereinafter specially appointed*, and the first Visitor of the said Institution shall be the Right Honourable and Right Reverend Father in God, Archibald Campbell, Lord Bishop of London.[2]

III.

The Superior shall be a fully admitted Sister, and shall be appointed in manner hereinafter mentioned and shall have the government of the Sisters and other Inmates of the said House and of the household thereof.

The first Chaplain of the said House shall be the Reverend William Upton Richards, the Incumbent of the said District of All Saints', and all future Chaplains of the said House shall be elected by the said Superior and Sisters, and shall be allowed and confirmed by the Visitor. The Auditor shall audit and pass all the accounts of the Society the first Auditor shall be Benjamin Lancaster Esq.,[3] and all future Auditors shall be elected by the Superior and Sisters.

---

[2]   Archibald Campbell Tait (1811–82), bishop of London from 1856, archbishop of Canterbury 1869–82.

[3]   Benjamin Lancaster (1802–87, variously described as a banker and as a 'wealthy merchant') and his wife Rosamira are considered to be the co-founders of the community of St Peter, Kilburn, established as a fairly 'protestant' sisterhood in 1861. He provided all the community's financial support until his death in 1887.

IV.

Harriet Brownlow Byron being the foundress of the said Society and having been elected by the said Sisters to be their first Superior she shall retain the Office of Superior during the term of her natural life and every succeeding Superior shall hold her Office during the term of three years from the date of her election.

V.

In every vacancy in the Office of Superior, the fully admitted Sisters shall by a majority of votes nominate one of their own number as successor, and in case they shall fail to nominate a successor within one calendar month from the date of the vacancy, then the appointment shall lapse to the Visitor, who shall appoint one of the Sisters to be such Superior.

VI.

Every Superior hereafter to be elected shall continue in Office for the period of three years but may at the end of that period _be continued in her office by the Visitor_, or may be re-elected by the sisters for another period of three years and so on from time to time at the expiration of every period of three years.

Removal VII. _see also XII and XV_

The Superior or any Sister may be removed from her Office or from the Society by the Visitor, on [the] complaint of the Chaplain or of the Superior or of the Sisters as the case may be, but the Sisters shall not lay any complaint touching the Superior, or a Sister, before the Visitor until it shall have been assented to by a majority of them, and shall have been signified in writing to the Superior, or the Sister complained against for fourteen days before the same shall be laid before the Visitor.

VIII. _of the Assistant Superior_

The Superior may from time to time appoint any fully admitted Sister to be her Assistant in the office of Superior for such period as she shall think proper, and during any vacancy in the office of Superior, or during the absence or incapacity of the Superior by reason of illness, such Assistant shall perform the duties of that office. – and if on any such vacancy, absence or incapacity there shall be no

Assistant, the Senior Sister in order of admission shall act as Superior for the time being.

IX. *Of the Assistant Superior*

The Assistant may be removed by the Superior at any time at her will and pleasure.

X. *Of Professed and Novices*

The Sisters shall consist of two classes:–
Professed – 1st. Confirmed Sisters after probation and *Novices* – 2nd. Sisters Probationers – the term and nature of probation shall be settled in the rules hereinafter mentioned but the Superior and Sisters, with the *advice of the Chaplain* shall be at liberty to shorten the period of probation at their discretion in any particular case.

XI. *Of Novices*

No person shall be admitted into the House as Sister Probationer unless she be a Member of the Church of England and in full communication with the same, and every such admission shall be made in such manner and form as shall be determined and set forth in the said rules.

XII. *Of leaving the Community*

Every Sister shall have full and uncontrolled liberty whenever she shall fit to leave the House and Society. *see also XV and XII*

XIII. *Of Novices*

Every Sister shall upon admission to probation agree to be bound by and observe all the Statutes and rules of the [said] Society applicable to herself and such Probationers shall not in any manner interfere or prefer complaints to the *Chaplain* or to the Visitor respecting the conduct of the House or the Members thereof.

XIV. *Of alterations in Internal Rule*

The Superior may with the consent of the majority of the sisters and the *Chaplain* make and vary such rules for the internal management and discipline of the Sisters as shall be consistent with the Statutes of the Society, and be approved of by the Visitor, and such rules shall be accessible to all Members of the Society.

Footnotes to Statute XII. *by desire of* **EDWARD, ARCHBISHOP OF CANTERBURY,** *the Visitor,* **1890.**[4]
An original rule ?
1st. 'Any Probationer or Confirmed Sister may quit the Sisterhood whensoever she pleases, and as her own conscience before God is the guide she ought to follow in this matter, no one can have any right to blame her for so doing.'
2nd. Every Sister is to have a copy of the <u>Statutes and notes</u>. *Rule?*

XV. *Of removal and expulsion see also VII and XII*

The Superior shall have full power at any time with the consent of the Visitor and *Chaplain* to remove or expel any Sister from the Society.

XVI. *Of Finance*

The *receipts and expenditure* of the Society *ie current or ordinary* shall be under the entire control and management of the Superior for the time being, who shall act as Treasurer, and the Superior shall pass her accounts from time to time before the Auditor. *See end of Statute XX*

XVII. *Of the property of the Society*

All the real estates and chattels real houses leasehold or copyhold estates and all monies invested in the public stocks or funds, and all household furniture, books, linen, china and other chattels personal, and effects respectively belonging to the Society shall be respectively conveyed and assigned unto and invested in the names of the Trustees for the time being of the Society, and be held by them upon trust for the benefit thereof and such Trustees shall from time to time

---

[4] These footnotes were added at the insistence of the visitor, and against the wishes of the Mother Superior.

dispose of such real estates and chattels, real either by way of absolute sale or by demising or leasing such real estates and chattels, real houses leasehold or copyhold estates or any of them, and also of such stocks or funds furniture, books, linen, china and other chattels personal and effects by sale, transfer, or other disposition thereof as the Superior, with the consent _of the majority of the Sisters_ shall from time to time direct but in order to facilitate every sale which may be made and every lease which may be granted of any such real estate or chattels, real houses leasehold or copyhold estates by the Trustees thereof for the time being such trusts and provisions shall be inserted in every conveyance and assignment which shall be made and be executed either on the original or on any other conveyance or assignment of such real estates and chattels, real respectively as well as effectually authorize and empower the Trustees or Trustee for the time being under such conveyance and assignment to sell and demise the premises therein compromised and to give effectual receipts to purchasers and others without the necessity of any consent of or direction by any other person or persons whomsoever, and also a power in case of the death resignation, refusal or incapacity of any Trustee or Trustees, or for the executors or administrators of the last surviving Trustee to appoint a new Trustee or Trustees without the consent of any other person or persons whomsoever and all such other powers and provisions whatsoever as the Counsel in the Law of the said Society shall advise as necessary for the purpose of relieving all Purchases, Lessees and others, from the obligation of inquiring into the necessity or propriety of any sale or sales, or seeing to the application of being answerable for the misapplication of any purchase or other monies paid to or received by the Trustees or Trustee for the time being under such conveyance or assignment; (and the first Trustees of the said Society shall be Walter Carew Cocks,[5] Philip Charles Hardwicke,[6] Benjamin Lancaster,[7] and John Edward Buller.[8])[9]

XVIII. _Of the Property of the Society_

No Sister whether dismissed or not, whether remaining or not, or her heirs, executors or administrators, shall have or be entitled either in her lifetime or after her decease to, or shall have power to claim either at law or in equity, any estate right

[5] Born 1824, and lived in Chester Place, Regent's Park. He was an auditor in the audit office.
[6] Sir Philip Charles Hardwick (1822–92), 21 Cavendish Square. Architect to the Bank of England and St Bartholomew's Hosptial, he designed the Great Western Hotel, Paddington.
[7] Benjamin Lancaster (1802–87). The first auditor of the Society.
[8] John Edward Buller was a solicitor in Lincoln's Inn. He may have been the brother of Anthony Buller, the author of one of the _Tracts for the times._
[9] The first trustee was originally written in as William Holland (1829–1927), and then crossed out. He donated much of the money that built All Saints' church, Margaret Street, consecrated in 1859. He was later Lord Rotherham. A textile manufacturer and Liberal M.P. from 1892, he converted to Catholicism in 1924.

title interest property or share whatsoever in or to the real estate, or chattels, real houses leasehold or copyhold estates, stocks, funds and monies or in or to the household furniture, books, linens, china and other chattels personal, and effects belonging to, or held in trust for, or used for the purposes of the said Society or any of them or any part or parts thereof anything herein contained to the contrary thereof in any wise notwithstanding.

XIX. *Of appointment of Trustees*

Whenever any Trustee or Trustees shall die or desire to be discharged, or shall refuse or become incapable to act, the *Superior and Sisters* shall appoint a successor or successors, but this provision shall not supersede the power of appointing new Trustees contained in such original conveyance, or assignment of any of the real estates or chattels real, being the property of the Society as aforesaid, and on every appointment of a new Trustee, or new Trustees, all the property then vested in the Trustees for the time being shall be dealt with, that the same may be effectually vested in such new Trustee or Trustees, and the surviving or continuing Trustees, or if there shall be no surviving or continuing Trustee, then in the new Trustees only.

XX. *Duty of Trustees see XVII*

The Trustees shall pay all rents, dividends, and other annual produce, and all other monies received from time to time by them whether capital or annual income, into the hands of the Bankers for the time being of the Society to the account and credit of the said Society, and such payment shall be a sufficient discharge to the Trustees for the monies so paid by them and the Superior shall have power to draw out monies from the Bankers for the use of the Society as may be required.

XXI.

The Trustees, Visitor, and Chaplain shall be Members of the Church of England, and in full Communion therewith.

XXII. *Dissolution of the Society*

If the want of funds or any other cause render it expedient to do so, the Superior and Sisters, or a majority of two thirds of their whole number (including Sisters and *Probationers Novices?*), shall have power to dissolve the Society, and in such case the houses and property of the said Society in Margaret Street, Canvendish Square shall be reconveyed to and vested in the said Harriet Brownlow Byron, her executors, and administrators, and assignees, if the dissolution shall take place in her lifetime;[10] but if the same shall take place after her decease, then the Superior and Sisters for time being shall have power on such dissolution to order the sale and conversion of the whole of the property and effects thereof both real and personal into money, and the clear monies produced thereby, after paying all expenses attending such sale and conversion, and all debts owing from or on account of the Society shall be disposed of to such charitable purposes in connexion with the Church of England and in such manner, and if thought fit in such shares or proportions, *the Trustees shall determine !* at a Meeting especially called for that purpose, and which shall be held not less than three nor more than six calendar months after the sale shall have been completed.

XXIII. *Muddle*[11]

Whenever the word 'Sisters' is used in the foregoing Statutes without the word 'Probationers' it shall be taken to mean 'Confirmed Sisters'.

In witness whereof the said WILLIAM UPTON RICHARDS as Chaplain, the said BENJAMIN LANCASTER as Auditor, the said WALTER CAREW COCKS, PHILIP CHARLES HARDWICKE, BENJAMIN LANCASTER, and JOHN EDWARD BULLER as Trustees, the said HARRIET BROWNLOW BYRON as Superior, and the several Sisters of the said Society have hereunto set their hands and seals this eighteenth day of January in the year of our Lord one thousand eight hundred and fifty nine.

Here follow the signatures of the above, and of the Sisters.

---

[10] This clause is found in the statutes of a number of sisterhoods; because founding a community was such an uncertain venture, and was normally financed from the income or capital of the foundress (for the first few years, at any rate), it was considered correct to return the assets to her, should the society fail.

[11] Phillimore clearly found this afterthought definition of a 'Confirmed Sister', a concept not found in the original rule, confusing and undesirable.

ADDITIONS TO THE STATUTES OF THE SISTERS OF THE POOR

TENTATIVELY ACCEPTED FOR 3 YEARS
FROM THE 18TH OCTOBER, 1890.
ADDITIONS TO THE STATUTES AND RULES OF THE
SISTERS OF THE POOR, ALL SAINTS.

OF THE LAY SISTERS.

THERE shall be attached to[12] the Community a body of devout women as Lay Sisters, who shall take such part in the work of the Community as shall be assigned to them, but shall not have a voice in Chapter, nor shall they be required to attend all the Offices in Chapel.

These Lay Sisters shall be divided into two Classes, Novices and Professed Sisters. They shall be admitted at the discretion of the Superior, and approved for Profession by the Superior, with the concurrence of the Novice Mistress and the Chaplain, without further election.

OF THE CHAPTER.

(a) Chapter is the assembly of the whole Society of Choir Sisters, and its acts are binding upon all members of the Society whether present or not.

(b) The Chapter may be summoned by the Superior whenever she pleases, but there shall always be a Chapter holden in close connection with the half-yearly Retreats of the Society.

(c) All the *fully admitted Choir Sisters*[13] have a right to be present at the Chapter, and those who are hindered from coming, either by occupation or distance, shall receive the *minutes* of the Chapter, and be *desired to send their votes to the Secretary upon any matter involving constitutional principles.*

(d) Any Sister who desires to bring some matter before the Chapter shall have leave to do so, on intimating her wish with written notice of motion, but such notice must be given before the Agenda paper is issued.

It shall be competent for the Mother Superior to forbid such motion being brought forward, unless one-third of the Council and the *Chaplain* are in favour of its being brought forward.

---

[12] Phillimore's marginal comment was 'To avoid their being called "Sisters" of the original foundation?'

[13] Fully admitted sisters had been professed three years or more.

(e) No Motion shall be brought before the Chapter of such a kind as to affect the Community at large, unless time has been given for receiving a communication upon the subject from the most distant of the Branch Houses of the Community.

(f) An Agenda paper of all matters to be considered at the half-yearly Chapters, shall be circulated to all Branch Houses of the Community whether in England or abroad, and if possible sufficiently early to obtain a reply, but when the business is merely a motion of routine, and not involving principle, it shall suffice that such notice be sent round a fortnight before holding such Chapter, to the Branch Houses within the British Isles.

(g) No Choir Sister shall have a vote in Chapter until after three complete years after her Profession. The words 'fully admitted' or 'Confirmed Sister' in the original Statutes and Rules must be understood to mean Sisters who have been Professed three years.

(h) After the Chapter is concluded the Secretary shall transmit a copy of any notification made, or resolutions passed therein, to the Sister Superiors of the Branch Houses, to be communicated to the Sisters working with them.

(i) The Mother Superior will preside in all Chapters when she is present. When she is not present the Assistant Superior, the Novice Mistress, or the Housekeeping Sister, will preside, or, failing these, the Senior Sister present.

OF THE CONSULTATIVE COUNCIL.

(a) A Council of 9 Sisters shall be appointed to prepare matters for the Chapter, and to advise the Mother Superior as to anything that may be desirable, but such Council shall not have authority to order anything to be done.[14] The Council shall consist of the Assistant Superior,[15] Novice Mistress,[16] and Housekeeping Sister,[17] and 6 other Sisters over 7 years of Profession, freely elected by all the Choir Sisters. The Sisters so elected shall remain on the Council for a period of three years, two members retiring annually either to be replaced by fresh members or re-elected.[18]

(b) They shall meet twice a year before the half-yearly Retreats, and at any other time the Mother Superior shall deem necessary, and say one of those Sisters, members of the Council, who may be at a distance, may write to the Mother Superior of any matters which she may wish to have discussed.

---

[14] This is unusual. Most other communities' council had more than advisory powers.
[15] The assistant superior was an office appointed by the mother superior and assisted the mother as second-in-command.
[16] The novice mistress was responsible for the training and supervision of the novices.
[17] The housekeeping sister managed the ordinary invoices and daily administration of the community.
[18] Phillimore recommended that the last two words be omitted.

(c) The business transacted at meetings of this Consultative Council shall be recorded in a book by the Secretary of the Council, but they shall not be divulged to anyone except members of the Council, *the Chaplain*, and the Visitor.

(d) No work shall be undertaken or abandoned without necessity, save by the votes of the majority of the Council, and the consent of the Chaplain. This does not apply to the necessary development of works in any locality, such necessary works rest with the Sister Superior, subject to the control of the Mother Superior.

OF ELECTIONS.

(a) Notice and Information of approaching Elections shall be sent to all distant Sisters, so that they may send in their votes or proxies to the Mother Superior in time for such elections.

(b) Those who are in foreign countries shall not be allowed to vote, except on the election of the Visitor, Chaplain, and Mother Superior. In the case of the election of the Mother Superior, as also in the Election of the Visitor, and Chaplain, a bare majority shall suffice.

(c) No Choir Sister should lightly excuse herself from the responsibility of voting with reference to the Profession of a Novice.

A Novice shall be elected by two-thirds of the votes of the Choir Sisters.

(d) In the case of the Election for a Mother Superior there shall be a preliminary election by all the Choir Sisters over 7 years of Profession. From this first election the four Choir Sisters who have received the highest number of votes shall be nominated for the general election by all the 'Choir Sisters'.

OF FINANCE.

(a) All the receipts and expenditure of the Community Fund of every kind shall be submitted to the Auditor once in every half-year, and his investigation shall be presented to the *Consultative Council*.

(b) Any accumulating Funds shall be paid over to the Bankers on account of the Capital Fund of the Community according to the discretion of the Mother Superior with the *concurrence of the Council*, and shall be invested according to the advice of the Trustees.

(c) *The Chapter* shall have power to vote a grant from such accumulating funds for any work of immediate importance to the Community.

(d) The Mother Superior shall have power to grant to any of the Branch Houses a sum not exceeding a Hundred pounds annually to any one Branch House for the benefit of such House.

(e) The Community, however, is not to be in any way made responsible for the maintenance of such Branch Houses unless an arrangement is made to that effect by the Mother Superior with the *concurrence of the Consultative Council.*

(f) Care must be taken that the furniture and decorations of all rooms occupied by the Community, and in all Branch Houses, be consistent with Religious poverty.

OF THE CHAPLAIN.

(a) The Chaplain has the oversight of the spiritual well-being of the Community, and all Members can have access to him.

(b) The Chaplain may be invited by the Mother Superior at her discretion, to be present at any Chapter, in which case he will preside, and he shall have a veto conjointly with the Mother Superior on the discussion at that time of any matter which may be brought forward a the meeting to which he is thus invited by the Mother Superior,[19] but he shall have no vote in any meeting of the Chapter.

(c) The Chaplain shall counsel the Mother Superior in her management of all the Sisters, and advise her on all matters of importance.

(d) The Chaplain shall also see that the spiritual needs of all the Sisters in the Branch Houses, at home or abroad, are supplied.

(e) No Offices, Prayers, or Hymns, not in use during the lifetime of the Foundress and first Chaplain, shall be introduced in any Chapel of the Community without the sanction of the Chaplain and Mother Superior. No Priest shall conduct any ministration whatever in any Chapel of the Community without the permission of the Chaplain, unless he be well-known to the Chaplain, or the Mother Superior, or the Sisterhood.[20]

(f) No religious objects not previously sanctioned by the Foundress shall be introduced into the Community without the approval of the Chaplain and Mother Superior.

OF THE SUPERIOR.

(a) The Mother Superior having the government of the Sisterhood, shall be supreme in all matters belonging to the management of the several Houses, taking care in all things to act in accordance with the Statutes and Rules of the Community. She must on no account add to, or discontinue, alter or change any of the customs, dress, mode of Offices, or any other observances which were in existence during the lifetime of the Foundress, without the concurrence of the

---

[19] This level of control was unusual. In most communities the chaplain had no power of veto, and in some, he was permitted to speak only by invitation.

[20] Phillimore suggested that this sentence be removed.

majority of the whole Chapter of the Choir Sisters in Great Britain and abroad, and also with the consent of the *Chaplain* and the Visitor.

(b) The Mother Superior assisted *by the advice of the Chaplain* shall appoint the Sister Superiors to all Branch Houses, and also the Sisters in Charge of such Houses.

OF THE ASSISTANT SUPERIOR.

(a) It pertains to the Office of Assistant Superior to represent the Mother superior on all occasions of the Mother Superior's absence from House, whether for any period.

She will take her place the first in honour after the Superior. She will assist the Mother Superior in the management of all the Sisters, and shall therefore take care to be present whenever the Sisters or any of them are assembled together in a general meeting, to ensure the respect and observance of the Statutes and Rules, and report any irregularities which require to be noticed. She shall report what is wanting in every department. She shall keep an account of the current expenditure for the Mother Superior, making a monthly summary of all receipts and disbursements, and do all such work as the Mother Superior may from time to time entrust to her.

(b) All members of the Community shall have free access to the Assistant Superior with reference to any matter on which it shall be undesirable to disturb the Mother Superior.

(c) She will have charge of the books, which she shall keep in good order, and distribute them to the Sisters, as the Mother Superior shall direct.

(d) She shall read in the evening to the Sisters the subject for meditation on the following day.

(e) As the delegate of the Mother Superior she should concur with her in all things for the good of the Houses, carrying out as far as possible the commands and wishes of the Mother Superior.

(f) She shall have charge of the Mother House whenever the Mother Superior is absent, and shall never, except through unavoidable necessity, be absent unless the Mother is at home.

OF THE MISTRESS OF THE NOVICES.

(a) The Mother Superior shall, with the advice of the Chaplain, appoint a Mistress of the Novices to whom shall be entrusted the training of the Novices during their period of their Novitiate.

(b) She will have spiritual charge of the Novices, and will report to the Chaplain and the Mother Superior whatever matter appear to her to be of importance.

(c) She may be removed by the Mother Superior at any time with the advice of the Chaplain.

OF THE HOUSEKEEPING SISTER.

(a) The Mother Superior shall appoint a Sister to be in charge of the household and domestic arrangements, subject in like manner to be removed at the Mother Superior's discretion.

(b) The Office of Housekeeper shall rank next to the Mistress of the Novices, and in the absence of the Mother Superior and her Assistant the Sisters must apply to her for all needful permissions.

(c) As occasion may require she shall consult with the Mother Superior on the necessities of the House, and receive her commands and instructions.

(d) She shall keep a correct account of all the money entrusted to her for the expenses of the House, and give in her account monthly to the Assistant Superior. She shall apportion the various employments among the Lay Sisters.

(e) She shall look after and superintend all the necessary repairs of the property of the Mother House, the improvement of the premises, or any necessary extension of the buildings or furniture for the same.

OF BRANCH HOUSES.

(a) Sister Superiors and Sisters in Charge shall be appointed by the Mother Superior assisted by the advice of the Chaplain, and may be removed at any time at her will and pleasure.

(b) The Sister Superior in the House over which she is placed is the representative of the Mother Superior, from whom she receives her delegated authority.

(c) The Sister Superiors and Sisters in Charge shall see that the Rules and Customs of the Community are faithfully observed, being careful to maintain the regularity and discipline of the House after the pattern of the Mother House. Such arrangements as are necessary for the carrying on of the Rules and Customs must be submitted to the Mother Superior for her approval.

(d) The Sister Superiors shall in all difficult and doubtful cases refer to the Mother Superior, and must take care to carry out her decision.

(e) The delegated authority exercised by the Sister Superior in a foreign mission shall be beyond that of a Sister Superior in England, inasmuch as her government shall extend over the Houses and works of the Community in that locality independently of the Mother Superior in England, in such cases where time does not admit of obtaining the order or sanction of the Mother Superior. The Sisters in all such Branch Houses shall look to her as the representative of the Mother Superior, to whom she is responsible.

(f) The authority of the Sisters in Charge is subordinate to that of Sister Superiors. They do not act as representatives of the Mother Superior, but are responsible to her for the good management of the Branch Houses, the well-being and happiness of the household, and of the Sisters working with them.

(g) The Sister Superiors and Sisters in Charge shall render to the Mother Superior an exact account of the spiritual and financial state of their Branch Houses once a year, submitting to her a balance-sheet of their receipts and payments.

(h) No Sister shall be made Sister Superior without first having had some charge, and therein proved herself fitted for the Office of Sister Superior.

OF AN AFFILIATED HOUSE.

1. An Affiliated House can only be formed by the General Chapter of the Community.[21] No Affiliated House shall at any time be formed in England.

It must be composed of a Mother, and not less than five Choir Sisters, with power to form a Noviciate, and elect Novices for Profession. They shall have their own Chaplain and Visitor. The Visitor of an Affiliated House shall be appealed to only on questions of local necessity. He shall have no authority to sanction the alteration of the Constitution and Rules, which power belongs only to the Visitor of the whole Community.

2. The Statutes, Rules, Office-book, and Offices for the Reception of Novices, and Profession of Sisters, shall be the same as in the Mother House.

3. An Affiliated House shall have its own Chapter, which shall decide all purely local matters, and such internal arrangements as would not affect the Constitution and Rules of the whole Community.

4. The first Mother of an Affiliated House will in every case be nominated by the Mother Superior for a term of three years, and every succeeding Mother shall be elected by a Majority of the Chapter of the Affiliated House, but such election much be confirmed by the Mother Superior, and must receive the sanction of their Visitor.

5. The Chapter of an Affiliated House will consist only of those Choir Sisters duly elected into it. Choir Sisters of the Mother House permanently living in an Affiliated House can only vote in the local Chapter, but in the event of their return to the Mother House, those of them who were elected for Profession in the General Chapter will resume their right of voting there. The Mother of an Affiliated House, as the representative of her House, shall have a vote in the General Chapter of the Mother House on all matters affecting the Constitution and Rules of the whole Community.

[21] The American affiliation was established in 1890. India affiliated in 1894. Anglo-Indians and Indians were then free to test their vocations.

6. It is advisable that the Mother of an Affiliated House should from time to time visit the Mother House, and that visits should also be paid to an Affiliated House by the Mother Superior or her delegate, in order that the spirit of the foundation of the Community may be preserved in the House.

7. The Mother of the Affiliated House while visiting at the Mother House shall take precedence immediately after those holding Office in the Mother House

All other Sisters will take precedence according to the date of their Profession in the Community.

8. Notices of the Reception of Novices and of the Profession of Sisters shall be forwarded as soon as possible to the Mother Superior, and similar notices of Receptions and Professions at the Mother House will be communicated to the Mother of the Affiliated House.

9. The entire dress of the Sisters as well as the Motto shall be the same throughout the Community, but this Rule admits of differences of material necessitated by variations of climate. All such differences must have the sanction and approval of the Mother Superior.

10. The real and personal property of the Sisters joining an Affiliated House and the funds thereof are entirely independent of the Mother House, but are subject to the same rules of property and furniture.

The annual income (if any) of Sisters from the Mother House permanently attached to an Affiliated House shall be transferred to that House, subject to the Rule of the Society, *vide* Rules III and IV.

11. If unhappily the Houses should ever separate, the above arrangement shall be carried out only so long and until a new Habit, and that of a different colour, be made and actually worn by the Sister-in-charge, or by any one of more of the Sisters of the said Affiliated House.

FOR THE HOUSE IN AMERICA ONLY.

12. The arrangement between the All Saints' Community in England and the Sisters of S. Mary and All Saints' Community[22] in America shall be carried out by the Affiliated House there.

The Sister in charge of that work shall rank as Sister Superior, appointed in the first instance by the Reverend Mother Foundress, and she shall hold such position until a change is deemed advisable by the Mother of the American House, their Chaplain, and the majority of the Professed Sisters of S. Mary and All Saints' Community, as stated in their Rules.

Succeeding Sister Superiors will be appointed with the consent of their

---

[22] This was the daughter community for black women established by All Saints in 1880; it became extinct in 1917.

Chaplain by the Mother in America, notice of the appointment being sent to the Mother Superior.

The Community in England shall, during the life-time of the four Sisters comprising the Community of S. Mary and All Saints', at the making of the above arrangement by the late Reverend Mother Foundress, hold itself responsible for all demands made upon it by the Mother of the American House, and the Sister Superior for the necessary expenses of the four said Sisters.

Here follow the signatures of the Mother Superior, the Council, the Sisters, and of RICHARD MEUX BENSON, Chaplain, and of EDWARD CANTUAR, Visitor.

Letter interleaved at the end of 1890 version.

> ~~The Coppice~~
> ~~Henley on Thames~~
> 86 Eaton Place
> S.W.
> June 1. 1896.

My dear Madam,

I send herewith your draft constitution back, with my notes and suggestions *in pencil* on the flyleaves. I have only made one or two suggestions, very tentatively, on such of the Rules as do not come into direct relation with the Statutes. These suggestions are rather with reference to good drafting than to any thing else.

But I have carefully gone through every point in which the Rules come into relation with the Statutes and have suggested alterations in the language wherever there is an apparent conflict between the two.

This must be avoided at all costs: for

The Statutes are Sovereign.

When the Sisters come to pass your Constitution, They will I suppose and advise, repeal the present 'Rules and Admonitions' and ~~declare~~ 'additional rules' and declare the period of the existence of the tentatively adopted 'additions to the statutes' at an end.

Then your new book should begin with the Statutes, follow on with the Constitution and perhaps end with the rule of Life.

If I can be of any further use you will let me know. Perhaps some modifications of my modifications will suggest themselves to you.

> yours with all respect
> Sincerely
> Walter G. F. Phillimore

P.s. I return also the book of Rules and Statutes and the loose print on 'affiliated Houses' wGFP

The Revd Mother Superior.

II. 3

Chapter

1885
Saturday May 16
Chapter of Faults[1]

Saturday May 23

At the Chapter held at the close of the Retreat,[2] F. Benson said: 'The principal matter w^h we have to consider is whether S. Christina[3] shall be received back into the Novitiate.[4] We must consider both as to whether it be desirable for her, and as to whether it would be good for the community. She, herself, desires it very much and has written and begged the Revd Mother to have her back, owning her great wilfulness during the time she was here before. She is so anxious to return, that she is willing even to come as a Lay Sister, if only she may be re-admitted. The Revd Mother did not like to reject her application without your advice, and would not give an answer without knowing your feeling as to its desirability.'

The Mistress[5] said: 'I can see no objection to laying the matter before the community for their consideration. When here before she seemed like a blind person, & cld not see her faults, but since she has been away, she has written to me very fully & seems now to realize them. She asks for another trial, not for an extension of her Novitiate; if she returned, it would be as a stranger to rejoin over again. I think the decision of the Chapter[6] was entirely conclusive, in the state she was then in, because she was rejected on account of her faults, but now she seems a changed person. She asked for another trial before she left, but I held out no

---

1   Chapter of faults, at which sisters acknowledged their breaches of rule before the community, was normally held on a weekly basis. No minutes were kept.

2   The community held an annual retreat, which provided the sisters with several days of concentrated prayer, meditation, and spiritual teaching, led by a variety of priests.

3   I cannot identify this novice. The community did not retain, if it ever kept, detailed records of the many women who tried the life but did not reach profession.

4   The All Saints noviciate at this period is well described in Alice Horlock Bennett, *Through an anglican sisterhood to Rome* (London, 1915).

5   The novice mistress at this time was Sister Clementina.

6   Chapter was composed of choir sisters: only those professed for more than three years had a vote. See statute 'Of the chapter', clause (g).

hope, thinking it was only the excitement of the moment; since then, however, the wish has gone on growing in her.'

S. Sophia[7] said: 'S. Christina, when she was going made me an apology for something she had done two years before, & acknowledged how just she considered the decision of the Community to be.'

S Harriet Mary[8] said: 'While she worked with me at St Elizabeth's,[9] the patients were all very fond of her, & no one did more for them spiritually than she did. One of the patients shed tears when she heard she should have no more instructions from her.'

S Cecilia[10] said: I think to receive her back would be a bad precedent. We prayed for the guidance of the Holy Spirit & hoped we had it, when we unanimously rejected her; it seems to me like taking her out of His Hands to receive her back. I think it would be better for her to go to another Community, where she would be less drawn by personal affection. I think it would also be bad for the other Novices & would tend to make them careless if they thought once after being rejected, they might still hope for another trial.

S. Winifred[11] said: S. Cecilia had quite expressed my feelings on this subject. I think it would be a bad precedent & would be more advisable she should go to another Community of wh: there are now many good ones.

S. Isabella wished her to go to another Community.

S Helen[12] & *S Grace Mary*[13] were of the same opinion. F. Benson & the Rev$^{d.}$ Mother said the matter must be referred to the absent Sisters for their vote. F Benson said, 'The Sisters must not think that by re-considering their decision about Christina, they are taking her out of the Hands of the H. Spirit. The Holy Spirit guided them then, & we hope still continues to do so, & His guidance is shown by His having opened S. Christina's eyes to her faults; – at the same time the Sisters must not be guided by a sense of pity for her, but consider primarily what is ~~good~~ best for the Community whatever is best for her is included in that.' 'One other thing the Revd Mother wishes me to speak of viz the manner of saying the Offices in the Branch Houses. It is very important they should not be hurried over, but said reverently & with deliberation. And here, in Choir, there should be no hurry, but a steady pace, thinking well, what you are saying, lifting up yr

7   Harriet Sophia Robinson (1837–1904), prof. 1868.
8   Harriet Mary Pleydell Bouverie (d. 1890), prof. 1869. She was related to E. B. Pusey.
9   St Elizabeth's home provided residential care for a number of elderly women, a few very small
     children (they may have been ill: they are described in the 1881 census as 'patients', and were
     aged at that time from two to nine years; most were toddlers), and a few industrial girls.
10   Frederica Philott Skillot (1844–1927), prof. 1870; an outer sister from 1862.
11   Secular name unknown. Sr Winifred later left. Since the first systematic list of professions dates
     from 1895, the earlier portions of the list are unreliable and there are many gaps, especially of
     sisters who did not persevere.
12   Helen Bowden (1827–96), prof. 1864; worked outside the community in the U.S.A. for several
     years in the 1870s, establishing the nursing school for Bellevue Hospital.
13   Grace Mary Webb (d. 1892), prof. 1875.

hearts & understandings, remembering that in every utterance of the Psalter we are partaking in the mind of Christ.'

––––––––––

Wednesday May 27th

Chapter of Faults. The Rev[d] Mother announced that S. Christina's application had been rejected; some of the absent Sisters had written most strongly on the subject. Some thought she had been hardly dealt with by the Chapter & the Rev[d] Mother was grieved to see amongst the votes traces of a fault she had spoken of before; viz that Sisters had consulted with each other & then had voted accordingly. Sisters must never speak, nor talk over, what has occurred in Chapter; every thing said there is sacred, & should not be talked over, not even with a Sister Superior. One Sister unintentionally cannot fail to bias another, when things are talked over by them & then the voting is not just, because one Sister had passed on her view to another, instead of leaving her to form her own judgement. The Sisters should all recollect the solemnity of voting.

The Mistress said she wished to rectify two mistakes in the report (sent out to the Branch Houses (of the last Chapter *NB* [these were afterwards corrected, & a second copy sent to all the absent Sisters & this latter report has been copied into this book] this led some of the Sisters to wish the Chapters could be taken down in shorthand to avoid mistakes in future; S. Cecilia said she had found that a remark of hers had been erroneously reported. It was therefore agreed that this should be done if possible, or at least that fuller notes should be taken down at the time in future whenever any subject of importance is treated of.

Friday June 5[th.]
Chapter of Faults.

––––––––––

Friday June 12[th.]
Chapter of Faults.

––––––––––

Friday June 19[th.]
Chapter of Faults

––––––––––

Friday June 26th Chapter of Faults

––––––––––

1885
Friday July 3rd Chapter of Faults

––––––––––

Friday July 10th Chapter of Faults

———————

Friday July 17th Chapter of Faults

———————

Friday July 24th Chapter of Faults

———————

Friday July 31st Chapter of Faults

———————

Thursday August 6

The Archbishop[14] addressed the Sisters in Chapter
as follows:–

The Revd Mother has asked me to speak to you because I have a very sad circumstance to communicate, wh: is not known to most of you & she wishes me to
speak about it myself. It is that one of the Sisters – S. Priscilla[15] – has left the
Community. It is, I am sure a great blow to you that such a circumstance should
happen; & I feel it acutely myself. I do very earnestly desire that there should be
none in this Community whose whole heart is not in the work to which she has
given herself. But one of the Sisters came to me some time ago by order of the
Revd Mother & I had a long conversation with her: it mentioned circumstances
so strange & mental states so unintelligible that I could but come to the conclusion that she never had any vocation at all; & when I put it to her, it was her own
conviction also that there never had been any real vocation.

I am sure you will none of you misunderstand me if I say how very solemn the
promise you make is & how earnestly every one ought to keep before them the
deep solemnity & gravity of that promise which is made not unto man, but unto
the Lord. Your own hearts bear witness to the great pains taken to make the Vocation real to yourselves as well as to others; – not only in the long Novitiate, but
the perpetual call during the Novitiate, that call, on no account to go further if
they do not feel called by the Holy Spirit to a special work: – then there is the ten
days' Retreat, & the solemn questions asked you all in Chapter, the solemn
prayers, constant exhortations, searchings into conscience – therefore I do think
the Sisterhood is quite clear in this matter – the Sisterhood & all who rule in it –
they have done all they could in every case to arrive at the truth, as to whether
there is a real vocation or not. And in this particular case the statements made
were so very strange as to how it was possible to make such a Profession without

14 This was Archbishop E. W. Benson. He was elected visitor by the community in 1883.
15 Secular name unknown. Sisters who left often had records of their time in the community
    destroyed, as leaving without the community's consent was considered a betrayal.

self-deception, that therefore I do tremble lest, at any time, there should be such self-deception among you.

But I am sure the right step has been taken now. – And to those now professed, I do most earnestly say that they must consider that in each & every course of life there is a real & very troublesome limitation somewhere or other. Some of us have several limitations – & if we could, even by a hair's breadth, depart from them, ~~we~~ sometimes we would. In every vocation, (it does not what it is) clergyman, married life, tradesman, shop-keeper, landlord, servant – every condition has its limit assigned by God, & we break the 10th Commandment when we only allow ourselves to think whether we should not do better to break that limitation. For the command 'Thou shalt not covet, thou shalt not desire' is not only broken when we wish for this or that, but when we think thus. We know that all limitations appointed for us by God are for our training. Remember that in all circumstances everyone who is tempted will most certainly rebel if they are not faithful. And you – so blessed amongst yourselves & those with whom you are working, are sure to have limitations of every kind & these are broken every time any one says: 'I dislike washing those dirty children' – 'I dislike this dreadful smell of this sickroom' 'I dislike these filthy children & places' 'I cannot bear this climate' 'I cannot get on with this particular clergyman' 'with this particular person appointed to guide me' – 'in other places I might get on better, but here I cannot bear this or that particular thing'. Here, if we are wise, we shall only hear the Voice of God saying, 'My child, here is the particular thing by which you are to be trained' & with that revelation to yourself come other revelations to others. Never, never let the thought come, still less let the words pass your lips 'I will give up, & seek something else'. If you have put your hand with much consideration into the Hands of our Lord Jesus Christ & He leads you on, over rough roads as well as smooth, & He will make the way plain, though it may be over many a rough road with bleeding feet. We are hindering all God's great, deep loving-kindness for us, if we turn round & say 'that the chosen limitations of my life are more than I can endure, & I must seek some other way' – & if such thoughts do arise, there is generally something else first, some little inner rebellion against the law; – I do not say so blaming anyone, but because I know it in myself. I do not rise so early in the morning as you do, for instance, not quite so early, but not much later, at 6.15[16] – but I know very well that if I do not spring from my rest properly, instantly, (but it very seldom happens now I am thankful to say) – or if I am tempted because the business of the day will be so great, & there are so many engagements to be met, & I feel there is that great pile of letters waiting for me, – if I am tempted to shorten my devotions, or to say my prayers & leave my reading, if so, I do know that that day will be spent (never mind how much God in His Love may forgive me, & help me in other ways) not so near Him as it might have been; & I know that if I do overcome these temptations & little

---

[16] The sisters rose at 5.30 a.m., according to the timetable which prefaces the 1859 rule.

self-indulgences, God's goodness is helping me & if not, I know that I shall fail – there will be something of temper – something wrong in my dealing with some one, I have to speak to, perhaps seriously, some loss of spiritual force.

So, if it ever comes to thinking 'I must give up, I cannot go on' – it is not only the repressing that, but it is a call to look further back & see 'In what way am I rebelling?' I do not mean that there never will be weariness & trial, but I do mean that when they come, then strength comes from waiting upon God. 'Put thy trust in Him & He shall bring it to pass' is true not only of great things, but of little things also. 'Put thy trust in Him.' –

I know that not one of you will misunderstand or misapply what I say. I only desire to enter into the trials which test some of you; – they must test you, because they have been too strong for one of you – I do desire that everyone of you shall see that having promised to God & not to man, that they cast away all those temptations wh: will arise.' [*sic*]

Friday August 7th

After the Chapter of Faults the Rev. Mother said that there were some Novices due for Profession[17] – that she had spoken in a previous Chapter that she thought S. Mary Theodora[18] & S Ethel[19] had better wait a little longer in the Novitiate because they were rather young. Since then S. Mary Edith,[20] & S. Mary Gertrude's[21] time was up – they were due in June. She did not think it fair to propose these over the heads of those two, as they were not put back for any faults, nor would she like to keep them back. Therefore she proposed to put up all four. S. Mary Theodora, S. Ethel, S. Mary Edith & S. Mary Gertrude. She thought from all she had heard of them that the Mistress was quite satisfied with them.

The Mistress said she was quite satisfied with all four that they had shown great earnestness, & striven faithfully to overcome their faults & that since the Rev[d] Mother had decided that S. Mary Theodore & S. Ethel were rather young for Profession & on that account wished them to wait a few months, their spiritual lives had very markedly deepened.

The Rev. Mother then said that as so many Sisters were dispersed about, she did not wish the Profession to take place just at present. She wished to have some Clothings first & the Professions might perhaps be in September. The votes to be sent in on Monday week[22]

---

17   The normal length of the noviciate for choir sisters was two years; for lay sisters, ordinarily three.
18   Dora Mary Fooks (1860–1935), prof. 1885. She was born in Bengal, where her father was a major-general.
19   Secular name unknown, (d. 1891), prof. 1885. She died in India, of consumption.
20   Edith Mary Hayes (1859–1943), prof. 1886. Died in India.
21   Mary Gertrude Knapping (d. 1889), prof. 1886. She died of consumption; her sister, Edith Mary Knapping, was professed as Sister Edith in 1896.
22   Only senior choir sisters had the right to vote for professions. A majority of two-thirds was required for election.

Friday August 14th
Chapter of Faults

———————

Friday Aug. 21st
Chapter of Faults

———————

Wednesday Aug: 26th

After the Chapter of Faults, F. Benson came in & announced that the four Novices had been elected.

The voting was as follows:–

S. Mary Theodora	12 yes, yes –	1 No, no
S Ethel	16 " "	2 " "
S. Mary Edith	14 " "	– –
S. Mary Gertrude	18 " "	– –

The Novices were then brought in one by one & F. Benson addressed each –

To S. *Mary Theodora* –

'The Sisters are willing to accept you for profession if it is y^r most earnest desire to go on to y^r Profession, is it so?'

'Yes, Father' –

'Do you feel thoroughly resolved in y^r own mind? It is a great step to give yourself wholly up to God? When it is done, the step is taken for the rest of your life in this world.'

'Yes, I do feel quite in earnest.'

'May God's Blessing rest upon you; & in the life that is coming look forward to a real increase of grace from your Profession, & at the same time look for an increase of trials, we must always remember that the girding on of our armour is not like the putting it off; we must be prepared for many trials & difficulties in our professed life, in wh: we must seek God's help & strength. I hope the Help & strength of God will be always ready for you.' –

To *S. Ethel.*

'The Sisters wish to know if it is your earnest desire to go on to your Profession?'

'Yes'

'The Sisters are willing to receive you, if it is your own desire. Consider well what you are about, it is not the work of a short time but the acceptance of a life-long bearing of your Cross; being prepared to take up y^r Cross & follow Christ; following Him right on to the end, just as Elisha followed Elijah as he went on his way saying "I will not leave thee", so we must follow our Lord J. C. carrying His Cross to the end, & so you will get the blessing which He gives. When you are professed & the step once taken for the rest of your life, you must remember that there is no turning back. The Sisters will be glad to welcome you & I hope God's Blessing will rest upon you for the rest of y^r days.'

To *S. Mary Edith*

'The Sisters wish to know from yourself whether you are really wishing to go on to be professed?'

'Yes'

'If it is y^r own earnest wish they are willing to accept you; & in the time that remains before y^r Profession, consider well what a solemn thing it is, the giving up of oneself to God to be wholly His, no longer to be your own but His to have no longer the choice of any thing, but to be entirely willing & ready to accept whatever is His Will: there is no other choice in the world but just to choose that which He marks out for you by those He sets over you as your Superiors in Christ; you yield yourself up entirely to that Divine Obedience that so you may have the full grace of y^r Profession, a fount of Divine grace to strengthen you increasingly; in proportion as we seek, we shall find, we are quite sure of that, & as we give ourselves up in entire Confidence to GOD, He will make His Grace the entire sufficiency of all our needs.'

To *S. Mary Gertrude*

'Is it y^r own decided wish to go on to y^r Profession?'

'Yes, certainly.'

'The Sisters want to hear it from your own lips; if you are really steadfastly prepared to go on, they are willing to receive you among themselves, & you may accept their votes & willingness to receive you as a token that God has given you a call. What a blessed thing it is to think that God has given us a call! but we must remember that it is a call to many difficulties & dangers wh: we must expect in the course of our vocation, & at the same time we must meet them in the strength of that vocation; God's call is to ring in our hearts all our life long, we must never let it go, or let our ears be deaf to it. The call goes on, but we may not hear it, because one ear may be deaf to it, so be watchful to keep the ear of your soul alive to that call, & I hope you will find that Voice wh: calls you to be indeed full of blessing. In the time that remains before your Profession you must be really considering well with yourself what it is you are undertaking, & that you under-take it with such fulness of heart that your acceptance of it may by God's Blessing be crowned.'

The Novices having been dismissed, F. Benson addressed the Sisters: –

'My Sisters, since last we met we have had a visit from the Archbishop, & he has spoken to you words, wh: tho' I did not hear, I have read. I am sure they are an encouragement to us all; it is a great comfort to have our Visitor speaking words of such intense sympathy & love. As we have fresh Novices professed amongst us, we must see that we really have a deepening sense of the greatness of our Profession, we must not think less of it, as more come to be professed, but with the Profession of others, we must have an increasing consciousness of what our own professed life means; & as others give themselves up to GOD & we are witnesses of their giving themselves, we must think increasingly what it is to wh: we have been so long pledged, & how we must be steadfast & true to our Religious vocation. As we grow in numbers, so we must also seek to grow in spiritual strength, earnestness & consciousness of what our life is, striving, by GOD's grace to persevere to the end in every good work to wh: He may call us.'

Friday. Sept: 4th
Chapter of Faults.

Friday. Sep. 11th
Chapter of Faults.

Friday. Sep. 18th
Chapter of Faults

Friday Sep. 25th

After the Chapter of Faults, the Rev. Mother said: – (Those Sisters who have no vote, having by her desire withdrawn.[23]) 'I wish to speak to you about something not generally known in the Community, concerning S. Winifred Mary.[24] – A short time ago she conceived an idea that she was called to establish a Sisterhood quite independent of her Community upon the estates belonging to her family. The idea became rooted in her mind, that GOD willed her to go & instead of putting away the suggestion as a temptation, she cherished it, & without telling any one of her purpose, she left the Hospital & went to the place to make arrangements for carrying out her plan. By GOD's mercy however she very soon came back, & is now thoroughly ashamed of her fall & sorry for it. I know she would ask the forgiveness of the Sisters, & is most anxious to remain in the Community. I hope she may be a better Religious in the future through her fall, for it has opened her eyes to herself. She saw F. Benson, who gave her absolution at once seeing that she was penitent; but he thinks she ought to have some punishment by way of discipline, & has decided that she shall have no vote in the Community henceforth. She knows her punishment & has accepted it in a right spirit, & thinks he has been very lenient.

---

[23] Junior professed choir sisters (of less than three years' profession) had no votes in chapter, but they attended and could take part in discussion. Neither did lay sisters, regardless of seniority; they did not attend chapter.

[24] Winifred Simeon, prof. c. 1873, left for good in 1892, due to mental illness, and the community gave her an annuity of £125 a year. The Benson papers at Lambeth Palace hold several letters from her and her brother regarding this payment.

I wish you all to feel it is a thing of the past, & not speak about it among your-selves. It is a great cause for thankfulness that she had grace to return. In speaking of it to me, she said; she thought she was undertaking a good work, & that the end justified the means – she took her office book with her, & recited her Offices & performed her other Spiritual duties as she would have done here, & could not see she was doing anything wrong –

'There is something else I wish to tell you, which is very sad but happily is no sin. You know we were expecting S. Pauline,[25] who was being sent home because her brain was in such an overstrained condition. The doctor in India thought if she remained there, she would become a confirmed invalid, but that in England she might be able to do some work. She ought to have returned home on the 21st September, but instead of that, I received the following morning a letter from her, of which this is a portion: –

'After much agony – I have arrived at the conclusion I am unworthy any longer to be called your child. My inward failure in India forces me away from all which is most precious to me, as their sin drove Adam & Eve from Paradise. . . It is nothing but my own unworthiness which moves me to what is to my soul, as the bitterness of death itself. Without money, friends, or talents or health. . . a soul such as mine would be a hindrance to a Community & I have no right to come. . . No one will hear anything about me. However I hope by deep repentance in my future life to gain GOD's pardon if possible. I humbly at your feet in deep peni-tence implore your pardon for my ingratitude & the sorrow I cause you.' –

'This letter alarmed me very much & I immediately sent to the Steamer to make enquiries. We traced her as far as the Liverpool St Station, but there all clue to her has been lost. She had only three friends, to each of whom I telegraphed, but they knew nothing of her. I heard from one of them, Sir W. Hill, who is as grieved as we are, advising us to apply to the police, he cannot suggest any other way of tracing her. I think there is nothing to be done, but to pray & I would wish you all to make your Communion tomorrow with this Intention. She has sent back everything – all her books. I had a card from her from Suez or Aden in which she said she was longing to be again among us, & I can only think the heat must have affected her head anew. S. Gertrude Anna saw her on board, she was then very ill & sick, but full of love for her Community & longing to be at home.' –

A Sister asked whether application had been made to the Police, the Rev Mother said it had not been made. (This was however done the following day). –

Friday. Oct. 2nd
Chapter of Faults

---

[25] Secular name unknown.

Friday. Oct 9.*th*
Chapter of Faults

Friday. Oct 16th

After the Chapter of Faults the Rev. Mother told the Sisters that S. Mary Gertrude's Profession would have to be postponed as her Mother refused her consent. Her Mother refused to allow her daughter to be bound by any Rule she had not read herself, & as the Revd Mother could not allow the Rule to be seen outside the Community, there was no alternative but to put off the Profession.

Friday Oct. 23rd
Chapter of Faults

Friday Oct 30th

The Revd Mother told the Sisters that F. Benson had put back S. Mary Edith,[26] & wished her to remain a Novice, six months longer; only two therefore would be professed on Nov 3rd. She also spoke very strongly of the sacredness of all that was said in Chapter, & said how grieved she had been to find more than one Sister had spoken of things which had lately been announced in Chapter. Sisters must also never talk over what has been said in Chapter with their Sister Sup^r.

Friday. Nov 6th
Chapter of Faults.[27]

F. Benson. 'Is there any other matter wh: any Sister present would like to bring before the Chapter?'

S. Harriet Mary. Rev. Father, some of us are very anxious to know with regard to S. Mary Edith whether our votes still hold good for her, & if she will be professed at the end of the six months she was to wait, without any further reference to us? as she was elected & brought before the Chapter? or whether she will have to be brought in again? – And also with regard to S. Mary Gertrude, we should like to know whether she is to remain always in the Novitiate?' [*sic*]

F. Benson. 'In the case of S. Mary Edith, it was an act of discipline on my own part putting her back. it was not for a fault of any kind to cause scandal, or to

---

[26] This was Mary Edith Knapping, whose profession was to be further delayed due to her mother's objections. Her sister, Gertrude Knapping, also joined the community and was professed in 1896.

[27] Some repetitive material is omitted at this point: the text resumes immediately after the election of several sisters at a chapter held on 22 January 1886.

cause in any way the overthrow of her election. She got into a trouble, & I felt that she would never look back to her Profession without a certain amount of scruple if she had been professed then & there. It was not a fault of any such kind as at all to affect the votes of the Sisters, so that I think she could not be elected over again, I think the election must hold.

With regard to S. Mary Gertrude, the difficulty has resulted from her Mother. Her Mother definitely says in writing, that she is old enough to act for herself, but that she (her Mother) will not give her consent; – now, our Mother does not like to set a parent aside so entirely as it would be doing, if she were professed, though she feels no doubt that if she saw the Mother, she could be brought to give some sort of assent to her Profession. That is the reason why S. Mary Gertrude has been delayed in this way, & I should hope that the Mother will give in. I do not think there is any hesitation on the part of S. M. Gertrude herself?'

S Clementina.[28] 'No, none whatever Father, not in the very least' – I feel, Father, that we could not possibly hold another election in both cases it has been a very great distress & surprise to me, their Mistress, that they should be kept back from their Profession, but in the case of S. M. Edith it was a matter of discipline, & does not affect the Community. I think that we could not hold another Chapter; it would, be like setting aside the Voice of God, if we did hold another, we should never know when God did speak by us or not.' – 'I feel very strongly about it.' –

[F. Benson] 'I do not think any thing could set aside a Chapter except some-thing in the shape of a public scandal, in that case we might very fairly open the question again; – but you might as well repududiate a Sister after Profession for a little act of discipline, as elect S. M. Edith over again' –

S. Harriet Mary. 'I am sure, Father, we are all very thankful to hear you say so.'

F Benson. I hope that this difficulty in the case of S. M. G. may be overcome.

S. Helen. 'May I say, Father, that the Mother has said quite recently to me, that she is very anxious some steps shld be taken in the matter. It is not just for the Novice herself, nor for the Novitiate to have a Novice always in it' –

F. Benson. 'I am very anxious indeed; if Mother had been about, she would have communicated with S. M. G's Mother.'

S. Helen. 'S. M. G's Sister spoke to me about it; she said her Mother had said she wondered that her daughter did not use her own judgement about it, & that though not giving her own sanction, she thought her daughter wld be quite justified in doing so. I remarked that I wondered she had not done so, & she said she was kept back by our Superior; but Mother says "No," she would much rather something was done.'

---

28 There was a Sister Clementina (also called Clementia and Clementine), born Emily Clementia Williams, a governess who was the daughter of the Rev. Bennett Williams, rector of Bramshall near Uttoxeter, who was professed in 1874 and left later (by agreement) to join the community of the Epiphany, Truro; she became their mother superior in 1901.

F. Benson 'I know Mother does not at all like keeping her back, but she does want to get some little more tacit assent from Mrs Knapping, if she cannot get a definite one; but if she says "I will never give my consent" – I think those were her words it is a strong measure to act in defiance of them. If she could be brought to say, "I wont express an opinion in the matter" it would be a different thing, but she rather drives her daughter to do it in somewhat of a spirit of defiance.'

S. Helen. Something might be done towards opening the question again.'

S. Clementina. S. Mary Gertrude writes continually to her Mother, entreating her to give her consent; she cannot do more – & puts it before her that she cannot disobey her, but her Mother says if she cannot see the Rule of the Community, she will not allow her to be professed, & will not give her consent to her daughter signing any Rule wh: she has not seen.'

F. Benson. 'The Rule is in print, is it not?'

S. Clementina. 'No Father, Mother told me to write & say that the Rule had never been given to a parent' –

F. Benson. 'What the Mother wants to see is in the Parliamentary Blue Book is it not? That would satisfy her, she would not care I suppose to see the spiritual rule,[29] & our Constitution is actually in a Parliamentary Blue Book.'[30]

S.C. 'That never occurred to me Father'. –

F.B. 'I think it would abundantly satisfy her Mother; I have never heard that [objection] before, & have no doubt she would be quite satisfied.'

S.C. 'Perhaps Mother would let her see that.'

F.B. 'I think she would do well to do so; I did not know that was the difficulty; no doubt it is the Constitution not the Spiritual life, she wants to see. I will suggest it to Mother; I do not suppose Mrs Knapping could really care about the other: for by "rule" no doubt she means the Constitutions.

S.C. 'The impression it gave both Mother & myself was that she meant the spiritual rule; because fr. time to time she asks S. M. Gertrude questions about her spiritual life; – all the time she has been here, she has been very curious, & very much opposed to anything like the Religious Life.' –

F.B. 'I suppose she is.' – Yes, I will urge upon Mother to try to bring the matter to completion.' –

---

[29] This is a reference to the first part of the rule, which deals with the objects of the society, and with the promises of chastity, poverty and obedience, and other spiritual teaching.

[30] He is referring to the *Report from the select committee on conventual and monastic institutions, &c., together with the proceedings of the committee, minutes of evidence, and appendix* (London, 1870), VII.

Friday May 28th [1886]

The Rev. Mother said: I wish to put up some Novices for Profession: – S. Bernadine,[31] S. Verena,[32] S. Mary Clare,[33] & S. Frances Emily.[34] They have all passed through their Novitiate satisfactorily. The three first were due for Profession some time ago, but it was thought better that their training should be lengthened, as they were young & would be going abroad when professed. S. Frances Emily has given much edification in the Novitiate, by her great humility, her health is quite restored & she has never required any dispensations – she has only just completed her two years. S. Katherine Rose, we do not think ready for Profession. I propose giving her another year's trial, & am going to send her for six months to a Branch House; – she will then return for six months in the novitiate. Votes to be sent in next Friday.

Friday. June 4th

Chapter of Faults.

The Rev. Mother said the votes were as follows:–

S. Bernadine	24 yes, yes –	3 no, no.
S Verena	27 "	–
S. Mary Clare	28 "	–
S. Frances Emily	39 "	–

The novices were then brought in, & were each separately asked whether she wished to be professed & each expressed her earnest desire for the same. The Mother then exhorted them to make a careful examination of themselves before taking so solemn a step, from which there is no drawing back, & desired them to make a good & prayerful use of the time which still remained for preparation. After this, she addressed the professed Sisters present: – I hope you will pray very earnestly for the Novices: – I think you do not pray sufficiently for each other; you are very apt to grumble about each other, not to pray. If you will only pray you will do a great deal of good. When you see a Sister doing anything wrong, you should at once go & pray for her; you can do no good by speaking, but a great deal by praying. So with these Novices, you should every day say a special prayer that they may be strengthened in the life that is before them, – it will be an immense help to them. If we spent more time in intercession we should be a much better Community. Some of you are so wanting in love & charity, & are so apt to speak of the faults of each other. I hope you will not do

---

31 Secular name unknown, prof. 1886, became 'enclosed' 1894, left to become a Roman catholic 1917.
32 Secular name unknown.
33 Secular name unknown.
34 Fanny Emily Walker (1832–1915), prof. 1886. She waited eighteen years before her family would permit her to enter, and was an intimate friend of the foundress.

this in future, but pray for each other. The Professions will not be just yet; F. Benson has fixed that time – so there is time for you to pray. As a rule I think if you remembered the Novitiate more in y^r intercessions it would be a very great help.

(The Professions took place July 15. & S. Mary Edith & S. Mary Gertrude were professed at the same time.)

Friday Octr 8th

Chapter of Faults

The Revd Mother said: 'I want to speak to you about something that has cropped up in Chapter the last two years, speaking of "*necessities*"[35] – I do not think it is necessary & some of the Sisters feel also with me about it. If you are *obliged* to be absent from an Office, it is not a fault & it is very unreal to speak of it in Chapter. But you must remember that you must tell your Sister Superior, (or the Assistant Superior, those who are here) at Obediences,[36] if you have been kept away – because it is well we should have something over us to keep us in check, for some might be inclined to make a "necessity" of nothing & perhaps say they could not go to Office, or a meal when they could quite well have done so. So you must be careful about that – you must not give yourselves too many dispensations from "necessity" & when you are obliged to be absent you must tell your Sister Superior at Obediences, you were very sorry you were kept from an Office or a meal for such & such a reason but do not confess any more of these necessities in Chapter & be very careful as I said before about these "necessities". Sometimes the "necessities" are almost longer than the Chapter itself & we are so very apt to give ourselves dispensations & think that we are not well enough to come to Office, or to sit through a meal & therefore you must always give account to yr Sister Superior at Obediences *why* you were absent from an Office or meal. I am quite aware that the Sisters at the Hospital[37] have a great many, "necessities", being a public work but I am not quite sure whether the Sisters here or at St. Elizabeth's need have so many "necessities".'

Friday Octr 15th

Chapter of Faults

In the absence of the Revd Mother, the Assistant Superior said. Dear Sisters, I have to speak to you from our Revd Mother, & tell you that there are four novices

---

[35] A 'necessity' was a minor non-observance of a rule, for a necessary purpose.
[36] Obediences were held once or twice a day; at them each sister received her instructions for the day's work. If a sister felt that what was requested was unreasonable, she had the right to refuse the work; if not objected to at obediences, however, the order had to be carried out.
[37] University College Hospital.

who have passed through their two years in the Novitiate, & are now due for
Profession –

> Sister Helen Agnes[38]
> Sister Marguerite,[39]
> Sister Mary Gladys[40]
> Sister Marie Albinia.[41]

The Rev[d] Mother would like you all to send in your votes by Thursday
morning next; she asked me to remind you all that there are some very momen-
tous subjects for us all to think of when we have to vote for the Novices; we must
spend the time in earnest prayer to GOD the Holy Spirit to guide us as to our
votes, whether we are to vote, or whether we are not to vote; whether we are to
vote for them, or whether we are to vote against them. GOD the Holy Ghost is
the Brooder over Vocations; it is by the Holy Spirit that we are united to JESUS
CHRIST in our Profession, & it is the Holy Spirit particularly to whom we must
earnestly pray in order to have a right decision with regard to our votes – therefore daily, up to the time when you make & send in y[r] votes, earnestly seek the
Guidance of the Holy Spirit as to what to do. This gives us a great rest from
responsibility, because if we are earnestly praying to GOD to guide us, we may
be quite sure we shall make a right decision; GOD will not let us vote, or withhold our votes, unless He sees it good; so day by day let us all unite in prayer,
each one of us, & especially at the Celebration of the Holy Eucharist we must
make it a particular intercession then; let us unite together to ask GOD the Holy
Ghost to teach us what to do with regard to these Novices. The Mistress has
nothing to say against them – they have all passed through their Novitiate without
any drawback; they are not perfect, none of us are; they have their faults even as
we have our faults – but even in the time left to them GOD can perfect them to a
far greater degree, if we only pray for them; so do not let us have any prejudice
against any one of them, & let us rest our anxieties about them in GOD.

Remember to send in your votes by Thursday morning, that the Novices may
be brought in on Friday to hear the result of them.

> Friday – October 22nd
> Chapter of Faults.

After the Chapter of Faults, Father Benson came in & said.

Dear Sisters, I have to announce to you the result of the election of the
Novices; & first I find that Sister Helen Agnes has been rejected; she has 15. 'yes

---

38 Helen Lawley. If this is the Helen Agnes in the community's records, she died in 1906.
39 Sarah Hardy Bates (b. 1849), prof. 1886, left in 1899 in the U.S.A. to become a Roman catholic.
    She later joined a catholic religious order.
40 Mary Gladys Farnum (b. 1858), prof. 1888. She became a Roman catholic in the U.S.A., in 1899
    or 1908.
41 Albina Robinson (1847–1927), prof. 1886. In some records she is Mary Albina, not Marie Albina.

yes' votes, & 14 'No No'; I do not know how that has happened, she has been a very excellent Novice, & it must not be considered to be any fault of hers – but we must take it as being an indication of GOD's will for her, & no doubt it will be a blessing to her. The other Novices have been elected . . .

. . . . . .

Saturday, Novr 20th after Retreat
Present 36 Sisters

The Revd Mother said –

'I wish to speak to you about a few things in w^h it is not generally known by the Community what is right & what is not right.

First, there is the question about making Communions on Vigils;[42] several Sisters have asked permission to make their Communions on Vigils, & several do not wish to do so – there is no rule about it – it is not in our rule, & I do not know how the *not* making Communion on Vigils got introduced – I have never yet found out that it is a rule of the Catholic Church, except on such *great* Vigils as those of Xmas, Easter, & All Saints: so I think the best plan is to decide it in this way – the Sisters shall do as they feel drawn about it, but the Sister who makes her Communion on a Vigil must not be condemned by the one who does not like to make hers, because there is no rule about it. The not making Communion on Vigils is a thing that has cropped up; some Sisters do not care to make two Communions running & that might be an excuse for not making It on a Vigil: I have been written to quite lately f^r America & India to know about it, so I thought it better to decide it, & leave it quite free for the Sisters to do as they shall wish about their Communions on Vigils.

The next thing I have been asked to speak about is Retreats; not that I do not allow the Sisters to have a day of retreat when they wish it, but you must not make it a rule to have one every month.[43] Some Sisters have gone abroad & said 'O it was the rule & they must have it', & whenever it is wished for, a Sister can always have it', but a Sister must not think that she can have it at the end of each month, that again is not a rule of the Community, but has been sanctioned because the Sisters have busy lives, but in most Branch Houses it is very difficult to manage it & causes a great deal of discomfort. At the University Hospital I feel that the Sister Superior there, is able to let the Sisters have a day's retreat on Sundays f^r time to time – & then it is very nice indeed for them, we know what a busy life they have there, living so much in the world, that a retreat f^r time to time is very important – I am ~~very~~ glad they sh^d have it; I do not want you to lose it

---

[42] A vigil is the day (strictly the evening) before a feast; there were eighteen in the standard Roman calendar, but there were some local variations. Catholic tradition expected the commemoration of a vigil to include a mass: it seems an excess of refinement on the part of those sisters who felt it inappropriate to make their communions then. The mother's decision is clearly based on Paul's teaching on the meat offered to idols.

[43] The 1855 rule included this; the 1859 revision did not.

altogether – but not to look upon it *as a right*: again another thing comes of it – those who ~~do not~~ take their day of retreat, are apt to judge others who have not been brought up to it, nor feel drawn to it, one Sister must not judge another; if the younger Professed wish to have their day's retreat, they must not judge older Sisters who have not been brought up to it.

Another thing w^h is creeping into the Community is about the reading in refectory. Now Father Benson told us the other day how very careful we ought to be that each branch house sh^d follow the Mother House: here you know we never read anything but the rule,[44] the Commentaries of the Fathers,[45] or Thomas a Kempis;[46] & I must beg all the Sister Superiors to keep to that rule & nothing else: I believe it is the rule in all the Communities all over the world, & that this is the reading in refectory, the rule, Thomas a Kempis, or the Commentary of the Fathers; so you must be careful about it, it is wonderful how these little things creep in, & one hears of them quite accidentally; quite accidentally I have heard of different reading in refectory at the fancy of the Sister Superior of the house.

The next thing I want to speak about is the clothing – we are all vowed to Poverty, but I find that very often the Sisters do not like practising it in their clothing, & if they cannot get things when they want, they get very impatient & very naughty, & have a habit of asking for things they do not want, because if they do not ask they will not get them; there is at this very moment a Sister wearing out the hoods of a Sister who sent them home because they were not good enough for her to wear! As the Community increases, this becomes a very serious matter, & takes a great deal of money & time, & you must be careful & not ask for new things before they are wanted: it w^d be well if the Sisters were to send a specimen home if they are bad, their hoods or collars, & if they were really bad they w^d have others at once – but it has become so much the habit for Sisters to send home for things before they are wanted, that they are not attended to, & so they lose by it. You know full well I do not like the Sisters to be untidy or shabby but I do want them to be more careful that they are, because the expenses are very heavy: I know some of the Sisters think that the Community is made of money, but if they kept the accounts they w^d not say so – one Sister who had a hundred pounds said to me the other day 'You do not want it, let me have it for a branch house, nothing under a thousand pounds is of any use to you'. Even the smallest sums are of use when we think of the enormous expenses of the Community & the heavy bills there are to meet – Then sometimes Sisters want to have two cloaks, but they must not without a special dispensation f^r myself they must be very careful to return all the clothes they have to the Mother House,

---

[44] The community's manuscript copy of the rule has the amounts to be read at each meal pencilled into the text.

[45] The edition used was probably *Catena Aurea, commentary on the four gospels, collected out of the works of the Fathers by S. Thomas Aquinas* (4 vols, Oxford, 1841–5).

[46] *The imitation of Christ* was first circulated in 1418.

otherwise they gather together more things than they ought to have – sometimes a Sister keeps three habits, & *two* is the allowance; they like to keep things *in case* they sh^d want them, but that is contrary to the Vow of Poverty.

Another little laxity has come up of late years, visiting about a good deal; our rule says we may 'visit a parent &c.'[47] but it does not at all tell us that we may go hither & thither; this has been gradually creeping in, the Sisters going about visiting brothers & sisters; we have always allowed a Sister to go to her sister's house when it has been her home – it is not necessary I think, but it is allowed – but it has got now to going to two or three brother's & sister's houses – & then perhaps a friend says, 'I will take you to the sea-side if you are not well'. I hope you will all try to keep up the rule amongst you of not visiting about unnecessarily. . .

I have also been asked to say that some of you do not quite begin y^r chapters properly, it is as well to have unity in everything. Some say 'I confess before almighty GOD', others 'in the Presence of GOD'; by 'unfaithfulness to the rule', or 'to my rule'. I have had the right form written out – 'I confess in the Presence of GOD to you – that I have sinned by unfaithfulness to the Rule'. I sh^d like each of you to have a copy & make it like that; it sounds so bad for one Sister to make it in one way, & others in another.

These are the principal things I wanted to speak to you about today. I hope you will all find that this retreat will send you out much strengthened in y^r spiritual life – be very careful – I so often find that after a retreat Satan creeps in, you all get together & begin talking after the time of silence, & say uncharitable things, & discuss one another, I hope you will all be very careful & watchful especially on these two points – curiosity & uncharitableness. So dear children think of these two things, for some of you fall into these faults very often, & specially after a retreat, wanting to know where Sisters are going to work & so on – remember how necessary it is to keep up our Religious reserve.

May 20th Friday [1887]
Chapter of Faults

After which the Revd Mother said:

'I am obliged to have Chapter today because it is so long since S. Mary Pauline[48] was put up for election that it is not fair to keep her waiting any longer – the votes for her have been 27 "yes yes" & not any "no, no" at all.

---

47 See rule XV.
48 Mary Ewart, prof. 1887. In 1907 the anglican Benedictine community at Malling Abbey asked All Saints to allow her to become their abbess; in 1913 she took the community, then at Milford Haven, to Rome virtually *en masse*.

I thought I would now put up the other four Novices whose time has expired, or will have expired in a day or two – S. Katherine Rose;[49] S. Maude;[50] S. Mary Monica;[51] & S. Augusta.[52] As regards S. Katherine Rose, you know she was put back for a year; I am sorry to say I do not think she has improved one bit; her temper is very bad, & she is a great anxiety to the Mistress & a very great scandal to the Noviciate, & therefore I think I will ask the Mistress if she has anything to say about her.' The Mistress – 'I think it is quite true that she has not improved during the last year in any way.'

The Revd Mother – The next novice that comes is S. Maude. I have nothing to say but that she is so very young, scarcely twenty one, that I am going to put her off, though her time is come, because I find it is very undesirable to have these very young Sisters professed, she has only just had her two years, & I think she is too young to be professed, & her character not sufficiently formed. I have always regretted those who have been professed too young & have made up my mind to keep them back.

Then comes S. Mary Monica; as far as I am concerned I am quite satisfied about her, I am sure she has a vocation, & have nothing to say against her; but the Mistress will speak about her.'

The Mistress. 'I think she is truly earnest & has tried throughout her Noviciate to overcome her faults & to give herself up to the Life, & I know she has always looked forward to her Profession.'

The Revd Mother – 'Now I come to S. Augusta, & I honestly say that I think at times she is not right in her head; she goes on very well for a little while, & then is quite insane may be for a week or ten days together; she is very peculiar in her ways, & has a very peculiar & difficult temper, & she is another who has given the Mistress a great deal of anxiety during her Noviciate – & as her time is come I put her ~~put~~ up, because I do not think that twenty years will make any difference to her. Has the Mistress anything to say?

The Mistress – No, except that I quite feel that what you say is true, she is thoroughly good & earnest in herself, but I do not think she has any power, any mental power to grasp the Religious Life at all.'

The Revd Mother. 'She is a very earnest good woman, but has not the power to grasp the life; she constantly has these fits, & I think she is not at all accountable. S. Maude of course you need not send any votes for; I only tell you the reason she is kept back; so it is S. Katherine Rose, S. Mary Monica, & S. Augusta who are put up. As. F^r Benson will not be here again until June 3rd, & as we like him

---

49   Secular name unknown.
50   Maude Crampton (d. 1900, South Africa), prof. 1887. She had previously been a sister in Mrs Palmer's irregular sisterhood, St Saviour's, which worked in central London, but as Mrs Palmer was a married woman, she took off her habit every evening and returned home to her banker husband.
51   Secular name unknown. Prof. 1887. She left in 1895, being dismissed under statute 15.
52   Secular name unknown.

always to receive the Novices himself when it is possible, we shall not require any votes to be sent in till June 2nd. I should like them to be sent in to myself on that day.'

The Rev. Mother to S. Mary Pauline. 'Sister Mary Pauline, I wish to ask you in the presence of the Sisters if it is your earnest desire to be admitted as a full Sister in this Community?'

S. M. Pauline – 'Yes Mother, it is my desire.'

The Rev. 'You are quite sure, that they may know that it is of your own free will?'

S.M. Pauline 'Yes Mother, quite entirely'

Rev. Mother. I am happy to tell you that the Sisters have elected you; you will not be professed for two or three weeks, but still it will not be any time lost, because you are going to take upon yourself the most important step of your life, one that you cannot retrace; so you must not think the time lost between this & your Profession, & I will ask the Sisters to pray for you.'   The Mother Foundress' last Chapter.[53]

TELEGRAPH
CROYDON-FOUR MILES

ADDINGTON PARK,
CROYDON.

4 Aug 1887

My dear Madam,[54]

You will necessarily be proceeding after a short time to elect a Successor to take the revered and dear Mother whom we have lost – or rather who has taken her place to pray in Paradise for those whom she loved and governed here –

When last I saw her she entrusted me confidentially as Visitor of the Sisterhood with her wishes – which I wrote out & to which she attested as to her Successor.

But it is important to say that she desired that her wishes should be made known *only if the Community wished to know them.*

Unless they themselves wished to be informed of her views before proceeding to elect she desired not to embarrass them by communicating them.

If they preferred to elect without this knowledge she wished them to do so.

I will therefore not send you the paper unless I hear that the electors wish to have it, and if in due time you will let me know their decision I will forward the paper to you – or I will destroy it – just as is wished.

---

[53] Added in another hand. The mother foundress died on 4 August 1887.
[54] This letter was addressed to Sister Caroline Mary, acting mother superior of All Saints sisterhood.

The Peace of the Lord be with you all in sorrow and in joy – for there *is* joy for those who love her.

Yours faithfully in Christ
Edw: Cantuar:

1887
August 8th Monday.

A Chapter was held at which 67 Sisters were present, &, with a few exceptions, all voted that the late Reverend Mother's wishes as to her successor should be made known to the Community.

Copy of a letter from the Assistant Superior to the Sisters

August 10th 1887

'The Archbishop sent for me this morning & gave me our Rev[d] Mother's wishes, & said I should now send a copy to each Branch House for every sister to see. The Archbishop has extended the time for voting until 9 weeks from this date, in order that the Sisters abroad may send theirs – he said we could depute the Chaplain to receive our votes & tell us the result, but that the mode of voting must be settled entirely by the Sisters themselves. He read Statute V & said he quite thought that the "majority of votes" meant "*the most in number*" not, "more than half the *Sisters* votes" – but he would let us know this point for certain later on – I enclose you a copy of our dearest Mother's wishes.'

Caroline Mary of All Saints
Assistant Superior

The wishes of the Mother
Superior as to her Successor
to be made known to the Sister –
hood if they desire.[55]

The Reverend Mother Superior

would wish one of the following three to be chosen as her successor with the approval of the sisters and Visitors

Sister Caroline Mary
Sister Cecilia
Sister Gertrude Anna –
Her X Mark
All Saints Sisterhood – Margaret St
19 July 1887 –

In the presence of Edward Cantuar.

---

[55] This piece of paper has been glued into the chapter book.

The Mother herself named
them in this order
EC[56]

Copy of a letter from the Assistant Superior to the Sisters.

August 16th 1887.

– 'Yesterday I received the enclosed from the Archbishop, of w[h] I send you a copy. This decides the question as to "majority of votes" —

LAMBETH PALACE.[57]
S.E.
13 Aug 1887

My Dear Sisters,

I enclose you the question asked in F. Benson's words, as repeated, and my legal advisers'[58] answer. To this interpretation I should adhere as Visitor

Yours sincerely

Edw: Cantaur:

The Acting Superior
All Saints Sisterhood.

Question 'In every vacancy in the office of Superior the fully admitted sisters shall by a majority of votes nominate one of their own number as successor.'[59]

Does this mean

'not only that all the fully admitted sisters shall vote but that the sister who is to be appointed must have a majority of these votes, more than half of the votes–?'

or does it mean

that the Sister elected must have a clear majority –?

Answer I think the enclosed means that the Sister to be elected must have a clear majority of votes among those voting but that it is not necessary that all the fully admitted sisters should vote.

I think the term majority would be taken to mean that the Sister to be elected must be nominated by a greater number of votes than anyone else but need not necessarily get more than half the votes.

As for instance if there were nine sisters voting & one of the fully admitted sisters was nominated by four votes, another by three, & another by two I think that the one who got four votes would be duly nominated as successor.

L.[60]

---

[56] This sentence is in the archbishop's hand.
[57] Page glued into chapter book.
[58] The archbishop's legal advisors were Lee, Bolton and Lee. All of the opinions with respect to sisterhoods were signed by Mr Lee.
[59] Sheet glued into chapter book.
[60] Mr Lee.

Continuation of the letter of the Assistant Superior to the Sisters[61]

August 16th 1887

— 'On Sunday at Cowley I saw Father Benson, & asked his advice with regard to when & how we should vote. He said I had better ask you all in England and Edinburgh to send in your votes on *Saturday Sept[r] 3rd* he will receive them, & will then wait until the arrival of the votes from abroad, after which, in Chapter, he will announce the result.

It is not necessary for us in England to delay in sending our votes till the end of the nine weeks which the Archbishop granted only for the benefit of our foreign Houses. Father Benson thinks we has better, as far as is possible, take a day's Retreat, or at any rate make it the special matter of Prayer and intention at our Communion on Wednesday the 31st of August. The Sister Superior, or Sister in charge of every Branch House will collect the votes of the Sisters under her, & they are to be sent addressed to "The Rev[d] the Chaplain All Saints Home, 82 Margaret S[t]', The Veni Creator[62] & Whitsuntide Collect[63] should be used by every Sister until her vote is written – the vote is to be written on our knees after our Communion on *Thursday, Sept[r] 1st* It is not necessary to send voting papers round to the Sisters. All that each sister has to do is to write "I vote for *m or n* to be elected Superior of our Community" signed so & so.

She must put her vote in an envelope fastened down & directed to Father Benson and give it to be sent with the other Sisters votes by the Sister Superior or Sister in Charge of the House to which she belongs. Any Sister who from circumstances cannot take August 31st as her special day of prayer, or get her Communion on those days, — must simply take it any day she can, but her vote will be reserved to be sent to the Chaplain until Saturday, September 3rd.' —

+Caroline Mary of All Saints
Assistant Superior

Sept. 29th Thursday

Father Benson –

'My dear Sisters, GOD guides us onward, & now we come towards the appointment of the new head of our Community; I have to announce to you the election which has been made; I have received the votes of all the Sisters, & Sister Caroline Mary has been appointed by a very large majority of votes.[64] Two or three other sisters have some votes given to them, but those given to S. Caroline Mary are several times more than those given to anyone else. I know it has

---

61 This is written at the top of the page, on which the ordinary use of the paper resumes.
62 The best known English version of this hymn is 'Come Holy Ghost, our souls inspire'. The Latin form is sung at the election of popes and the ordination of priests, among other occasions.
63 This collect asks for wisdom and God's guidance.
64 This simple announcement does not reveal R. M. Benson's attempts to get another sister elected as mother; nor does it reflect the community's concern that their chaplain was eager to interfere in the election. The story is told in Lambeth Palace Library, Benson papers, 42.

been a matter of prayer amongst you that GOD would guide us aright, & I know it will be continuously a matter of prayer that our new Superior may be guided in all things to act according to God's will. I cannot doubt that He Who has blessed the Society so greatly hitherto, will continue His Blessing. He will certainly never draw back His Blessing from those who seek it, & I feel quite sure that you will be seeking his Blessing both for yourselves individually, & for the Community at large, as well as for our dear Sister now appointed to take charge. It will be arranged with the Archbishop as to when it will be possible for her to be installed in the Office of Mother, but I was anxious that there should be no delay in letting you know how the Election had terminated. May GOD indeed pour upon us all the Spirit of Unity, & truth, & love, quickening us with fresh strength, that as one generation succeeds to another we may not be feeling the weakness of earthly decay, but may rather feel the strength which is to be found from having those who were with us here, now dwelling in the closer fellowship of Christ; we must feel that our roots are indeed struck deep in Paradise, & as those who have been with us here are taken to be there, we must take care that we are putting forth the continual energies of Divine Strength; GOD's grace is renewed to us time after time, & if we are really looking for Him we shall find that He will never fail us. I am sure that the Election w^h has been made is one that will be very much welcomed by you all; we must see that we are really working together with holy energy, & continuous hope, & earnest confidence, looking for GOD to lead us onward in all ways of holiness & truth & love; we must see that everyone in the several positions to w^h GOD calls any are really losing all thought of themselves in the thought of the well being of the Community; all of us, from the Superior downwards, must have the thought of GOD's glory as the primary object of this Community, & the Community as a special means through w^h GOD's glory is to be manifested, & all thoughts of self must be entirely forgotten.'

To S. Caroline Mary

'I am sure dear Sister in speaking to you whom the others have now elected, this will be your endeavour, to lose all thought of self in the well being of that Community w^h will be entrusted to you & that you will seek that well being not as any mere matter of earthly aggrandizement, not as if the Community were a mere institution of earth to be measured by any outward considerations, but as a real trust f^r Almighty GOD for the manifestation of His kingdom & the advancement of His Power. Will it be y^r wish to say anything to the Sisters ?'

S. Caroline Mary

'Father, I cannot say any words just now, they all know what I feel about it; I will try, GOD helping me, to do my duty; I will try and take it up in the spirit of love, for the Glory of GOD, GOD helping me.'

Father Benson

'May GOD indeed grant you the fulness of His Blessing; the rule of Religious Community is indeed the wearing of a crown of thorns; many are the troubles & anxieties of a Community w^h none but the Superior can possibly know – & that is such an important thing for all the Sisters to bear in mind; how many considerations there are w^h a Superior has to weigh w^h may often seem to hinder this or that, so that what anyone in the mere consideration her own work, or her own knowledge, might desire, might not in the Superior's judgement be a good thing of the Community at large; it is indeed a crown of thorns, but we may be quite certain that He who gives it, will give along with it a special participation in the blessing of His Sacred Passion; we can only rule as we are united with Him, & we can only be united with Him first in proportion as we share in His cross. The union shall be ours by & bye, but we have to prove His Strength here while we are upon earth by enduring many trials & difficulties in its power, & every fresh office must be a free opportunity of bearing the Cross & thus becoming united with Him. Dear Sisters, may GOD's Blessing indeed be with you & strengthen you fr all the difficulties of coming years. We will now go up into Chapel[65] & there make the announcement to the rest of the Community.[66]

Sepr. 30th Friday.
Chapter of Faults

———

Octr 7th Friday
Chapter of Faults

After which S. Caroline Mary said:

'Dear Sisters, I have to tell you, 1st Our Retreat is fixed to begin on Monday Nov. 14th I do not know whose turn it is to be in Retreat, but I daresay the Sisters will let me know in due time – 2nd The Archbishop has said he will come on Wednesday afternoon, Nov.16th whilst we are in Retreat, to place me in the Office to w^h you have elected me.[67] It is the only time & day he can spare, & for my own part I am very thankful it will be during our Retreat. If possible, all the Professed who have not yet received the Benediction of the Visitor had better be presented to Him then, so any Sister who has not received his Benediction will please let me know. 3rd There are four novices who have passed the full time of their Noviciate, I wish to know if any of you think it W^d be unconstitutional to put them up for election now, & if elected to have them professed before the Retreat & therefore before the Archbishop has appointed me?'

S. Sophia & S. Cecilia were the only sisters who made reply, & both said that they did not think it could be unconstitutional, as S. Caroline Mary had been duly elected to act in Mother's place.

---

65 This was literally the case. Chapter was held in the refectory; the chapel was directly overhead.
66 This would mean the junior professed, lay sisters, novices and postulants.
67 At the installation of Caroline Mary, she received a ring from the archbishop as visitor, saying 'Receive this ring, the sign of faith, and be careful so to exercise the authority so entrusted to thee that the Church, the Bride of Christ, may receive no hurt through failure of faith or laxity of discipline in this Holy Community.'

Novr. 19th Saturday.

At a general Chapter following the Installation of Sister Caroline Mary as the Reverend Mother Sup^r she said

Dear Sisters, I thought we could best get over the pain of this Chapter, if I spoke to you in coming straight out of Retreat. I want to tell you first that I have chosen Sister Gertrude Anna[68] for my Assistant. I know that she will be a great help to me, & to you too. I know that our dearest Mother would have advised it. F^r· Benson will be here on Thursday, and will make her Assistant Sup^r then, but until then she will help me – there are a great many papers to look over, & letters to write, so Sr Gertrude Anna will take the place of Assistant at once, but will not be put in Office till Thursday. On Thursday there will be a general Communion for the Sisters going to the Cape on that day.

With regard to the other Offices, I am sure that dear Mother would have said that they ought all to abide as she left them. The Mistress will remain in the Office of Mistress, & Sr Eliza in the Office of housekeeper, & all the other Sisters Superior in the Office in w^h Mother left them, until any necessary or special cause should come for change, & all the Sisters, not only those in the Office of Sr Sup^r, but all the Sisters, I hope will be content to rest in their various posts, because Mother arranged, & put them in those posts. Of course if anything occurs in w^h we know that she would have advised a change, it is different – only we are not going to be so foolish as to leave our place and work, unless there is any real cause – let us all stay just as she left us. I want now to speak to you about a little business affair – the money matters of the Community.

Mother of course knew about every thing, what each Sister contributes to the maintainance of the Community, & I know next to nothing. I dont know how much we have with regard to income or how much we spend during the year, so I am going to ask you all, those who do contribute to the maintainance of the Community, to let me know between this, and Christmas, how much you each give, that I may have it clearly what the income of the Community really is.[69]

There is a project that came into my mind a little while ago, w^h I want to put before you – which is – that if our funds will allow it after a while, we should build a wing to the Cowley Hospital, as a memorial to our darling Mother, for the sick & infirm Sisters.[70]

As the Community increases, may be many of us will be ill, & not able to work for some time before death comes – & why I thought of Cowley is simply

---

[68] Secular name unknown, (d. 1904, in India), prof. 1873.

[69] Rule V states that the mother superior and the chaplain are both informed of the financial contribution of individual sisters to the common fund. Either this had not been carried out, and Benson was not informed of the amounts they contributed, or he was refusing to pass this information on to Mother Caroline Mary.

[70] The Cowley hospital was handed over to the society after it proved too expensive for private philanthropy; it was originally for incurables 'of a better class'. The extensions, which increased the number of beds to fifty-five and also made provision for infirm sisters, cost over £25,000. It is now the Society's motherhouse.

because it is so near the Fathers, who are constantly ministering at the Hospital, & therefore any sick Sister would have great privileges in their constant ministrations. Then I want to tell you that I have asked Father Benson, & he says I am not to make any Chapter of faults as Superior, he is sure it is not the right thing for a Superior to do.

I am sure dear Sisters we shall all of us try in our daily lives, & in our intercourses one with another, to carry out all Mother's teaching with regard to little details of Rule. You know how often she used to tell us about courtesy – we must try not to forget our curtseys when we meet one another – we must be courteous, respectful & considerate to one another – at Recreation – one Sister not monopolizing all the conversation. These little points of Rule Mother was very particular about. She always taught us that if we looked after these little things, we should not leave the greater things undone.

Nov 23rd 1887

'Extract from a letter from W Ford[71] Esq. in reference to the Election of the Mother Superior of the Community'

'Dear Mother Superior.

In accordance with the request contained in your letter of the 21st I enclose a form of Election which I suppose should be lithographed, & sent to every Sister entitled to a vote, whether resident or non resident. There are two ways in which a Superior may be continued in office under Statute (6) of which a copy is enclosed.

(a)   By the Visitor's authority continuing her in office, or

(b)   By Election of the Sisters.

The enclosed form is applicable to (b)

I suppose form (b) would be practically the course adopted because the Visitor would probably hesitate to continue the Superior in her office, unless he is made aware in some way of the wishes of the Sisterhood – which way could be so satisfactory and effectual as an Election?'

Extracts from Statute referred to. N°. 6.

'Every Superior hereafter to be elected, shall continue in Office for the period of three years, but may at the end of that period be continued in her Office by the Visitor, or be re-elected by the Sisters for another period of three years, and so on from time to time, at the expiration of every period of three years.'

Form of Election for Superior
To be signed by each Sister.

'In pursuance of the power exercisable by me contained in the Statutes of the Society of the Sisters of the Poor, commonly called All Saints' Home, I hereby

---

[71] Of the legal firm Ford, Ford and Chester, Gray's Inn. Mr Ford gave evidence on the Society's behalf at the 1870 parliamentary investigation into conventual institutions.

nominate and elect .... to be Superior for 3 years from the 29th day of September 189...'

To be signed and returned in an envelope addressed to the Chaplain

All Saints' Home
82 Margaret St
Cavendish Sq.

Friday Febry 24th [1888]
Chapter of Faults

After which the Revd. Mother said. 'There are two things I want to speak to you about. The first is that the University Sisters have been asked to join a British Association of Nursing, a national association that has been organized headed by the Princess Christian.[72] It has for its object to draw together all the Nurses of the various Hospitals, & band them together in a Profession. All the heads of the different Hospitals have been asked to become members. It did not seem right that University,[73] wh is a large school of Medicine should hang back.[74]

Fr Benson & I have thought it over, & I am perfectly certain our dearest Mother would have wished it, and it does not bring our Sisters into any greater contact with the world than they have now.[75] The other day there was a great meeting at wh S. Cecilia & our Asst Superior attended – the object was to take measures to obtain a charter making it lawful for no nurses to go practise as trained nurses unless possessed of a Govt certificate.

The Revd Mother said 'Of course if we hang back, it will put us in a very difficult position with other Hospitals. Sr Cecilia has become a Member, & probably other Ward Sisters will do so as well. You need not be afraid it will secularize our Sisters any more than nursing in a public Hospital does.

The next thing I want to speak about is quite different. – During my absence from Home, I visited S. James the Less Liverpool,[76] where in the house, working with S. Mary Milicent[77] is our rejected Novice Sr Helen Agnes. She has been there ever since she left us. Sr M. M says 'Her life is simply beautiful, she is most

---

[72] This is how Princess Helena, Queen Victoria's fifth child, was known after her marriage to Christian, prince of Schleswig-Holstein.

[73] University College Hospital.

[74] Founded in 1887, the Royal British Nurses Association began registering nurses in 1890. An attempt to professionalize nursing, it demanded three years' hospital training before admitting names to its register. It also lobbied for sick pay and pensions for nurses. Over 3,000 nurses joined in the first two years, including most of the University College hospital and All Saints' Nursing home nurses.

[75] This, as it turned out, was not strictly correct. Sister Cecilia was on the R.B.N.A. executive from 1890, and by 1892 was also on the registration board, which scrutinized the credentials of candidates for registration.

[76] All Saints had an orphanage for sixty girls in Liverpool, called St Margaret's home and orphanage.

[77] Mary Melicent Hine (1839–1928), prof. 1874.

devoted to the poor, does not mind what she does, & is the most unselfish worker she has ever had, she is always pleasant, cheerful, & ready to undertake anything; she does not mind what changes she has in work, & fills up all gaps, she seems to be quite a different person to what she was in the Novitiate, so much so that I did not know her, & addressed her as one of the other ladies there. S. M. Milicent is looking forward with dismay to her leaving, as in June she is going to the Sisters of Bethany. All the Priests who know her, think she has a Vocation, & I have been thinking ought we to lose such a Sister without at least giving the Community one more opportunity of receiving her. She was rejected entirely on the score of health; not as much of body, as fear of her brain giving way, and apparently this year has quite restored her. The Mistress says she was as good a Novice as she ever had, & the young Professed Sisters say they never knew a more unselfish, or a more capable person. Under these circumstances shall we put her for re-Election? She knows nothing about this, so she will not be disappointed, if not elected. I spoke to F^r Benson about it, and he seemed to think we might consider it.

S. Cecilia said, on being asked by the R. M what she knew about S. H. Agnes, that she had taken her to a doctor while she was a Novice, who had said that if she took off her habit for a year, she would probably then get well, and recover from the great strain, w^h family troubles had caused her. S^r C also asked if she had been living up to our life while in Liverpool?

The R. M. said. 'Yes S. M. Milicent treats her like another Sister. She says her office, is at Prime every morning, does everything with S. M. M. that a S^r w^d do, makes her meditation, & takes her time for devotions & spiritual reading.'

Sr Cecilia 'Still she is free, she has taken no vows, & she can do all that or not as she pleases.'

The R. Mother 'But she does do it.'

S. C. 'Yes Mother but there is a difference.'

The R. M. 'Any how she feels as convinced that God has called her into Religion, & the desire she has had since she was eight years old, is so great that she is going to the SS. of Bethany, though it is a great grief to her even to leave St James's because she feels it is the last tie with us.'

Sr Winifred asked if she could not be placed in the Novitiate again?

The Revd Mother said she should not dream of such a thing, & was quite sure that if she was Professed, & sent straight back to Liverpool, where she is a great deal out, & about in her work, she would do perfectly well.

S. Helen asked it if was not a Rule that Sisters should not be put up for Election a second time? It had been proposed once, & it was then said that having been rejected once would be a bar to anyone being put up again.

Sr Cecilia said that in the case mentioned by Sr Helen the question was one of conduct, & not of health.

R. Mother said 'This is an unprecedented case, her conduct was exemplary in the Novitiate, not only the Mistress, but all who knew her speak most highly of her sweetness & unselfishness, & her powers of governing others, because she had a gentle way of helping them. I put this before you, & you can take a week to think about it, & I will look in the back Chapter notes, & see whether she can be re-elected.'

Sr Winifred said the proposal in a former case had been that the S^r should go back into the Novitiate.

The R. Mother said that she did not see why she should go back into the Novitiate, She had had her full time & a year out of it.

Sr Gertrude Anne said that what Sr Helen had mentioned c^d not apply in the present case, w^h was purely a matter of health. The question was whether as the D^r had said that a year of freedom would make her well, she c^d now be put up again.

S. Winifred said that as a year out of the Novitiate had made her well, might it not show that it was the life that made her ill.

S. H. Mary[78] said she remembered our dearest Mother having said she w^d never put up a Novice for re-election. It would be doing away with the validity of the votes. S. Helen said the same, & added that F^r Benson had said in telling them of the rejection of S. Helen Agnes that it was mysterious to him & to the Mistress, but that He felt it was God's doing, & he hoped she w^d be accepted elsewhere.

The Revd Mother 'The reason why I have thought about this is that S. M Milicent has such difficulty in finding anyone who has got sufficient self-sacrifice & endurance to bear the life of poverty, disappointment, & hardship of that Mission, year after year goes by, & she has no Sister to help her, & here is a Novice we have rejected. She seems untiring in her devotion, & is an example as well as a help, it may be of course that GOD has ordered that she shall go elsewhere, we may not be worthy of her.

March 2nd 1888.
After Chapter of Faults

The Revd Mother said.

I cannot tell you the result of the voting for or against the re-election of Helen Lawley as we have not yet got in all the votes – at present there are more votes for than against. I have looked back in Chap. to see about a re-election & this is what F^r Benson said with regard to the re-election of a Novice who had been sent away because of her faults, & wh asked to be taken back.

'The SS must not think that by reconsidering their decision they are taking the Novice out of the Hands of the Holy Spirit; the H.S. guided them, & we hope still continues to do so, & His guidance is shown by having opened this particular Novice's eyes to her faults, at the same time the Sisters must not be moved by a

---

[78] This is Sister Harriet Mary.

sense of pity, but must consider primarily what is good & best for the Community, & what is good & best for her, is included in that.'

Then with regard to a Sister, now Professed, who was put back after her Election by F^r Benson, I find the Mistress did speak very strongly about not having a re-election under those circumstances. F^r Benson said it was an act of discipline on his part, & not for any fault to cause scandal, or in any way overthrow her election. – In the case of Helen – she has no faults w^h. keep her back – it is not a question of pity, she does not know what we are doing, & has made up her mind to enter another Community. The question is whether it is right to reject such a good & holy person. Sr Anne[79] writes. I shall be very glad indeed for S.H.A. to be put up for Profession again. I remember our Mother saying she considered her quite a Saint, & also that she thought she w^d be unable to bear the strain of the Novitiate, only because she had been broken down by family troubles – As she was rejected solely on acc^t of her health, & is now quite well, I cannot see why we should be afraid to have her, it is not even as if she had ~~sp~~ been spending the year at home doing nothing but she has been keeping up the Religious Life, & her having done so without any vows speaks in her favour. A Novice rejected for her faults is in quite a different position. . . .

S. Gertrude[80] says. With regard to S.H.A. I was sorry she was not Professed. She worked with me at S. Gabriel's,[81] & was very helpful with the girls. I saw a good deal of her, & voted for her then, & have done so again. The only question is Can we vote for any one who is not actually a Novice? I cannot help thinking she would be better in the Novitiate for a time.

S. Edith Anne[82] wrote that she w^d willingly vote for the re-election of S.H.A, & said she thought her keeping up her spiritual life, without the aid of vows was a strong test of her earnestness.

Sister Sophia[83] urged that the Sisters were kept too much in the dark about the Novices, & mistakes in voting were made in consequence.

The Revd M. said she had been talking to a very wise Priest who said that when a Novice was completely approved by the Mother, the Mistress, & especially the Director, the Sisters took a very grave responsibility on themselves in rejecting her. Sr Sophia says 'we see something we do not like, in expression, or manner, & know nothing more, & so vote against a Novice.' – no doubt S.H.A.'s outward manner was depressed & morbid, but it is not right to go only by outward manner. If the Community had known about the debt, it might have altered the case.[84]

---

[79] Elizabeth Anne Wigram (1830–1918), prof. 1864. She became an outer sister in 1858.
[80] Gertrude Annie Baty, prof. 1865, left 1895.
[81] I have not been able to identify this branch house.
[82] Secular name unknown.
[83] Harriet Sophia Robinson (1837–1904), prof. 1868.
[84] This suggests that the family troubles were financial in nature, but they may have been temporary: no one of the name of Lawley went through the bankruptcy courts in the 1880s.

The Mistress said she had had no opportunity of telling the SS when S. H. Agnes was put up, how thoroughly earnest she had been. She had never given her a moment's anxiety, the strain was entirely caused by her family troubles, as for the Rule, it was a joy to her to keep it; a re-election should not take place when a Novice is rejected for her faults, but when it is only a matter of physical circumstances, & they are removed, there would be no reason to prevent it.

S. Cecilia asked if there was any insanity in the family of S.H.A.

S. Catherine[85] said 'I do not see that it makes any difference whether it is health, or conduct; a wicked person may become a Saint in a year, but I object to any person being put up a second time for Election; when a Novice is put up we are desired to make it a subject of special prayer for direction, & when we have voted, it is considered a matter of GOD's ordering, whether she is elected, or rejected & there it rests; it seems to me like tempting GOD, & following the example of Balaam to bring the matter forward again. With regard to the present circumstances I for one, could not be as ungenerous as to try to deprive another Community of a person, because we had just found out her value.'

S. Winifred asked if the matter of insanity could be found out. The R. Mother said she w^d make enquiries.

Friday March 9th. 1888.
Chapter of Faults

After w^h The Revd Mother said

With regard to the questions we are considering as to the re-election of S. Helen Agnes for Profession. I have first to tell you that F^r Benson has decided that in any case she must come into the Novitiate again for a year, so the question is now whether we will admit her into the Novitiate – of course it is really the same thing as we should do it, intending to put her up at the end of the year, F^r Benson says. 'I do not think we are acting contrary to the H. Spirit in subjecting a Sister to re-election if it can be done consistently with our constitution, my doubt w^d be not the re-election, for a Novice might be fit at one time, who had not been fit a year before, but my doubt w^d be as to the constitutional character of the election, I do not see how the Sisters can vote for her on the mere report of her behaviour in a Branch house. If she is received back for a twelve month's probation, the Sisters might vote to that effect, & then proceed to her election at the end of the time. I do not see my way to sanction her return unless it be for as Novitiate of twelve months.

She might be put at the head of the Novices, as having left through consideration of health. We ought not to grudge her to another Community, but I should think it would be unprecedented to receive a rejected Novice, back at the end of as long a time, otherwise than as a Novice requiring a prolonged probation. I

---

85 Catharine Williams, the author of the Franco-Prussian war diary.

wrote to M^r R M Grier[86] as to the sanity of her family, & he says he never heard of there being any insanity in the Lawley family, & thought if there had been, he must have heard of it. I also wrote to S. Mary Teresa,[87] & asked her if she had said anything against the sanity of Helen's family, & her answer is that she had said nothing of the kind. I also wrote to the Arch Bishop,[88] & told him we were considering whether we could re-elect a Novice rejected in /86 under apprehension of impending brain affection he says he has no doubt as to the answer to give, relying on our LORD's guidance – GOD did intend by the painful doubt as to her assured sanity that the Sisters using their reason should not at the time elect her to be a full Sister,– why for the sake of herself & the Community He should thus have prolonged the time, we do not, & cannot know. Now that the ground of delay for acting in such a way is gone, the delay is over, & doubtless has worked His Will. He adds 'no stronger case could arise for exceptional treatment – she in life & spirit has been all you wish, & has answered so lovingly to the Divine Guidance & trial' – he says he should not think it necessary that in all such cases there should be a prolonged new Noviciate, but it must be left to the wisdom & love of the Community as to the time still to be waited, but as to the advisability of a second election I can feel no doubt.' The Archbishop is very plain that it is not against the H. Spirit of GOD that we shld make a re-election, & F^r Benson is not ag^{nst} it, only wishes for a year's probation, & the majority of the votes being for the election, I shall take them to be the votes for her re-admission into the Novitiate. I have decided that she shall be admitted for a year, if she is willing to come, & then she will be put up for a second election.

July 20th

Chapter of Faults

After w^h the Revd Mother said – Dear Sisters I have to tell you two or three very sad, & grievous things. – I can only feel that Satan is very busy trying to do what he can in our Community just now, as we are coming to the close of our first year of bereavement. A sort of stillness & hush came upon us all, & in our great sorrow we were united, & now as the year is getting over, Satan is trying to find out who amongst us is faithful. He is walking up & down our ranks to see whether we are really true in heart, or whether we are really standing upon ground that is only sand.

The first thing of w^h I must tell you is the defection of Sr Edith Anne.[89] She has only been Professed 4 years. She has left us to join the Church of Rome, & it

---

[86] Richard Macgregor Grier was vicar of Rugeley, Staffs., where the Lawleys lived, from 1865. In 1876 he became prebendary of Lichfield. He was a high church liberal and the author of controversial pamphlets.

[87] Mary Theresa Suckling (d. 1910), prof. 1875. Her sister (Mary Augustine) became All Saints' third mother superior.

[88] This letter does not appear in Benson's letterbooks in Lambeth Palace Library.

[89] Secular name unknown.

has been done in a very wilful & obstinate manner. She would not come into Retreat, she would not see F^r Benson, & the only Priest whom she would see, when her saw her, said that it was of no use, because her mind was quite made up. She would not hear reason or try to settle her faith in the Sacraments, & order of our Church; she would look at things only in her own way – and so she went. – & since she has left she has not behaved truly, she has not kept promises that she made to me. She not only wrote, but telegraphed to a girl working with us at Eastbourne to come to her, & then wrote to me that the girl had called upon her, & as I knew from Sr Anne that the girl had not only been written to, but telegraphed for, it is only the old story, that when people lose their faith, they go down in the scale of truthfulness. I do not go into the question of joining the Church of Rome but this I say that if we religious join the Church of Rome, it must be at the expense of breaking our vows. – Our Profession, our Vows – become as nothing – & that is a most awful thought. I cannot dwell upon it dear Sisters, but as these things must come to yr ears, I want you to know that I think Sr Edith Anne's departure a most wilful act.

The next great sorrow that has come upon us is, that Sr Frances Anna[90] wishes to leave us. That is an old trouble. Last year even before our dearest Mother left us, even on her death bed, she was most anxious abt Sr Frances Anna, but hoped that she might recover herself and that we might keep her. It is just the old story of going down by unfaithfulness in little things, until she has lost her faith in her vocation, & in the power of recovering herself. She says she can never rise up to our standard or Rule, & to the Vows, & she therefore wishes to go. Of course it is a great sorrow to us all, but especially to her Sr Superior at the Hospital, who has done everything in her power to keep her true & faithful. I only hope it will be a help to us all dear Sisters, in one way, to become more watchful & true, for if we will become independent, taking our own line about things, & get into the habit of scorning little customs & old rules, we shall of course weaken our spiritual life.

Then I have to pass on to another trouble, w^h is about the insubordination & rebellion of a young Sister, young in age though she has been in the Community some years, & I feel I ought to bring it before Chapter, whether a Sister ought to be so very disobedient & impertinent without receiving any correction or disgrace in the Community. It is Sr Mary Stanislaus.[91]

She was taken into the Novitiate when only 18 straight from school having barely finished her education. She was educated at our school at Clifton,[92] & our dearest Mother was most charitable in receiving her. She passed through her

---

[90] Secular name unknown.
[91] Secular name unknown (1857–1926), prof. 1879. She evidently continued to be a problem: the community took away ten years of her seniority in 1895.
[92] The school at Clifton was for young ladies, and was opened in 1870–1. Maria Rosetti taught there during her religious life; it seems to have closed by the 1890s.

Novitiate & was Professed when she was 21. and ever since then she has given great trouble to her Superior wherever she has been placed, through her conceit & stubbornness & rebellion.

At Edinburgh,[93] Wolverhampton,[94] Liverpool, & America, it has been the same story, & now because she cannot get her own way about the time & manner of her return to England, she writes of her Superior that she has the bitterest feelings towards her, says she has acted in a most mean manner, crosses her will only in order to be spiteful towards her, & says how to endure another month with her she does not know, & this notwithstanding the greatest forebearance on S^r F Helen's side. She adds 'if I was to remain in America, I shall as a matter of course join the Roman Church, it being the Catholic Church of this country. The Church of Rome is a very great attraction to me, & I should like to talk the matter over with a Roman Priest. I thought of going to the Cathedral to speak to the Bishop, but thought it not quite open, as I should not have spoken to Sister first, but I will leave all this now, & try & endure this month. You see I do not know you, or you me, & I might not be happy if I was at Home, & she goes on to say that there are many things in the Community of w^h she does not approve. – such as the admission of widows[95] &c says she would never have joined the Community had she not hoped to rise up to daily Communion,[96] it being the custom of the Ancient Church – and complains of our continuing to pray for the soul of our Rev^d· Mother Foundress,[97] saying that the prayer is a real aggravation to her. Then later on I get a <worse> letter from her. She says 'Our passage has again been changed, & I simply cannot endure waiting any longer.' If you can send a cable gram to say that S. Frances Hilary & I can sail by the Pretoria I will wait, if not, I am quite sure that I shall act for myself in the matter, & feel justified in so doing. I think that we can work our passages over as stewardesses. I never met with any one so untruthful as S. Frances Helen & S. Anna Maria. I hope you will tell S^r not to send us later than the 3rd, if not, you do not know what terrible temptation you will be exposing me to, & go with S. F. Helen I will not, rather than that I shall take off my habit till I get Home.'

I never in all the course of my Religious Life have heard or received such letters or sentiments as these from a Sister old or young, & I do not think it is right to let it pass. I thought this Sister ought to be given the opportunity of remaining in the Community either by being put down to the last Professed, or by

---

93   All Saints worked in Edinburgh from 1870 to 1932.
94   Here they worked in the parishes of All Saints and St Andrew's.
95   All Saints admitted widows from the very beginning. The Visitation order was founded by a widow.
96   Members of the society seem to have communicated every other day in this period.
97   This prayer has not been preserved. Prayer for the dead remained contentious in anglican circles until World War I. This protestant objection sits oddly with the Roman-leaning complaints listed above; the sister seems to be in a state of considerable theological confusion.

being put into the Novitiate again. She has written me a note of apology but I still think her conduct ought to come before the Community.

The Revd Mother then asked each of the senior Sisters what they thought about it, and the feeling was unanimous that some very decided step should be taken. 5 Sisters thinking she ought to be expelled, the rest wishing that the opportunity should be given her of redeeming her character by being put down below the lowest Professed.

Having found out the mind of the Sisters on the subject the Rev^d. Mother said she should lay the matter before the Chaplain to be guided by his advice. She also added that whilst in Edinburgh she had consulted with Sr Mary Augustine[98] who had been S. M Stanislaus's Mistress & she was most strong on the need of her having some humiliation, as if the matter was passed over now, she w^d go off at some future time in a pet or naughty mood, & that it was better to take the matter in hand now.

The Revd Mother then said 'Of course, it is a most terrible step to take, to remove a Sister, & I wanted to say one word about that bit in the Rule w^h says that a Sister is at liberty to quit the Community at any time.[99] Of course you all know it simply means that you are not kept as prisoners in the Community, you are not hindered *legally* from leaving it, you are not *bound by law* to keep in the Community, but when, in union with the Holy Sacrifice we ask to be received into the Community in *Poverty, Chastity* & *Obedience*, (and remember these are the first words we utter after we have made our Communion with that intention) *for the rest of my life in this world*, when we have made these solemn vows at our Profession, it is of course the gift of our free will to GOD – & when a Sister withdraws from the Community, & breaks her vows, it is just because that gift of free-will is withdrawn. We can of course withdraw, whenever our *will* is withdrawn, from the sacrifice we have made to GOD, but it is a taking back of what *has been given* to GOD, and consecrated to Him for ever.

I feel dear Sisters that now, if ever, we must all be on the watch, & be faithful, true & earnest in keeping up our life of Consecration, striving to live in obedience & submission, & in love one towards another.

One thing more, I do wish to remind you of.

Did not our dearest Mother always say, it was so bad for Sisters to try & pump one another, & try & find out what this one, or that was doing. – If a Sister comes from a Branch House, she is immediately set upon to know where this or that Sister is, a habit Mother used always to say was only idle curiosity. What is good & useful is sure to be made known through Superiors, this cross-questioning is a

---

[98] Anna Maria Suckling (1841–1923), prof. 1875. She was later to be mother superior for twelve years.

[99] This is a reference to the much disputed addition to the rules, inserted by Tait when bishop of London and All Saints' visitor. See the appendix to rule I, and the letters on vows.

very bad habit to get into. Never let us neglect our dearest Mother's exhortations to us, if we lose her spirit, & care & thought about the little things w^h make up a hedge round our Religious Life, we shall be sure to become lax & fall to pieces.

This is a most sorrowful Chapter, but we must ask GOD to watch over this Community, & pray very much that He will give us the spirit of wisdom, deep charity, & a pure intention.

Sepr 7th

Chapter of Faults

After w^h the Revd Mother said she was grieved to have to tell the Sisters of another falling away from the Community. S^r. Florence[100] had for most trivial reasons withdrawn. She gave as her reason that the Community encouraged a love of acting amongst the children, and the guilds under their care. She was much upset at being asked to go & see the little orphan Boys at Lewisham[101] act, & objects to a little children's dressing up & acting at Liverpool,[102] & she thinks this a sufficient cause for leaving the Community. The Rev^d. Mother then went on to warn the Sisters against allowing in themselves a judging & criticizing spirit, & in questioning the actions of their Sisters Superior.

When they saw things of w^h they could not approve, they were to seek counsel about it, but not allow themselves to fret or be disturbed about it. They should be in their Community as a wife who trusts her husband.

She begged the Sisters in Charge not to force the Sisters working with them to any of the entertainments with w^h their work was not concerned, & she exhorted them all to have a more charitable spirit amongst themselves.

The Rev^d. Mother begged the Sisters to pray very much for those who had fallen away from their cross, that GOD w^d give them a merciful judgement at the Last Day, for it was very terrible to think of souls who had so solemnly dedicated themselves at the Altar, falling away after many years of Profession, & breaking those vows.[103] It was a most solemn warning to us all.

---

[100] Secular name unknown.

[101] The boys' orphanage was founded in 1877 and closed in 1926. In the 1890s it held 130 boys. Acting and related entertainments were normally acceptable to anglo-catholics, who found disapproval of such activities excessively 'protestant'. The community of the Sisters of the Church also regularly entertained the children in their care with such diversions, and there is a description of such an event in Bradford in Bennett, *Through an anglican sisterhood to Rome*, pp. 85–6.

[102] This would be the girls' orphanage, St Margaret's home.

[103] It is clear that the mother superior viewed the vows as life-long.

Sep^t 14th 1888.

Chapter of Faults.

After w^h The Rev^d the Chaplain said.

I am very sorry to have to speak to you as I am now doing but the matter does not allow of delay. It refers to S. Louisa.[104] It is not a trouble of yesterday, as many of you are aware, it has been a long trouble in various places, this self-will of hers. I dare say many of you have known how it was at Eastbourne, when she left the organ silent, & gave way to her temper; now matters have culminated, & while at Liverpool her conduct has been such, that Sr Emily had often in Chapel to take up both sides in Choir, because S. Louisa was simply dogged & sullen.

When she first went there S. Emily told her to be cantrix & she went on much in the same way she did at Wolverhampton, until one day at the Nunc Dimittis she was simply making such a noise with the instrument that it was an act of irreverence to go on, & she was told to stop altogether. After that S. Louisa asked S. Emily's leave to go home to her family who live in Liverpool, & said she would write to the Mother. S. E. allowed her to go. An hour after her return to her family S Louisa wrote to the Mother, saying she had thought the matter over very seriously, & could not wear the habit any longer. She said S. Emily had no right to give her leave to go to her sister's house – she having herself asked her for leave. The Mother telegraphed to her to come home at once, & getting no answer telegraphed a second time 'By what train shall we expect you'. Then came a letter from Sr Louisa saying she was not coming at all, & would send her things home – she must persist in leaving the Community. Now it seems after this that we scarcely ought to allow her to go of her own self-will. No doubt it is better – not for her – but for the Community that she should go, because those who are in a state of perpetual ferment, can be no real help to the Community, but it seems both to the Mother & me that she ought not to go off just because she chooses, but that the Society ought to dismiss her.

The matter must be under consideration, & you can vote upon it at yr next Chapter.

I ask you to vote as to whether we accept her resignation, or whether we consider that the Society has expelled her. We must feel however sorry we may be to lose this or that Sister, that such a state of insubordination ought not to be tolerated for ever. It is not the case of a Sister feeling herself unworthy to be a Sister, & unable to live up to a Sister's life, & therefore requiring the encouragement of the Society. Those who feel unable to live up to their ideal of a Sister's life, are just those one wants to encourage & cheer, but one feels that a Sister who goes on as Sr. Louisa has done, in dogged self-will ought to be dealt with by the exercise of some kind of discipline. The exercise of discipline is always a very sad thing, but at the same time while sad to individual hearts, it is a matter of

---

104 Secular name unknown.

strength to the Community to have the Society purged of those who are simply setting it at defiance. One of the great leaders of the Religious Life said that what gave him the greatest pleasure, next to admitting a Novice for Profession, was expelling one who had proved himself utterly unworthy, not that his going was a pleasure, but that it was such a relief to the Community that unworthy members should be sent off. We may hope that such an act of discipline may be a blessing to S Louisa, & that she may be made to see that putting off the habit, is not putting aside a plaything she is tired of, but that the habit is the symbol of Religion, & of an abiding covenant with GOD. I hope you will all feel this more & more, & realize that the Habit is the symbol of tremendous responsibilities, & of a Covenant of wondrous grace.

Those that seek GOD's grace in His Covenants shall surely find it. We must not be surprised at temptations. Any of us may be liable to some terrible temptation at any time, & it is then that the grace of the Covenant is so great, one member of the Community giving a hand to the other – we feel ourselves sustained by the whole Community. Oh the marvellous power of our mutual devotions, our mutual intercessions, of our Rule – of our life – of our work given to GOD under the three vows. We ought to realize this when we feel our weakness, we ought to feel the strength of the Community holding us up.

Sepr 21st 1888.

Chapter of Faults

After w^h the Revd Mother said that she thought the Chaplain had not quite understood what was wanted in regard to S. Louisa. It was not as much a vote of censure on her general conduct in the Community, that was wanted, but a vote of censure on this last act of wilful disobedience to an order thrice repeated. I want you all to vote with me that we cannot look upon such impulsive conduct as she has shown as withdrawal from the Community; & that we think her conduct worthy of dismissal. Of course we cannot dismiss her, as she has already sent back her Habit, but if she was to repent, & be sorry for what she has done, & want to come back, we could not overlook her conduct, & what I ask for is a vote of censure for her conduct to the Community, & for the insult to the Religious Life.

All the Sisters who have sent in votes (except 3 who did not understand the matter) about 45 have said that they do censure her conduct, & consider it worthy of dismissal. Among all the votes there is scarcely one dissentient one. We all feel alike that as far as we are concerned we are better without one who w^d do such a thing as she has done.

––––––––––

Oct 12th 1888.

Chapter of Faults.

After wh the Revd. Mother said

I have to put up 4 Novices for Profession.

S. Muriel[105] & S Mary Blanche,[106] are both over their two years. They have been kept back because of their youth. S. Muriel nearly a year, S. M. Blanche 7 or 8 months. They have both been at work in Branch Houses. S Muriel has been 6 months at Wolverhampton, & since then has been working very well at Westminster, till she was called away to her dying father, where she is still, as he is at the point of death.

S. Marion[107] is the next. She is over her 2 years since Augst. Her Profession was delayed because the Mistress was away so much.

S. Frances Adelaide[108] comes next. Her two years will be up on the 22d of this month, & the time being so nearly up, I thought she ought to be put up with the others. The Mistress says that every one of them have given her entire satisfaction, & she considers that none of them have any faults that would exclude them from being good & faithful & holy members of the Community. They are all very much in earnest not of course without faults, I suppose none of us were when we were elected.

This is what the Mistress says.

'S. Muriel has given me entire satisfaction, though her character has taken a long time to develope [sic]; she has given herself up to being prepared for the Religious Life. She has never wavered from her vocation; she has given me no trouble whatever. I have never seen her give way to temper, all the faults she has she has tried to correct.

S. Mary Blanche, S. Marion, & Sr Frances Adelaide have also given me entire satisfaction in their Novitiate. Our dearest Mother had a special appreciation of S. Frances Adelaide, & looked forward to her becoming a member of the Community. She is not only a very earnest person, but a very capable person.

Revd Mother. Has any one any thing to say.

S. Catherine Some time ago it was said that if any one knew anything about a Novice they should speak, & say what they know, so I say what I know of Sr Muriel when she was sent to S. Elizth. I thought her officious & interfering, & very determined to get her own way. I asked to have her removed because of these grave faults – she was so disobedient, & very disedifying.

S. Cecilia. I think we ought to ask how long ago that was? The faults of two

---

105 Muriel Constance Dale. Prof. 1888, she left in 1908 to become a Roman catholic.
106 Secular name unknown. Prof. 1888, left 1896.
107 Secular name unknown (d. 1923), prof. 1888. Her family made its wealth from pottery manufacture.
108 Adelaide Frances Carpenter (1852–1929), prof. 1888. The daughter of a protestant Episcopal church bishop, she was American by birth.

years ago may have been overcome. If we were all judged by faults we committed in that way, it w^d go very hard with us.

S. Catherine. It was at the time of our dearest Mother's funeral I mean.

S. Cecilia That is more than a year ago. I heard that she had tried to accept the discipline of being sent from S. Elizth's in the right spirit.

The Revd Mother. Yes she did, and also being sent to Wolverhampton, & then from Wolverhampton being sent to Westminster. The other day too she had gone to her father, & was appointed to come home at a certain date, & she came at that date although her father was supposed to be at his extreme end. She did not shirk her work, & that shows she has the spirit of obedience at least.

The Revd Mother. S Frances Adelaide is a widow. I ought to speak of that, because I have heard it said by some Sisters, that we do not have widows in our Community, but neither our Foundress, nor her Co-Founder, our late Spiritual Father ever said we were not to have widows. On the contrary two were trained in our Novitiate to take the head of other Communities. Our Mother never thought twice about it, & accepted S. Frances Adelaide at once.

Our Community is very much formed upon that of the Visitation, & S. Frances de Sales was not against widows coming into Religion.[109] If we are not to have widows then, we must make it a law, but it will be a law contrary to our Foundress's spirit. –

Some Sisters think it is contrary to the Roman custom to have widows in Community, but this is a great delusion. Community after Community in the Roman Communion was founded by widows. "The companions of Jesus" was founded by a widow who had a son. S. Frances de Chantal had children. I want this point to be clearly settled, otherwise it places me in an awkward position, if Sisters give out that we do not receive widows, & widows come to me & ask to be received. If they are given the Habit, they cannot be black-balled simply because they are widows. I was told in my Novitiate, that a widow's vocation was a wonderful grace, & her response a wonderful co-operation with grace.

S. Cecilia. Have any of these Novices been in any other Community.

Revd Mother. None of them.

———

Ass^t Sup^r. The Revd Mother wishes me to add that since Chapter she has had a letter from S. Jane Margaret[110] in w^h she says. I was in Charge of S Elizth's House when S. Muriel was working there, just before she entered the Novitiate, & I am struck by the humble way in w^h she accepted the position in w^h she was placed. She never showed any unwillingness to do any of her appointed work, &

---

[109] De Sales' Visitation order was founded by a widow, Frances de Chantal. All Saints modelled itself upon the Visitation to some extent.

[110] Jane Margaret Handley (1831–1919), prof. 1881.

always appeared good-tempered. There had been a mistake I believe as to her position, & she was treated as if she was going to enter the Lay Novitiate. S. Mary Louisa[111] also said that what S. Muriel wanted was time. She was very slow at taking things in, but she was always ready to do what she was told. S. Maria[112] has written that S. Muriel was most obedient & most retiring-[113]

Oc^t 20th 1888.
Chapter of Faults

After w^h the Rev^d the Chaplain announced to the Sisters, the Election of the 4 Novices. Two of them he said had a small number of negatives, the other two had none, & all four were Elected by a large majority of votes. He then added 'I wish to say in reference to the admission of widows amongst you, that the fact of two widows having at different times trained in your Novitiate, with the consent of the Foundress, that point is already settled, & the mind of the Community pronounced on that point. There are Communities that do not admit widows, but the generality do – there is therefore no reason why we should go against the general habit of Communities in Christendom.

The Revd Mother. Then Father you do not think I am wrong in admitting widows as Postulants.

F^r Benson No you may consider that point as finally settled. –

Novr 17th
Chapter of Faults

———————

After w^h the Rev. Mother said

There are two or three important matters to bring before the Community.

1st The question of our training, & bringing into being of an Anglo-Indian Sisterhood. The first proposal about this came from the Bishop of Bombay[114] last April. He writes saying 'Sr Gladys has asked me to lay before you the possibility of opening a Novitiate in Bombay for Sisters belonging to the Country, and in some cases of mixed blood. The question of the vocation of individuals is not one I would pronounce about, nor would you wish it – the point in w^h I feel my experience may be of use to you are these.

---

[111] Louisa Blackman (1838–1908), prof. 1876. She was sister in charge at Christ Church, Wolverhampton, for twenty-five years.

[112] Maria Roempke. Prof. 1883, died 1915.

[113] This is the one point (other than the pasted-in correspondence with the archbishop at the time of mother foundress's death) where the chapter minutes deviate from being a record of chapter discussion and activity.

[114] Louis George Mylne, priested 1868; tutor of Keble College, Oxford 1870–6; bishop of Bombay 1876–97. He was vicar of St Mary Marlborough 1897–1905 and vicar of Alvechurch, Birmingham, 1905–17. A prolific author.

Such persons would not be sent to England without great danger of their vocation, supposing them to have one – the invariable experience of this country is that its inhabitants do not bear transplantation, and that they could not stand the severity of the English climate, nor go through the trial of life under totally new conditions. I do not know the rule of yr Community in sufficient detail to be able to judge of the demand the Novitiate makes on physical strength, but if it is at all a severe strain, that is a double reason for feeling sure that Anglo Indian, and Eurasian women c^d not go through it; besides this, grades of social life are so different here to those in England, that inhabitants here lose a great deal by going to England.[115] I do not think even a novice w^d be free from such difficulties.

Another point is, that I think few things w^d tend <so much> to make one hopeful as to the future for work here, & thankful also, as to know that the Religious Life had stuck its roots into the actual soil of the country – that the introduction of it here, should have led even to hopes of it with one who has such a strong unsentimental knowledge of them as Sister Gladys, is a great satisfaction to me'. The Bishop called here, when in England and spoke again about this, saying that it was his most earnest desire.

F^r Page, S Gladys, & S M Dorothea,[116] & one or two others have written, urging it very strongly.

S. Gladys says with regard to an Anglo-Indian Community – 'We have two Anglo-Indians anxious to become Sisters. I feel they have true vocations, but I do not think it would do them any good to be trained in the Community at Home. What we want is to be allowed to have a Novitiate for them out here.

Few people of this country could stand an English winter. They have in them much that is good loving & docile, & are very devotional, but weak, and not naturally truthful. We have found that a good bringing up does much for them. If they were trained here, they might in time be formed into a Community of their own, & do an immense deal for the land; It w^d be better for them to be trained here 1st because it is doubtful if they could stand the English climate, 2^{ndy} because we want to give them a truer love for this Country. They have always been despised by the English, & we would seek to give them a feeling of self-respect, which would come as they saw that from within themselves they could do a work for the land, w^h no imported elements could do, for they can stand the climate as we cannot, & understand the manners & customs of the natives. 3dly they would cease to ape after what was English, & their characters

---

[115]   The women referred to in this passage as Anglo-Indians were of mixed race. It seems that the English communities at this time (with perhaps one or two exceptions, such as Wantage) were reluctant to accept mixed-race or non-caucasian women into their choir novitiates. Since these women were well educated and the daughters of professional men, they were not suitable candidates for the lay order, nor presumably would they have wished to join it. Most communities faced with the situation established separate noviciates or separate daughter communities for non-white women.

[116]   Mary Dorothea Cope (d. 1927, in India), prof. 1878.

w^d be strengthened by discipline, 4^{thly} it would do a great work for their Church in India, to have Institutions w^h would be independent, & the love of the Catholic Church w^d strengthen & grow. I w^d ask that the Anglo-Indian Novitiate might be in all ways as like ours as the climate would allow, our Rule, our Office Book, & only a slight change in the dress. They w^d have no vote in the Community, & be like our Lay Sisters, except that they might go to all the Offices, as they are very devotional. The R.C's have done a great work for the Eurasians, & have formed an order for them.[117] *Catherine Pearson* one Postulant, has been most faithful to us, ever since we have been in India, has longed . ɔr 10 years to be a Sister, & would be a good one to begin this work.

Gertrude Wheeler another one is the nicest Eurasian I have ever seen –

S. M. Dorothea says 'I am so glad the question of an Anglo-Indian Novitiate is at last brought forward. It has been constantly in our minds for the last 3 or 4 years. We feel that nothing will do more for the Eurasians than to see Religious vocations responded to, and the life lived out by their own people.

I am sure there is more than one amongst them, who has it in her mind to devote her life to GOD's service, but they do not see their way to it, & we could not encourage them in it, as unless they c^d be trained here, it is impossible for them profitably to enter the Religious Community. S. Gladys also adds in another letter, that Gertrude Wheeler's grandfather was a Brahmin, a Priest of our Church, & very much respected, her father an Englishman, also a Priest in Calcutta.[118] The Bishop knows her family, & he spoke very warmly of her Brother, a Professor in the Bishop's College at Calcutta.

When I was at Home, I talked of the Eurasian Novitiate to our Mother, & she said she w^d send us a Mistress for the Novices when we were ready, so I feel in a way it had her sanction.'

The Revd Mother then asked the Ass^t Sup^r to say what she thought of the matter, as she had been in India & she said "I quite agree with all that S. Gladys and S.M.Dorothea have written. The Anglo-Indians are not fitted to be amongst our Lay Sisters, & yet are not wholly fit to be Choir Sisters. The modified rule to my mind is exactly what is needed, & I believe it will be responded to by many."

Rev^d M "I w^d ask you all to think about this, & I shall ask for yr votes at a future time.

2nd subject The Affiliation of our House in America. Some years ago the subject was put before the Community & it was judged that it was certainly not the time for it, & that Americans who wished to be Sisters must come & be trained at the Mother House. Many have done so, & some have returned. The Community out in America has grown in number, & spread out. They have a House now near New York, as well as at Philadelphia, & Baltimore. Those most interested

---

[117] Not identified.

[118] There was a Charles Edward Wheeler at Gowhatty, in the diocese of Calcutta, from 1869. He was the only priest named Wheeler in India in this period.

concerning the growth of the R. life in America F^r Maturin & several Priests are most anxious that our Branch out there should grow, & be more fruitful, & they think it will become so if it is affiliated, in the same way as the House belonging to Clewer & East Grinstead. I have applied to both these Communities for information, & I will now read what are their laws of affiliation.[119]

Revd Mother In both these cases, nothing must be decided in a hurry. Our Community will become crippled if we act hastily in such weighty matters. I know there is a great feeling in the Community about many of our Sisters being sent off to foreign works when there is so much to be done at Home, but if we are never to grow *in* the countries where we are planted, & do not make use of the people of this land, & draw them into Religion, naturally the life is being sapped out of us. We are obliged to send our best Sisters abroad, & the poorest are left at Home in consequence. In every good Community there is always growth. In the order of the Sacred Heart, they have grown in this way. Branches have gone out & planted themselves in foreign lands, & then the people of the country have come into Religion, & Branches have been formed after the pattern of the Mother Houses. The SS. we send to these foreign works, ought to become foundation stones of a Community growing up in that country. We have now nearly 20 Sisters in America & if they are not strong enough to form a good House it does not speak well for their Novitiates.

The Revd Mother then went on to speak of *Dundee* & said that the Bishop of Brechin[120] – wanted to know if we would take up the work there as a Branch House & whether in that case, we should be willing to yield it up, if he & his Clergy wished to form a Scotch Sisterhood – or whether we would form it into an Affiliated House, & train Sisters from Scotland. – She thought that at present we could only take it up as a Branch House, sending a Sister Superior, & a certain number of Sisters there.

The Ass^t Sup^r asked if that would mean that we renounced the idea of having a Scotch Novitiate, or whether it was only a temporary arrangement, as the Scotch character seemed so specially to need a separate training. The *Revd Mother* said it w^d only be a temporary arrangement – & after a time we might be able to form a Novitiate. The question was now whether we should take it up as a Branch House. It was put to the vote, & the Sisters unanimously agreed to the proposal. –

---

[119] The minutes then go on to quote from the rules of the Society of St Margaret (East Grinstead) and Community of St John the Baptist (Clewer) regarding affiliated houses.

[120] Hugh Willoughby Jermyn (1820–1903), priested 1845; elected bishop of Colombo 1871; elected bishop of Brechin in 1875; elected primus of the Scottish Episcopal church, 1886–1901.

March 29th
Chapter of Faults

After w^h the Revd Mother said

Dear Sisters I wish to consult you on a certain subject. It seems to me quite clear that a Mother Superior elected for 3 years, in order to have the confidence of the Community needs different powers, & different safeguards to the Mother Superior elected for life.

The Community can never again have another such a Mother as our loved Mother Foundress. Our constitution of Triennial election makes it seem wise that we should agree together that for the future, the Mother Superior should have what is called a Consultative Council?

This Council to consist of 12 Sisters
The Assistant Superior
The Novice Mistress
The Sister Housekeeper
The Sister Superior of H.C.H.
    "   at Eastbourne
    "   Cowley
    "   Edinburgh
    "   S Eliz^{th's} Home
    "   S John's House
The Sister Superior at America
    "   Cape Town
    "   Bombay

that is 12 Sisters holding the most important offices in the Community provided that no one of them is of less than 5 years standing in the Community. The Mother Superior should have absolute right as to when to consult them, with 4 exceptions, when she would be required to consult them.

1. As to dismissing a Sister.
2. As to taking up or resigning a work.
3. In the appointment of a Novice Mistress.
4. As to putting before the Community any very grave faults on dismissal of a Sister. On these or other occasions should the Mother-Superior desire it, their votes would be *authoritative*. On other questions their opinions would help the Mother Superior to decide. The Community would thus know that they were being governed constitutionally, & not autocratically. Our Mother – who was always our Mother – did not need this to receive the full confidence of the Community, but a Mother who has hitherto been one of the Sisters, & is suddenly elected to be over them (and it might be over a last years Mother) seems to need this safeguard to her authority. Then again every good mother Sup^r is not always a good women of business – it would be a safeguard, & relief of heavy responsibility, if there were 3 or 4 – or 5 Sisters formally Elected by the Chapter to be

consulted by the Mother Superior as to the expenditure of the Community. If these proposals are agreed upon in Chapter by a majority of ⅔^{rds} of votes, it is to be understood that it is with the desire & intent that through the blessing of GOD, the principles on w^h our Constitution has been founded, & our Statutes & Rules for the due order & government have been established, & the traditions, customs, & spirits of our Community given to us by our Revd Mother Foundress, & first Spiritual Father & Chaplain, may be always preserved unchanged, & inviolate amongst us. I would ask you to think out this subject & be prepared to give yr votes at the Chapter we shall hold on coming out of Retreat May 4th 1889.

Should any of the Sisters wish to get a clear understanding of the respective powers of the Authorities in the Community; the following will assist them.

1. *The Mother Superior* is within certain defined limits absolute – 'The Superior shall have the government of the Sisters' Statute III.

2. *The Visitor's* powers relate to

(a) The management

(b) The Discipline of the Community, but in the following particulars *only.*

(a) *Management* – he *may*

        1. enforce obedience to Rule (Statute 2)

        2. continue Superior in Office after 3 years (Statute 6)

        3. Remove Superior (Statute 7)

he *must*   4. Give consent to remove a Sister (Statute 15)

     "   5. Confirm election of a Novice (Rule 2)

(b) *Discipline*

        1. He can sanction the use of books (Rule 6)

        2. He can control the rule of fasting (Rule 19)

———

The Chaplain's powers relate to the

(a) *Management* & (b) *Discipline* of the Community in the following particulars only

a   Management & (b) Discipline of the Community in the following particulars alone

a   *Management*

     1 He may complain to Visitor of Superior (Stat. 7)

     2. He must consent to removal of a Sister (Stat. 15)

     3 He must approve of the Profession of a Novice (Rule 2)

     4 He must consent to receiving a probationer (Rule 1)

     5 He must consent to any altering of Rules & c. (Stat. 14)[121]

---

[121]   There was a bitter struggle between the community and their chaplain in 1890, as the community revised its statutes. R. M. Benson wanted the power of veto over all decisions (including the right to overrule the mother superior); the Society resisted this, and Archbishop Benson supported them.

(b) *Discipline*

1 He (or the Mother Sup^r) must consent to admission of books into the Community; unless expressly sanctioned by the Visitor (Rule 6)

2. He can (with the Sup^r) control fasting (Rule 19)

3 He may (with the Sup^r) & concurrence of majority of Sisters, appoint a Silence (Rule 22)[122]

4 He 'advises' the Sisters spiritually, & is to be obeyed by them as their *spiritual advisor or director* Statute 10. Rules 8 & 21.

April 5th
Chapter of Faults

After w^h the Revd Mother said that having received so many different opinions from the Sisters concerning the Council, she had decided to defer the matter for future further consideration at a Chapter to be held at the end of the next Retreat May 4$^{th.-}$

April 12th
Chapter of Faults.

April 26th
Chapter of Faults.

May 4th [1889][123]

The Revd Mother said. Dear Sisters we have met to consider the advisability of having a Consultative Council. I want first of all to say to some who thought the Chaplain would be at this Chapter, that when I asked him, he agreed with me that according to our Statutes, it was more constitutional for the Superior & Sisters to talk over matters by themselves; it is no slight to him – he does not feel it so. In the early days of our Community, when our beloved Founder & Foundress were with us, our first Father & Chaplain did not come into Chapter.[124] He *advised* with Mother, & afterwards approved, & gave his consent to things. I have

---

[122] Corrected in pencil to '20'.

[123] '1889' has been added in pencil.

[124] It is clear from the correspondence at Lambeth Palace that there was a conflict between the mother superior and the chaplain. Benson was attempting to change the statutes in the direction of giving the chaplain the ultimate authority in the community; Mother Caroline Mary and the sisters resisted this, and Benson ultimately resigned as chaplain, after he failed to win the archbishop's support. Benson seems to have been less than straightforward in his actions: he forwarded his revision of the statutes to the archbishop for approval before informing the mother superior that he had re-written them.

received letters from 30 Sisters, all differing in opinion as to details, but with 3 exceptions unanimous

1 As to the advisability of a Consultative Council.

2 Most are against the Sisters abroad being on the Council, or that it should necessarily consist of Sisters Superior.

3 Most seem to wish that the Sisters forming the Council should be elected freely by votes.

4 Many are anxious that it should not infringe on the present powers of Chapter.

———————

The questions raised are

1. Who should nominate the Sisters for Election?
2. Who should Elect?
3. For how long should the Council be Elected?
4. What should be its function?

———————

Gathering up the mind of the Community, & bringing into harmony the various opinions as far as possible with the Statutes that is with what is 'consistent with the Statutes of the Society' (as the 14th Statute expresses it), the following is the proposed plan I wish to lay before the Chapter –

1. Only Sisters of at least 5 or 7 years full standing now in G^t Britain should be eligible for Election. A list of the Sisters to be sent to each Sister having a vote whether at Home or Abroad, to be returned to the Mother Superior, with a mark against the name of the Sisters for whom she votes. This would be a strictly *private* communication between the Mother & the Sister.– The Mother should then nominate her Council according to the voting – the 6 Sisters having been freely Elected by the Community – the Ass^t Superior, the Novice Mistress, and the Housekeeping Sister making up 9 in all.

———————

2. The Council should be for 2 years – Three of the Sisters (elected members) retiring annually. In the first instance the 3 juniors to retire at the end of twelve months.

———————

3. The Sisters forming the Council may always be re-elected; it is not necessary that the Sisters should vote always for fresh members, if they are satisfied they can elect the same again.

———————

4. The one function of a consultative Council is, to advise the Mother Superior when she seeks its advice–

No council according to our Statutes, nor according to our Statutes, nor according to the idea of our Revd Mother Foundress, or of the Co-Founder, our first Chaplain M^r W Upton Richards, can absolve the Mother Superior from the responsibility of *personal rule of the Community.* It must be clearly understood that the Council is Consultative, not Executive, & that all it can give is *advice,* not *direction.* The Statutes place the government of the Community in the hands of the Mother Superior, with the Chaplain as guide in all spiritual matters. To tamper with this principle, would be to overthrow the idea of our Community. The idea in the mind of our dear Rev^d. Mother Foundress, which was upheld by Mr. W Upton Richards, was that of the *Family* – A Mother does not give power to guide or restrain her, to a Committee of her daughters, although *as* a Mother, she certainly *consults* the wishes & interests of her daughters and is glad to learn their minds. –

But we must not alter the position of the Mother Sup^r. doing away her office as *Mother,* & making her into a Sister Sup^r only, by making this Council executive, instead of Consultative. *Constitutionally* all it can do is *advise* the Mother *on points* on w^h she consults it.

5. But *such* a Consultative Council would be a great advantage to the Mother Sup^r, because through it she would gain a knowledge of the mind of the <whole> Community on any point on which she desired to ascertain it, & her responsibility would be, not removed, *that it must never be*, but lightened.

The Mother Sup^r would call her Council together, to consult, & put into shape any business questions that had to be brought before Chapter

––––––––––

6. The whole plan must be tentative. We must try how it will act for 2 years, before laying it before the Visitor for his approval, as it might not work well, & we might have to alter its formation.

––––––––––

7. As to the Finance Committee that had better be one of the things to be talked out, & put into shape by the Mother, with her Council, before bringing it into Chapter.

Statute *XVI* says –

'The receipt & expenditures of the Society shall be under the *entire control of the Superior for the time being*, who shall act as Treasurer, & the Superior shall pass her accts from time to time before *the Auditor.*

Statute I says – 'The Superior & Sisters shall be assisted by *Trustees*, an *Auditor*, & a *Chaplain* & such other offices as the Superior & Sisters shall hereafter think fit to appoint.' We have at present no Auditor. Our first Auditor was

Mr Benjamin Lancaster.[125] Statute III says 'all future Auditors shall be Elected by the Superior & Sisters. –

Before making any fresh arrangements as to Finance, it strikes me the first thing to do, is to obey our Statutes, & Elect an *Auditor.*

Statute *XVII* also contains very clear direction as to the ordering of the funds & property of the Community, & the way it is guarded by the Trustees of the Society. *Statute XX* says 'The Superior shall have power to draw out monies from the Bankers for the use of the Society as may be required'

What would help the Mother Sup^r would be to have 3 or 4 Sisters who understood business matters, with whom she could consult on money matters; & whom she could initiate into all the money matters of the Community, so that her own responsibility in these matters might be lightened.

The Assistant Sup^r & several of the Sisters expressed their hearty agreements with what the Revd Mother had said. –

There was then some discussion, in the course of w^h one Sister said she thought that one of the Statutes allowed changes to be made, without its being against the spirit of the Community, & that therefore if at any time a change was made it w^d not be contrary to the Statutes.

The Revd Mother said of course it would not be contrary to the Statutes. It was in the 14th Statute, and as an instance at one time there was no Novice Mistress, & nothing about it in the Statutes, but it was arranged in Chapter that there should be one, & also the Housekeeping Sister's office was arranged in Chapter, so that the Statutes do allow of new officials being appointed, but do not allow of any infringements upon the rule of the Mother, making it quite plain that she is to be the Superior & consult with her Sisters, while the Chaplain approves of matters to be consulted upon, which must be brought finally before the Visitor. Statute 14 shows the great wisdom, trust, & generosity with w^h they were formed, & for w^h we cannot be too thankful[126]

Another Sister said she could not help feeling that there was too much tradition, & not law in the government of the Community to w^h the Revd Mother replied that when any matter had been settled in Chapter it became a law, & must remain so until it was unsettled – A Sister then added that in Statute 14 there was a paragraph w^h said that 'these Rules must be accessible to all the Sisters', & a third Sister asked if Sisters in Charge of Branch Houses could if necessary refer to Chapter notes on points of discipline. The Revd Mother said that this had always been allowed although the Chapter 'Notebook' must not be lent about to Sisters, & in answer to another question she said that Chapter notes w^h had been sent round to the different Houses on matters of discipline might always be kept,

---

[125] Benjamin Lancaster (d. 1887), a banker, who, with his wife Rosamira was co-founder and patron of the community of St Peter, Kilburn.

[126] Statute XIV makes it clear that it is for the community to formulate their regulations, and that the chaplain's and visitor's roles are largely advisory.

but that those about the elections of Novices, or any containing particulars about the misconduct of a Sister must be destroyed.

The Revd Mother then put the following questions before the Sisters, on w^h she asked them to give their votes.

1. Whether the members of the Council shall be comprised of Sisters of 5 or 7 years standing?

> It was unanimously carried that
> they should be of 7 years standing.

---

2. Whether the members should be freely Elected?

> This was almost unanimously carried

---

3. Whether the foreign Sisters should be on the Council, either by election, or the 3 Sisters Superior '*ex-officio*'.

> After some discussion it was decided by a large
> majority that the Sisters should not be on the Council.

---

4 Whether the Council should consist of the 3 Office bearers at Home, & 6 or 7 Sisters freely elected.

> Unanimously carried 6 Sisters & the office bearers.

---

5. Whether the Council should be of 3 years' standing, the 2 juniors retiring annually, but eligible for re-election.

> Carried by a considerable majority

NB. The answers to these questions are in accordance with the opinions of the majority of the 30 Sisters who wrote to the Revd Mother on the subject of the Council.

A Sister then asked if the Council would have power to lay questions before the Mother for consideration at their meeting, which had been brought to their notice by other Sisters?

The Revd Mother answered that the consultees might severally suggest anything to the Mother, who w^d then if she thought fit, bring it into the Council – one of the objects of the Council was that the Sisters might speak to a Consultee of things they wanted brought before the Mother, but the members of the Council themselves must not consult together to bring anything collectively before the

Mother, for that would be holding a Council on their own acc[t] independently of the Mother.

The Assistant Superior, the Novice Mistress & others agreed that if the Council consulted together, it would be a Council within a Council, w[h] would be most objectionable, & that the Council was meant to be a help to the Mother, & not an authority.

It was also carried that the Council should be a tentative thing for 2 years, before being brought ~~before~~ formally before the Visitor for his approval.

Aug 23rd
Chapter of Faults

The Rev[d] Mother said she had received all the votes concerning the Consultative Council, & that she found the 6 Sisters having by far the largest majority of votes were

Sister Elizabeth[127]	Sister Cecilia
Sister Helen	Sister Mary Teresea
Sister Anne	Sister Mary Augustine[128]

& she therefore nominated them members of the Council[129]

Aug 30th
Chapter of Faults

After w[h] the Rev[d] Mother said she wished to tell the Sisters that as she intended leaving home for America on Sep 10th she was putting up 3 Novices for Election (Sister Helen Agnes,[130] S. Johanna Maria,[131] & S. Frances Teresa[132]) in order that if elected no time might be lost before their Profession on her return, w[h] she hoped w[d] be by All Saints Day.

With regard to S. Helen Agnes she said that during the 14 months of her re-admission into the Novitiate her conduct & spiritual life had been as earnest, & faithful as during the 2 years of her former Novitiate, & during the time spent out of her Habit at S. James the Less Liverpool with S.M.Milicent she in no way

---

[127] Elizabeth Simcox (1830–1919), prof. 1863. From a very wealthy family, she had trained as a nurse and served as an outer sister before entering All Saints.

[128] Mary Teresa and Mary Augustine were sisters (surname Suckling), and Mary Augustine became the community's third mother superior in 1893.

[129] These sisters were all quite senior: dates of profession varied from 1863 to 1875, with most being professed in the mid 60s; the two Suckling sisters were a decade younger than the rest.

[130] Helen Lawley had been discussed at length in chapter in 1888. She was elected to profession in September 1889 and died in 1906.

[131] Johanna Mary de Villiers, prof. 1889. She left to become a Roman catholic in 1919.

[132] Secular name unknown, prof. 1889, died 1907.

relaxed her Rule. 'She has been with us as either a Novice or worker over 4 $^{1/2}$ years, & those who have seen most of her, & have had the best opportunities of judging testify not only to her being perfectly sound as to the brain, but also to her uniform unselfishness, humility, sweet temper, usefulness, & quiet influence for good amongst those around her. The witnesses I can bring forward for proof of what I say are specially S.M. Milicent with whom she worked after her non-Election in 1885 till she was received back in 1888 & S. Mary Georgina,[133] whose life of poverty & roughness amongst the very poor & degraded women at Newport Market refuge[134] S. Helen Agnes has cheerfully & ably shared for some part of the last year she has again been a Novice, & also the Professed of 3 years' standing who were fellow Novices with S. Helen Agnes.'

I had better remind the Sisters of a few facts.

1. That the idea of there being insanity in S. Helen Agnes family cannot be corroborated as a fact.

Last year I made enquiries, & they were satisfactorily answered by Mr Grier of Ragley [sic] who knew her family well, & said he must know if there had been insanity in the family, & that he had never heard of it.

He had known S. Helen Agnes from childhood.

2. That the Archbishop writes strongly as to the advisability of a second Election in her case. 'Now that GOD has rolled the cloud away which hung over her – the ground for acting as you did, is gone. The delay is over, & has doubtless worked His Will. – No stronger case could arise for exceptional treatment. She in life & spirit has been all you wish, i.e she has answered lovingly to the Divine Guidance & trial. Do I put it clearly? that you were right in rejecting in 1886, but that delay, not ultimate rejection has been its working. As to the advisability of a second election I can feel no doubt.

2 F^r Benson says in his letter on the subject of her re-admission as a Novice 'I do not think we are acting contrary to the Holy Spirit in subjecting a Sister to re-election' & he then goes on to say that this however could not be done until she had had a twelve months' Probation in the Novitiate – This she has had fully, as she re-entered the Novitiate in June 1888.

I hope the Sisters will seriously consider these facts, & not allow pre-judgement to bias them in giving their votes. When S.H.A. was first up for Election in 1886 few Sisters pr voted at all for her, from the fact of her being so little known. Now I think all have heard fully about her, & several junior Sisters who knew her work in 1886 have now attained their Seniority.[135] –

The Mistress was then asked her opinion of the Novices *of S. Helen Agnes* she said. My opinion is quite the same as that of the Revd Mother. All through her

---

[133] Mary Georgina Heale (d. 1895), prof. 1887.

[134] For an account of the work at this hostel for homeless women in Soho, see Agnes Harrison, 'The under side', *Macmillan's Magazine* XIX (1869), pp. 331–9.

[135] Choir sisters did not get a vote in chapter until three years after profession. This custom was regularized in the revised statutes put into effect in 1891, and discussed later in this document.

Novitiate she has been thoroughly docile, simple, & unselfish & has never given me a moment's anxiety.

Of S. Johanna Maria she said she was most steady-going & dependable, all through the time of her Novitiate.

Of *S. Frances Teresa* she remarked that there was one special feature in her character worthy of notice, & that was her humility in taking reproof, & that she was always ready to acknowledge her faults & she added that all three Novices had passed through their Novitiate thoroughly satisfactorily.–

The R.M. asked the Sisters to send in their votes before Friday Sep^t 5th

. . . . .

Nov 16th 1889

At the end of the Retreats a General Chapter was held, at which the Revd Mother said she found there was a strong feeling in the Community, that it would be well for us at this period of our history to draw up certain additions to our first Constitution. She said this has been done in most of the old orders, after the death of the Founderess or Foundress as for instance the Order of the Visitation from w^h our Statues & Rule are largely drawn.[136] These Additions w^d form a sort of Appendix to our present Statutes, the words of which w^d still remain untouched.

The object of these Additions are

1st as safeguards against innovations which might arise through our Triennial Elections of a Supr.

2^{ndly} To encorporate into law in the Community what has hitherto only been tradition, & bye law.

The Revd Mother proposed with the help of the Chaplain & the Council to draw up these additions, which should then be laid before the Chapter for consideration, & if the Sisters agreed to vote for them, they would be submitted to the Visitor for his approval & consent.

Later on at the Chapter, on the same subject, in answer to a question put by one of the Sisters, she said that F^r Benson had drawn up a scheme for alterations & additions to the Statutes, & had sent it to the Visitor, who had written to say that he deferred giving his opinion until the matter had been agreed upon by the Sisters, when he w^d go fully into the question. The Revd Mother told the Sisters that she had consulted her Council, and that it had been decided by the majority that they did not wish one word of the original Statutes to be touched, but all had agreed on the necessity of an Appendix or Codecil.

The R.M. said in answer to a wish expressed by two Sisters, that F^r Benson's paper should be sent round to all the Sisters, that in a conversation she had had with him, he had explained to her that he only meant his suggestions to be a help and guide for the Community, in adding to the Constitutions what was necessary for their consolidation, and that until the scheme was more matured, it would be

---

136 While the rule and statutes, etc. of All Saints may reflect something of the spirit of the Visitation order, there is no overt borrowing, or even strong textual similarity.

unadvisable to send it round to all the Sisters, but that any Sister who wished to see it, could do so.

She then said there were two points upon w^h she would be glad to have the Sisters' votes at once–

1. As to the meaning in Statute 5 of 'the fully admitted Sisters'. In the Foundress's lifetime it was settled that only Sisters of 3 years' standing should have a vote, and it was proposed that henceforth the term 'fully admitted' should be taken to mean Sisters of three years standing, and who had the privilege of voting, and the Revd Mother added that as far as the life of dedication & consecration went, a Sister was a full Sister when she had made her vows, but that she was not admitted to her full privileges of voting, until she had been professed three years.

2^{ndly} The necessity of deciding whether Sisters who, either from illness, or other causes are living indefinitely out of Community life (S. Winifred[137] who is invalided, S Emily Catherine[138] partly invalided, & partly for the sake of an aged parent, S. Eliz^h Margaret[139] also on acct of her aged parents) ought not to lose the power of voting in Chapter, until they are able to return to Community life, when they would resume their powers of voting.

The next subject that the Revd Mother brought forward was the affiliation of our house in America, which had long been thought about.

The Assistant had visited America for the special purpose of finding out what the minds of the Sisters were on the subject. She was then asked to speak, and said 'that she found there was a very unanimous wish among the Sisters in America, that the affilation should take place without further delay, & that the work there must languish, if they were not able to train Novices in their own country. The Revd Mother also added, that they felt in their present position they could not expand, that many postulants for different reasons were unable to come to England. They were consequently hindered from taking up new works, & not being regularly planted in the Country, people were unwilling to help them with funds. This was also the experience of the other Communities in America. She then read the proposed Rules for Affiliation, and asked for the Sisters' votes on the subject. The Revd Mother then went on to speak to the Sisters on certain points of Rule, on w^h she found there had been some little laxity, & irregularity. For instance in one House the evening Offices had been put off till nearly 10 pm. on acc^t of work, as the Sisters liked to say them together. In another House, Terce & Lauds are daily said together and nothing marks the mid-day hour but the Angelus.[140]

---

[137] This may have been Winifred Mary (secular name unknown), who was professed in 1884, and left the sisterhood in 1892, due to mental illness.

[138] Secular name unknown, prof. 1868, and dismissed under statute 15 in 1897 or 1899.

[139] Elizabeth Margaret Black, prof. 1878, left the community in 1893. She had formerly been a member of community of St Thomas Martyr.

[140] At the ringing of a bell, the angelic salutation to Mary is repeated three times in honour of the incarnation.

The Office must be treated with dignity, and there must be fixed times for saying it, which should be arranged so as to fit in with the work, and when once fixed, the hour must be kept. One Sister must be responsible for the regularity of the Offices. The Sisters must not wait for the Sister Sup[r] or Sister in Charge. At Home no one waits if the Mother Sup[r] is not up at the moment, but the Office begins at the right hour. There must not be one moment's delay beyond what is necessary for the private prayer.

The Rev[d] Mother said that no change in the habitual hours of saying the Offices in the Branch Houses in England, should be made without reference to her. The foreign Houses referring of course, in the same way to their Sister Superior.

———

The Rev[d.] Mother forgot to mention to the Sisters in Chapter, that with the advice of her Council she proposed asking M[r] Walter Champion,[141] a confidential clerk in M[r] Ford's[142] office, to be our Auditor. She believed him to be a person well suited for the post, and she wishes the Sisters to send in their votes upon it.

———

NB as Mr Champion was not a Chartered Accountant he was not eligible, & M[r] W. Kitson[143] was subsequently chosen.

———

April 11th [1890]

Chapter of Faults

after which the Rev Mother said that there were 7 Novices who had come to the end of their two years but that she thought it well to keep S Mary Alma[144] back for a time before putting her up for election.

The 6 Novices were S Mary Rachel,[145] S. Mary Emily,[146] S Anna Fidelia,[147]S. Florence Anna,[148] S Mary Constance[149] & S. Mary Gabriel[150] –

The Mistress – S. Mary Rachel has passed through her Novitiate very satisfactorily, as has S Mary Emily – I have nothing to say against either of them.

S. Florence Anna has striven earnestly against her faults. She has a rough

141 Not identified.
142 Mr Ford was the Society's lawyer.
143 Not identified.
144 Secular name unknown; prof. 1893, left in 1899 to become a Roman catholic.
145 Kathleen Templeton (1846–1910). An American by birth, she was professed in 1892. Her profession was delayed because her family insisted that she return to the U.S.A. to care for her widowed brother's children.
146 Emily Chatterton Legg (1863–1929), prof. 1890, mother superior 1905–29.
147 Secular name unknown.
148 Secular name unknown, prof. 1890, left 1893.
149 Florence Jean Constance Trench (1859–1915), prof. 1890.
150 Secular name unknown.

manner, but that is only superficial, as her character is gentle, and she has always borne correction well for her faults of manner.

Sr Mary Constance is very earnest & devout.

S. Anna Fidelia's health is the great hindrance to her Profession. She has never been able to keep the Rule, without frequent dispensations.

S. Mary Gabriel has not improved. I do not feel that she has overcome the faults for which she was put back for a time. The Rev Mother asked the Mistress what she thought of S Anna Fidelia's health.

The Mistress. I think her earnest & devout, but her health is the great difficulty. She has a great desire for the R. life, & knows what the life of a Religious ought to be.

S. Helen – I wish to speak of S. Mary Rachel. She has worked for some time at S. Elizth, & I have always found her most earnest & good, & all the patients are much attached to her. She has not a very strong character, but I think most highly of her.

S. Cecilia – Was not S. Anna Fidelia under treatment in a house for hysteria? Revd Mother – I think not for hysteria but nervous prostration. S. Cecilia – may I ask what the doctor's opinion was?

The Mistress. He said that she would require rest, & constant food, and that she would always be liable to a recurrence of the attacks.

Sr Helen. Nervous prostration arises from overstrain.

S. Mary Agatha.[151] Nervous prostration is not the same as hysteria, but is more serious, and arises from mental overstrain.

The Mistress – Her mind is very active, and it may be that it reacts on her body.

S. H^t- Mary – Did the doctor say that she would be an invalid for life? The Mistress – She would never be able to keep the Rule, it would have to be modified. The Revd Mother asked for the votes on the following Thursday.

————

April 18th
Chapter of Faults

The Revd Mother said, 4 of the Novices have been elected, and 2 have been rejected.

S. Mary Rachel has 39 yes yes. & no negatives

S. Mary Emily – 40 D^o D^o

S. Florence Anna has only 32 votes altogether, $\frac{2}{3}$rds & 4 over of yes yes.

S. Mary Constance has 41 yes yes. & no negatives.

S Anna Fidelia & S. M. Gabriel have been decidedly rejected; the former I suppose on acc^t of her health, the latter because I suppose her vocation has not been considered sufficiently sure.

---

[151] Mary Louisa Shute (1845–1922, in South Africa), prof. 1885.

To S. Mary Rachel I am glad to tell you the Sisters have elected you almost unanimously into the Community. Is it yr wish to come into it, if GOD Wills it? Yes Mother. I know a difficult question has sprung up for you,[152] but yr own wish and will is to come in, and I am sure GOD will fulfil yr wish, even if you have to wait, sooner or later.

To S. Mary Emily We want to know dear child whether you really wish to be Professed in this Community?

Yes Mother with all my heart. I am glad to tell you that the Sisters have elected you almost unanimously which shows that we shall be glad to receive you. You must seek to prepare yourself very earnestly during the next few days for yr Profession. You must ask GOD to show you if there is anything you w^d withhold from Him because when we give ourself up for Profession we sacrifice every thing, & have no reserves, and are ready to go where GOD wills, & work under any Superior, we make a whole burnt offering of ourselves.

To S. Florence Anna Is it yr wish dear Child to be Professed into this Community? 'Yes Mother I think so.' You know it involves a complete sacrifice of self, of yr will and inclinations, embracing the Cross. The Sisters have elected you. I hope during these few days before the ~~election~~ Profession you will weigh the matter well over once more, to be quite sure what you are about. – You cannot turn back when once you have made your Profession & promise GOD to give y^r.self up to Him for the rest of your life in this world in Poverty, Chastity, & Obedience. Be very earnest in prayer to GOD to show you that it is indeed His will for you.

To S. Mary Constance. Are you quite sure that you wish to be Professed. 'Yes Mother I am quite sure.' I know that since you have entered the Novitiate you have been desiring to give yr self up to GOD & now that you have made trial of it, do you feel quite sure that it is the life GOD means you to lead. 'Yes Mother' – The Sisters have elected you unanimously & are very pleased and glad to receive you. Now let gratitude come into yr heart, & offer up thanks – giving to GOD – a Eucharist offering –

The Revd Mother then told the Sisters that S Mary Rachel had that very day heard of the sudden death of her Sister who had left a family of orphans. Her parents had taken over the family, but it was a question whether S. Mary Rachel ought not to put aside her Profession, & take care of the second family her willingness to do whatever is settled for her, seems a proof of the reality of her vocation. It rests with F^r Benson to decide whether she goes back to America at once, or remains to be Professed.

---

152 This difficult question was the request of her brother (later a bishop co-adjudicator in the U.S.A.) that she return to care for another brother's children, whose mother had just died. She reluctantly obeyed, but was professed when the community told her that she would have to make a choice. Her family, according to the community's first historian, Sister Elspeth, continued to 'torment' her with demands for her time for the rest of her life.

The Revd Mother begged the Sisters to pray very earnestly for her.

With regard to S Anna Fidelia & S. Mary Gabriel I hope you will not think it strange if I do not take away their habits at once. I suppose S. Anna Fidelia has been rejected simply on acc^t of her health, & think myself that her health would have improved when the strain of the Novitiate was over; she is most broken hearted at her rejection, & feels that she can never go back to the world again, & has asked to be allowed to remain on, & work in a Branch House; neither can I turn out S. Mary Gabriel into the world, but must wait & see what she can do, & where she can go. She will not remain in the Novitiate, but will be at my disposal for the present – she too is broken hearted at her rejection, and says she can never go back into the world. I ask you all to pray for them. It is GOD's Will for them, but still it causes them deep sorrow, & is a great wrench in their lives. We must pray that it may be for their purification.

The Profession is fixed for May 1st.

———

II. 4

Letters on Vows

Letters from some of the Senior Sisters as to the early Comty [Community] *teaching on the subject of Life-vows.*[1]

London House
SW
Feb. 27th 1862

My dear Miss Byron,

I have carefully considered your letter and proposition of Feb. 20th,[2] and have been obliged to delay my reply.

It appears to me that the alteration which you propose makes too great a change in the bearing of this rule.[3] The right of each sister to leave should be asserted, and I see no reason for changing the rule in that respect. There is no reason however against adding as a modification, that 'It is expected that no sister shall leave the sisterhood, without a month's notice, during which, if thought necessary, the matter may be referred to the Visitor.' The rule will then stand as in the enclosed paper.

I remain,
Yours faithfully,
A.T. London[4]
[endorsed on reverse: B. of London].

---

1 Material in italics is in the handwriting of the community's third mother superior, Mother Mary Augustine (Anna Maria Suckling, 1841–1923). Professed as an All Saints' choir sister in 1875, she served three terms as mother superior, 1893–1905.

2 This letter does not appear to have survived. The proposition was a proposal that statute XII be modified so as to suggest that life-long observance of the vows to the community should be considered normative.

3 'This rule' is rule I of the community rule. It had been amended in 1861 to read: 'Any probationer or confirmed sister, may quit the sisterhood whensoever she pleases, and, as her own conscience before God is the guide she ought to follow in this matter, no one can have any right to blame her for so doing. It is expected that no one shall leave the sisterhood without giving a month's notice, during which, if thought necessary, the matter may be referred to the Visitor.' Lambeth Palace Library, Tait papers 121, fo. 306.

4 Archibald Campbell Tait (1811–82), ordained 1836, headmaster of Rugby school 1842–50, dean of Carlisle (1849–56), bishop of London 1856–69; archbishop of Canterbury, 1869–82.

10 St. Andrew's Place
Regent's Park N.W.
Dec. 11th 1863[5]

My dear Lord Bishop

Having been away from home since Monday I only received your note of the 7th last evening when I returned to Town. I have seen Miss Byron, who I am sorry to say is still very unwell & the Doctor[6] has ordered her to go at once to Brighton for change of air. Will you allow me to answer your letter for her.

I can assure you that the rule to wh. you refer is not considered a dead letter. Within the last few months I have more than once told a sister that she was at full liberty to leave the Home-that in accordance with the rules wh. your Lordship has made, a sister had only to write a letter to me stating it was her wish to go, which I might forward to you, and that you would see her within two months & advise her how to act – As regards the rule itself, I have from the first differed from your Lordship, but yet I have thought it my duty in no way to think it.

When your Lordship consented to be the visitor of the All Saints Home,[7] Mr. Buller[8] told both Miss Byron & myself that you had mislaid the copy of the office wh. we had sent you, that you had glanced over it – that it was not ~~what~~ really what you would like to use yourself – that you would have preferred an office taken from our own Liturgy – but rather than pain the Sisters by altering it you would allow me to admit the sisters & the sisters should be taken by Miss Byron to London House afterward for your Lordships blessing. I as well as Miss Byron understood him to say from you, that you gave us full permission to use that or any other office for the reception of Sisters, with this one restriction – *you simply prohibited vows.* We have used the office of wh. we sent you a copy and in wh. no vows are taken.[9]

---

5   Note that more than a year has elapsed.
6   Mother Harriet's doctor was Sir William Gull (1816–90).
7   Tait became visitor, in his capacity as bishop of London, in 1859.
8   This was probably Anthony Buller (*c.*1809–81), who wrote one short pamphlet in *Tracts for the times* (LXI): 'The Catholic church a witness against illiberality'. He was also a signatory to the Society's original rule and rector of St Mary, Devon, 1833–76. Another Buller was one of the Society's original trustees.
9   The relevant portions of this service, titled Office for a sister fully admitted after probation (1860s), are the questions and their answers:
[officiant] . . . I put to you these questions, touching your future course and conduct:
1. Will you, so long as you shall fill the place of Sister in this Community, be diligent to frame your life, your temper, your conversation, according to the Doctrine and Example of Christ seeking only and wholly to follow Him in this Office, to which we trust God in His Providence has called you?
answer: *I will endeavour to do so with the help of God.*
2. Will you reverently obey all who, by the Constitutions of this Community, are set over you n the Lord, following their godly admonitions, and observing all the appointed Rules?
answer*: I will do so with the help of God.*

I shall be most happy to give your Lordship any further explanation wh. you may require.

I am always

Your Lordships faithful Servant

W. Upton Richards[10]

[endorsed on reverse: copy answer B. London. W.U.R.]

From Sister Eliza,[11] the senior surviving Sister.[12] Professed in Aug. 1859. Jan/95

My dearest Sister

I am afraid I shall not be much help but I will tell you what I can.

1 When I was Professed it was not with the Office we now use,[13] but I fully understood my vows were for life. I remember Archbishop Tait questioning me particularly for he thought me too young to have made up my mind so that he must have understood it as well. There were no annual renewal of vows in those days.[14]

2 I should have said the same teaching had always been carried on.

3 I believe the Sisters were given to understand they were pledging themselves for life & the fact of receiving the *ring*[15] & the coronal of flowers with the words

---

3. Will you strive to live in love, gentleness, forebearance, and humility with your Sisters?
answer: *I will endeavour to do so with the help of God.*
4. Will you do all that lieth in you, for the interests of this Community, and to the good of those who are committed to your charge?
answer: *I will do so with the help of God.*
5. Will you give yourself to prayer, to the reading of God's Word [and] of all the studies of a Holy Life, that you may be the better enabled to fulfil these promises?
answer: *I will do so with the help of God.*

10 William Upton Richards (1811–73), vicar of All Saints, Margaret Street, 1849–73, and first chaplain of the Society of All Saints.

11 Eliza Crofts (1830–1906), clothed as All Saints' novice, 1856, prof. 1859, assistant superior, 1862.

12 Choir sisters were ranked by seniority, calculated from the date of profession.

13 The 'office now in use' was presumably the first printed form (undated), where the key passage is as follows:
[officiant] My daughter, what desirest thou of the LORD?
And she shall answer,
My Father, I desire grace and mercy of our LORD JESUS CHRIST to devote myself to His service in this holy Community in poverty, chastity and obedience for the rest of my life in this world; and *(turning round to the Mother and Sisters,)* I pray you, dear Mother, and you, my dear Sisters in JESUS CHRIST, to receive me into your Society for this purpose.
The Reverend Mother having taken previous counsel with the Sisters, shall answer, My daughter, we are content to receive you if such be your earnest desire.

14 Annual renewal of vows began very early.

15 The custom of receiving a 'wedding' ring at profession was adopted in 1861.

"Be thou faithful unto *death* &c seems to make it very clear & all through it implies that one is giving up ones life by ones vows –

4 I never entered into any alterations made after dear Mothers death I never read the Adgenda [*sic*] nor can I tell why no. 1 was altered into no. 5[16] I am very sorry to be so unhelpful –

About Sister Gertrude[17] having given any money I think there must be some mistake *I* never heard of it. I should ask when it was & to whom it was paid & who by because we could easily find out what became of it & *if* she did, according to Statute XVIII we cannot claim anything after having given up all at our Profession, *this* I am very clear about –

I have tried hard to remember & I hope the little I can tell may help you.
From your loving
† S. E.

From S. Elizabeth[18] *– the 2nd surviving Sister. Professed June 1863.*
S. John's Hosp.[19]
Cowley S. John
Oxford
July 18th 1895

My very dearest Mother,

With regard to the subject of vows, the teaching of the Mother Foundress was *always* most strong on the point that they were distinctly and decidedly *for life* – This was also the uniform teaching of the Community from the beginning, both during the Noviciate and on Profession – When I was Professed (in June 1863) I was most clearly taught to consider that I was taking '*Life Vows*', and so were all the Sisters – I feel quite sure that many would never have entered our Community had it been otherwise –

In speaking of Statute XII & Footnote[20] the Mother Foundress always said that the subject of the Vows was only so worded and treated, in order to meet the wishes and objections of the Visitor – I, for one, should heartily rejoice to see both Statute and Footnote expunged – Personally, I object to them extremely, & I consider it most unfair to the memory of our dear Mother Foundress to retain them, as future generations of Sisters would be mislead to think that Mother never taught *life*-vows when in reality she was unswerving in her teaching on that point –

16 See the rule.
17 Annie Batie, clothed as novice of All Saints 1863; prof. 1865, left the community, 1895.
18 Elizabeth Simcox (1830–1919), prof. 1863.
19 St John's hospital, Cowley, was run as a convalescent hospital for incurables by the community after 1880.
20 The footnote, added in 1890 at the request of Archbishop Benson, stated that each sister was free to leave the Society without blame.

I hope I have expressed clearly what I *know* to have been the mind of our dear Mother on this most important subject.

Ever dearest Mother

from your loving child

† Elizabeth

From S. Etheldreda[21] – Professed Nov. 1863
All Saints Boys' Orphanage[22]
Lewisham, S.E.
July 14 1895

My dear Mother

I am so much surprised to hear that any Sisters think that we old Sisters had any idea that our Vows are not life long – I date back to 1859[23] – When I told our Mother Foundress that 'I wished to be a Sister' she said *most* strongly that I must remember I should be bound 'for the rest of my life in this world' – 'Although there was a Statute which *verbally* released Sisters, it had been put in by the Bishop,[24] and really was never intended in the founding of the Comty, but our Vows were *binding for Life*.'

Then the 1st Sister Charlotte,[25] Sr Mary Eth[26] Sr Harriet,[27] always used to be telling me 'though you are a kitten, if you come in it must be for *always*' it was in the days we all sat in the Comty Room – In the 1st year of my Noviciate (S. Etheldreda 61 to 62) Sr Harriet repeatedly told me this – then Sr Sarah (/62 to /63)[28] on S. Etheldreda Day when I was taken into Chapter to hear I was elected, was more emphatic still & added 'not *only now* as we are, but in days to come when there might be changes a new Superior &c &c' Mother said just the same on the Eve of my Profession Nov 17 – 63 only more strongly & I was made to tell my friends that I should be bound as indissolubly as if married – Mother was most strong too in Chapter – I remember the PtScrpt [the Appendix] *to the Rule* being very much discussed, & objected to, by the 5 or 6 old[29] Sisters in the Comty Room.

---

21 Etheldreda Russel (1840–1918), prof. 1863.
22 This orphanage was established in 1877.
23 This is the date of her becoming an outer (associate) sister, a lay woman with special ties to the community.
24 The mother foundress described Tait as 'utterly ignorant of anything to do with the Religious Life'.
25 Charlotte Smith (1833–65), prof. 1859, died of consumption.
26 Mary Elizabeth Kergwin, prof. 1861, died 1865.
27 Harriet Brown (1826–76), prof. 1857, novice mistress 1860–2.
28 Sarah Easton (1831–1914), prof. 1856, novice mistress 1862–70. Left 1878 because she objected to the election of Richard Mieux Benson as community chaplain, but wore the habit until her death, and is described as 'sister' on her tombstone.
29 In community usage, 'old' normally means 'senior' when applied to sisters.

In the face of all this I do not see how anyone can make any stand in regard to Statute XII especially if the Archbishop agrees –

The only difference I realise is that we old 1st Sisters were trained for *work* & not for the Religious Life therefore I think sometimes the Sisters could be a little more charitable to the older few, left. Sr Harriet, Saint that she was, was always saying *Work* & Pray – or, that work must come first, & Meditations, Devotions, &c must make way if work came. I was just coming out of the Noviciate when the more *Religious* training developed – I was then 22½.

Yours in loving Obedience

† Etheldreda Sr of All SS

One thing comes more & more home to me how one was made to see 'changes and all development was to be accepted as part of ones Life long Vow'.

S. E.

From S. Anne[30] – Professed Nov. 1864

All Saints' Hospital[31]

Eastbourne

Monday

Jan 1895

My dearest Mother

I don't think there can be a difference of opinion as to our Mother Foundress's views about 'life vows' but still, she often said to me that if a Sister was <u>really</u> naughty – (such as S. G.) – it was better for her to leave the Comty than to remain in it, causing scandal, & under mining & unsettling other Sisters –

S. Sarah's teaching was *most* plain. I don't think she ever read the Rule without giving a homily upon how wrong it would be to leave – If Sisters have not understood that they were taking life vows, it is entirely their own fault as it has been most plainly put before them. How to reconcile the teaching with the Rule is a difficulty! Whatever the Mistress teaches each Sister has this *Rule* before her & can feel that she is not breaking the Rule & is leaving with the Visitor's sanction & ought not to be blamed – May not this be what has been put before the ArchB.P.? Perhaps the 'blame' we have put on the action has been kept in the background & he has simply been told that so & so has left. He cannot think there is any great difficulty in getting away after all who have left! Some people say we do not take life vows because we renew them every year – That *may* be the A.B.'s idea – It was ArchBP. Tait who put the Rule & footnote in.

[30] Elizabeth Anne Wigram (1830–1918), prof. 1864.

[31] When opened by All Saints in 1869, this was the first seaside convalescent hospital to be established in England.

Although S.G. told the A.B. *she* had never been taught about life vows she told me she never meant to break her vows & could keep [them] quite as well where ever she went – I hope you will be able to satisfy the A.B. I think it would be a far greater 'blow' to the Comty for him to resign than for S.G. to leave. I think F.P.[32] is quite wrong in his views! S.G. will do us far more harm than if she had left – she *will* leave as soon as she gets some money[33] & she is writing begging letters & of course making her own story good – with her great want of truthfulness one never knows what she may say & I shall never be surprised at seeing her story in the papers – I have to be so _very_ careful what I say – She came in only 6 months after I did & therefore her teaching was the same as mine – I wish the A.B. could know S.G.'s propensity to exaggerate – In the letter she showed me she told many *lies* but I made her promise to write it again – Of course she explains it by saying she did not mean it to be taken as I read it, – & quite plainly too! I am afraid I have not been able to 'help' you in any way.
Your very loving
S. Anne

From S. Anna Maria[34]
Professed February 1868
Germantown[35]
Aug[st] 6/95

My dear Mother,
    It never occurred to me for one moment that our Vows were not for life, or that we could at any time break them without sin, such was certainly the teaching when I was a Novice –
    I hope this comprises what you wanted dear Mother –
Believe me, your loving Sister
† Anna Maria

[32] Robert Lay Page (1839–1912), ordained 1863, joined S.S.J.E. 1870. He became second superior of the Society of St John the Evangelist and All Saints' chaplain in 1890.

[33] The community occasionally made permanent financial provision (usually in the form of an annual income) for sisters who left after many years' membership.

[34] Anna Maria Gutch (d. 1906), prof. 1868. American by birth, she was sent to help found the American affiliation in Baltimore.

[35] The community's house in Pennsylvania was here for a brief period.

From Sister Sophia,[36] *Professed Feb: 1868*
Kelsey[37]
Sunday
Jan 1895

My dearest Mother,

I am so sorry for all your worries, & this is indeed serious. Our first Mother always asked each Novice publicly at Chapter whether she understood that the vows were for life. And my Mistress taught us the same & explained the 'foot-note' then in the Rules, by saying this is a free country & if any one chose to break their vows, they were at liberty to do so, but we were taught it was a deadly sin, at least that was always the impression conveyed to me, as a Priest or a married woman may break their vows. At any rate we were always taught that the vows were life-long, & she said that clause was put in by our first visitor, the Bishop of London. We have never liked it & always wished to get rid of it. I believe in one old copy of Rules, it is, or was, in the Bishop's own handwriting.

I doubt whether the latter part of the Rule 1 is kept now, but no doubt it was when S. Gertrude was professed, as the Bishop was then alive.

I hope after this treachery on the part of S. Gertrude that you will let her stay or go as she likes, but allow her no money by Statute 18 which she has signed.

Ask her which year her aunt died & there must be some entry of the money if ever received by us. And could you not get a list of the works she has had & why she left them showing how she has always disgraced us.

It seems to me that in a free country no one can compel vows to be kept, or forbid them to be made if we like to do so. Surely the freedom must be allowed to both cases.

If it can be found that S. G. gave money it might be well to let her have it back, though we are not obliged to do so, but not a penny more with my consent. Others no doubt will advise you differently but I never liked hush money & once begun there is no end to it. After all, the mischief is done now, & give what we may, it will not help us in the matter of vows with the Archbishop.

The skating on Saturday morning was a great success, all seemed gentry & there was no annoyance, but the mid-day thaw was a great disappointment & the lake had to be cleared about 4 p.m. about 12 went in but nothing serious, I saw gentlemen were on the ice before 7 am & all seemed most thoroughly to enjoy it.
Your very loving Child
Sophia

It is such a lovely day. I have just been out & the little snowdrops & other flowers are coming up so prettily.

---

[36] Harriet Sophia Robinson (1837–1904), prof. 1868.
[37] A home for old women in Beckenham, Kent, opened 1895.

S. Caroline Mary[38]
Professed Nov. 1868

Mission of the Good Shepherd
12, St. Matthew's Street
Westminster, S.W.
Sunday night, *9:30 p m.*

My dearest Mother

Your letter reached me late yesterday evening & there has not been a moment today in which I could answer it. Sunday is filled to brim & uses up all ones energy.

It seems to me the best way to answer the Archbishop is to say that Sister Gertrude's case is not that of 'her conscience before GOD &c'[39] which we have no right to blame – but that she is leaving her Community because she wants her own way & will not consent to the work or place assigned her –

If S. Gertrude had been advanced by you to the office of Sister Superior or been chosen on the Council it would have no doubt taken away the determination to leave the Community.

There *are* exceptional cases of Sisters leaving their Community for 'conscience before GOD': such I suppose, was Sister Priscilla's case[40] – When after careful consideration it was decided by priests of note, & the Archbishop that a grave mistake had been made as to her Vocation.

And so again when Sister Mary Alma[41] & other really conscientious Sisters, have left on account of Roman convictions. Mother & Mr. Upton Richards always taught us from the beginning that when we devoted ourselves to GOD & asked to be received into the Community for the purpose of devoting ourselves to Him in Poverty, Chastity and Obedience for the rest of our lives in this world, we did it with the full intention of carrying out our solemn vows & we were like consecrated Churches set aside for always. But mother always said our Vows were what are called 'Simple Vows' as is the case with most of the Roman orders & that was one reason why the practice of Renewal of Vows was brought in, almost from the first – There is a book, I think you will find in English which explains all about Vows – the Mistress had a copy, & there was one I marked a good deal when we were considering whether S. Mary Monica[42] ought to return to her mother, to support her – Cases of that sort are considered in Roman vows

---

[38] Caroline Grace Millicent Short (1839–1929), prof. 1868. Novice mistress 1870–7. Elected as second mother superior of the community for two terms (1887–93).
[39] This is a reference to rule I.
[40] This was probably Phillipa Nicoles (b. 1833), prof. 1864, left around 1869. She was professed as Sister Phillipa. There was a Sister Mary Priscilla who died in the community in 1925.
[41] Secular name unknown, prof. 1890, left in 1893 in order to convert to Roman catholicism.
[42] Secular name unknown, prof. 1887, left in 1895 under the provisions of statute 15.

& Simple Vows dispensed. There is also a very helpful French book of Mother's on the subject & on the Constitution of Religious Orders – I left both books in your room.[43] The subject of Vows never came up between the Archbishop and me – nor as far as I know between him & Mother – The proviso about 'any Sister quitting the Community whensoever she pleased & her conscience *before GOD* being her guide & no one having any right to blame her' never troubled me or appeared the least to be contrary to the fact of our life-long dedication – Exceptions prove the Rule – & this proviso is distinctly for *exceptional* cases – Such cases arise from time to time in the Roman Church as with us –

Also it endorses our free-will offering & to English minds especially removes all idea of compulsion – or prison –

Our most wise Foundress thought it *most* essential that we should be under Episcopal Visitation from the first, and Bishop Tait, then Bishop of London, ruled that this proviso should be added to our Rule as well as the XIIth Statute – otherwise he wd. not have consented to become our Visitor –

Our present Visitor, the Archbishop consented to our changing the position of this Clause in the Rule at the time when the Appendix was under his consideration – but he would not allowed it to be omitted as some Sisters desired – he would not sign the Appendix unless we consented to place the sentence as a foot-note, & that a printed copy of Rules & Statutes should be in the hands of every Sister – All this was made quite plain to Chapter & Council at the time & all the correspondence, & the original letters & original copy of the Appendix with the Archbishops corrections & notes in red ink were left by me in your possession & you will certainly find them in your room.

I should think Fr. Benson[44] must have impressed on the Archbishop that we by no means coerced Sisters to remain in the Community, for he was always ready to tell them *to go* if they would – You know he urged Anna Dodsworth[45] *to go* he gave S. Emily[46] his Blessing & hoped she wd. get on well in the world, when she went to him in a temper one day & said she meant to leave the Comty – & he was quite angry with me when she *had* not gone. S. Frances Anna[47] was another & Fr Osbourne[48] has

---

[43] The community has not retained copies of any of the books mentioned and I have not been successful in identifying probable titles elsewhere.

[44] Richard Meux Benson (1824–1915), ordained 1849; vicar of Cowley, Oxon., 1850–86. In 1866 founded the Society of St John the Evangelist (the 'Cowley Fathers') and served as superior of S.S.J.E. 1865–90.

[45] Sister of the Revd. William Dodsworth, vicar of Christ Church, Upper Albany Street, 1837–51, who converted to Roman catholicism in 1851.

[46] This is probably Sister Emily Raphael, Emily Mandel Norris (1841–1922), prof. 1879, who was confined to a lunatic asylum in 1899 and 1903. She had formerly been a sister in the community of St Thomas the Martyr, Oxford.

[47] Not identified.

[48] Edward William Osborne, ordained 1870, member of S.S.J.E. He worked in Boston 1877–90 and in Capetown 1890–6, and was superior of the American S.S.J.E. 1898–1904. He was consecrated bishop of Springfield, Illinois, in 1906.

not only told S. Bertha Mary[49] but others that she has no vocation & would do better as a lady of good works in the world, so it is not to be wondered at, that the Archbishop does not understand –

I cannot but think that you would be wise to allay his fears, as to any departure from our Founders' spirit & intention & stick to the fact of its being a wrong act to break away from self-will – a very different thing to acting *on your conscience before GOD* – It is a very serious affair altogether – I am so sorry about it.
Ever your very loving S. C. M.

I believe Bishop Tait saw & sanctioned our Profession Office – it has been in use *as it is* for *over 30 yrs* if the Archbishop has not seen it – but I should think he must – cd. you not send it him?

Vows

Memorandum

The Sisters of Bethany[50] have always taken life vows from the beginning of that Society's existence. When the Bishop of London became Visitor[51] an addition was made to the Rule to the effect that –

No Sister can release herself from these promises she can only be released by the Bishop after the case has been heard by him.

---

[49] Bertha Mary Hodgson (1859–1931), prof. 1889. She disregarded his advice and remained in the community.
[50] The Society of the Sisters of Bethany was founded in 1866 at Clerkenwell by Etheldreda Benett, who had gone through the All Saints' noviciate (1864–6) as preparation for the establishment of her community. It was the first to embrace openly and explicitly the 'mixed' (semi-contemplative) life, and offered the first retreats for women in the anglican communion.
[51] Temple became visitor in 1889.

PART III

LIFE AND TRAINING

III. 1

Rules for the Mistress of Novices

The well-being of a Religious Community depends mainly on the good training of the Novices. The Mistress should not only be wise, gentle, and devout, but humble, patient, and considerate, taking good heed that her Office occasion no feelings of pride or self-sufficiency, but studying by the grace of God, to lead her novices on, step by step, in true devotion with a view only to His Glory, and not of her own self-exaltation.

RULES

1. There shall be two Instructions for the Novices daily, morning and evening, for the purpose of guiding them as to the best method of performing their prayers and meditations and other spiritual exercises.
2. There shall be 3 public obediences[1] daily, at 9.30 a.m; 1 p.m; 6 p.m; at each of which the Novices will make all necessary enquiries respecting their duties and work, and ask for all they may require. The will also receive directions as to the employment of their time until the next obedience, in order that the Rule of Silence be not unnecessarily broken.
3. Each Novice shall have one private Conference with the Mistress per week. The daily faults committed against the Rules must be acknowledged and corrected in public ~~but not in the presence of the Lay Novices~~.[2]
4. The Mistress must earnestly discourage any confidences which involve condemnation, either directly or indirectly, of the Confessor, Superior, or any of the Community, she should strive to impress upon them that all the Community should have but one heart and one mind, remembering that our Lord, by His Holy inspiration, has so joined and united them together, that they can never be disunited, but continue together in unity of mind, and the tie of Charity, which is the very bond of all perfection.
5. The Mistress must not in any way usurp the office of Confessor,[3] or the

---

[1] Obediences was the giving of orders for the day's work.
[2] The novices had their own chapter of faults, separate from that of the professed.
[3] The chaplain heard the confessions of the sisters. Some communities had a different confessor for the lay sisters: All Saints' practice on this point is not clear.

Mother Superior, or have any secrets from them, as regards those under her charge.

6.   Although the Mistress may vary the spiritual exercises according to her judgement, she may not introduce any new ones without the Mother's sanction – for example devotions that might be fitted for the Mistress, might not be such as would be suited for the Novice, She is also cautioned against overburthening them with devotional exercises.

7.   The Mistress is exhorted to treat all those under her charge alike, and to permit no difference in her behaviour towards any of them, no matter for what cause, she must not allow any of the Novices to follow her about, or have frequent private conferences, without *grave* necessity, or talk overmuch, or unnecessarily about their spiritual *feelings*, as this is apt to deteriorate into self-indulgence and self-contemplation.[4]

8.   The Novices must apply to their Mistress for all they require, but she must apply for what they want to that Sister who may have the charge of that particular department.[5]

[4]   'Morbidity' was greatly feared in religious communities. It was believed to be a sign of incipient mental imbalance.

[5]   The vow of poverty meant that great stress was placed on the careful husbanding of the Society's resources. Waste was discouraged, to the point that even paper was reused, thus destroying many documents that would be of value to the historian.

III. 2

Notes on the Novices' Rules and Regulations

CHAPEL[1]

Lay Novices Customs & Bye Laws

RULES

1. A novice should read her rules carefully once a week.[2]

2 If in doubt about a rule, she should refer to the Mistress[3] or the Senior Novice

3 When a Novice knows she has broken the Rule, she should confess it at chapter;[4] if of Necessity, say so.

4 She must not refer to anything said in chapter.

5 At obediences she should tell Sr Eliza of any failure in work, to the inconvenience of another, either from forgetfullness or neglect.

6 No Novice should speak to anyone of her interior temptations & trials, except to the Mistress.

---

[1] This document is a collection of untitled manuscripts. While the commencement is clearly intended for the lay sisters, it is probably the instructions given them by their novice mistress (Sister Eliza) rather than their formal rule, which does not appear to have survived. This set of instructions on their rule is probably as close as we can come to reconstructing their rule. Many of the tiny pages are numbered separately. While a good many of the rules apply only to lay sisters, we are also given some hints as to the practice of the choir noviciate. In terms of discipline, although not of work, their rules must have been similar. This document should be read in conjunction with the rules for the mistress of the novices.

[2] All novices were given a copy of their rule upon clothing; each was expected to study it carefully over the period of the noviciate, in order to ensure that she was fully aware of the Society's discipline and regulations when she was put up for election to profession (or in the case of lay sisters, was accepted for profession).

[3] Since the lay and choir sisters had separate noviciates after the community had grown to a sufficient size, this would be a reference to the lay novice mistress, a post filled (appropriately enough, given the duties of the lay sisters) by the housekeeping sister. The lay noviciate normally lasted about a year longer than that of the choir novices.

[4] This (and further references to chapter in the text) refers to chapter of faults, not the decision making chapter. Lay sisters did not attend chapter; neither did lay or choir novices.

1. Novices must be in Chapel before the Office begins, or say they are late.[5]

2. Each Novice goes straight to her own chair. Novices should not kneel out of their place at devotions, unless their chair be filled by a Professed Sister.[6]

3. Novices must be in Chapel at 11.30.a.m. if the gong has not been rung. They may go at 11.20. Those Novices whose work prevents them from making their Examen[7] after 12.0. must be in Chapel at 11.15. If there be no Instruction, the time is spent in Prayer, Spiritual Reading or copying out instructions.

4. The Novices ought to be in Chapel at 4.15 p.m. & not leave till the Gong rings.[8]

5. ~~The Novice whose turn it is to take the Compline Key, if in chapel should leave at 8.25.~~[9]

6. No novice may be fetched out of Chapel without leave from the Mistress[10] or Sr. Eliza, nor may the Portress give any message during an Office without leave from the Mistress or the Assistant Superior.

7. In coming out of Chapel the Novices do not pass before Professed Sisters or Choir Novices ~~but in going to obediences, they may come out before the Lay Professed Sisters.~~ In going up to Chapel they must not go before Professed Sisters.

8. The Novices curtsey when the Revd. Mother, the Assistant Superior, the Mistress or Sister ~~Eliza~~ pass their seats. If Novices be out of their place, they curtsey to every Sister on passing, & return Lay Aspirants' curtsies.

9. Lay Novices blow the Organ for Prime & Compline, for Thursday Litany, & Sunday & Festival Vespers – ~~Vespers are divided~~. Any Novice may offer to help another.

10. At Offices or Services in Church every Novice should follow the Service, & join in it, [remainder pasted over]

11. ~~If late for meditation, the Novices go to the Instruction Room. S. John~~

---

[5] In other words, to arrive just in time was to be late, and needed to be acknowledged in chapter of faults. The recommencing at number 1 indicates a new sheet of paper.

[6] Novices also took precedence by seniority; in this case by date of clothing. If many sisters were visiting the mother house from the branches, they could spill over into the area reserved for the novices.

[7] This was their examination of conscience.

[8] Choir novices would attend all the offices; lay novices (and lay sisters) were ordinarily expected to attend two. There was a constant temptation for the lay sisters to leave early, in order to ensure that their work (serving up the dinner, for example) would be done on time.

[9] This rule has been pasted over the original number 5, and then struck through.

[10] This would refer to the mistress of the choir novices.

12. Novices make their Confessions fortnightly [pasted over: unless they have special permission to do otherwise]

13. Only one book besides the Office Book may be left on one's Chair in Chapel, but (The Bibles may be left, as the one book) the Reading book[11] may not be left.

14. No notes may be written, given, or read in Chapel without permission.

15. The Senior Novice takes the Meditations out of the Case,[12] & they are passed first to the Postulants, then to the Juniors & only kept a few minutes by each. The Meditation is made from the one prepared [Pasted over: the night before].

16. Meditations may be made before or after Breakfast in the week, except on days of Receptions or Professions, when it is made after the Service or after the Breakfast or 11.30.

17. During the Afternoon devotions & the reading should be on the morning Instruction, or *Scripture*, *not* the Reading book; Preparation before & Thanksgiving after Communion & extra Prayers in the afternoon out of the Imitation.[13]

18. All should take their Bibles to Instruction. All should take Notes at Instruction & Addresses, except at Receptions & Professions. No pencil should be sharpened in the Chapel or the Instruction Room.

19. The Novices should not leave the Instruction Room till the Dinner Bell rings & on their way from Mid-day Prayer, they may not stop in the Noviciate or in the Yard to talk: On their way from dinner the Rule is the same, unless they have to give a short message.

20. On the first Sunday in the month, the Mistress gives the Novices their Reading books, these may not be left about nor lent to each other. No one may read another's Reading book. They must be kept on the shelf in the Noviciate. No Book may be left long in the Cloister.

21. In the Cloister the Novice only curtseys to the Novices coming towards her.

22. No Novice may be absent from Offices, Church or the Refectory without leave from the Mistress.

23. When the Bell rings for the departing soul of a Sister, all the Novices working in the house should go straight to Chapel.

---

[11] The novice mistress gave each novice a book to read during the course of the month, see rule 20. The book was chosen according to each novice's capacity and needs.

[12] Meditations were written out on pieces of paper, and reused at intervals.

[13] *The imitation of Christ.*

24. The Novices go to Chapel directly they come in from the celebration on Festivals.

CHURCH

1. Directly the first gong rings the Novices go at once to dress & do not loiter about; if not going to Church, they go to their work at once after the first gong, unless they have special leave to stay in Chapel.

2. Novices coming in after the gong, go straight to the Cloakroom, not wait in the Hall.

3. The Senior present gives the signal when to start, & when to ring the Bell, & if there is no Portress, passes the key to the Junior.[14]

4. The Seniors walk to the right, the Juniors to the left, each waits for her Partner on the step, all cross straight over the street to the Clergy House, in going, & to No. 78 in coming from Church.

5. No Novice is to go to Church alone, after the rest. If asked a question, on the way to, or from Church, answer briefly.[15]

7. All are to get ready in time for the Mid-day Celebration, leave work at 10.50 a.m. & when ready, wait in the Hall, not in the Noviciate, standing in a line with the door, two & two in their right order.

8. If the Blessed Sacrament is on the Altar, the Novices genuflect on passing into their row of seats.

9. Bible, Prayer book & Hymn book are taken to Mattins & Evensong; the Treasury[16] or the C.B.S. Manual[17] & Prayer book to Celebration. (or 'Imitation')

10. The chairs are not moved forward, except at the early Celebration, & then must be lifted, not dragged.

11. The mats are not used to kneel on, without special permission.

12. All kneel & rise together.

13. No empty chairs may be left between the Novices.

---

[14] The junior is the most recently clothed novice. All the novices who had been clothed less than a year were known collectively as the juniors.

[15] There is no number 6 on this sheet.

[16] This was *The treasury of devotion*, a manual of prayers, compiled by Edgar Hoskins in 1857 and edited by T. T. Carter, the co-founder of the Clewer sisterhood. Immensely popular with anglo-catholics, it went through at least twenty editions by the 1880s.

[17] The Confraternity of the Blessed Sacrament, abbreviated C.B.S.

14. No one may lean against the wall, put their feet on the chair in front, or their elbows on a chair, or sit or kneel in a lounging position during any devotion. All kneel upright at the Altar, & receive the Chalice in *both* hands.

15. ~~The Junior, who leads to church, before celebration, should count the novices in the cloakroom, & leave the two back rows for 22 Novices,~~[18] ~~to go far enough to let the rest come in.~~

16. Novices go to Mattins & High Celebration on Sunday; if work prevents this they go at 9.0. a.m. All go to Evensong on Vigils, & to High Celebration; ~~& Evensong or festivals, even though it be not their regular night;~~ unless work prevents.

17. ~~A novice must tell the Sacristan~~[19] ~~when going to omit her communion, or make an extra One in Chapel, if making her Communion on a day when the others do not, she must sit at the end of the row.~~ All make their Communions on Saints' Days.

18. The head is bowed at the Name of JESUS, occurring in the Lessons or in the Sermon, ~~we do not curtsey at 'we worship Thee', in the Gloria in Excelsia.~~

19. No one may look at her watch in Church.

20. Novices should go up to the Altar from the right end of the row of chairs, unless few in number, & seated at the left end. If waiting in the Chancel, lead right up to the Sanctuary steps & kneel there close together.

21. When there is a Lecture in Chapel Novices do not go to Evensong.

22. Novices may not speak after Church, or go to the Noviciate to put their books away, till they have taken their Cloaks & Hoods off. + No one is to stop & talk in the Noviciate after Evensong.

23. If the Novices have made their Communion, & there is a General Thanksgiving, they follow the Choir Postulants to the Cloister, if there is no General Thanksgiving, each Novice makes hers silently in Chapel, or if, as on Sundays, the Chapel is engaged, in the Instruction room. If a Novice has only been present, she goes unless prevented by work, to the Chapel ~~or the Instruction Room~~ for Devotion, until Breakfast; when the Breakfast Bell rings, all go straight in their order to the end of the little Cloister, unless they have to put their books away in the Noviciate. ~~Notes of instructions may be copied in the Noviciate before breakfast, but no work may be done,~~ nor may Novices sit about, doing nothing.

---

[18] Some of the novices lived in 22 Margaret St.
[19] The sacristan was in charge of the furnishings and ritual of the chapel.

+The Refectory Novices[20] may give their cloaks and hoods to the next Novice, instead of going down to the cloakroom.

NOVICIATE

1. ~~The Junior in the room answers the 79 bell~~, no Novice may let herself out without first ringing the Bell, & waiting a little, & must mention it as 'of necessity', when out, they should ring twice at 78 & wait for someone to answer the Bell, before going to 82.

2. If a Novice wants the Portress in 82, she should ring the Call Bell, & not open the Swing door, to see if she is there.

3. The Novices may not go into the Noviciate with their hoods on.

4. The Novices may not go to the Noviciate before Prime, or after Compline, except on Sunday evening after Church to put their books away.

5. Always knock before entering a room.

6. No one must go through the Yard, when it rains.

7. [pasted over]

8. No one must speak with the door open.

9. No paper must be burnt in the Noviciate & Instruction Room. The Gas must not be lighted with paper.

10. No Novice may ever sit in the Mistress' chair.

11. The drawers & work baskets must be kept tidy, nothing may be left about in the Noviciate or Cloakroom.

12. No good note-paper may be used for Confession or Chapter notes, unless no common paper can be found. If note-books are wanted, the Novices must ask for them from the Senior Choir Novice, or the Store drawer keeper.

13. Letters are generally written on Sunday by S^r. Eliza's permission, if there are no Obediences they may be written & it is mentioned on Monday. Novices do not ask permission to write to their Mistress or S^r. Eliza, when away from Home.

---

[20] These were the novices in charge of preparing meals.

CLOAK ROOM AND CLOTHES

1. After washing their hands, the Novices must empty the basin wipe it, & put the towel straight.

2. Only Recreation Work is to be kept on the shelves on the Cupboard, nothing else, no collars or other soiled things for mending.

3. Collars are to be hung tidily on the pegs.

4. Aprons may not be put in the Boot-boxes, nothing but Boots.

5. All clothes must be sent to the wash before breakfast on Monday unless by permission. Leave must be asked to send Petticoats, Habits, or anything beyond the usual number of garments to the wash, or to sew on a clean Boddice.

6. All clothes must be kept well mended.

7. No clothes or watches may be lent or borrowed.

8. ~~The clean clothes for the Novices sleeping out of the house, are put in the Cloakroom on Saturday afternoon & must be taken away before Sunday~~.

9. On days of Professions or Receptions, & on Festivals only best Habits should be worn, & no scrubbing done.

10. Each Novice has two pair of boots, which must be marked distinctly L.⁺S. & the number. Boots must be cleaned once a week, & taken off to be cleaned.

11. Collars must not be pinned.

12. Loops of Cloaks must be mended when broken.

13. It is a fault, carelessly to tread on a Sister's Habit.

14. Nothing must be accepted, given, or destroyed by a Novice, without permission.

15. Nothing belonging to the Common Box may be kept by a Novice, except just for the time she is using it.

CELLS

1. A Novice must be tidy in her person, she must keep her locker tidy & roll her hair up tidily in paper.

2. A Novice must not sleep with her Cell door open.

3. A Novice may never leave her Cell without her Habit, Cap & Cross on; not

even go to a child, sleeping in the next partition of the same Cell, to give her medicine, unless dressed.

4. A Novice must never take off her Cap, except in her Cell.

5. The head must not be washed without permission.

6. No needlework may be done in the Cell without permission.

7. The mattress must be turned daily.

8. A Novice must get up directly she is called; if she is forgotten, she may get up at the Angelus.

9. A Novice may say her regular morning Prayers in her Cell, or in Chapel.

10. While dressing, or undressing, the blind must be drawn down, but it may be up during the night.

11. All those sleeping in the same house, come in, & go out together, at night & in the morning. In the morning they wait for each other till 6.25. a.m.

12. ~~Novices may go across to Nos. 3. 4. or 5 without their cloaks at night, but never to 69 or 70 & must never carry cloaks over the arm~~.

13. A Novice should say her Night Prayers directly she goes to her Cell before commencing to undress.

REFECTORY

1. The Novices curtsey to the Crucifix on entering.

2. No Novice must refuse any food brought to her, if she can possibly eat it; if she cannot, she must ask to be excused. If she cannot finish what she has, she must tell the Novice who waits, who will carry the plate up to the Mistress, & it is left on the dumb waiter.

3. If a Novice has not time to finish, she must return as soon as the Refectory is clear & finish. Nothing eatable must be left on any plate or on the floor.

4. If a Novice has to help herself at Dinner or supper, she must take of meat & pudding just as she is usually helped by the Mistress.

5. Tea or Coffee must not be poured into the saucers to cool.[21]

---

[21] Most of the lay novices were of the domestic servant class, and part of the training of the noviciate was to give them more middle class manners but without instilling a middle class dislike of domestic work.

6. If there are eggs, the egg spoon should be used for the Pudding; forks for any solid pudding, nothing unnecessary must be used.

7. The Bread Boards are not moved at Breakfast or Tea; at Breakfast the bread is passed down on a plate, in slices; at Tea each Novice may go to the Board above her seat & help herself. If there are small pieces on the plate, never cut a fresh piece of bread.

8. The Novices go up to help themselves in Refectory in their right turn.

9. If on the same form with Professed Sisters, Novices go in & out at the Novice's end.

10. Half the Novices help in Refectory after Dinner on Sunday & the other half after Tea, unless their work prevents them; some help after Breakfast. The night before a Reception or Profession, Novices who have done their own work, should help in the Refectory until 8.30. p.m., they should also help after Dinner & Tea on the great Festivals, such as Christmas, the Ascension, or the Birthdays, so that their Sisters may have time to share in their pleasure.

11. Novices may talk in the Refectory Pantry, if a Professed Sister is in the Pantry or Refectory.

SILENCE

1. There is silence after the first gong for Church, or for Instruction, when the Office Bell rings, & before going to a Celebration. No unnecessary Conversation may be held before Meditation.

2. ~~If Novices go to Vespers on the Eve of a Festival, There is no silence from that time till 8.0.p.m.~~

3. There is no silence for the Refectory Novices during the Outer Sisters' Retreat.[22]

4. Silence must be kept at Obediences.

5. Silence is to be kept in the Dormitories.

6. Silence is to be kept in the Cloak room and in the area.

---

[22] The outer sisters had a large annual retreat at the convent. The refectory sisters needed to be available to answer questions and requests about food, tea and accommodation.

IN THE STREETS.

1. If a Lay Novice is sent out with a Choir Novice, she does not speak in the street; if she goes any distance with a Lay Novice, or in talking time to houses in the same street, she may speak. If she goes out with Girls or Orphans she always speaks, & in the Parks she may speak to a Sister.

2. If asked a question or spoken to, in the street, the Novice should answer courteously but briefly, & not stop, but rather walk on, if necessary, a little way, with the one who speaks to her.

3. A Novice should not trip [later altered to kiss] in the streets or any public place.[23]

4. A Novice may read in a train or omnibus, if she can avoid being overlooked.

5. Novices curtsey in the street, to Priests & Religious of our own Community.

RECREATION

1. The Novices keep silence before Recreation, till the Choir Novices come down, when they rise & remain standing, till the Mistress is seated.

2. Novices should be silent, at the entrance of the Mistress, when the letters are being given out, & when the Mistress is reading or speaking.

3. Novices should avoid sitting apart from each other, they must not sit, day by day, by the same Sister, or in the same place.

4. The Novices take regular turns, beginning with the Junior, to sit by the Mistress, except on days of Reception, when the places on either side are left for the new Novices; on week-days they sit on the left, on Sundays at the right side.

5. Novices may not read each other's letters.

6. Novices may not talk about work at Recreation.

7. Novices must never be idle at Recreation; they may string their caps, mend stockings & any clean linen, but not anything soiled. Not bind Habits or mend Petticoats; these they must ask to do in S. Dorcas. A quite clean, *under* Petticoat may be mended at Recreation.

8. Lay Novices should not be forward in speaking to the Choir Novices, but if spoken to should answer simply.

---

[23] This is puzzling. While kiss is easily understood as a kiss of greeting, it seems as if the original instruction was that novices should not walk with a bouncy step.

9. The Novices must not hurry to put their work away before the Choir Novices, or go through the Cloister till the Bell has ceased.

10. Cotton, tape &c out of the Common Box must be put back, immediately after each Recreation.

S. DORCAS[24]

1. If working under a Professed Sister a Novice should notwithstanding her leave from a Superior, ask to be excused by the Sister. In S. Dorcas ask the Lay Professed only.

2. Do not sit in a Professed Sister's chair during her absence.

3. Between 6.0. & 7.0. silence is to be kept, unless a Professed Sister is present. To her the Novices should refer about the work, for leave to change their seats, or to come away.

4. No private conversations may be held.

5. No Novice must repeat anything of Noviciate arrangements or Rules, nor talk of anything she has heard or seen in the Noviciate to a Professed Sister. No Novice is ever to mention what a Superior has said to her privately.

6. As the Novices come down to meals, they must go to their places.

PORTESS

1. The Portress may not open the Back Door after dark.

2. The Portress in 82 Yard need not get up when a Choir Novice passes.

LINEN ROOM

1. Novices should apply to the Linen Room, Store Room & take dirty things to the Pantry before 10.0. a.m – on Monday to the Laundry not later than 9.0. a.m. without special leave from Sr. Eliza.

2. Boots to be mended should be taken at the end of the week.

3. Nothing should be asked for, from the Linen Room on Saturday, unless necessary.

[24] A Dorcas society was a ladies' group for sewing clothes for the poor. The name for the needlework room evidently derives from that.

AWAY FROM HOME

1. If a Novice is away from Home for Rest, she should be careful to observe the Rule as if at Home; but she may get her Devotional time as most convenient. She only keeps the Great Silence, & silence to & from Church.

2. A Novice does not lie on couches, or sit lounging in easy chairs, or sit at a window looking out into the street, at passers by.

3. If on a visit to friends, or when visited by friends, a Novice is asked questions as to her work & Rule, or about the Community, she should answer simply & briefly, avoiding any seeming mystery.

SENIOR NOVICE[25]

1. The senior Novice makes out the List for Confession & weekly list for Compline ~~key~~, Blowing the Organ, Kitchen Sunday~~, & fetching the milk. A Novice may, if prevented from fetching the milk, ask the next to go for her, & her turn is then passed over.~~ Novices working at 69 or 70 do not take the Kitchen Sunday or Compline key.[26] If there is any reason why a Novice can not take her turn, it should be stated to the Senior.

2. The Senior Novice sees that there is Note Paper & Envelopes in the Case, if there is none, she asks for them.

3. The Senior Novice sees that all is tidy in boot-boxes, drawers, & pegs, & takes away anything left about.

4. The two Seniors in turn get the Mistress' water after dinner.

5. The Senior Novice cleans the Mistress' boots, & mends Her clothes, which the Sister working in 80 gets for her.

6. Before Receptions, Professions & Festivals the Senior Novice asks the Mistress & S^r. Eliza what the Novice[s] are to do, & tells the others.

7. In going to Obediences the Novices wait for Sr. Eliza, unless the Senior Novice tells them they need not.

---

[25] This is the novice closest to profession.

[26] The key was taken by the novice who needed to arrive first in the morning, to light the fires and then unlock the door for the others. Caroline Mary describes doing it as an outer sister, in the very early days of the Society (before there were lay sisters) in her 'Memories'.

GENERAL RULES

1. A Novice must go punctually at 4.0. p.m. to tea & Devotions.

2. A Novice should go straight to her work, unless she has some explanation or apology to make, ~~or to correct a fault,~~ which cannot be put off; but she may not neglect her work for it.

3. Novices should not go through Passage Rooms, nor to the upper part of 79 or 80, unless Houseworkers or unless sent.

4. Novices should be modest, not putting themselves forward, or commencing conversations with Choir Professed Sisters, but may answer naturally, if spoken to. They should avoid talking to any Visitor in the house; whether they knew them previously or not, except by permission.

5. Novices should curtsey to a Superior before & after addressing Her, whether at Obediences, or in giving a message.

6. Novices may exchange pictures among themselves.[27] They may not give pictures or cards to the Girls, unless working at 70.[28] Nothing may be enclosed in a letter without permission. *By permission* a lace picture may be given to a Sister on the Day of her Profession, but pictures must not be given to or received from Professed Sisters at other times. Novices do not ask to keep pictures given them at the Day of Reception, nor at any time, those given them by their Superior.

7. Novices should not discuss or compare Sisters, or repeat, what they have said.

8. Novices should not correct their Seniors, nor their Juniors when a Senior is present, unless the matter admits of no delay, such as stopping an improper conversation. If they see any grave fault habitually committed, or not acknowledged, they should tell the Mistress.

RULES[29]

6.30 p.m. is *obligatory* Chapel time.

8. Must not omit a Com^n, or make an extra Com^n without leave.

---

[27] These were holy pictures, not photographs.

[28] There was a small orphanage and industrial girls' training school at 70 Mortimer St.

[29] The following notes (to the end of the document) are written in a very small hand on tiny paper; they are obviously meant as notes for verbal instruction of the novices. I have not expanded the abbreviations, thinking them obvious. The first twenty-one points seem to be intended to apply to both choir and lay novices. Rules 1 to 7 are missing, as are 11 and 12.

9. If ill in morning, must send by the caller[30] to ask to stay in bed, – not stay without asking. Sh^d. not go into Noviciate or cloakroom after Lands or bef: Prime without necessity.

10. Sickness. Not *readily* ask dispensation – we are called to self-sacrifice.[31]

Sh$^{d.}$ let Mistress *know* if are ill – not, keep silence ab^t. the matter to her, & complain to everyone else! Not to be overcareful – ab^t. health (it is a charge, a gift, ∵ not to be reckless), – but not to be anxious, dreading heat, dreading cold, – wanting dispensations ab^t. clothing etc – Continually wanting medicine etc – All this a want of Poverty.

Our health belongs to the Com^{ty}, & must never allow ourselves to be fussy. . . .

– Wrong to run needless risks, – yard in evening or in rain, just to save trouble, this is not ascetic, but slothful.

If asked ab^t. health, sh^d. answer truthfully & fully. Very unsimple to evade questions, & keep back things – pretend to be well. . . When *asked*, – responsibility taken off you, – you have simply to answer.

– Those who are given dispensations ab^t. food or rest, – sh^d. not be always asking to do without – *Should* say if think it is no longer required, & then leave it.

13. Not to *run* up & down stairs etc. – Walk recollectedly in street, not rushing along – Silence when walking in the streets.

14. Care of clothes – books – crockery – things entrusted to our care etc. . Waste nothing, eg. gas etc. 'due regard'. . .

Leaving food on plate, little bits etc. all a want of Poverty. Personal neatness, – not leaving things ab^t., as if the whole place was your own.

Curtsey on meeting *each other* . . . .

15. No such thing as *holidays* . . . go for a rest if needed. Visit *parents* only. When at house, not to go out to public places, not to visit friends (though they may come & see you). Not to walk with brothers. Not to speak before Com^n.[32] – Not to stand to talk round the Church door.

16. Let friends know they can only come on right days. In waiting room, sh^d. be careful ab^t. manner, – not sitting on the floor, or kneeling on the ground, or talking loudly.

17. Not *enclose* letters without leave, except to brothers & sisters in same house.

---

30   The caller was the novice who awoke the others.
31   A dispensation was a relaxation of the rule, due to personal frailty.
32   This must have been a hardship in low church parishes, where communion could be at noon, or in the evening.

Seek to check letter writing. 'Use all *due* reserve', ie. not to be mysterious, but not to think the Comt^y. a sort of public Institution to be freely canvassed. . . . .

Not to show notes of Retreats or Instructions to seculars without leave. Shut bk on going to altar. Not to enter into conversation to strangers when travelling – speak if courtesy or charity demand it, – but otherwise be silent.

Avoid lounging postures, familiarities one with another, – nick-names, – kissing in the yard etc. etc. – Never go to Chapel or refectory to give messages, with cloak & hood on. All intercourse with Priests passes through Sister-in-Charge, – & when necessary he comes to the house at proper times & hours. Sister never waits to speak after Church etc. Intercourse sh^d. be brief & upon matters of business.

Curtsey when meeting Priests of the Parish, & always return salutations.

19. Not to keep fast days according to private fancy, eg. if butter is on the table it is meant to be eaten etc. . .

No mortifications contrary to rule, or which w^d. make the doer of them singular, – this wd. tend to spir. pride.

When away, sh^d. not eat between meals except by the express wish of a parent. Sh^d. not eat of a variety of things, – at the same time shd. avoid singularity, & not be rigid ab^t. the matter. Be watchful for mortifications & crosses wh: arise day by day in the Providence of GOD.

[Avoid] talk standing about at odd times, – standing by the fire, sitting down by it; – all this is self-indulgent & opposed to the spirit of mortification. Also *grumbling* ab^t. little things, e.g. taking medicine, the weather, boots, companions, companion in work, Noviciate in general.

On coming in from District, girls or Orphanage, sitting down in a self-indulgent position in the cloakroom, instead of at once taking off things; – even coming into the Noviciate cloak on, hood in hand, & standing idly talking, just as if in own home.

Standing about in cloakroom after supper.

20. Orphanage, girls & District Novices must remember that though they may have to talk in Silence hours to those in their care, yet their Silence is binding towards *each other.*

21. 'Comply unhesitatingly & cheerfully' etc.

LAY NOVICES[33]

8.[34] To go to the Instruction Room after mid-day prayer till dinner time; – never to come down & chatter to one another – not to go into yard or cloakroom and talk between breakfast & Meditation. To *rise up,* & let each other pass *into* places in Chapel – not step over each other.

9. Sh. not go into Noviciate or cloakroom after Compline or before Prime without real necessity. Rise directly when called.

13. Keep Nov: door shut – Not *run* up & down stairs.

14. Curtsey on meeting *one another.* Not to be familiar with one another, pet names etc. Not to clean boots in the cloakroom or on the stone steps. Take Compline key *bef:* bell begins. Not keep things in boot box.

19. Be watchful ab. self-indulgence. e.g. not sit over the fire with feet on fender. Not sit in Church or Chapel with book in lap & feet on chair in front. In food, taking what least like when there is a choice. Never being fanciful ab^t. food, leaving pieces on edge of plate. Not cutting bread unfairly to get all the crust for oneself etc. – take what comes first.

20. In returning from Church, remain two & two until enter the house, not stand in a group round the door.

21. Great danger of little unfaithfulnesses in things wh: do not come under Superior's eye – e.g. – going to work *directly* after Obediences in the morning, not standing about to talk. Going to work *directly* at 2 p.m., not speaking after Mistress has left Recreation. Not standing about in cloakroom.

23. Not to disparage another – not to be uncourteous, bear & forbear with one another To be careful ab^t. passing remarks on one another, either to them or of them. Passing remarks & commenting on Superiors. Talking egotistically. Avoiding little things we know cause annoyance to others – teasing others – rough or familiar to others – interrupting others.

5. Gossiping, frivolous, inquisitive remarks or conversation shd. be specially guarded against. If hear any little thing said in disfavour of another *never to go & repeat* to them what you have heard. Much mischief made in this way, & Lay Novices often fail to realise the sin of repeating these remarks, because they are apt to regard it as a mark of friendship.

4. Careful not to hoard little treasures as private possessions, or to retain things

---

[33]　While headed lay novices, most of what follows is clearly intended to apply to both types of novice. Some applies only to choir novices (no. 26).

[34]　The following numbers are not completely in sequence. This seems to be a list of points to expand upon when discussing the numbered rule.

apart fr: the Noviciate – eg bottles of glycerine[35] to keep privately in cell, instead of using the general bottle provided for the Noviciate.

Must be obedient not only to Mistress, but to the Novice in charge of the work in all concerning the work; – even though she may be junior, – not as clever etc. etc.

22. 'The Sisters shall hold no rank among themselves.' Precedence is for order's sake, not rank. Not to be aggrieved if a junior is put in charge of any work. . . Never to complain of work being distasteful. . .

23. Never complain to one another.

If anything is wrong speak ask (deleted) freely to the Mistress – put away school-girl notion of 'telling tales', – only be strictly *accurate* in what you say; – & do not speak on the very first occasion, wait & see if it occurs again. . . . .

Never use a sharp sarcastic tone to one another. Sarcastic speakers sh^d. *never* be heard in a Religious House. Sh^d. avoid little tricks or habits that cause annoyance to others. Talking when others want to read or write; – interrupting conversations between 2 others, – contradicting others, (when no principle is involved it is always best to yield the point).

Expressing strong likes & dislikes.

25. Avoid curious questions, or even idle objectless questions. Never repeat things from one to another; giving out little pieces of gossiping information ab^t. things external to your own business, – which though they may be no secret, yet are not necessary to be communicated & talked over.

26. Recreation. Come unselfishly & in a generous spirit. Try to make the conversation as general as possible – try to include the Lay Novices. 5p.m. is *not* recreation, simply it is not Silence time.

Novices who are not naturally in the Noviciate at 5 p.m. sh^d. not arrange work at Chapel time with a view of being there at that time for the sake of talk.

(*Omitted from 13.*) Not to rush about with arms swinging, but when not otherwise occupied the hands to be folded in front of the person. Never to leave cell without Habit & cap. Say private prayers with Habit & cap on.

(*Omitted from 9.*) Rise directly you are called.

---

[35] Glycerine was used to rub on cracked skin and on chilblains. Very few rooms in the convent had even a fireplace, and fires were rarely lit.

III. 3

Rules for Visitors and Outer Sisters[1]

RULES FOR VISITORS AND OUTER SISTERS, 1872

I   To keep silence until after Terce, and also from 10 till 12, and from 2 till 4, and after Compline. On Sundays and Festivals silence is to be kept only until after Terce and after Compline.

II   Not to speak on the stairs, or in the passages, and to go about the House and shut the doors quietly.

III   Not to ask any inmate of the House to do an errand[2] without first obtaining permission of the Superior or Assistant Superior.

IV   To ask no questions concerning any of the inmates of the House, or the arrangements or discipline of the Establishment, except of the Superior or Assistant Superior.

V   Not to speak of, or canvass the affairs of other religious Houses, nor to talk of what they did, or of what happened to them whilst they were inmates there.

VI   To retire to their bedrooms at **8.30 P.M.**, unless they go to Compline, and then at once from the Chapel to their bedrooms.

VII   Not to go into each others' bedrooms at any time without special permission, or to speak to each other through the partitions.

VIII   Not to lend books to each other without permission. No Roman Catholic books to be left about either in the Common Room or in their bedrooms. No newspapers to be brought into the Common Room.

IX   When desirous of speaking to the Superior or Assistant Superior they must inform the Portress: but may never waylay any Sister in the passage, or on the stairs, or go after her when at her work: neither may they go to any of

---

[1] Outer sisters (or associate sisters) were women who could not join the community, but who wished to help in in its work and enter into a special relationship with it; the Society had outer sisters from the first decade of its existence. They followed a simple rule of life. This was kept in the common room at All Saints. The 1872 version printed here was a revision of the original rule, dated May 1871, which also instructed outer sisters not to wear crinolines while staying at the convent. A third version of the outer sisters' rule dates from about 1894; it follows immediately after the 1872 version. The increase in Roman practice and terminology over this twenty-year period is instructive.

[2] Used to commanding servants, ladies who were visitors or outer sisters might have been inclined to send the industrial girls, or even worse, the lay sisters, on errands.

the appartments appropriated to the Sisters, or to the Superior's room without permission. The Portress must be summoned by ringing the bell in the Common Room, *not* the call-bell.

X Not to talk over the District,[3] or any poor person, or any other work with each other. Those who visit in the District must receive their orders from the Assistant Superior, and give in their reports to her. This extends to all works connected with the Home.

XI There must be *silence* in the Common Room after the first gong is rung for Church. At the sound of the second gong, *all* the Outer Sisters going to Church must leave the Home: so as to put a stop to the incessantly running in and out of the Home.

XII The Outer Sisters must be careful not to disturb the Sisters when they are in Chapel at Meditation, by going in late.

XIII Plain black dress and bonnet must be worn when living in the Sisterhood; but when going out to see friends it can be changed, only before entering the Common Room the black dress must be resumed.

XIV The Outer Sisters will take precedence according to the time of their admission, except in the case of any stranger coming in accidentally – and the Senior one present will take the head of the table in the absence of the Sister.[4]

XV All letters for the post must be in the box by **4.30 P.M.**

XVI It is requested that the Outer Sisters should put away their work etc. before going out, and help each other to keep their room tidy, and particularly not leave their boots about.

XVII Outer Sisters living in the neighbourhood must not be constantly coming to the Common Room for the mere sake of meeting their friends, and having a talk, as it causes much distraction, and tums the Religious House into a secular one, and those living in the House are not to be inviting other Outer Sisters into the Common Room, especially after the 5 o'clock Service.

These Rules must be read on Mondays and Thursdays at Breakfast.

All Saints Day, 1872   (signed) † Brownlow
                 Mo. Sup. of All Saints

---

[3] Districts were areas of urban poverty visited by sisters and other philanthropic women.

[4] Precedence was observed at the dining table as well as for the seats in chapel. The original version gave married women, as well as visitors, precedence over the single associates.

RULES FOR OUTER SISTERS, *c.* 1894

Outer Sisters of All Saints[5]
Sisterhood of All Saints
I.
This Religous Community aims at the perfection of a life hidden with God in devotion and charity.
II.
The Sisters associate with themselves Outer Sisters, i.e., ladies who desire to be joined to the Third Order of a Religious Community, with the view either of preparing for a religious, or of sanctifying a secular vocation.

The members of a Third order partake in the prayers and works of the Community; enjoy access to the Divine Office,[6] and so far as is possible to the superiors for comfort and counsel; and subject themselves to a Rule of Life. They are divided into two classes.

1.   Outer Sisters leading a life of special piety and mercy, whether in their own dwellings or in those of the Sisterhood.
2.   Outer Sisters married or unmarried, fulfilling duties in the world.
III.
Persons wishing to become Outer Sisters must be approved by the Chaplain and the Reverend Mother.[7]

RULE OF THE THIRD ORDER OF ALL SAINTS.

1. Of the Spiritual Life.

The one great law of an Outer Sister's life must be, to live daily more and more in the Presence of God and in the spirit of her Christian vocation. She must, so far as the wishes of her parents or her husband will admit, study moderation in dress, diet, habits, amusements, and general demeanour; avoid all singularity; be very watchful against all sins of speech, and especially against all gossip and detraction, whether the subject of conversation be secular or religious. She must keep early hours, both morning and evening, in proportion to her strength and circumstances, with a view to devotion.

2. Of Community Prayers

Every Outer Sister is bound: To say daily the appointed Prayer for the Community, by whom the Third Order is also remembered in prayer. To examine herself by her Rule before making her Communion (if possible) on the first

5   This version is *c.* 1894.
6   In other words, unlike mere curious onlookers, outer sisters could attend divine office in the Society's chapel.
7   From a very early date, the Society kept a record of the names and addresses of all outer sisters. There were a very large number of them.

Sunday in the month; and in her intentions at that Communion to include the Sisterhood and its works.

3. Of Community Work.

Every Outer Sister is bound to help the Sisterhood in any way within her power. The following will be the most usual modes: – Personal aid in works of mercy. Gifts in money and in kind, according to her ability. Collecting alms. Providing work, receiving orders for it, and promoting its sale.

4. Of Community Allegiance.

No Outer Sister may, in England, attend services not of the Church of England.[8] Nor may she become an Associate of any other Community while retaining her position in this Third Order. Nor may she, without leave from her Superior, assist at the services or in the works of another Community; nor do so at all with prejudice to the aid due to her own. If allowed thus in any degree to help other Sisters, she must while doing so observe their Rule, and in a loving spirit abstain from all comparisons, criticisms, and remarks on differences.

RULES FOR OUTER SISTERS

while living in any Community House.

1. To be punctual and exact in the observance of rule and time.
2. To render to the appointed Sister of the Common Room the obedience due to the Superior, asking her permission before doing anything not included in the Rule of the House, such as visiting friends, lending books, &c.
3. Never to waylay any Sister at her work or about the House. To inform the Portress when they need to speak to any of the Superiors. To summon the Portress by ringing the Common Room bell, not the call bell.
4. To wear a cap and plain black dress in the House.
5. To give no unnecessary trouble, not to speak to the Inmates, nor send them on any errand without permission from the Sister of the Common Room.
6. Never to go without permission to the Superiors' or the Sisters' Rooms, nor to any other bedroom than their own.
7. To retire to their bedrooms at 8.30 p.m., unless they go to Compline; if so, at once from the Chapel to their bedrooms.
8. To leave about no Roman Catholic books in any room, not even their own; and to bring no newspapers into the Common Room.
9. To study quietness and noiselessness in all their movements.

---

8 This suggests that All Saints subscribed to the idea of a 'national church': thus in England it was one's duty to be anglican; whereas if born in a catholic country, it would there be one's duty to be catholic. Many anglo-catholics extended this reasoning to include attendance at catholic churches when abroad as a duty; I doubt whether they attended lutheran services in Scandanavia, or presbyterian ones when in Scotland, however.

10. To contribute a guinea weekly to the expenses of the House.[9]
11. Of Speech and Silence.
    In a Religious House, Silence is the Rule, and Speech the exception. Most
    places – the passages and stairs especially – are places of silence; most times
    are times of silence. The exceptions are, when sent for to a Superior or to the
    parlour, and when engaged in work requiring speech, such as teaching. Con-
    versation is also allowed in the Common Room as follows: on Sundays and
    Festivals, from after Terce till Compline. On other days, from after Terce till
    10 a.m.; from 12 till 2; from 4 till Compline. But all conversation must be
    strictly regulated; there must be no frivolity, no gossip or murmurs about
    anything in or out of the House, no controversy and no curiosity.
12. Of avoiding Secularity.
    Seculars admitted into a Religious House must regard their privilege as a
    means of sanctification, and guard most watchfully against introducing the
    spirit and habits of the world, either by frequenting the House for mere con-
    venience, inviting friends for profitless conversation, or in any other way.

THE DAILY PRAYER
OF THE THIRD ORDER OF ALL SAINTS

1. O Lord Jesus Christ, we give Thee thanks for all Thy handmaids whom Thou
hast chosen in the Community of All Saints to the good part of Mary: and we
beseech for them Thy grace to be faithful unto death, that Thou mayest give them
the crown of life. *Amen.*

2. Pour down, O Lord, Thy Holy Spirit upon the Sisters in all their counsel and in
all their work: and grant mercy and salvation to all the souls for whom that work
wrought. Amen.

3. O most loving Lord, we bless Thee for our own vocation in the Third Order:
and we pray Thee to accomplish in us Thy Will, even our sanctification. Who
livest and reignest with God the Father in the Unity of the Holy Ghost, God,
world without end. Amen.

OUR FATHER.
OR THIS:
O LORD JESU CHRIST, we pray Thee, bless, and sanctify those among us who

---

[9]   Since the board and lodging of a sister cost about £15 a year, a contribution at this level more than
      covered the cost of the outer sister's visit; it seems intended to ensure that a substantial portion is
      available for the community's charitable works.

have been called to a closer life with Thee, as Sisters of the Poor in All Saints' Home; and mercifully grant unto them the grace of perseverance.

Raise up unto them Sisters that their numbers may be multiplied, and make them a blessing and a comfort to Thy poor, the orphan, the sick, and the sorrowful.

Bless all who may be brought under their roof for holy training, care, and discipline; and grant that they who leave it to enter upon their worldly callings may never forget the holy lessons they have been taught, never fall away from Thee and be led into sin.

And bless, O Lord, all in whose hearts Thou hast put the longing to live more and more to Thee alone, and give them grace to follow Thee, when Thou callest, and whithersoever Thou callest; and to us all who are associated in Thy Name for this service, vouchsafe, we beseech Thee, the increase of faith and love; and in Thine own good time bring us to the everlasting joy of Thy Presence, in the mansions of eternal bliss. Amen.

RULE OF DEVOTION FOR OUTER SISTERS OF THE SOCIETY OF ALL SAINTS[10]

1. To attend Mass on all Sundays and Holy Day of Obligation unless lawfully hindered.[11]
2. To observe the rule of fasting Communion.[12]
3. To be obedient to the precepts of the Church in regard to days of fasting and abstinence.[13]
4. To make regular use of the Sacrament of Penance.[14]
5. To receive Holy Communion at least weekly and on the greater festivals, and if hindered from Sacramental Communion to make an act of Spiritual Communion.[15]

---

[10] This folded sheet of paper was interleaved in the original. It is unclear whether it is of the same date; it is considerably more Roman in its requirements than the outer sisters' rule as given above.

[11] Anglo-catholics were advised to observe fifteen of these by the editors of the *Kalendar of the English Church*, an annual publication associated with the English Church Union. The concept is borrowed from Roman practice; strictly speaking, an anglican was required by ecclesiastical law to take communion three times a year, including Easter. Walter G. F. Phillimore, *The book of church law* (10th edn, London, 1905), p. 105.

[12] Again, an indication of how high the community was by this time. Fasting communion was considered by many anglicans to be a modern Roman innovation.

[13] Fasting and abstinence are not the same; to fast is to abstain from food for a certain time; to abstain is to refrain from certain types of food, normally meat. Examples of fast days in anglo-catholic practice were vigils, Lent and the Ember days. Examples of abstinence days were the three Rogation days, and all Fridays.

[14] Confession.

[15] An act of spiritual communion occurs when an individual is legitimately unable to take the sacrament in its physical form during a celebration of the eucharist; in a spiritual communion the person 'partakes' metaphysically, by putting themselves in the mental and spiritual position of communication, even though physical participation in communion is impossible.

6.   To offer the Holy Sacrifice and to communicate with intention for the Community[16] on All Saints' Day or within the Octave, and at least once a month, and to use daily the prayer for the Community.
7.   To make a yearly retreat when possible.
8.   To have a rule in regard to the daily practice of mental prayer, and to give a definite time each day to intercession.
9.   To avoid such late hours in rising or retiring as would hinder devotion.
10. To use moderation in dress and amusements, being careful to maintain a demeanour befitting one, who, as a Christian, is pledged to renounce the pomps and vanities of the world.
11. To be watchful against all uncharitable, detracting speech and to avoid wasting time in frivolous, idle talk.
12. To endeavour to manifest a loving spirit towards all around, thinking of their needs before gratifying personal desires.

RECOMMENDATIONS

1.   To attend Mass daily where possible.
2.   To read Holy Scripture daily.
3.   To practice examination of conscience daily.
4.   To make a day's retreat in private from time to time as opportunity offers.
5.   To recite two of the Canonical Hours daily, unless attending Evensong.

---

[16] To communicate with intention means to take the sacrament with some special purpose in mind.

PART IV

WORK

IV. 1

The Franco-Prussian War Diary

17 Sept: 1870. Left Charing Cross Station by the 8.45 P M – Arrived at Dover about 11 P M & embarked immediately in a Steamer for Ostend. We were nine in all – Mother,[1] Seven Sisters,[2] & our Chaplain the Rev[d] R. Porter.[3] Several friends & representatives of the Society as well as some of our poor people, Hospital nurses and Sisters came to see us off from Charing Cross. We all stayed on the deck of our boat for some time – there were no berths, but Mother & the other Sisters retired for rest one by one, or rather by ones & twos until Sister Cecilia[4] & I[5] were left alone – we with M[r] Porter remained on deck all night reposing on our rugs. It was a lovely night & we had an unusually good crossing – not one of our party being ill.

18th Sunday. Reached Ostend about 4 – Washed our faces in some curious little Cupboard at the corner of the Salle where we had some Coffee. After Coffee four of us set out for a little walk – hearing a Bell we were guided to the fine old Church of S. Vincent de Paul – we found several people at their devotions although it was only 5.A M – the Bell was tolling for a Funeral. On our return we found Mother anxiously looking out for us fearing we should be late & M[r] Porter was desirous we should not separate again.

6.45 From Ostend by Train to Brussels 9.30. We intended to go to Church when we had had some breakfast but the town was so full that we had to go from place to place before we could be accommodated & the people were so dilatory that we did not get breakfast till near 11 & Mr Porter assured us there was no

---

[1] Harriet Brownlow Byron (1818–87). Foundress of All Saints Sisters of the Poor. Served at Balan and Épernay ambulances.

[2] Sisters Helen Bowden, Harriet Brewer, Rosamund Buckley, Eliza Crofts, Cecilia Phillott, Catharine Williams and Sr Mary Ann. An eighth, Sr Charlotte Kripe, arrived later in the year. (There is a curiosity – the Red Cross listed a Sr Emily-Mary Howe from All Saints as being present, but she is not mentioned in the diary.) Sister Emily Mary was professed in 1863 and died in 1876; she was almost certainly a lay sister as she is described as being 'utterly illiterate'.

[3] Reginald Porter (1826–1904), ordained 1850. He became the storekeeper at Balan ambulance from 20 Sept. 1870 to 14 Oct. 1870. He was curate, St Barnabas, 1851–8, perpetual curate, Purbrook, Hants, 1861–86, and rector Laindon Hills, Essex, 1886.

[4] Cecilia Phillott (1844–1927), prof. 1870. Served at Balan and Épernay ambulances. She and Sr Catharine were professed on the same day.

[5] Catharine Williams, author of the diary (1817–1917). Born in Wales, prof. 1870. Served in Balan and Épernay ambulances.

time for Church going. We breakfasted at the Hotel de l'Europe [added in pencil but the same hand] the landlady was delighted to hear we had come out to nurse the Sick & wounded & she brought in several American ladies who were staying at the Hotel to see & admire us as we fed. We are each supplied by the Society[6] with a black leather bag for our clothes a small pouch containing brandy flask – Lint strapping & a rug & shawl: our bags & pouches marked with the red Cross. We also wear the red Cross Brassar[7] [sic] on our arm. The wounded are being brought in by Train from Arlons[8] & then covered on Stretchers to the different Ambulances,[9] followed by troups of people eagerly peeping under the cover to get a glympse of the sufferers within. Left Brussels for Arlons at Alors between Brussels & Ghent we were reminded of the war by seeing a detachment of soldiers on parade – the Belgium National Guard, farther on at the several Stations we saw wounded Soldiers waiting to be sent on by Train.

6.30 P M Reached Arlons. No one to meet us & no Conveyance to be had – we felt rather flat after our long day – however with bag in one hand & Rugs in the other we proceeded in search of L'Hotel de l'Europe which we found within half a mile of the Station. On enquiry we found that Captain Blackenbury was away – another damper – We were shewn into a room marked with the red Cross where we waited some little time before the Hon[ble] R. Capel[10] – Capt B's representative came in – It was evident at once that he looked for real work – he spoke decidedly as one used to command & had no words to waste in compliments. He said five of us were to go to Buznel[11] & be at D[r] Frank's[12] disposal – he first thought of our going tonight, but as that might be rather unmerciful we might

---

6   The British National Society for Aid to the Sick and Wounded in War, i.e. the British Red Cross Society, founded in 1870 in response to the Franco-Prussian war by Colonel Loyd-Lindsay under royal patronage.
7   Brassard, an identification badge worn on the arm by a volunteer. Dr William MacCormac, a surgeon serving with the Red Cross, commented that 'at the outbreak of war the French military surgeons disdainfully rejected the protection of the Red Cross badge. After the first battle was fought it was eagerly demanded by all of them'. *Report of the operations of the British National Society for Aid to the Sick and Wounded in War during the Franco-German war, 1870–1871* (London, 1871), p. 17.
8   Arlon, Belgium. Near the border with France, the town served as a Red Cross depot.
9   'Ambulances . . . the term ambulance is limited to an ambulant hospital formed in the time of war, and that such establishments are attached to corps and divisions, the movements of which they follow, for the purpose of affording the primary care upon their sick and wounded . . . [they are] ordinarily transported by means of wagons'. Charles Alexander Gordon, *Lessons on hygiene and surgery from the Franco-Prussian war* (London, 1873), p. 60. Gordon was the deputy-inspector of hospitals in Britain. When stationary, ambulances formed field hospitals.
10   The hon. Reginald Capel (1830–1906). Late Queen's messenger, and superintendent of the Red Cross depots in Arlon and Château-Thierry 3 Sept. 1870 – 30 Apr. 1871. The second son of the sixth earl of Essex.
11   Bazeilles.
12   Dr Philip Frank M.D. (1830–1913). Head of Anglo-American ambulance branches at Balan, Bazeilles and Montvillet. Afterwards set up Red Cross ambulance at Épernay; later went on to Switzerland to assist the interned French army of General Bourbaki. Originally an army surgeon 1855–62, he served in the empire, but went home because of ill health. He lived in Cannes, France

remain until the morning if we would start early – how early should we be ready? he was told that our time was his. He settled for us to start at 7 A M. Three Sisters were to remain until further orders Mr Capel does not think we shall all be wanted at Baznel & probably the others will have to go to Metz[13] which is expected to capitulate daily. Had supper & went to bed – probably our last bed for some time.

19 Sept: Up at 5. our Chaplain giving us a Celebration in the red Cross room at 6 before our separation. Neither breakfast or Omnibus being ready at the time appointed we did not start until 8. Mother, S. Eliza,[14] S Rosamond,[15] S. Cecilia, & I inside Mr Porter outside. We carried a white flag with the red Cross. Met & passed several waggons & other conveyances with similar flags[16] also people on horseback & foot wearing the badge. It gives us a kind of brotherly feeling towards all – here & there we pass a house with our banner flying marking a Hospital or place in some way connected with the Society: at Dourey[17] Mr Chater[18] came out & welcomed us – He & his Wife[18] assisted by Mr Crookshanks[20] one of our dressers[21] from U.C.H. have had an Ambulance here – several of the houses are still marked with the red Cross; but most of the patients have been evacuated.[22] A little further on we met Captain Blackenbury[23] on his

1868–98, retiring to London. Fellow of the Royal College of Surgeons 1871. Capt. Brackenbury paid the 'highest tribute to Dr Frank for the care with which his patients are tendered, the cleanliness and purity of his hospitals and the evident love with which he was regarded by his wounded'. *Report of the operations of the British Society*, p. 62.

13 The sole remaining French army, under Marshal Bazaine (1811–88), had allowed itself to be trapped in the fortress of Metz since 17 Aug. 1870. Eventually 173,000 soldiers surrendered on 27 Oct. 1870 after a 54-day siege.

14 Eliza Crofts (1830–1906), prof. 1859. Served at Balan and Épernay ambulances.

15 Rosamund Buckley (1824–79), prof. 1865. A University College hospital nurse, described as 'an excellent surgical nurse'. Served at the Saarbrucken ambulance.

16 The Red Cross operated volunteer ambulances from a variety of countries. These operated under the jurisdiction of either the French or Prussian army medical services.

17 Douzy.

18 Dr. Sidney Chater, surgeon at Douzy, and then Balan, ambulances, 1 Sept. – 7 Nov. 1870.

19 Mrs Annabel Chater, nurse at Douzy, and then Bazeilles, ambulances, 1 Sept. – 7 Nov. 1870.

20 H. Crookshank, dresser at Balan and then Épernay ambulances, 2 Sept. 1870 – 8 Feb. 1871. A medical student from University College hospital, London.

21 A surgeon's assistant.

22 Ambulances dealt either with casualties direct from the battle, or from the battlefield medical stations, depending on their location. Patients, if badly wounded, went home; French patients who were not too badly wounded went to prisoner of war camps in Germany.

23 Captain, later General, Sir Henry Brackenbury (1837–1914). An officer of the British royal artillery, and a professor of military history at the Royal Military Academy, Woolwich. He was the Red Cross chief of the north eastern district 3 Sept. 1870 – 31 Jan. 1871. He was responsible for the distribution of supplies and the maintenance of the ambulances in Belgium, the war zone around Sedan and Metz, and north eastern France. He went on to become director of army intelligence 1886–91, and director-general of the War Office Ordnance 1901–04. He was considered to be the 'cleverest man in the army', Anne Summers, *Angels and citizens. British women as military nurses 1854–1914* (London, 1988), p. 321.

way back to Arlons from Bazunil.[24] He was delighted to see us – wished the other Sisters had come on[25] – there was work for a dozen & more – the most fatal mistake the Society had made was in not having sent out Sisters & nurses at first[26] – how much might have been done he now fully realized after seeing what Mrs Capel[27] had accomplished. Capt. B. was quite affected as he spoke of the dreadful scenes he had witnessed & the little relief they had been able to afford the sufferers then – now he had seen a different scene & beheld with admiration Mrs Capel's[28] devotedness – how she had done the most menial & filthy offices w^h men shrank from.

4 P M Baznel[29] – the burnt Village – a picture of desolation. Church burnt – roofless houses. Chateau Baznel[30] the only house in the Village not burnt a beautiful Chateau now used as an Ambulance. Dr Webb[31] begged us to stay he had work for us all – we told him we were under orders to report ourselves to Dr Frank & could not undertake anything without his sanction – he was at Montviller[32] about a mile distant. Mr P.[33] walked there to consult him while Dr Webb's servant made us some tea & produced a Can of Australian beef as the only thing he had to offer – the house was completely gutted by the Prussians & then they departed leaving their sick & wounded destitute of everything – they are lying on the floor still but have been provided with bedding by the very people whom they had burnt out of house & home. On Mr Porter's return we learnt that Dr Frank had arranged for Mother & 2 Sisters to remain at Baznel & that S. Cecilia & I should go to Sedan. Started immediately in the same Omnibus for Sedan Mr Porter going with us. The battle Field[34] was on either side of us –

24 Bazeilles. Sometimes referred to as Baznel or Buznel. Site of a Red Cross ambulance, near Sedan.
25 Sisters Helen Bowden, Harriet Brewer, and Mary-Ann had stayed behind in Arlons.
26 The sisters arrived seventeen days after the decisive battle of Sedan 1 Sept. 1870. Thus they had missed the bloodiest fighting.
27 Wife of Mr Reginald Capel. See note 34. She commented that 'two All Saints Sisters are here now . . . which is a great comfort . . . the work would have failed from my want of experience, and I should soon have knocked up'. Summers, *Angels and citizens*, p. 139.
28 Presumably Mrs Capel.
29 Bazeilles. It was the scene of heavy fighting, before the main battle of Sedan, on 31 Aug. 1870. Captain Brackenbury described it as a 'heap of blackened ruins'. *Report of the operations of the British National Society*, p. 62. The villagers had helped the French troops against the Bavarian soldiers, and, if found with weapons, were shot out of hand. Michael Howard, *The Franco-Prussian war. The German invasion of France, 1870–1871* (London, 1961), p. 208.
30 Château Bazeilles. Sister Catharine spells this in a variety of ways throughout the 'Diary'.
31 Dr William Woodham Webb M.D., surgeon at Sedan and Metz ambulances, 28 Aug. 1870 – 8 Feb. 1871. Educated in Scotland, after the war he eventually moved to London, where he was hon. physician at the Soldiers Daughters home, Hampstead.
32 Montvillet.
33 Rev. R. Porter.
34 The Battlefield of Sedan 1 Sept. 1870. The French army of Châlons, under Marshal MacMahon (1808–93), was trapped at Sedan and defeated by nearly 200,000 Prussians. Overall 94,000 French surrendered, and 17,000 suffered death or wounds. The Prussians lost 9,000. The war correspondent, Archibald Forbes, described how he 'saw where MacMahon lay wounded and also how full the town was of troops. They were swarming, densely packed, everywhere. Of the

strewn with helmets, knapsacks & all kinds of relics, the unburied carcases of several horses still remaining with wheels of gun Carriages & heavy material. At Baloun[35] we found Dr Frank – the Mayorie[36] several houses here are filled with sick & wounded chiefly french. Dr Frank took us in to some of them the sufferers were lying on beds on the floor – Dr Frank wished he could keep us as there was great need of us but they wanted help so badly at Sedan that he felt it would be selfish not to send us on & he desired us to report ourselves to Dr Sims[37] there.

Sedan 6 P M Dr Sims out but Mr Mac Cormac[38] received us but having been directed to Dr Sims we said we must await his orders. Mr Porter then left us & Mr Beauclerc[39] kindly conducted us through the Wards of the Asfalt[40] a great Military Hospital now used as an Ambulance for french prisoners. There are 14 Wards & 2 half Wards as they are called & several out in Tents besides. Mr Mac Cormac kindly invited us to mess but we felt rather shy of sitting down with 30 or 40 people & said if it were not inconvenient we should prefer not joining so large a party. Dr Sims then arrived & it was arranged we should dine with him at 7.30. The Hon. Mr Wood,[41] whom I should have said met us in the Wards & hailed us with delight as All Saints Sisters, dined with us as well as Dr Parker,[42] Miss Nellingen[43] & a person who went by the name of the Crimean nurse[44] &

wounded, some were in churches, the houses, public buildings and others lying unheeded and jostled in the courtyards: the dead were everywhere – in the gutters trampled on by the living, in the swampy margins of the moat, littering the narrow way through the glades and the fortifications, lying some of them on the steps of the church, the sight was one never to be forgotten'. John S. Haller Jr, *Farmcarts to fords. A history of the military ambulance 1790–1925* (Illinois, 1992), p. 18.

35 Balan.

36 The mayor's residence.

37 Dr James Marion Sims (1813–83), an American surgeon. Head of the Anglo-American ambulance, formed by eight U.S. and U.K. doctors, leaving Paris on 28 Aug. 1870 and setting up at Sedan two days later. He left on the 25 Sept. 1870 to go to England.

38 Dr William MacCormac (1836–1901). Surgeon at St Thomas' hospital, London. Second in command of the Anglo-American ambulance at Sedan, 25 Aug. – 25 Sept. 1870; then chief of the ambulance when Dr Sims left, 25 Sept. 1870 – 10 Oct. 1870. Educated in Belfast, Dublin and Paris. He wrote a memoir, *Notes and recollections of an ambulance surgeon* (London, 1871). He had volunteered to see 'what military surgery was like'. *Ibid.*, p. 1. He left the ambulance to fulfil a lecture engagement in London. Awarded the Legion d'Honneur. He later served with the army in South Africa 1899–1900. He was considered the 'best decorated practising surgeon of his generation'. *Parr's lives of the fellows of the Royal College of Surgeons of England* (London, 1930), p. 748.

39 There is no record of him in the Red Cross reports. Possibly a nurse or hospital orderly.

40 Also known as the Caserne D'Asfeld, a 400-bed hospital at Sedan. Dr MacCormac noted that the hospital attended to 610 cases, of which 137 died. There were 138 operations, of which 61 subsequently died. MacCormac, *Notes and recollections*, p. 132. Sister Catharine also calls it the Asfalt.

41 Hon C. L. Wood, superintendent of hospital orderlies and nurses at Sedan, and elsewhere, 28 Aug. 1870 – 13 Feb. 1871.

42 Dr Robert William Parker M.R.C.S., surgeon at Balan ambulance, 15 Aug. – 14 Oct. 1870.

43 Kate Neligan, nurse at Bazeilles and then Metz, 15 Aug. 1870 – 13 Feb. 1871.

44 Possibly Mrs Holteman, a nurse at Sedan, and listed in the *Report of the operations of the British National Society*, p. 35.

who has charge of the nurses' Stores. We begged Dr Sims to give us definite
work or we could do little good – everything being in a State of confusion with
no organization – Mrs Beauclerc[45] told me she visited more than 100 Wards a day
on explanation I found, she meant that number of patients – Dr Sims says poor
little thing she knows nothing. He promised to arrange matters for us with D^r
Mac Cormac next morning. We were told that the D^rs had forbidden the ladies
going into the Wards after dinner or before breakfast – they all slept in the town
excepting Miss Nellingen & the Crimean – they allowed us to share their room
there being no other we could have. In the centre of it was a table covered with
bottles of medicine &c as the room was used as a kind of Dispensary during the
day – in each corner was a bed – we lay down in our Habits in spite of the remon-
strance of the Crimean who said she was quite used to Sisters having seen those
of East Grinstead[46] during her wanderings. I got no sleep from bugs which travelled in shoals over me & up & down the walls.

20th Up soon after 5 & wandered outside not liking to interfere in the Wards
until our work had been arranged. – Met a Dominican Father a little before 7.
who said he was just going to say Mass if we like to come – we followed him &
soon found ourselves in a Chapel attached to a Convent of S. Vincent de Paul –
here I heard my first Mass:[47] several of the Sisters were present coming in
through various side doors. On our return at 7.30 found Dr Sims & M^r
MacCormac arranging about division of work. They gave us each 3 Wards – the
rest being divided between 2 little Sisters of the poor, Miss Nellingen & another
lady. I find that 2 of these Sisters are here for the day & two for night – the night
nursing seems to be entirely left for them they have a Convent in the town which
they retire to when their watch is over. The Doctors are all very kind & glad to
have us – Dr Sims told us to ask for anything we wanted & he would get us as
many people to help as we liked as what he wanted was people of experience to
direct – such of the prisoners as are well enough act as infermiers[48] & are very
handy. Mr Beck[49] who used to be Mr Erickson's[50] house Surgeon is here. We find
that the French Sisters take their meals as they can & we have had permission to
join them – for to sit an hour or two over a sumptuous repast leaving our poor
patients dying & suffering cannot be right & we sat down with much more Satisfaction to cold boullon after serving out or rather assisting the infermieres in
giving the patients theirs, than in joining Dr Sim's table supplied with excellent
skill by his black Cook. In the afternoon Miss Pearson[51] came up roused as it

---

45 Not identified.
46 This was the Society of St Margaret. They did not go abroad, so she must have encountered them
    in Britain.
47 Sr Catharine's first Roman catholic mass.
48 Hospital orderlies.
49 Dr Marcus Beck, M.D., of London. Surgeon at Sedan 8 Sept. – 12 Oct. 1870.
50 Not identified.
51 Emma Pearson, nurse at Sedan 15 Aug. – 27 Oct. 1870. The Red Cross dismissed Emma Pearson

appeared by the intelligence of our arrival. She lives at an Hotel at Sedan & had not been to the Asfalt for days – the D[rs] talked of her as their hysterical patient in a very uncomplimentary manner. She came up to me in one of the Wards making a Military Salute said 'I am Commandant here'. I believe she is jealous of the attention the D[rs] pay us & is anxious to get rid of us though the poor men are dying from neglect – those in the tents especially being constantly forgotten & lie in filth unchanged & unfed. Miss Pearson tried to get the Doctors to consent to our being sent back to Bazaelle in exchange for two ladies now working there who had come out with her but the gentlemen objected. She then tried to appear civil to us &c by persuading us that we should find it more agreeable to be with our own party &, Miss Byron[52] as she was pleased to call Mother, to get us to coincide with her wishes, but I told her bluntly that we had been sent to Sedan & at Sedan should remain until we were recalled or dismissed by the proper authorities – at last she brought us word that D[r] Sims had consented to the exchange – I said I must hear it from D[r] Sims himself – D[r] Sims a most good tempered easy going man who can never say no to anyone – appeared very uncomfortable & evidently bothered. I asked whether we were to understand that we had been dismissed – he could not answer the question in that form – but said something about Miss P's wanting her own people back – but he was very sorry to lose us &c. Between 4 & 5 we started in an Omnibus with Miss Pearson & Miss Mac Coughlin[53] – found D[r] Frank then tried to appear civil to us & by persuading with M[r] Porter & S. E.[54] at Balaun[55] – Miss P tried to enter into an explanation with D[r] F but he cut her short & went on with his business. M[r] P. however entered into an angry altercation & said that he could not have 'his Sisters' moved about to suit her whims. Reached Bazuelle about 6. D[r] Webb most indignant & spoke his mind in no qualified terms to Miss Pearson. He said that these constant changes were most unfair to the patients for no sooner did they get used to one person than she was withdrawn for another at the same time he must say he would be very glad to have us. He then ridiculed Miss Pearson for being afraid of entering the part of the Chateau alloted to the fever patients w[h] made her very wroth – & the two ladies M[rs] Mason[56] & Miss Barclay[57] did not like going away so altogether there was a sad state of confusion & discord. After all this it is refreshing to turn ones thoughts towards those little Sisters of the Poor, doing their work so

and her fellow nurse, Louise McLaughlin, because of inefficiency and insubordination. Both were critical of the Red Cross's neutrality, and displayed pro-French leanings. They co-authored, *Our adventures during the war of 1870–71* (London, 1871). See also Summers, *Angels and citizens*, p. 137.

52 Harriet Brownlow Byron, mother superior of All Saints.
53 Louise McLoughlin, nurse at Sedan, 15 Aug. – 10 Oct. 1870.
54 Eliza Crofts, the assistant mother superior.
55 Balan.
56 Nurse at Sedan, 15 Aug. – 10 Oct. 1870.
57 Miss E. A. Barclay; nurse at Sedan, Sept. – Oct. 1870.

humbly & simply – no one had taken the trouble to inform them about the distribution of work – they came into the Wards as usual but found us fully employed
&directing things there – they enquired if there was anything for them to do &
we told them of the arrangement & they fell into their places at once – it was
enough for them to be allowed to minister to their suffering countrymen & they
seemed not only content but pleased that others who had been more trained in
Hospital nursing should take the lead. I found a Breton[58] among the patients but
he was delirious.

20 Sept: Chateau Bazuelle – After Miss Pearson's departure S. Ce & I were
left with a french Deaconess Mother & the other Sisters having gone before – the
Doctors are Drs Webb & Tinker.[59]

21. Slept on the floor. Up about 6. Breakfast – Coffee with condensed milk –
Australian beef & bread – no butter – Dr Webb said it was necessary we should
not go from room to room – he had divided the Surgical patients from those who
had fever & dysentry he took the latter & Dr Tinker the wounded – it was settled I
should have them & S. Ce Dr Webbs – The french lady sees to the housekeeping
& is ready to help us if required. She is very nice & talks German – her brother is
a Minister at Sedan. All the patients are Bavarians.[60] Hard at work all day trying
to get the place a little clean & straight. In the evening walked to Chateau
Mountviller[61] about a mile to get some clean Caps & Collars as we could not
divide them before going to Sedan. Met Dr Frank at the door impatient to see
Mother, who with S. Rosamond had been sent to help Mrs Capel there. He
wanted to send for the Sisters from Arlon immediately as S. Eliza was alone &
worked to death at Chateau Paupar[62] an Ambulance at Balaun which the Prussians had just given up to Dr Frank with their Sick & wounded. I offered to go at
once as it was uncertain how soon the Sisters would arrive from Arlon but D^r
Frank was unwilling to withdraw me without Dr Webb's consent – walked back
& got it – through Dr W. was unwilling I should undertake the walk after a hard
day's work & more work in store he feared I should be knocked up & useless
there was no conveyance of any sort. I proposed a horse but none was to be got –
however go I must & with a man to carry my bag & act as guide I set off walked
about 3 miles & appeared much to the relief of S. Eliza & the Doctors M^{ssrs}
Thomas[63] & Chater – Mrs Chater not yet arrived. All the patients here as at
Mountviller [are] Bavarians.

[58] Sr Catharine felt an affinity with the patients from Brittany, possibly based on the belief of a
       common Celtic origin shared by the Bretons and the Welsh.
[59] There is no record of a Dr Tinker. There was a Dr Tilghman (1846–1906), an American, in the
       ambulance.
[60] The kingdom of Bavaria supplied two army corps to the Prussian army, the I and the II, which
       together numbered 52,000 soldiers. They were involved in the fierce fighting in Bazeilles, at the
       battle of Sedan, and suffered heavy casualties.
[61] Château Montvillet.
[62] Château Poupart, Balan. Sr Catharine primarily worked in this field hospital.
[63] Not identified.

22. The hardest day yet – about 40 patients almost all helpless & only S. Eliza & I assisted by a French boy to do everything for them. Sister Helen[64] & S. M.A.[65] arrived in the evening. Mr Porter is stationed here as Store Keeper. S. Harriet[66] has gone to help at Montviller.

23. Walked to Montviller – the Chateau is surrounded by a beautiful garden & Park – it is in very good preservation as the proprietor offered it to the Prussians for an Ambulance before it was ransacked. The brushwood & branches of the fir trees have been formed into little sheds or rather wigwams where the soldiers bouvocked[sic].

Helmets, Knapsacks &c are lying about in all quarters here & there the raised earth marks graves here as in the grounds of the other Chateaux. Had tea in the kitchen with Mother & the other sisters – Mrs Capel in her thick Cap & Check Apron I did not recognise at first. Returned over the battlefield to Chateau Poupar & finished up my Birthday by making a bonfire of an infected Mattress & having my health drank in Cognac by the youths who assisted.

24. We are getting a little more straight – Dr Frank came to inspect & congratulated us on the improvement. This afternoon our french boy was taken prisoner by a Prussian in the garden but S. Helen explained & got him off – it seems that a Frenchman stabbed a German as he was posting a letter & the culprit was traced to our Garden – Poor Dudu was quite innocent & greatly alarmed – he begs he may have the red Cross Badge & follow us wherever we go. This house was very well furnished – but the velvet chairs have been used by Common Soldiers. the eider down Quilts rolled up for pillows, handsome rugs & petticoats used instead of sand bags. The reckless waste & ravages is quite distressing – the old lady, a widow, to whom it belongs comes to try & rescue what she can of her property accompanied by her maid or companion, holding bags of camphor to their noses. Of course they did not venture until the Prussians had cleared off & now we are beseiged with beggars – the people around are lying on straw as the bedding has been taken for the sick & wounded. It was quite pathetic to hear a young father, who looked not much more than a boy himself, plead for an infected bed condemned to be burn for his pauvres enfans. Mr Butler[67] called & brought us letters from England. His employment is to visit the different villages & to report to Capt. Blackenbury wherever there are wounded in want of help. Mr Porter

64 Helen Bowden (1827–96), prof. 1864. A U.C.H. nurse, she was described as 'a good medical nurse and first rate linguist' in 'Memories of an old woman', p. 60 above.

65 Sr Mary Ann.

66 Harriet Brewer (1826–76), prof. 1857. It was noted that she 'spoke French and was educated. Not trained as a nurse'. Sr Catharine also recorded in her memoirs that Sr Harriet was 'anxious to go' to France.

67 The Rev. W. J. Butler (1818–94) served with the Red Cross, 20 Sept. – 19 Oct. 1870. Co-founder of the Community of St Mary the Virgin, Wantage. Ordained 1840, vicar of Wantage 1846–80, diocesan inspector of schools 1849–80, honorary canon of Christ Church, Oxford 1872, canon of Worcester 1880–5, dean of Lincoln 1885–94.

tried to get Mr Butler to lend him a surplice[68] but as M^r B has only one he could not spare it. Mr Porter left his at Arlouns. Wrote this sitting up.

25. Sun: Mr Porter failed to arrange for a Celebration – he spoke of evensong but it could not be managed – we had an unusually busy day with an amputation in the afternoon. The Doctors are very nice & regret having nothing to mark Sunday. Having sat up last night I got my work over early & went to S. Marie at Balan for Mass & Sermon at 10.30. During luncheon a Prussian in full uniform walked in, our doors being always open, – the gentlemen immediately arose & we followed their example rising from table & receiving him with the most profound bows & curtsies as we stood in a semi-circle. I thought that at least he was one of the royal family, but afterwards learnt he was Dr Youchan[69] one of the first German Surgeons. We invited him to join our repast but he declined having already dined. He wished to see the Hospital but was in no hurry & sat down until we had finished chatting very pleasantly in french & German. In a little time Dr Frank & a train of Doctors arrived & took Dr Youchan over the place – he seemed very well pleased & said he should come another day & dine. We are constantly having people looking in upon us in this way.

26. Mr Butler came on his way to Arlons. Two English gentlemen said to be inspectors or reporters came & lunched. Mr Porter has fitted up a spare room at the top of the house as an Oratory – M^r B laughs at his distress about a surplice & says we could easily run one up – I do not see how we are to get the time.

27. Had a towel for the first time – such a luxury. Two Sheets on my bed – w^h consists of a hay & Straw Mattress on the floor – no pillow. Slept in a Nightgown for the first time since I left England. I have a brass pan to wash in. Got up with a headache & hard work to drag through my morn^{gs} work – went to lie down after giving the patients their dinner, but now I have had some tea & am able to write. Just heard the report of a Cannon. We are told that a town only 5 miles off is to be bombarded tomorrow & we may expect some wounded here – but we hear so many reports that we do not know what to believe. You know much more about the war in England than we do. The wounds are in a very bad state – some having been left 5 others 8 days without being dressed when we come. So you may imagine the smells. We are on the trot all day in this atmosphere but I am thankful to say we keep very well on the whole – & the Doctors are very careful

---

68 A loose, full-sleeved white linen vestment descending to the knees, and worn over a cassock by clergy.

69 Not identified. Allied bombing in world war II destroyed the military archive with records of German doctors in military service. The Prussian army had an efficient medical service, in comparison to the French. Each corps had a surgeon general, and two division surgeons, as well as a number of regimental surgeons. They also had civilian consultant surgeons attached to their medical units. The field hospitals were subject to Prussian medical inspection. 'The great civil surgeons who hold the highest posts in the German armies visit the different field ambulances at fixed times, when there are regular consultations with the surgeons attached to each on all cases of importance, and at these visits the operations are performed, which are decided upon after consultation'. MacCormac, *Notes and recollections*, p. 124.

of us. They have forbidden us to encounter the stench of the Wards on an empty Stomach but we cannot always avoid doing so. I have at present 12 patients all Bavarians but one a Prussian Infermiere attached to the Ambulance whom they made a great fuss about, & Dr F. has given orders that he should have the greatest attention, which he takes pretty good care to exact – he is in a room by himself with velvet chairs – his friends have stowed away a quantity of the old lady's choicest preserves in one of the cupboards of which he keeps the key in bed. He has not been wounded, but had gastric fever followed by pleurisy & inflammation of the Lungs: his room is at the top of the house & my other patients are in a granary on the same floor – they are all wounded. They seem to have quite a Jay's fancy for stowing away things. I turned out a lot of the old lady's petticoats out of their beds yesterday. They lie on Mattresses on the floor side by side in two rows. My room cuts off the granary from my other patients' room & I distinctly hear the groans on either side of me during the night. S. E. shares it. The other patients are scattered about in different rooms & divided between S. Helen & S. M. A. – S. Eliza & Mrs Chater, who has now joined us are Cooks & parlour Maids in turn. We have 2 men by day & 2 by night to help with the patients now. There are 2 or 3 women in the Kitchen but they do not do much more than talk & steal. Two Surgeons & one dresser Mr Crookshank from U.C.H. complete our establishment, we have to dress a great many wounds ourselves. I did all mine but only yesterday & all but three the day before so you may imagine we have enough to do. The patients meals are 7.30 Breakfast Coffee & bread. 12 Dinner – Soup with Meat & Potatoes. 6.30 Supper Coffee, soup, or Arrowroot, Eggs & Wine & biscuits besides with Cigars & Chocolate Each man has half a bottle of Claret a day. This is the ordinary diet but special cases are different as may be ordered. They do not like Brandy so port wine is generally given for such cases as require it. Our own meals are not very regular – the time fixed is 8 Breakfast. 1 Lunch. 7 Dinner. Some of us generally manage to get an early Breakfast so as to have our Wards straight before the Doctors come in. Some have to be up at 6 or earlier to make the patients breakfast cut bread &c. We used the preserved milk almost entirely in the Coffee. The Cans of preserved meat too are very useful but we can generally get enough meat from the butchers here – some of it is very like horse flesh. We have 10 rooms of different sizes for the patients & a barn for Cases of pierexia[70]

28. Only allowed to get up on condition I w^d go off duty[71] – the doctors always on the look out for fever after sickness, so I am sitting out writing on a garden seat – in a sort of glade looking down on the house over a tiny fountain & pond surrounded with beds of double geraniums & a row of Orange Trees on one

---

[70] Pyrexia, an infectious febrile disease, and highly contagious. Pyaemia, which was a combination of blood poisoning and fever, was also common and 'occurred only in cases in which the bones had been injured, or when amputation had been performed'. Dr Frank's report, *Report of the operations of the British National Society*, p. 111.

[71] Sister Catharine seems to have been ill the day before, as there is no entry for the 27 Sept. 1870.

side. It is so peaceful & pretty – it is hard to realize the scene of Carnage so recent here, but the vestiges remain. Helmets, boots, Caps, Knapsacks But ends of guns, Cartridges strewn about in all directions. Here & there the pots & pans as if the soldiers had snatched a hasty meal. When walking in the wood w^h is thick with brushwood I feel as one does on the Sea Shore after a Storm – a dread of coming unexpectedly on a body or mangled form – pieces of cloth with suspicious looking fragments of bone & flesh letters & diaries are also to be seen – Some of the trees riddled with Shot others cut in two by a Ball. Yesterday about 20 frenchmen were busy in burying the body of a Prussian they found here. I think it is wonderful how these french people render offices to their wounded & dead enemies – our men wait on them as tenderly as brothers Some of the wounded french come to our gates, & shake hands cordially with those of our patients that can get about – we have only 2 or 3 that can, 'he is wounded' seems sufficient to quell all animosities. But to return to my present peaceful picture. the quaint irregular old Chateau – the Village of Balum[72] with its Church – beyond the house a beautiful blue & then the background of hills. Troups of Prussians have been marching past today & yesterday. A Waggon has arrived with letters from England – & Mr Porter's Portmanteau all from Arlons. We are to have a Celebration tomorrow.

29. 7.15 A M HC.[73] at Chateau Montvillier – Mr Crookshanks drove Mr P. S. Helen & me over for it – we returned directly after. The french Ambulance has gone by – I sh^d think a dozen Waggons 7 drawn by mules. Prussian Troups are passing & repassing daily. Mrs Chater provided us with a Goose for dinner.

1 Oct. Mr Capel came yesterday with orders that 5 or 6 Sisters should go to Saurrebruck[74] to organise a new Hospital there. The Dutch have given it up & the Doctors are particularly anxious we should undertake the nursing there, but so many cannot be spared. It was settled that Mother & S. Eliza should go & S.E. wished us good bye this morning & went as far as Montviller there at the last moment it was arranged for Sisters Harriet, Helen & Rosamond to go instead.

2. Like all Sundays an unusually busy day. We had however a Celebration at 7. Miss Goodman[75] who wrote a book against English Sisterhoods joined us yesterday she has come to work with us & is particularly civil & obliging. We were told that the Prussian Inspector of Hospitals[76] would be here at 3 but he did not arrive until 5.30 we were kept in a state of suspense & again failed to have evening Service as was proposed. The Inspector was well satisfied several

---

72 Balan.
73 Holy communion.
74 Saarbrucken, Germany, which had a Red Cross ambulance.
75 Margaret Goodman, *Experiences of an English Sister of Mercy* (London, 1862). A nurse at Balan, and then Carignan, 20 Sept. – 7 Nov. 1870.
76 Prince Hans Heinrich Pless XI, born 1833. 1864 leader of the knights of the protestant Order of St John – a voluntary medical order. 1866 appointed to the second army for the war against Austria. 1870 appointed royal commissary and military inspector of hospitals and the voluntary orders aiding the sick and wounded.

German officers came with him – two spoke a little English & one said 'God bless you' in going away.

3. Walked to Montviller for some clothes. Mrs Capel who sat up last night heard Canon at 4 this morning. Dr Frank has gone to Sedan today to attend a meeting which will probably decide our future movements. The question proposed is – Are we to continue in the Anglo American Ambulance? or to have an Anglican Ambulance headed by Dr Frank?[77]

3. Dr Frank just returned from Sedan – nothing settled until he has communicated with Colonel [illegible] Lindsey.[78]

12. I have not kept my journal since the last I sent home w^h I think was about 10 days ago. There has been nothing particular to note from day to day – The Inspector General of the German Hospitals paid us another visit about the begining of last week & was perfectly satisfied – he told us the Prussians would take up the house again in six days but a day or two after he came & said he hoped we would stay on – Dr Frank told him civilly that we could not remain much longer for after the Inspector had offered to release us Dr F. had entered on other engagements. The Prussians are anxious to get their own Ambulances forward to the Seat of War & to get us to look after their old Cases but our Doctors are also desirous of moving on. They had a grand Meeting at Sedan about a week ago to arrange matters. Dr Sims an American & Mr MacComac an Irishman have been at the head of the Anglo American Ambulance – Now they have both retired[79] & the English men wished Dr Frank to be head but Dr Platt[80] the American thought he ought to be so there has been a split Dr Platt with some of the Doctors accompanied by Miss Pearson & Miss Maclouchlin have gone on to the neighbourhood of Paris[81] while we remain here awaiting orders from England. Dr Franks says it is foolish to go on to Paris where there are plenty of doctors, Sisters & nurses & of course supplies would be stopped & therefore we should be rather in the way than otherwise. He has been to Brussels to arrange matters & we shall probably go on to Brussels in a day or two. When we came here first we had 42 patients now by death & evacuation they are reduced to 15 including 3 we yesterday received from the Mayorie – we sent off 13 Convalescents this morning – they had each a new Flannel Shirt & red blanket of which they were very proud – one had no Cap so I soon picked one up for him, in the wood. They went in 3 Waggons attended by one of our Medical Staff, M^r

---

77 The work of the ambulance was winding up, as patients were transferred home, if German; or to P.O.W. camps, if French.

78 Colonel Robert James Loyd-Lindsay (1832–1901), later Lord Wantage. Chairman and founder of the British Red Cross Society. He was a veteran of the Crimean war 1853–6, and had been an equerry to the future Edward VII.

79 See nn. 37–8.

80 Dr T. T. Pratt, chief of the Anglo-American ambulance. He led the ambulance to Paris, and then on to Orléans.

81 Paris was besieged by the Prussian army from 19 Sept. 1870 to 26 Jan. 1871.

Wyman.[82] They are all Bavarians – we have had only two Prussians out of 45.
you would be amused by the jargon of language – the Bavarians speak a sort of
German patois – our Servants are french & so is Mrs Chater – Sometimes I try a
little Welsh when my German & French are exhausted & my English not understood – however we get on very well generally but when in real difficulty have
recourse to Mr Porter or Mr Chater who both speak German – Dr Frank speaks it
as well as English but his head quarters are at Montviller – They have sent
several patients away from there also – Chateau Bazaalle has been evacuated
some time & the Mayorie & other houses at Balan[83] are nearly empty. The
Mayor Monsr Sauvage is connected with the Ambulance & he & his Sister seem
to devote all their energies to it. His official residence has been filled with
wounded as well as several of the surrounding houses – Balau is a sort of Suburb
of Sedan but as they have a Church & Mayor I suppose it is an independent town.
The spire & roof of the Church are full of shot holes. The Curé[84] has just returned
from prison where he was sent as it was supposed he had incited his parishioners
to rise against the Prussians.[85] He is a Stern looking old man rather deaf – I called
at his house to ask the hours of Service. He asked if I was a Catholic? I replied an
Anglo Catholic – he said he did not understand. was my Bishop Bp of Westminster?[86] & was Dr Pusey[87] a Catholic? I am surprised at the want of reverence here
– I expected it to be so different in a Catholic country. A man & woman were
cleaning the Church the man with his hat on. Sunday one would hardly remark
unless perhaps from cleaner Caps than usual. The absence of Priests amongst the
sick & dying Struck me forcibly at first – we met them along the roads & in
every place but the sick Wards – the Dominican at Asfallt[88] being the only
exception but when one came to consider it the reason was clear, at the Asfallt
the Sick French would naturally have their own Priests & Sisters, on the other
hand it was doubtful how they would be received besides not understanding the
language of the enemy. However now we are visitted by German & French
Priests & Protestant Ministers. Our dead are however buried without any Service
simply wrapped in a Sheet & buried in the wood. We have had several people
from England enquiring for Col^r. Pemberston's[89] Grave. He fell 3 or 4 miles

---

[82] Dr John Saunderson Wyman, surgeon at Sedan, and elsewhere, 28 Aug. 1870 – 8 Feb. 1871. He
      qualified in 1867 and, after the war, practised at St Bartholomew's Hospital in London.
[83] Balan. The chateau is Bazeilles.
[84] Parish priest.
[85] Probably responding to the republic's call to arms by Leon Gambetta (1838–82), minister of the
      interior of the new republican government, which condoned resistance of any type against the
      Prussians. Howard, *Franco-Prussian war*, p. 240.
[86] The catholic archbishop of Westminster was Henry Edward Manning (1808–92), archbishop
      from 1865, and cardinal from 1875.
[87] E. B. Pusey.
[88] Caserne D'Asfeld, the main hospital at Sedan.
[89] Lieutenant-Colonel 'Kit' Pemberton, a correspondent with *The Times*, who was shot whilst out
      riding with Prussian officers on 1 Aug. 1870. See Sir John Furley, *In peace and war* (London,

from here between this & Dousey – Capt Stracey[90] & a friend of his came last week & Mr Chater took them to the supposed spot & they had the grave opened & are quite satisfied that it was the Colonel – but as he was buried without his clothes & has been a month under ground it can hardly be possible to identify him. There are 3 single graves – 2 have the names & date & are evidently cared for but the strangers grave has no mark. Mr J. Adams[91] called one day *en route* – he had just been round Paris & brought deplorable accounts of the state of destitution there – he said that they could only get one Pigeon & no other kind of meat between four or five of them for dinner – he said that it was absurd for people to go on there. Mr Adams came out for a month & has been riding on an average 35 miles a day during that time & now he is going back to England. Mr Job[92] has also called by 2 or 3 times to see how we were getting on bringing us Letters & Newspapers. His work is to report the state of things to head quarters & so get assistance & supplies where necessary. Chateau Barzaelle has been evacuated[93] – Sister Ce: has gone to Montviller. There has been a great deal of dysentry & some fever at Bazaelle but most of the Typhus has been at Montviller & have been nursed entirely by Mother & Mrs Capel. Mr Hewitt[94] one of the dressers has it now. We have no cases of fever here. I hear that Mr Wyman took our men to Bouricour[95] a Station about 12 miles beyond Sedan & saw them into Trains for Rous[96] & Munich – he did not know what w^d be their final destination but the men were hoping to be sent to their own homes. Dr Frank came & told us what he had arranged – M^r & Mrs Chater are to remain here with some ladies to help them, one of those he mentioned was Miss Goodman but she refuses in spite of all that is said & says she is going to stay with her friends the Nuns of Cursquon,[97] so Miss Veitch,[98] who is at Montviller is to come & Mrs Capel & Mr Watson to remain there with 5 patients, including Mr Hewitt who cannot be moved at present. Dr Davies,[99] an American with Color came from Pont[100] for Miss Goodman as Mrs Capel had said she was to assist him. Dr Davies is a

1905), p. 39. The *Times* report of his death (10 Sept. 1870) says he was buried between two trees on the Sedan road. A further account (11 Oct. 1870) describes his rather comfortable lifestyle while reporting on the conflict.

90   Captain Hardinge Richard Stracey, 98th regiment of foot, British army.
91   Mr J. Adams, a Red Cross official.
92   J. Robarts Job, convoy agent, 9 Sept. 1870 – 10 March 1871.
93   I.e. the patients were evacuated home to hospitals.
94   Fred Hewitt, dresser at Sedan, 28 Aug. 1870 – 19 Jan. 1871.
95   Boulzicourt.
96   Possibly Rouen.
97   These were probably the Soeurs Penitentes at Kerchsken, celebrated for their embroidery and fine needlework.
98   Zepherina Veitch, a U.C.H. nurse. She wrote that she was part 'nurse, dresser, surgeon and everything else'. Summers, *Angels and citizens*, p. 140. She later founded the Matrons Aid Society, which became the Midwives Institute.
99   Not identified.
100 The remainder of this word has been crossed out.

Westleyan (*sic*) & I believe his Ambulance is supported by dissenters in a great measure – he is well supplied with stores but wants hands or rather heads to relieve him of some of the work – he seems most energetic & self-denying, very gentlemanly & agreeable. Miss Goodman was out so he came again the next morning in his carriage to drive her back, but she positively declined – She cannot have come out on the same terms as ourselves – we having had to sign a paper declaring we w^d go wherever the Society wished us. I am sorry we have not been able to have Chateau Poupart photographed – the man promised to come but has not. Chateau Montviller has been done. This is such a curious old Chateau so full of little odd places I do not know if I have found them all out yet – such queer little room & closets with hardly perceptible doors opening out of the walls & partitions. The House was well peppered my room at the top of the house joining the granary seems to have been used for drying grapes as there are wires all across a little below the ceiling – in one Corner there is a Cupboard full of iron pots & pans out of w^h I selected an iron pot as a washing basin for Sister E.[101] & I found a large brass boiler for myself – the few washing basins which we have we have been obliged to devote to the patients & very queer use of them some of the men made. After we had been here some time I hunted up a bath amongst the rubbish w^h was a grand find & we used it in turn. I also found a great folding screen w^h I put up between us & we called it the fortification. There are two gunshot holes in the glass of one of the windows one of the balls lodged in the bedstead & I have extracted it & keep it as a trophy. I laid my mattress under the gunshot widow as I liked the air & put the bedstead behind the barricade for S. E. it had neither sacking or bars so like the Sedan Chair of old, except for the honor & glory of the thing you might be as well without for the mattress rested on the floor.

14 Oct Up at 5.30 to get Mr Porter breakfast he left at 6.30 for Brussels hoping to get to London at 6. A M tomorrow. He took a Sword & other trophies, chiefly brass ornaments off Helmets home for me. Gave the patients their breakfast & said good bye – The parting was quite affecting – they poured forth their thanks & good wishes – their eyes full of tears – I said to one you will not forget us – he sat up in bed, took my hand in his & with brimming eyes said no not so long as I live. We have given one man the name of Mermaid as he is so fond of combing his hair – he was most pathetic. Sister E. went to Montviller yesterday & as I carried her bag past him he cried out Sister you are not going to leave us. Taking them altogether we have had an exceedingly nice set of men – brave simple fellows. The Bavarians have been placed in the front of the battle & then when wounded been left for us or anyone else to attend to while the Prussian Ambulances took care of the Prussians. Our patients were about equally divided. Catholics & Protestants – all equally regular in their Devotions. When I came here

---

[101] Eliza Crofts (1830–1906), prof. 1859.

first I had 12 patients in the Granary. On going in of a morning I might have heard a pin drop – each man having his book of prayers or Testament in his hand, unless too ill. Every man can read & write. Mermaid occupied a room with another Catholic – it was most striking to hear them saying their Prayers regularly morning & evening Ý & Rʒ[102] in Latin all without books. Most of the men were fair with blue eyes but a few were dark with coal black eyes & seemed a superior race & class to the others. Mermaid was one of these – on the first evening that I arrived here I found him looking at some illustrated papers something like our Art Journal, & he called me to admire a Copy of one of Raffael's. I do not think I have told you of the tents we had put up in front of the house for severe cases Dr Frank hoping that the fresh air would keep off pyrexia, they lay on mattresses put upon stretchers & were brought out in the sun during the day – at night a lantern was tied to the pole in the centre of the tent & we paid them constant visits to see if they were comfortable or in want of anything – & of course supplied them with nourishment – I forgot to say that we had a barrel of porter[103] sent, by Miss Barclay I think, this & beer several of the men preferred to wine & asked for English bear.[104] I forgot to mention a troup of Prussians w^h I saw go by with 5 pieces of Cannon[105] one day – they returned the next & it was reported they had been defeated but we have heard no more of it so conclude the rumour is false. The people have been pilfering terribly from us – our Cook made away with a Sack of flour. They seem to think it fair that as the Prussians have taken their goods that they sh^d pay themselves back when they can – but it is rather too bad to make us suffer. We have been much tormented with flies here w^h swarm the place & get into everything, but we have been wonderfully free from vermin. I have seen nothing worse than fleas since I left Sedan. I suppose soldiers are everywhere particular in their persons but considering how long these have been lying here I think great credit is due to them for keeping themselves free from various intruders. Spitting is of course general.

8.45 A M Bid Adieu to Chateau Poupar – driving with SMA in a Waggon to Montviller a distance of about 2 miles.

11 A M left Montviller[106] in an Omnibus & P^r of horses w^h took us all the way to Arlons where we arrived at 9. P M We stayed an hour & a half at a Village about half way to bait[107] & dine. We passed n^r the supposed spot of Colonel

---

[102] Versicles and responses.
[103] A type of bitter, or beer.
[104] This appears to be an attempt to describe their accented English.
[105] The Krupp-made steel artillery was particularly deadly, being accurate and quick firing.
[106] The ambulances at Balan and Bazeilles finally closed on 27 Oct. 1870. The ambulances had treated 161 German and 119 French patients. There had been thirty-eight major operations, including twenty-six amputations. Fifty-five patients died. *Report of the operations of the British National Society*, p. 118.
[107] The horses were fed and watered.

Pemberton's Grave. We had several times projected a visit to it but had not been able to accomplish it. Our party in the Omnibus comprised Dr Frank, M^{ssrs} Wyman & Thomas,[108] Mother & 4 Sisters.[109]

10 P M Had supper & went to bed. sleeping for the first time on a bed & bedstead since I left here a month ago. It seems a long time & we have had very hard work & much to go through – but not what I consider real hardship – we have always had plenty to eat & a Mattress & blanket whenever I have been

15th – Arlons. It was supposed when we left Balan that we sh^d have to wait here some days for orders, but Dr Frank was delighted to learn on arriving here last night that it had been settled for us to go on to Meaux.[110] We are to start this morning but I have not yet heard how far we are to go today. Dr Frank has been engaged with Mr Capel all the morn^g.

10 A M Told the Omnibus is ready & we must get in at once or shall be too late for the Train. We did not know what had become of Dr Frank until we passed him & Mr Capel on our way to the Station. The gentlemen have taken our tickets we know not to what destination – they being in a different carriage. Namur.[111] Dr Frank gets out – we enquire if we are to alight? 'No go on to Brussels'. Dr Frank comes on too.

3.45 P M Brussels. Reported ourselves to Colonel Brakenbury. Orders to remain here until Monday – we are looking forward to a quiet Sunday for the first time since we left England. Walked to the Church of S. Joseph & then to the Cathedral conducted by a little french lady, although she said her dinner was waiting she w^d just show us the way & pay a visit herself to the Blessed Sacrament. Vespers had just commenced at S. Goudure's. We then walked back to our Hotel w^h we had some difficulty in finding as we did not know the name – however thanks to a kind flyman[112] who volunteered to drive with us & show us the way to the Luxembourg Station as we knew it was near that we got back in time for dinner & then wrote letters home.

16th Sunday – A day of rest at last – 8.30 AM. Breakfast. 9.30 S Goudar where we heard High Mass. 1.30 Started for L'Eglise des Carmes on foot the others going in a Fly.[113] A most beautiful Church belonging to the Carmelite Brothers. Splendid Service & Procession followed by a French Sermon preached by a Dominican – This is their Fete as they are keeping the Octave[114] of S. Teresa. On our way back to the hotel met Mr Bluett[115] who s^d Dr Frank had gone

[108] Dr Frederick Aubrey Thomas, surgeon at Balan and elsewhere, 3 Sept. – 26 Oct. 1870.
[109] Sisters Catharine, Cecilia, Eliza, and Mary Ann.
[110] Outside Paris, behind the besieging Prussian armies.
[111] In Belgium.
[112] A coachman.
[113] A one-horse hackney carriage.
[114] The Carmelites are observing the octave of St Theresa of Avila, their foundress.
[115] Dr Byron Blewitt, surgeon at Sedan and Épernay ambulances, 20 Aug. 1870 – 26 Feb. 1871. After the war Blewitt practiced in London, for a while at the London Hospital. He passed

to London to arrange matters respecting the Ambulance so we shall not leave here before Wednesday at any rate. Dr Frank had called when we were out.

17th Went out walking at 9 & did not return until near 12. Saw the Church of S Nicholas a very curious old building surrounded by Stalls for merchandise. Went over the Hotel de Ville After dinner took some letters to the General Post Office – meeting a courier who walked with me & shewed me the way – The people here are most polite in shewing us about – they seem to have plenty of time on their hands, so different to the business air of London. Visited the Church of S. Boniface where some men were erecting a Bier[116] & canopy on the top of a high table with a Pall of Black & Gold for the Coffin of Madame —[117] to be buried tomorrow. A Priest was catechising some boys in one corner of the Church & the girls were being instructed in another part. 7. P M Went again to L'Eglise des Carmes for Salut[118] & a Sermon by the same Dominican.

18th S. Luke's.[119] 7 AM. S Josephs. After Mass a Lay Brother entered into conversation with me – wished to know where we are staying, where we have been so so – the usual mode of questioning we undergo here. We wear our brass-ards & so are recognised as belonging to an Ambulance & are considered a sort of public property – everyone is most kind in going out of their way to help us to find ours. After breakfast I walked alone to L'Eglise des Carmes as I wished to examine the Frescoes. They are very beautiful. One of the Apostles on each of the twelve Pillars of the Arches supporting the Roof: one of the Articles of the Creed is illustrated under each Apostle. Round the Church are Frescoes of the Stations. S. Teresa is represented as patroness supported by her nuns. The wood-work is of carved oak & the whole Chapel quite a little gem. The fine voices of the Monks from time to time reciting their Office from the Monastery within adds not a little to the whole effect.

5 P M Telegram from Dr Frank, a Committee is being held in London today when the desirability of our going forward or not will be settled so perhaps after all we may return to England this week. Mother has just met Suigi.

20th Went to the Cathedral at 10. There is an especial High Mass in all the Churches today. Prayers for Peace & the Pope. The Doctors called but no news further than that Capt: Brackenbury is going to London. Found a most curious little Chapel up a great flight of wooden Steps & was told it belonged to Les Frères Anglais. The rest went to the Cathedral in the afternoon. I kept guard.[120]

---

through the bankruptcy courts twice, in 1879 and 1885. (*The Times*, 28 June 1879, 14 Nov. 1886.) He was still listed in the *Medical directory* for 1908.

[116] A moveable frame on which a coffin is placed.

[117] Sister Catharine apparently did not know the name.

[118] The exposition of the Blessed Sacrament, accompanied by the hymn 'O salutaris Hostia'.

[119] Feast day of St Luke.

[120] Presumably on their possessions.

21st Had a conversation with the most Saintlike SubSacristan[121] at L'Eglise des Carmers & find he can talk English.

22nd My boots cleaned for the 2nd time since I left England, so could not go out before breakfast. Went at 9 to the Chapel of the Carmelites – the Sisters joined in the Service from inside & received their Communion through the grill – there were only 2 or 3 persons in the Chapel besides myself – one an elderly lady spoke to me after Service in good English, remarked on my bearing the red Cross & gave me 2 francs for the sufferers. Mr Bluett brought us some letters but still no orders or further news – the suspense is very trying day after day we are expecting to be ordered off & are quite ashamed of being seen about but it is no fault of ours.

23rd Sunday. 9 A M L'Eglise des Carmes. 2.30 L'Eglise Saint-Sacrament – Sermon by Pére Boom. Mr Mansfield[122] called about 12 to tell us that he & Capt: B return^{ed} this morning, & it is settled we are to go to Chabourg[123] he proposed our starting tomorrow & not waiting for Dr Frank who is not expected before Tuesday, but it w^d not do for us to be separated in these times. Mr Mansfield said he was going to get pots & pans to take with us as he did not think we sh^d be able to get any again. Mr Wyman called & is very flat at the idea of going back to Chalons instead of proceeding towards Paris.

24th Mr Bluett called between 11 & 12 & took our passports. He has given me a note to Monsr Fourdrium[124] the head Doctor at the Ambulance de la Cambre as I am anxious to see some of the Hospitals here.

1.15 A M S M A.[125] & I started for the Ambulance. In the Boulvards we got into the 'American Railway' a larger Omnibus running on a train-road – our fare 40 Cent^o each. We drove on & on right into the country – at last we stopped in the middle of the road & the Conductor told us hat if we took a path across a field down a very steep hill we sh^d find the place we were in search of. The path was very slippery after the mornings rain & on either side was bounded by muddy ploughed ground, but we trudged on as best we could until we came in sight of a large Hospice at the bottom of the hill. The buildings were very extensive divided by various quadrangles – a large Steep roofed Church overtopping the rest date 1609. Originally it had been a Carmelite Convent but of late been occupied as a poor house. You may judge of the size when I tell you that at one time more than 2000 paupers were accomodated there – at present there are only between 5 & 600 & the authorities have given up the spare quads to Dr Foudrian for an Ambulance for wounds. The Church was used as a Stable at the time of the battle of Waterloo & is bare of almost all ornament & has straight forms like those in the

[121] The sacristan was in charge of the furnishings and ritual of the church.
[122] F. Mansfield, clerk with Dr Frank's ambulance 8 Oct. 1870 – 19 Jan. 1871.
[123] Châlons (sur Marne).
[124] Dr Foudrian. Probably with the Belgian Red Cross.
[125] Sr Mary Ann.

Chapel of an English Union. There are a few monuments to the former Sisters. The patients are all French. One Ward had 8 Officers but it differed in nothing from the other Wards. Several of the men came from Sedan & one I met with from Balan. I distinguished 2 Bretons but we were not able to get on very well in our Mother tongue.[126] The patients were tended by very poor kind of infermieres – I think they must have been from the work-house. We only saw 2 or 3 nurses who seemed to give their whole attention to knitting stockings & chatting to some 2 or 3 old Crones who were there but for what purpose I could not devise. After visiting the Ambulance I obtained permission to see the Establishment. Dr Foudrian & Madame were most kind & obliging wishing us to take some refreshments & presenting us with pears. I left SMA, who was tired, to rest with them while I went over the Union. It was most interesting – first we visitted [sic] the women some 30 or 40 old crones mending Shirts in another place they were spinning – others knitting. Then there was the Laundry with its various appliances – the refectories the kitchen – the Storehouse & the bake-house with its enormous ovens – here we met Madame, I suppose the Matron, who said her daughter could speak a little English. She was a girl of about 12 – who had been taught English at School but I found it much harder to understand than her Mother's French. The men were variously employed some mending the machinery, others Carding-weaving &c. The chief commodity was cow hair-brown & white which was worked up into a very strong kind of blanketing, as well as clothing for the inmates. They had lace looms but they were not at work. Bidding Adieu to Dr Foudrian & his Wife we returned home by 5.

25th – 7 A M L'Eglise des Carmes for the last time. Returned by 8 & to my surprise found S. Charlotte[127] just arrived from England with Drs Frank & Webb. She has brought letters from the Princess Xtian[128] to the Princess Alice[129] & is to proceed to Durnsladt[130] tomorrow – there she will be joined by the Sisters from Saarbrucken. After dinner I went with Mother in search of some essence of Celery, w^h Dr Frank wished us to get to flavour Leibig[131] with, but after going into about 20 Shops we gave up the Search as fruitless & after paying a last visit to L'Eglise Saint Sacrament returned to our Hotel for Coffee & went to the Station by 4. Here we found Drs Frank & Webb – the former went with us. Dr Webb waits to see S. Charlotte off tomorrow. The other gentlemen came with the

126 Presumably Welsh.
127 Charlotte Kripe (d. 1879, in South Africa), prof. 1870.
128 H.R.H. Princess Helen of Schleswig-Holstein (1846–1923), daughter of Queen Victoria, married to Prince Christian of Schleswig-Holstein, head of the ladies committee of the British Red Cross.
129 H.R.H. Princess Alice of Hesse-Darmstadt (1843–78), daughter of Queen Victoria, and an organiser of the Darmstadt ambulance.
130 Darmstadt, Germany.
131 Sister Catharine is referring to Liebig's extract of beef, invented by Baron Justus von Liebig (1803–73) about a decade earlier.

waggons. Mr Thomas returns home. Took Tickets for Namur it being doubtful if we can get on further by rail.

7.30 P M Givet[132] – Find that we can get on part of the way by train tomorrow, so hope to get to Chalouns[133] on Saturday instead of Sunday as was thought. The Waggons & horses did not arrive until 12 P M as they came by a *Slow* Train – leaving Brussels at 12.30. I though we travelled very Slowly but I afterwards learnt it was an Express.[134] The Town gates were drawn up before they arrived – permission for the men to come through was obtained with difficulty but the poor horses had to remain locked up in their boxes – the authorities said they w^d have given leave if there had only been 3 or 4 horses but *17* might be part of a Cavalry Troup.

26th Givet. 7.30 Church. Returned 8.30 but no preparation for Breakfast w^h is not until 10.30. People taking Coffee in their rooms so we had some to wait – & amused ourselves in admiring the large Glass Cupboard in the Sal à mangé[135] full of such pretty China – Cups, figures & all sorts of curiosities.

10.45 Breakfast. First Slices of Beef & Potatoes. D^o of Mutton. Then Chicken & apple Sauce. Butter, Cheese, Pears, Walnuts & Claret. This is such a queer old Hotel. We had 2 bedrooms between 5. One room had 2 Bedsteads with 3 Cupboards fitted in between with glass doors lined with chintz. Givet is a strongly fortified town & very interesting but as it has poured all the morning we cannot walk out. When we reach Chareville[136] we shall only be a few miles from Sedan – we all feel rather flat at the thought of returning to our old neighbourhood as it would have been better for us to have waited at Balan & gone direct from there to Chalous[137] if we had known. It seems the Society in London took a panic about money as so much has been spent but finding how very economical Dr Frank had been they have allowed him to have an Ambulance of his own the expenditure limited to £2000. Of course he is anxious to do as much as he can for the money. The ladies of the Committee, especially the Princess Christian, interested themselves much in his favor & he proposed it sh^d be called the 'Ladies' Ambulance'. It is a very pretty turn out – first a most elegant little Omnibus with

---

¹³² Givet is a town in northern France. It is situated on the Meuse, and is bounded on three sides by Belgian territory.

¹³³ Châlons.

¹³⁴ Dr MacCormac described how 'for a moving ambulance, the smaller the quantity of stores taken the better, and these without exception should be carried on horses or mules. The wagons are a serious impediment . . . what is most needed are a few cases of surgical instruments and appliances, some medicines, chloroform and carbolic acid, one moderate sized tent, and half a dozen stretchers of the simplest construction to carry the wounded and to serve as beds. These, and some tins of preserved foods and biscuits, are all that need be carried about. For whatever else may be required, one must trust to the supplies of the place in which one may happen to be'. MacCormac, *Notes and recollections*, p. 27.

¹³⁵ Dining room.

¹³⁶ Charleville.

¹³⁷ Châlons.

Cane Sides & is supposed to be large enough for 6 Dr Frank & our 5[138] selves but 4 is as many as can travel comfortably – it belonged to Mad^m Courobert the Marechal's Wife.[139] We are followed by 6 Fourgons[140] – light covered waggons on Springs – One four in hand – one Unicorn & the rest drawn by pairs – the Waggons are quite new & bright painted in different colors & each carrying its red Cross flag. We have eleven men headed by Mr Laws the Foreman of Transport – he is the Coachman of the Waterloo Coach from Brussels – two of the men are Pensioners acting as Commissionaires.[141] Our medical Staff Dr Frank, Mes^{rs} Kane[142] & Crookshank.

26th – Dr Webb with Mes^{rs} Wyman & Bluett[143] are to follow us with additional Stores some of w^h have not arrived from England. Mr Mansfield our little Store keeper also accompanies us. This has been our hardest day such a trial of patience. First the long waiting for breakfast – Next having got to the Station at one we had near an hour to wait before Starting for Nouson[144] w^h we reached about four. We had pouring rain all the way but as far as we could see through misty windows the country was very picturesque, by far the most beautiful we have passed through. The Ardennes peaking Cliffs with hanging woods in bright Autumnal foliage in some places down to the very edge of the river w^h the railway skirted the greater part of the way. At Nouson the only accommodation was a dirty little Waiting Room or rather slip of a room – the 1st Class being divided by the 2nd & 3rd by a partition with a hole in the centre for a Stove w^h thus served for all. On the opposite side was an old grandmother with her grandchildren who had escaped from Charlville their mother preferring to remain there & share the fortune of her soldier husband. They were nice looking children & peeped at us through the opening above the Stove. Dr Frank induced by degrees all but the youngest to come in to us but the little one was resolute in spite of biscuits & sugar. Here we stayed in this dirty pokey place from 4 till 7. There was no Refreshment room – the gentlemen had some bread & butter at a Café but we declined waiting in the expectation of being off every minute. About 6 Mes^{rs} Kane & Mansfield rushed in in great excitement, what D^r F calls a panic, & said the Station Master had forbidden them to go or in getting the Fourgons off the Train – he had given them no assistance but the gentlemen & men had been hard at work until now when the Station Master bade them stop & walked off with the keys in his pocket leaving the poor horses for another night in their boxes. To add

138 Mother superior, sisters Catharine, Cecilia, Eliza, and Mary Ann.
139 Possibly Madame Canrobert. Marshal Canrobert (1809–95) was VI corps commander, who had repulsed the élite Prussian guard at the battle of St Privat 18 Aug. 1870, until outnumbered five to one. The remainder of his corps surrendered at Metz.
140 Ambulance carts.
141 Uniformed convoy attendants.
142 Henry Kane, dresser 28 Aug. – 28 Nov. 1870. A medical student from Dublin.
143 Drs John Wyman and Byron Blewitt.
144 Nouzon.

to our perplexity we were told that the gates of the town,[145] w^h was about half a mile off were probably shut for the night & even if we did get in there was small chance of our finding room. So Dr Frank who takes things very easily & makes the best of everything – said we could sleep very comfortably on the *floor*. I looked down & made an internal resolution not to quit my chair – for by this time we had been provided with chairs of one sort or another – the filthy floor in the stifling atmosphere of a charcoal Stove was to say the least of it not inviting. In a little time the gentlemen returned with fresh news – they had found a most obliging man who had duplicate Keys & said he w^d get the horses out if we decided on going on in the Omnibus in such tremendous weather hail, sleet & rain – he thought the gates of Charlville w^d probably be closed & we sh^d in that case have to spend the night in the Omnibus & at the same time run the risk of falling into the hands of marauders[146] who were scouring the country. We waited in breathless silence for the decision of our chief & to my unutterable relief the word was 'forward'. I think Mother cast rather longing glances towards the Stove & floor but she had a sick headache & a slight operation of Dr Frank's by pressure on the nerve incapacitated her from taking any part in the matter. Our poor tired people resumed their work & a little before 7 we were told that the Omnibus was ready – but now a fresh obstacle arose our French Coachman did not know the way – so the next thing was to go to the Mayor for a guide – a man volunteered to come & at last we were on our road & reached Charlville in about an hour. driving up to a good Hotel without opposition. The Landlady apologised for having no soup as she had given it all away to a boy who had met with an accident but Dr Frank delighted her by producing some extract of Beef & thus enabled her to complete her dinner.

27. 9 A M Went to a fine old Church with Mezzotinto[147] paintings of the Stations. We have to await the arrival of the Fourgons here – & then the horses will need rest until tomorrow.

11 A M We walked with Dr Frank to Mezieres a good mile from Charloille.[148] He was stopped by the Centinel & his passport & credentials had to be produced: we have not had ours asked for yet since we came out. Mr Bluett took them to the authorities at Brussels but they civilly declined looking at them. Dr Frank asked to be directed to the Commandant's & a soldier with gun & bayonet conducted us to his house by the barracks: we walked up & down while Dr F. had an interview with the Colonel until his Wife beckoned us in from the window & begged us to

145 Charleville-Mézières was a two-town conurbation. It was a fortress with a French garrison, which fell to the Prussians on 2 Jan. 1871.
146 After the defeat of its main armies, France sanctioned the *francs-tireurs*, an irregular body of troops, more like a guerrilla force, to operate against Prussian supply lines. However lawless brigands also operated under this guise. This blurred the distinction between combatants and non-combatants, and increased the suspicion of foreigners.
147 Mezzotint painting – a print produced by a method of copper or steel engraving.
148 Charleville.

rest. After some time D^r F joined us with the Colonel who was all politeness & had given a safe conduct to D^r F for ourselves and all our belongings. He also gave us permission to see the Military Hospital. On our way there we were over-taken by the other 3 gentlemen who had just arrived in the Fourgons. The Hospital was nursed by French Sisters – there were few wounded chiefly cases of Typhus, Dysentery, & Small pox[149] – the latter Wards D^r F prohibited our entering – The beds Struck us as being very close together & as all the windows were shut the atmosphere was stifling: I found one or two Bretons among the sick – I can generally tell them – they are such a wild looking race. We after-wards visitted an Ambulance at Charlville. It was a most interesting building – a Monastery of the Christian Brothers – who had given it up to the sick whom they ministered to though part seemed to be nursed by Deaconesses. The building was lofty & well adapted for the purpose but the windows were all closed as usual – in other respects everything seemed very nice & clean – the patients had hair mattresses the first I have seen since I came out.

28th – S. Ce. was stopped by the Superintendent of the Police as she was going out for Church this morning, he said we must all keep indoors, so she ran up to us followed by the landlady in a dreadful state of fright & excitement. Mother went down with our Passports & Papers from the Society & soon put it quite straight with Monsieur who was full of bows & apologies hoping we w^d excuse it in time of war &c &c & gave us permission to go out in future without let or hindrance, w^h we immediately acted upon by going to Church at once. There was a crowd of the Guard Mobille[150] outside but on the Superintendant's speaking to them they dispersed. Hotel Ducal is very comfortable & beautifully clean – the people most civil & obliging. It seems quite empty as we have the Sal a manger to ourselves. Mes^rs Kane & Mansfield are seized with another 'panic' they say that the french people are annoyed by our being at this Hotel as the people are considered to favor the Prussians – & the Colonel at Givet was very angry we had not asked for a safe conduct from him – he told Mes^rs Kane & Mansfield he knew we should not get on without & no doubt we sh^d be sent back like another Ambulance some time before. This Hotel with many of the houses here are most picturesque with unusually Steep roofs.

9.30 A M Started for Attigny a distance of about 25 miles the Fourgons having left at 8. our route lies through *Merzieres*. Here we found Mes^rs Kane & Mansfield in high excitement – the Fourgons had been stopped by the soldiers who presented their guns & threatened to fire if the[y] moved on. We were

---

[149] The Prussians, unlike the French, had vaccinated their troops against this disease. During the war, the Prussians had 483 cases of small pox; the French had 4,178 cases, as well as some 2,000 deaths from the disease. Valentine A. J. Swain, 'The Franco-Prussian war 1870–1871: voluntary aid for the wounded and sick', *British Medical Journal*, III (1970), 514.

[150] *Garde Mobile* – untrained army recruits aged under 30; originally, a reservist force, but now forming a large part of the new French armies.

surrounded on all sides by armed men in the greatest state of excitement[151] –
Why we knew not – had the Commandant proved false? Or had our men by any
mismanagement provoked hostilities? There was no opportunity for explanation.
At last we saw the Commandant a fine old man – his grey locks uncovered & his
whole deportment one of rage & fury. Certainly his appearance was not calculated to mitigate our worst fears. He passed the Omnibus like a furious Tiger but
french politeness still held possession of him & he bowed in passing notwithstanding his wrath. We followed in the Omnibus at a Funeral pace the Commandant clearing the way until we came to the Fourgons & found Dr Frank who had
jumped down at the first stopage & gone we knew not where. At last we all
moved on headed by the Commandant & aided by his Staff. When we came to
the last Bridge there was a tremendous skuffle an Officer was arrested & carried
off kicking & struggling & expostulating.[152] When we were clear off D^r F
explained to us what had taken place. The Fourgons had been stopped as I
mentioned – the gentlemen went immediately to the Commandant who gave
them a written order so that they might proceed unmolested – this had no effect –
the Guard Mobille was on Guard & their Officer paid no attention to the Colonel's Order. The man rummaged the Fourgons & opened several packages. one
contained Salt w^h they said contemptuosly was not fitted for the Sick. M^r
Crookshank, who is always ready in his own quiet way, took off his hat &
making a low bow said pardon Monsr. I was not aware that you were a Doctor.
Another Case they affirmed contained Champage w^h on being opened &
disclosing a quantity of empty tins caused great amusement. They also tapped the
bottoms of the waggons w^h they declared were false & that ammunition was
stored between. The gentlemen continued running backwards & forwards to the
Commandant who wrote 3 Orders successively but finding they were not heeded
he came out himself & put the Officer on guard under arrest. The Com^t. told D^r F
that he was ashamed of his countrymen. This is the first time that the red Cross
has not been respected. We proceeded without further interruption until we
reached the Prussian Outposts about ¼ of an hour from Meziers – Francheville[153]
– here we were challenged by the Centinels, & Mr Mansfield who speaks german
& french perfectly alighted & asked to be conducted to the Officer in Command
– he was marched off to the Village between two Soldiers & we had to wait his
return. Mr M. shortly made his appearance having found the Officers most agreeable & ready to facilitate our movements as far as they could. At Boussor[154] a
railway Station & Village 12 miles from Sedan every house seemed full of

---

[151] Dr Frank reported how 'an excited mob surrounded our wagons, crying out that we were taking
       provisions to the Prussians'. *Report of the operations of the British National Society*, p. 119.
[152] Dr Frank commented that 'we were allowed to proceed on our journey, followed by the hootings
       of the crowd'. *Ibid.*, p. 119.
[153] Florenville.
[154] Boulzicourt.

soldiers – the officers most kind & gave us a dragoon who rode before us to the next Station. Here we were told that the country was infested with maurauders who were constantly shooting at the Soldiers on every opportunity 19 were wounded yesterday –The Soldiers are in a terrible way they are brave fellows & do not shrink in the Field but to be potted from behind a hedge is quite another thing & they are much exasperated – they have caught 16 of these marauding peasants, & they are to be shot at 1 o'Clock today in a neighbouring field tied hand to hand.[155] The Officers said they would gladly give us a guard but they thought it might only provoke hostilities – they thought we sh^d probably be plundered but hoped we should not be fired upon if we did not make any resistance – they sent however a soldier with us to explain to any Prussians we might meet: we soon met a large troup & our guide quietly slipped down from the Fourgon & returned with his companions. We met several Waggons driven & guarded by Soldiers. We stopped at a farm house for the horses to get wind & water & we went in & had some beer & bread & curd cheese – w^h was about the consistency of cream cheese – Sharp but not bad tasted when you summoned sufficient resolution to do so – the outside being all mildewed & smelt like – I won't say what – the gentlemen brought part of a leg of mutton stuffed with garlic w^h they had secured from dinner. We stayed here about half an hour thinking it w^d be our only rest, but when we were ready to start we learnt that there was a village a couple of miles off where the horses c^d be put up. Mr Laws said the horses required an hour & a half or two hours rest so we had to turn out notwithstanding the risk of so far delaying our journey. We paid a visit to the Church w^h was nothing remarkable – then some of the Sisters went into some cottages where they were offered wine &c. We left the Village about 4 & drove on & on through a barren unininteresting country for miles without seeing a human being or habitation gradually the twilight came on – then the moon rose & we speculated on the probability of a change in the weather, it had been wet of late, my thoughts however were far distant – I strained my eyes through the failing light expecting each moment to see the maurauders appear on the horizon – until at last even that was shut out & we drove in silence through a dark wood – there was no ambush – & we clattered up the Streets of Attigny without opposition. We no sooner halted than we were beset with invitations from the inhabitants who wished to house 'Mes chère Soeurs' but we declined all with thanks & went to the quiet old-fashioned Hotel w^h we found very clean & comfortable. We arrived at 7 – the landlady apologised for not been able to procure any meat as the butcher had

---

[155] Helmuth Von Moltke (1800–91), the Prussian chief of staff commented that 'the newly formed French armies have now all been gradually defeated on the open battlefield, but we are unable to be everywhere; minor ambushes cannot be prevented and are punished by pitiless severity. A handful of loafers singing the Marseillaise with guns and flags break into houses, shoot out of the windows, and then run away out of the back doors, and then the town has to suffer for it. How lucky are those places which have a permanent enemy garrison in occupation'. D. G. Williamson, *Bismarck and Germany 1862–90* (London, 1998), p. 105.

gone to bed – so we dined on Omlet & poached Eggs. A french Doctor who has an Ambulance here called as we were Sitting down to dinner & remained for some time chattering away as frenchmen do chatter much to the detriment of D^r F's dinner. The frenchman wanted opium &c for his patients – all Prussians. The Prussians have marched through this town twice – once on their way to Metz & afterwards to Paris when they marched through for 8 hours consecutively – they met with no opposition here & so have treated the inhabitants very kindly, but they pillaged the Ambulance even taking the utensils w^h had been provided for the Sick – drank what they could of the wine w^h had been bought for the patients & carried off the rest – leaving their own wounded behind wholly unprovided for.

29. 7 A M Church. On our return we found the french D^r waiting for D^r F anxious to show him the Ambulance so poor D^r F had to go off before his break-fast. The Ambulance was nursed by french Sisters & every thing was very clean & nice. D^r F was taken to see one of the Sisters there who had caught Typhus fever from nursing the Soldiers & was not expected to recover. There were no wounded among the patients all fever & dysentry.

9.30 A M Started all right our Fourgons having been watched during the night by 4 men procured from the Mayor – Suippe[156] is about 25 miles from Altigny[157] we baited at a house rather more than half way it was a lone house & the only place we were told we could put up at. the gentlemen brought some raw sausages w^h Mr Mansfield enjoyed in that State but Mr Kane had some cooked for the more fastidious. The people of the house brought us bread & cheese & wine & also some Veal w^h was brown outside but quite raw within. There were a lot of cones[158] stowed away in one of the lofts for winter firing. There was a very deep well in the farm yard – one of the men threw a stone in & it took 4 seconds before we heard it struck the bottom. I got leave here to ride in one of the Fourgons w^h was a great relief – two days cramped in the Omnibus was not pleasant – My driver a native of Brussels c^d. not speak any german & only a little french – his native tongue being Flamand[159] – however we were able to converse quite as much as I wished – I held the reins for him to light his pipe – he asked if I was not afraid but seeing that I could handle them he asked me how I had learnt to drive & if we kept horses at our Convent. He told me that English & german were taught in the Schools at Brussels now as well as french & flamand.

5 P M Reached Suippe as the clock Struck but had to wait near an hour while matters were arranged with the authorities. The town is in the hands of the Prus-sians who have entered without opposition & consequently have treated the inhabitants with great consideration, as they usually do when unopposed – only

156 Suippes.
157 Attigny.
158 Presumably pinecones.
159 Flemish.

making requisitions for money &c. two neighbouring villages have been burnt to the ground – in one of them two Zouaves[160] had fired on the troups from a window – a Priest who had incited his people to oppose the invaders was dragged through this town tied to a Cart wheel. The Prussian Officers received D^r F here as in all other places most courteously but they wondered we had reached the place in safety & said we had run the greatest risk in coming without an escort. Some of the gentlemen went to the mayor for a watch for the Fourgons. In the meantime we were beset on all sides with invitations for the night. A Sister who had followed us up the town pressed us to return with her to her Convent. She said their shutters were shut as they always are of course in the evening, but hearing our Fourgons pass she looked out, not from curiosity she assured us, & seeing Sisters she was immediately inspired with the desire of offering them hospitality as far as her resources would admit of – so she begged Madame to accompany her & they followed us until we stopped in the Market Place. I was much taken with the idea of a night in a Convent, but Mother foreseeing difficulties likely to arise declined the invitation with many thanks but ma Soeur was not to be repulsed & still implored us to grant her request in the kindest manner. Our conversation was interrupted by Mr Mansfield, who had been seeking accommodation for us – he said that all the Hotels were full excepting one outside the town which had one very bad room containing 6 beds disengaged – he therefore strongly advised our accepting the Sister's offer but Mother said it could not be. In this dilemma Mr Kane came up & said there would be no difficulty in our getting lodgings as everyone was offering beds for mes chères Soeurs. A worthy ironmonger Monsr Camus was first in the field & came forward with Madame his Wife – Mother closed with this proposal at once – their house was close to the Market place & in sight of our Fourgons – so we alighted & followed our host the Sister accompanying us & chattering all the time most good naturedly without any apparent displeasure at our preferring her more favored neighbours. We passed through the Shop into a snug little parlour with a bright fire on the hearth & in a little time we were each presented with a chaufrette.[161] After the affairs of the morning Mother said there was to be no Church going tomorrow, however the Sister, who sat with us until dinner was served soon suggested that we should wish to go to Mass in the morning – Mother enquired the hour & our hearing the first was at 8 said we should not be able as we had to start early – the Sister then proposed we should call on the Curé who she knew would give us a special Mass if on our informing him of our case. Here was a grand difficulty – our entertainers had taken us in supposing us to be good Catholics – it w^d never do to hurt them by informing them that they had housed a lot of heretics – for Sisters not to go to Mass on a Sunday w^d be a scandal to go & not to make our

[160] These were the Papal Zouaves, élite soldiers, who came over from Rome with the withdrawal of the French garrison from there. Their emblem was the cross and the sacred heart.

[161] A footwarmer.

Communion remarkable but nothing daunted Mother simply stated that if they could oblige us with breakfast at 7.30 we sh^d then be able to attend Mass after. In due time our Supper was served by the Grandmother a dear old woman who wept alternately tears of distress for the misfortunes of her country & those of joy at the honor of entertaining our poor selves – She was assisted by Marie a pretty girl of 14 – I fancy the only child of Madame Camus – Marie is being educated at a Convent at Rheims but owing to the troublous times she has remained at home this half. When our meal was served the Sister wished us good bye or rather good night & we sat down to most excellent Soup, followed by a Kind of Omlet – Marie's best preserved gooseberries & wine. We soon retired to rest in rooms & beds: equal to those of a gentleman's house – the Camus seem well to do – everything is very good & Madame quite a Superior person.

30th Sunday. Up soon after 6 & descended to Café au lait & long rolls – Madame insisting on our taking the rolls that were over from our breakfast to eat by the way.

8 A M. Marie conducted us to Mass – Afterwards outside the Church door we found our Sister friend & two other Sisters waiting for us – She returned with us & sat some time until she said she must go home for breakfast, so with many adieus & a picture from Mother the Sister took her leave. Mother says this is the nicest foreign Sister she has met for years. – She asked no questions & was over-flowing with Kindness. I took her for about 30, but Madame said she had been Sister Superior in this place for 20 years. We sat expecting to be summoned to Start every minute – Mother & the Sisters presenting pictures. – At 10 we were off – I still Keeping to my beloved Fourgon & little brown horses – the distance to Chalons is only 28 Killomaitres about 18 miles. After driving about two thirds of the way we pulled up at a village where the peasants seem to have just come out of Church – the horses were baited on hay & water without being taken out. We have travelled very slowly the road being on the collar the greater part of the way – from Mezieres we have crossed the Ardennes a fine open Champagne country, but the hills [were] of that smooth undulating form common to chalk foundation. A great deal was tilled & sown with wheat – but yet we seldom saw a habitation of any kind & a human being was a rare sight. Here & there the land-scape was broken by a windmill or solitary tree something like the country around Brighton occasionally we passed deep hollows lined with trees – in other places there were plantations of tiny Firs – on the whole the country was most dull & uninteresting D^r F tried to create a little interest by telling us it was infested with wolves – it w^d be a pleasant country for a gallop but easy riding. In one place we met a Shepherd followed by his Sheep. The rails of the railway between this & Nouzan have been taken up by the french – the telegraph wires have also been cut. A red cross flag was tied to one of the posts – probably dropped by some Ambulance on the road – I must not forget to mention a Soli-tary buzzard we saw perched on a tree. At last I spied the Spires of Notre Dame of Chalons – the square towers of the Cathedral appeared at the other end of the

town. D^r F, who had ridden with the other gentlemen in the four-in-hand Fourgon today alighted & got into the Omnibus telling the drivers to go slowly as we sh^d probably be stopped – we proceeded at a Slow funeral pace until we reached the town Hall without opposition. 1.30 P M

6 P M Chalons sur Marue.[162] We are prisoners[163] – the town is in the hands of the Prussians, but we are in the hands of the French – But this requires explana-tion – We arrived at the Town Hall between one & two & drew up in a line – you may picture our little Omnibus & 6 great Fourgons in front of a Town Hall in a large Square – the Hall apparently full of Soldiers – On the foot pace above the Steps are Sentinels with their bayonetted guns – D^r F is of course surrounded by Prussian Officers in various uniforms – the inhabitants crowd round anxiously trying to gather what this new arrival portended – the medical men are in a great state of bustle – the Ambulance men of different nations distinguishable by their red cross badges – that man with a red rose on his white cap is we are told a Polish Count – that fine looking man with a grey beard is my zealous countryman Dr Lewis[164] – he is in anxious conversation with one after another drawing them aside & whispering what to judge from the mystery may be most important communications – at last he has got D^r F & there seems no end to their conversa-tion. In the meanwhile we have been delighting the populace by our various manoeuvres three times we drove round the Square & arranged ourselves in various positions our horses were next taken off & then put on again. An old man from one of the neighboring houses came to the Omnibus & invited the Sisters to visit his house & refresh themselves, but they w^d not alight & finding we were going no further I dismounted from our Fourgon & joined them a little before one of the gentlemen came up with a billet[165] for 5 Religieux on S. Joseph's, 2 Soldiers w^h had been put on previously being crossed out. All the Hotels are full so this billet was provided for us. We were accordingly conducted to S. Joseph's & after some explanation we were shown into a Sitting room to await the arrival of Mademoiselle Grignon the head of the house – She enterred, a tall woman of between 40 & 50 wearing a black Cloak with quilted hood drawn over her bonnet, & received us with cold politeness & said she had only one small bedroom for us all – 5 – She was accompanied by an attendant & others followed on various pretexts – They were all dressed much alike with Cardinal Capes like their dresses & white Caps tied closely round. About 4 we were served with

---

[162] Châlons sur Marne. The town was an evacuation site and receiving station for the Prussian armies investing Paris.

[163] This refers to their experience when accommodated in an orphanage in the town under a misunderstanding.

[164] Dr James Lewis (1817–90), a surgeon with the Red Cross, whose 'advice on sanitary matters was greatly prized by the authorities', *Report of the operations of the British National Society*, p. 120.

[165] A practice by which soldiers were accommodated free of charge in the homes of an occupied village or town.

broth & the beef w^h made it on a separate dish – it was boiled to rags & so
Stringy that we called it charpee – Curd Cheese, Pears Grapes & a bottle of wine
(this was our usual dinner.) One of the old women sat with us during dinner &
then she was relieved by another – if we went out of the room we were followed
by one while another kept watch in the parlour – We asked to be shown our
bedroom but were told it was not ready. Mother & S. E. went out hoping to get
Salut at the Cathedral – I went to Notre Dame w^h is close by – there I learnt that
the only Salut at this hour 5 was in the little Chapel of the Sisters of Perpetual
Adoration a man volunteered to shew me the way & I got in just in time – to our
mutual Surprise I found Mother & S. E. there – After Salut one of the Sisters read
out a Meditation. On our return to S. Joseph we found that our Sleeping apart-
ment was a long Corridor, with a little Cell for each of us curtained off – there
was a bed across the upper end commanding a view of the whole – this was occupied by our night watch. Mademoiselle G. said she did not wish us to go about
alone & therefore she w^d give us one of her women as a constant companion –
this old body was more benign in appearance than the others but she kept a strict
surveillance & always accompanied us up & down to our Cells &c. She took
snuff largely w^h did not improve the atmosphere of a small room with 6 persons
having meals as well as sitting there. At 8.30 we retired to rest having been
desired to go up together. We were conducted by a guard before & behind to our
Dormitory where our day watch resigned us to the one for the night who after
lighting our Candles retired to the bed at the end.

Vigil of All SS.[166] 5 A M – a regular tramp past us, the Orphans coming from
their dormitory. At 6 our Cells were enterred [sic] by our Keeper who lit our
Candles & said it w^d be convenient for us to arrange to go down together. We
therefore asked to be conducted to the Chapel for Mass at 7. Our attendant knelt
beside us & kept guard the whole time – then she conducted us to the Sitting
room for breakfast & there resigned us to the other. We were asked in the most
supercilious manner 'of course you eat meat today' Mother answered 'no' but
they w^d not believe it & another came to ask again – Mother said 'why it is the
Vigil of All SS we are not heretics' – this shut the old dame up so completely that
she did not open her mouth for some time. They have had two Prussian Deaconesses billeted on them here & took us for the same – S. Josephs had been an old
Benedictine Convent & when the Nuns left – Mademoiselle Grignon seems to
have bought it & with some other women, not Sisters devoted themselves to the
maintenance of 40 Orphans & as many old women, now a small Ambulance for 8
wounded is attached. Mes^rs Kane Crookshank & Mansfield called in great wrath
– they said there was nothing to be done here – that D^r F was being talked over by
the Commandant & Dr Lewis who is cracked. Mademoiselle told Mr M. that our
being here was contrary to the Convention of Geneva & she c^d not keep us after

---

[166] 31 October, the day before the feast of All Saints.

Tuesday. Presently D^r F & Dr Lewis arrived – D^r F so bright & sanguine – he had just seen 600 wounded come in & he was going to take a large house for 200 beds at once & had had 60 beds in another Ambulance assigned to him but as there were french Sisters already working there we sh^d not be wanted, but we sh^d have plenty to do in getting the new Hospital ready. Mr Capel whom we were to have met here has left. Still no tidings of Dr Webb with Mes^{rs} Wyman & Bluett, they were to have followed the next day & joined us at Charlville with money & another waggon load of goods. Dr F. has telegraphed to know what has become of them. The railways & wires are in the hands of the Prussians.

2.30. Vespers & Salut at the Cathedral – a good Organ accompanied by a Trombone – the Choristers voices a shrill wail – the Choir men handing snuff to one another. Fat old Canons with red faces warming their feet & hands on Chaufrettes – one of them so like Dr Webb that we call him his Uncle.

All SS Day.[167] 7 A M. Notre Dame. 9.30 Cathedral – the Bishop officiating – Grand Procession – the Choristers in red cassocks, worked muslin Albs,[168] red Shoes, Skull Caps & Sashes. The Bishop having Mitre & Crosier of course. Such a simple holy looking man – so patient as he was pulled about by his attendants & dressed & undressed by the fumbling old Canons. 2.30. Vespers & Salut The Bishop in procession carrying the Host. A beautiful boy with a lovely voice sang a Solo.

All Souls Day. 7 A M Cathedral – the Bishop Celebrating. The Choir hung with black with white pear shaped tears. D^r F & L called – poor D^r F who has hitherto been the life & stay of the party quite down cast. He can get no work – he finds on examination that we have been forestalled there are plenty of doctors & nurses. Here we are without money our horses eating their heads off at the Hotel although poor animals they have been put on short commons – no tidings of Mr Bluett & Co with the most essential part of our Stores. Mr Capel who was expected today has not turned up. D^r L still holding out promises of work w^h D^r F now finds from experience are not to be relied on – The Depot of Stores we were to have found here has been emptied by Dr L. who has been giving things away wholesale. Metz has capitulated.[169] When we arrived at Arlons seven weeks ago the bombardment of Metz was daily expected three of our Sisters were retained at Arlons to be sent on there, but afterwards joined us at Bazuelle & Balon. Again the same cry was raised when we got to Brussels & instead of going on to Meaux & Dammartin as was first settled & D^r F's wish, we have been sent back here D^r F's visit added to our constant surveillance has so depressed Mother that at 8 she went to bed with a headache, & we had all to go upstairs at the same time – I had not undressed like the rest who were snug in their beds when a woman came up to say there were two gentlemen below wishing to speak to us – I went down &

---

[167] 1 November, the Feast of All Saints.
[168] White eucharistic vestments, long-sleeved and reaching to the floor.
[169] Metz surrendered on 27 Oct. 1870. 173,000 French went into captivity.

found Mr Bluett with D^r F once more bright again. He came to ask for the letters
to the german Princes w^h he had brought out from England & had given Mother
to take care of as she was not so likely to be searched as himself & therefore they
w^d be safer in her keeping. Dr Webb had arrived with the other gentlemen but
they had been obliged to leave the stores at Charlville – the man whom they had
engaged at Nouzon to bring them here refused to come on & they could not get
another Waggon – they had had great difficulties with the authorities at
Charlville and Mizieres, at the latter place they went to the general of the forces
who was very crusty – however our friend the Commandant helped them
through. They travelled in a light carriage & when they reached the Prussian
lines had a Uhlan[170] to gallop before them – this must have been rather morti-
fying to Dr Webb who is thoroughly french at heart

3 Nov: 9 A M. Cathedral Mass for the dead – a Sham Coffin covered with a
black Pall on w^h a Mitre was placed – in the centre of the Choir surrounded by
Candles. Mother thought it might be the anniversary of a Bishop's death –
Monsigneur was there – he did not Celebrate but gave the absonts[171] round the
Coffin. Doctors F & W called – Dr F. each time has found fault with the atmosphere of the room – he says we shall all catch cold & be ill & when we told him
the old dame objected to the window being opened he said we must smash a pane
then – I have found it rather a good plan to open the window whenever she makes
an exit w^h makes her clear off on finding it so on her return & she then keeps
guard from the waiting room opposite. She carries her chaufrette with her – this
seems as much a winter appendage for old women as a muff is for ladies – they
bring them to Church as a matter of course. – Our attendant has been mending
Soldiers' old Coats & trousers making our parlour still more oderiforous. But to
return to our guests – Dr F did not know we had been billeted here or he w^d not
have accepted it – he considered it placed us in the same position as the invading
Army & he had refused billets for the gentlemen. We knew nothing of this & had
taken ours as a matter of obedience much as we disliked it. D^r F therefore sent D^r
W. to explain matters to Mademoiselle & ask her to state which she required in
compensation. As D^r W is a R C[172] & entirely sympathises with the french he
found her very agreeable – she w^d not make any charge but was willing to accept
a present for the orphans & we were not to stay after Thurs: or Friday – so
matters are arranged & our entertainers visages are rather relaxed towards us but
we are still guarded as before – I have however been allowed to go to our Dormitory unattended once or twice. D^r F asked us to meet him at the railway Station to
see the wounded come in & the wooden huts w^h have been constructed for those
Soldiers who arrive at night to rest in until morning. After seeing the huts D^r

[170] The term commonly applied to all Prussian cavalry, but it was originally the name for the
Prussian lancers.
[171] Possibly absolution.
[172] Roman catholic.

Lewis took us to see the Ambulance Carriages[173] – beds slung up on hammocks in some two rows the upper ones fastened – by Indian rubber ropes – the lower row have springs like those of a carriage – part was fitted up as a Kitchen – Doctors & nurses were aportioned to certain Carriages. When we got back to the platform we found the Train from Metz had come in & brought Mr Capel. There are 6000 Sick at Metz – a few are wounded but the greater part are cases of Typhus & Dysentery. As there are 300 Doctors & plenty of Sisters we are not wanted there.

3rd Mr Capel & Dr F left this morning to searci. for work[174] – they have gone towards Paris – Mr Mansfield left yesterday for Charville to try & get the remainder of our Stores – Everybody thinks it is a very arduous undertaking – He & Mr Kane made us laugh at their account of the Table d'hote at their Hotel with all the German Grandees. Mr K. said he was kept so perpetually bowing that it had become his normal state. They have a variety of Titles from the Prince of Sax[175] downwards – Counts are thought nothing of Mr M. declared he had had one to pull off his boots. Two ladies dine at the table with all the Officers – one is a Baroness the other a young english girl in a most anomilous position I believe she was a Governess out here & now Stays on independantly going to the huts alone night & morning to help the Soldiers to Coffee &c. Mr Markham[176] called today before going to Metz & has promised to make enquiries for Mother's friend Monsr Duval who was in Bazuine's Corps[177] & has not been heard of since the 18th Aug: Mr Markham took us to see the Ambulance at Hotel Dieu a Convent of the Sisters of S Vincent de Paul. Mr Markham had served as House Surgeon in different Hospitals in Paris for 4 years & I was amused to hear him dilate to Mother as we walked along on the superior excellence of Sisters of this Order over others: he said they were not bigotted like the rest, but wd carry out the Doctors directions without setting up their own opinions & attended to their work instead of always running off to their prayers. On our way to the Hospital we were overtaken by Lee[178] the Irish Commissionaire who with a Military Salute informed us that Drs Webb & Lewis were looking for us – we waited for

---

[173] Both sides used railway ambulances. These were specially adapted or constructed hospital carriages. The French service was the Train Sanitaire Permanent; the Prussian system was the Lazarett-Zunge, known more widely as Lazareths. The Prussian system was efficient. See Heller, *Farmcarts to fords*, p. 68.

[174] Dr Frank travelled to a number of places, including Versailles, seeking permission to establish a field hospital.

[175] Possibly refers to Albert, crown prince of Saxony, who commanded the XII Saxon corps.

[176] Dr Alf Markheim, surgeon, Sedan, 1 Sept. 1870 – 24 Nov. 1870.

[177] Marshal François-Achille Bazaine. Originally commander of II corps, before being appointed commander-in-chief of the French army on 8 Aug. 1870, after Napoleon III's collapse. He controlled the army of the Rhine, which surrendered at Metz. In 1873 Bazaine was court-martialled and imprisoned as a result of this defeat. He escaped and died in penury in Madrid.

[178] Michael Lee, commissionaire, 13 Oct. – 26 Dec. 1870.

them & found they only wanted to ask us to go with them to see the Champagne Cellars at 2. o'clock. The Sisters received us very graciously & showed us over the ambulance – the patients were all Germans with the exception of two French prisoners. The Germans had each his gun & helmet by his bedside. At the door we met such a bright Bavarian boy Soldier on Crutches he did not look more than 16 & was overjoyed at the prospect of going home. All those who were deemed fit for evacuation were sitting on their beds or walking about ready dressed for the move. None of the Sisters could speak German but they seemed on very good terms with their patients who brought out what broken French they knew – one of them hearing the word Paris said saucily to one of the Sisters – ah! 'Paris caput'. After we had seen the Soldiers the Sisters took us to the Wards set apart for poor old men from the town – they looked so clean & comfortable in their beds which had white dimity curtains from the ceiling down. Mr Markham here left us to bid adieu to his friends – he & Dr Lewis were sent out by the Society, but now they are not attached to any Ambulance & pick up work as they can – Dr L thinks he is doing a great work he seems to have constituted himself as Whipper-in in general to the Ambulances here. He goes about with a leather pouch full of opium Morphine, & Quinine Pills wh he gives to the Soldiers at the Station as they arrive & depart – he cannot speak to them but says he can see at once by their eyes what they require & administers a dose accordingly.

2 P M. We were conducted by Dr L to Monsr Jacques's Cellars – he – Dr L – takes a fatherly interest in us during Dr F's absence our medical staff followed. The Cellars are all underground in solid rock the greater part being natural Caves – here & there the sides were covered with Cobwebs & Lichen there were openings for light at certain distances & there a few Solitary ferns had taken root – Vines are planted everywhere in this great Champagne country – some trained on walls – others under hedgerows – besides whole fields tied to short poles like raspberries – The Prussians have protected the vintage & we were told there were 3000000 bottles here. From the Cellars we ascended to the upper part of the buildings – those in which the Champaigne is made is now converted into an Ambulance & they were busy sending off their Convalescents Monsr Jacques had given up the place for the french sick Soldiers but when the Prussians became Masters of course they sent their own men wh one of the nurses a native of Guernsey thought very hard. We next proceeded to the railway Station passing by a new Mansion wh Monsr Jacques had built for his Son, who died & therefore the house & grounds are left in quite an unfinished State – this was the house Dr L. had proposed for Dr F & Staff – a long line of barracks close by for the patients who were to be brought up on trucks on a tramroad from the Station – the idea is grand & worthy of the man but wd require months to be put in practise, & therefore unless we intend making a Settlement for life here quite out of the question. We reached the Station in time to see the wounded off – Amongst them we recognised the Bavarian boy in a state of wild joy – snugly packed in his hammock – Mother asked if he was going home & he shouted out Ja, Ja, Dr L

gave me a Feld postCard[179] they are used by the Soldiers & are thought to go safer than a sealed letter. The officers are very obliging in allowing us to send letters but the inhabitants may not. Amongst the 2000 Sick & wounded brought in here last week there were not more than 20 Frenchmen. Bismarc's Curassiers[180] have arrived here such tall fine men in white uniform.

4th 7 A M Chapel of the Sisters of Perpl Adoration. Took a Feld post Card to post at the Station – the Officers were very civil & did not require my signature as is usual. On my return I found that Dr Webb had procured us lodgings & left £4 with Mother to present to Mademoiselle she was quite overcome by such a handsome donation. Mademoiselle sent us a french Paper with an account of ourselves. It mentioned our arrival with 6 Fourgons & taking charge of an Ambulance with 700 Sick & that we laboured without distinction amongst those of either nation. Also that the Director of the Ambulance finding the Chemists of the town short of medicaments had supplied them gratuitously from his own stores – Mother assured Mademoiselle that the greater part of the Statements were untrue but nevertheless this with the £4. has changed her aspect towards us, & she took us over her establishment wh is very interesting & of great extent & forms a large quadrangle surrounded with Cloisters. We ascended Staircase after Staircase & went from corridor to corridor everything beautifully clean & orderly & excellently arranged. The old women had each her little cell curtained off like ours but larger & better furnished & supplied with cupboards – the broad Corridor in front formed a sitting room – beyond a tiny Kitchen & Stove for their little comforts – their meals being cooked below – there was also a small dispensary attached. On each flat there is a kind of gallery looking down into the Chapel, which is open to the roof – so those who cannot get down stairs can thus join in the Services. One of the old women is 90. The Orphans Dormitory was quite beautiful – more than 40 little iron bedsteads with quilts as white as snow each packed in the peculiar french fashion without a crease. We afterwards saw the garden which is very productive – an immense length of wall is covered with vines. Our old Sentinel seemed quite sorry to part with us & gave us each a little scapula[181] as a Keepsake We are once more free – the two Commissionaires carried our baggage & we took up our residence at a small Hotel next door to our Doctors. It is a little pokey place not near so clean as our late abode but we are free & can go about as we like. Mother & S. E already breathe more freely the imprisonment depressed them sadly & they could not Sleep or eat. I do not think

---

[179] Field postcard.
[180] Prince Otto Eduard Von Bismarck-Schoenhausen, or simply, Bismarck (1815–90), the Prussian chancellor. Cuirassiers were the heavy cavalry, and wore an armoured arm and breastplates. There were a number of heavy cavalry charges in the war, most of which were destroyed in a hail of fire. The 'only choice before horsed cavalry lay between idleness and suicide', Howard, *Franco-Prussian war*, p. 119.
[181] A badge of affiliation to an ecclesiastical order.

I minded the restraint as much as the others I went out more & the brisk mountain air soon dispelled any depression & I quite miss my little cell now that it comes to sleeping 3 in a room. Dr Lewis called & brought relics that he had picked up at the emperor's[182] Chateau at Mourmulon[183] – the only thing I thought of interest was a Map with the different battles marked on it – besides this there are bits of bellropes &c &c – We passed near Mourmielon & the Camp on our way from Suippe but did not see any remains of the Camp.[184]

5 Nov: We were disturbed in the night by great Knocking & tramping but did not think much of it supposing the Soldiers in this house & the next were moving. This morning we learnt that there had been a fire in the adjoining Hotel one of the rafters in an Officers room having caught fire & gone on smouldering until he was nearly suffocated by smoke – however it was soon extinguished. D^r L is always running in – I think he means to be Kind, but is very eccentric I think poor man that his head has been turned with grief from the death of his only child a most promising young man – Capt of Eton & afterwards a Postmaster at Merton.[185] D^r L caused great amusement in the Square today by mounting one of our Fourgon horses, having first furnished himself with a Switch from our fire. He is most anxious to do all he can for us & after having offered Champagne & different delicacies in vain he asked S. E. confidentially if there was no little comfort she c^d. suggest for him to bring Mother or had we taken a vow of perpetual austerity. Hundreds of Troups leave for Paris every day – we saw a truck full of spades & mallets going off today. Such very long Trains often two Engines – Troups of Soldiers are now flocking in from the neighbourhood of Metz.[186]

6th 7 A M Cathedral – the Bishop said Mass & was again present at High Mass at 9. when we had an excellent french Sermon on Charity the Text taken from the Gospel. 2 Choristers carried a loaf of bread on a kind of bier to be blessed – they were preceded by a girl bearing a lighted Candle followed by another child of about 7. these girls collected the Alms a beadle in Scarlet with Cocked hat &c going before them. On All Souls Day 2 pretty young ladies in black took the Alms. The Bishop's Palace is close to the Cathedral – he passes through one of the small Chapels to get to it – this was today full of boys, who were brought to Church by some Xtian Brothers, the Bishop in passing held out his hand for the boys to kiss, so lovingly & with such a heavenly smile. One of the side Chapels was dedicated to S. Vincent de Paul & was full of little girls conducted by some of the Sisters of that Order – they came again in the afternoon

182 Napoleon III (1808–73), emperor of the French, 1852–70.
183 Mourmelon.
184 Marshal MacMahon used the camp to muster the Army of Châlons, which at 130,000 strong, set off to relieve Bazaine at Metz, but met defeat at Sedan.
185 An undergraduate scholar of Merton College, Oxford. This was Robert Hely James Lynch-Blosse Lewis (1846–69), who died shortly after beginning his legal studies.
186 The Prussian army was regrouping, to strengthen the siege of Paris and to confront the newly raised French armies, forming in the Loire valley, south of Paris.

when one of the Sisters Catechised them. Different Priests took boys. Still no news of D^r F or Mr Mansfield – Mother very flat at this prolonged idleness & letters from home are so urgent for her return but we cannot help ourselves. Dr L. has been in 4 times today – he is constantly running in with a book or paper for us to look at. Today he brought a plan of his proposed Hospital – he asked if we could direct him to an English Church or w^d we allow him to join us when we read the Service.

7th 9 A M. All the D^{rs} came in bringing Mother & S. E. a letter each posted in London on the 3rd. Letters have been so scarce of late that the receipt of these created quite a sensation amongst the Doctors – they were expected to gain intelligence of D^r F from them in spite of London & Ostend postmarks. Dr Webb called again between 11 & 12. the Polish Count who had accompanied D^r F has come back. D^r F has gone on to Versailles. Mr Capel stopped at Chateau Thierry. The Fourgons are to leave for Nogent tomorrow. We are to wait here for orders.

8th – The Fourgons went off at 7.15 A M. the Pole & one Commissionaire went with them. Seeing a Funeral Procession when I was out today – I followed at a distance until we reached the Cemetery, the Priest had scarcely left the Grave when another Funeral arrived – this was a Soldiers – a Priest & the little Sacristan from the Cathedral bearing holy Water came first the Coffin of rough deal with sloping lid on which was a piece of paper with the name about 20 Soldiers followed with an Officer. There were 3 bodies brought in this way one after another & laid side by side in a pit with their comrades & then covered over. A black Cross with a number is placed over the head of each. The Protestants are buried in another part hedged off but still with the same black Crosses. I counted more than 100. Among the Protestants there was a Stone Headstone to Carl Knack 25 Oct/70. The French Soldiers are buried separately amongst their countrymen – there were not more than 6 or so & their crosses were not uniform like the Germans'. In the afternoon I took Mother to the Cemetery & afterwards we walked out of the town across a larger field here we met 4 Soldiers bearing a Coffin on a Bier – We soon came in sight of a large Barracks & a little beyond a new Asylum built on a large scale with a Chapel in the Centre – A Convent was being built near. Mr Mansfield returned this evening & relieved our fears we were quite anxious about him he had been away so long but he had gone through Rheims to Chateau Thierry where he left the Stores – Mr Capel having set up a Depot there.

12 Nov. This has been such a week of contradictions, mismanagement & misunderstanding. On Monday the Pole returned with an order from Mr Capel to send the Fourgons to Chateau Thierry – Tuesday. 7.15 A M they start for Epernay. Then comes a telegram from the Prince of Hess[187] at Versailles 'The

---

[187] The prince of Pless, the inspector general of hospitals, is probably meant here (see note 76). Prince Ludwig (Louis) of Hesse-Darmstadt (1837–92) helped his wife, Princess Alice, organize the Red Cross hospital at Darmstadt.

English Ambulance to remain at Chalons'. Dr Webb dispatches 2 of the gentlemen in a Carriage at 12 o'clock at night to catch & bring back the Fourgons but the orders from Chateau Thierry are so peremptory that the Fourgons proceed – & the disconsolate gentlemen return. Next orders from Capt Blackenbury to proceed to Metz, where he had just arrived with Madame Courobert. Mr Bluett goes to Metz to explain our dilemma. Dr F. returns to Chateau Thierry from Versailles & to his disgust finds the Fourgons there.[188] D^r F had obtained an Order from the prince of Hess for our Ambulance to accompany Prince Frederick Charles's[189] Army but the Fourgons having been withdrawn from Chalons has thrown the whole Scheme out as if they were brought back it w^d then be too late. The mistake had arisen from some of the telegrams being misconstrued & others c^d not be read. On hearing the State of things Count Blücher[190] the Prefect at Epernay telegraphs to ask the Prince to send the Ambulance there in consequence of w^h D^r F receives orders to move to Epernay & thus the grand idea of our bivouking with the Army has ended in our having to take up our quarters in a pokey little place like Epernay – You may imagine the wrath of the Doctors.

13th – Sunday. We had looked out for D^r F day after day until we were Sick at heart – Mother spied him in the Place about 5 o'clock this afternoon & it was not long before he was ushered in by Lee the Commissionaire. D^r F looked very worn & tired but still disposed to make the best of things – everything seemed to have gone against him but still he has battled on The letters he had brought out from England to the King[191] & Crown Prince[192] D^r F took with him hoping to present them himself but when he got to Colonnieres[193] & there seemed no liklihood of his having an opportunity of doing so he posted them. 2 days afterwards Dr F. finds himself at Versailles – but the letters had not arrived & he did not like presenting himself without introductions. The next disaster was the

---

188 In his report Dr Frank commented that 'to my great surprise . . . the Ambulance wagons were at Chateau-Thierry', in *Report of the operations of the British National Society*, p. 120. Captain Brackenbury noted the difficulties in 'obtaining sanction to render aid and [in] obtaining proper information on where to give it'. *Ibid.*, p. 31.

189 Frederick Charles, prince of Prussia (1828–85), known as the 'Red Prince', nephew of Wilhelm I, king of Prussia. Commanded the siege of Metz, and took the field against the 'new' French armies in the Loire Valley, around Orléans and Le Mans. He was nearly responsible for a great defeat at the battles of Rezonville-Gravelotte, 18 Aug. 1870, but Bazaine, the French commander, was unable to recognise the opportunity and retreated into Metz.

190 Count Ulrich Blücher (1836–80), a descendent of Field Marshal Blücher (1742–1819), the Prussian general at Waterloo. The Sous-prefect would have been responsible for the military administration of the occupied department. Dr Frank noted that he 'treated us throughout with most distinguished courtesy.' *Report of the operations of the British National Society*, p. 122.

191 Wilhelm I of Prussia (1797–1888).

192 Prince Friedrich William (1831–1888), later Kaiser Friedrich III, 1888. Married to Victoria (1840–1901), daughter of Queen Victoria. Army commander at Sedan, and the siege of Paris. Father of Kaiser Wilhelm II.

193 Coulommiers.

Fourgons having gone to Chateau Thierry. & he said he was in daily expectation of a Telegram from Mother to say we were going home w^h would have brought his trials to a climax. His cheerful endurance in spite of all is quite an example to us.[194] He says that a part of an Ambulance's work is waiting – patient waiting – & if we are not resigned to this waiting it shows a want or faultiness in ourselves – we are envious of others who are at work, or dissatisfied that there are not Sick & wounded enough to employ us in such a case An Ambulance is attached to an Army & like the Army must share its several fortunes – The Soldiers are not always engaged but those in peaceful quarters are necessary appendages to the rest. Such was D^r F's homily. In going upstairs tonight after dinner, which we have in a sort of hall by the Stable yard, we met a French Officer, who politely held his Candle until we had all passed. It immediately occurred to us that this was an opportunity of gaining some intelligence of the Mother's friend Capt. Duval & finding from our landlady that the Officer had just arrived from Metz we urged Mother to ask for an interview, but it was some time before she c^d. overcome her fear of intruding upon a Stranger. At last she consented & then learnt that Capt Duval had been sent a prisoner to Germany as he was one of those, who on the capitulation of Metz, refused to promise not to carry arms again.[195] The Officer spoke very sadly just answering the questions & no more so unlike a Frenchman. Mother was quite nervous for the rest of the evening fearing she may have taken too great a liberty.

14th – Breakfast 7.45 as Mother & S. E. were to start with D^r F for Epernay at 8.15 to arrange things & procure beds &c by the time we arrived by an afternoon Train. Of course the conveyance was not forthcoming at the appointed time, & then they had to wait for D^r F to finish his letters &c At 9.45 the creaking door of the Fly[196] was shut & the signal given to start but the wretched starved horses were of a different opinion & no persuasions of the driver by whip or tongue were of any avail – the horses turned right round & looked in at the window. At last urged from behind by driver & landlord & dragged by the bit by Lee they c^d no longer resist & a start was made. I believe the same scene was gone through at every place on the road w^h had the appearance of a Stable. Mother was anxious to have a Copy of the Bishop's Charge w^h was read from the Pulpit before the Sermon last Sunday & before leaving she told me she hoped I c^d manage to get it. I went twice to the Cathedral before I could meet with my little friend the Sacristan but that was nothing as I generally went to some of the offices there & after Vespers I spied him & asked him where I could get a Copy of the Charge –

194 John Furley, the Red Cross representative at Versailles, said of Dr Frank that 'his presence is sunshine in every room he enters'. *Report of the operations of the British National Society*, p. 11.
195 Officers who promised 'not to take up arms against Germany' were set free. See Howard *Franco-Prussian war*, p. 222. By the end of the war, the P.O.W. camps held 372,000 soldiers and 12,000 officers. Some 5,000 P.O.W.s escaped from Germany to rejoin the war. *Ibid.*, p. 391.
196 The carriage.

he told me to follow him & before I knew what he was about he had rung the bell at the door of the Vicar of the Cathedral a woman answered it & on being informed of my request brought me a Copy but said that as it was the only one left I must return it when I had finished it but I said I could not do so as I was going away today. However my guide was anxious to oblige me & so skipped off & rung the bell of a door at the back of the Bishop's Palace – a woman opened the door & having explained matters he departed leaving me with the woman who bade me come in while she rushed off – I waited in a kind of Court Yard in a State of terror lest Monsigneur sh^d appear.

I believe he was out – I felt I had undertaken to get the mandement[197] & must abide the issue – the messenger returned saying there was not one left. I had yet one remaining resource, in glancing at the Copy produced I had caught sight of the address of either printer or publisher so off I went in quest of it & at last for 20 Cent^s secured my prize. We left our Hotel about 3 in an Omnibus with our luggage & waited about an hour at the Station while Dr Webb arranged for our transit – he had failed to get a conduite[198] from the Procfete[199] in the morning but on shewing our papers to the officials at the Station they allowed us to go in a Soldier's Train free – The Platform was crowded with Soldiers waiting for the Train to Paris – they seemed on very good terms with Lee although they c^d only communicate by signs. When they understood that he was going there was great shaking of hands & expressions of regret – the new Comers admired his Medals & asked if they were french or english – Lee in reply turned out the side with the Queen – Some ignorant Bavarians asked if it represented Napoleon – Lee drew himself up as a proud english Soldier – & sneered contemptuously at their 'bits of copper'. At length the Train from Metz arrived & there was a rush & a crush but we got into a carriage with Dr Webb where there were only two Officers & another gentleman – they were remarkably civil quite putting themselves out to make way for our packages & arranging them for us. One of the Officers who was quite young asked 'Are you from Ireland my Sister?' & on being answered in the negative persevered 'Are you not then Catholics my Sister?'.[200]

Epernay

14 Nov: Arrived at 5 P M & were met by Mr Mansfield & Mr Wyman at the Station. M^r M presented us all with billets as he said we could not possibly get room at any of the Hotels & that when they came here a few days ago they could not get a bed until 6 A M when some one else turned out. We started from the Station carrying our own bags, the gentlemen packed their luggage on a barrow. This caused a good deal of confusion as the barrow had to go to different

---

[197] An obsolete form of 'mandment', meaning 'that which is ordered'.
[198] A safe-conduct.
[199] Perhaps a misspelling of préfecture.
[200] Southern Germany, including Bavaria, was mainly catholic. Northern Germany was predominantly protestant.

quarters, M^r M not knowing how to direct us & was well scolded for not having brought the Omnibus & learnt our various destinations better. At last Mr Wyman undertook to go with the other two Sisters & myself in search of our house. At the door we met a number of German women all dressed alike possibly deaconesses – then a frenchwoman came & told us there were no beds as they had already 18 Germans quartered there. We asked permission to rest there while M^r W went in search of our chèfs & arranged what we were to do. The people were very civil & asked us into a room where one of the Germans was sorting clean clothes & then promised to bring us some tea – the first time we have been offered any abroad. Dr Frank had taken Mother & S. E. to call on the Préfect Count Blücher & to see the house or rather schools he thought of for an Ambulance.[201] They had arrived about one & after getting some refreshment turned in to a Stationers. Mother & Madame conversed fluently in french until S E made a remark in english, which made Madame exclaim 'Oh! are you English?' She proved to be a country woman of ours who had married a French man 13 years ago & has lived here ever since. She is a cousin of a bird Stuffer in Vere St: – Upon hearing of the difficulty of finding lodgings Mother returned to the Shop & asked Mme Fiérvet if she could recommend us any. She at once begged us to go there as she w^d most thankfully take us in for nothing as she w^d be so glad of our protection. Her Husband died 6 m^ths ago, her little girl of 12 is in Paris with an Aunt & so Madame was left alone with her boy of 9 – a maid servant & an apprentice girl – when the Prussians arrived several soldiers were billeted on Mme F. her servant ran away & Madame was almost frightened to death. However she says she must in justice to the soldiers confess that during the time they were there she never experienced the slightest incivility or impropriety in their conduct towards herself – requisitions they made – but then it was war time & they followed as a matter of course – At first the soldiers walked into the Shops with a cocked pistol in hand & made their demand – one came to her so armed & required a match to light his pipe. After a few days Madame went to the Prefect & represented her case & he in the kindest manner removed the Soldiers & said she should not be molested again. The rooms had not been cleared or cleaned since the soldiers had occupied them – the Straw on which they Slept being still there; but they are to be prepared tomorrow & Madame has promised us another little room for tonight. Mr Wyman came back to us with this intelligence & conducted us to the Hotel where Mother & S. E. had secured one little bedroom between them. At 7. we sat down to the Table d'hote but waited half an hour before anything was served & then had to endure nearly two hours over a very indifferent dinner served in the slowest most uncomfortable style. Dr Frank

---

[201] The ambulance established itself in a schoolhouse, with a capacity for thirty six beds. Dr Frank wanted to establish a 100-bed hospital in the wine shed of Messrs Moët & Chandon. *Report of the operations of the British National Society*, p. 120. The Caserne du Genie became the main hospital, with a capacity of 150 beds.

ordered a bottle of champagne to try & cheer up his party but it was all in vain every one felt flat & showed it. We were not sorry when the ceremony came to an end & we were able to retire to our sleeping apartments. We three shared Madame's little room – about 8 ft x 10 – finding my sheets were quite wet I wrapped myself up in my travelling shawl for the night.

15 Nov.[r] 7 A M Church. 8 Breakfast at the Hotel. Mother in bed with a sick headache. We could not get into our rooms until they had been cleared of the straw & dirt left by the soldiers. The 3 rooms open from one into another & are quite bare of furniture of any kind – Madame had all her things packed away in her cellars before the invaders arrived – all her linen was stowed away in casks there & our damp Sheets were brought from them last night. We went to look at our new Ambulance but could not get in as it is still occupied by the Soldiers. We can do nothing until the Soldiers are gone so I availed myself of the opportunity of having a good walk. I am very agreeably surprised in Epernay which we were told was a more pokey town than Chalons – but I think we shall like it better – it is smaller than Chalons & has no pretensions to architectural beauty but it is large & clean – the Hotel de Ville at Chalons is superior to any building here but the houses are not so squeesed up many having a garden or courtyard in front. Epernay is very prettily situated in one of the Valleys of the Marne surrounded by vine clad hills extending for miles varied here & there by a cluster of houses nesting round a church – I followed a winding path over one of these hills – as far as I could see on either Side were vines closely planted after ascending a little way I came to a wooden Cross. In Belgium one meets with wayside Crosses & Crucifixes at every turn, but in the parts of France we have been in they are very rare. It soon began to rain & my muddy path became more & more slippery at last by taking a sharp turn down a very steep pitch, I landed on the high road in safety & returned to our lodgings. These were beginning to get a little more into shape – the Straw had been cleared away & the rooms scrubbed – Madame had lent us two bedsteads & S. E. had hired two others & some Mattresses. Mother came about 12 & looked the picture of misery in one of the empty rooms – we sat on the floor in another to eat our lunch some bread & brawn we had bought. 4.30 we went to Church for Vespers & Salut – Madame cooked us some dinner by 6.30 & at 7 we went to bed to be out of the way.

16 Nov.[r] 9 A M Ambulance having first been to Church & breakfasted. The workmen are beginning to whitewash – the Soldiers Still in one of the Wards & Kitchen grumbling at our turning them out. We worked all day trying to scrub off some of the dirt – first having gone with Mother to buy Soda & brushes with which she & I were quite loaded.[202]

19. We have been hard at work at the Ambulance from 6.30 A M daily

[202] Dr Frank reported that after 'four days hard work, and an expenditure of £40, we converted a schoolhouse, situated near a railway station'. *Report of the operations of the British National Society*, p. 120.

scrubbing till night & taking it in turns to run home for our meals – the Soldiers have at last turned out – the boards we have scrubbed on our knees but the greater part of the floor is brick these we have scrubbed with long hand-brooms – swilling them over with water & then rubbing the bricks with all our might – Mother taking the lead & scrubbing like any Charwoman – it is wet work & our boots & petticoats are well saturated by night & we go to bed hanging them out to dry by morning. Some French Sisters called & kindly offered to lend us their sabots[203] but as the principle part of our work was done Mother declined. The head German Doctor D[r] Levine[204] has been here today to inspect our progress, indeed he has paid us daily visits, & suggests having slips of Carpeting up & down the Wards & the whole length of the place from Ward to Ward. We thought this a most inconvenient arrangement considering the Spitting propensities of the nations but D[r] F thinks it best to carry out Dr Lavin's views. Count Blücker the Prefet has also come to see us every day – he is very nice speaks english & is more like an english Gentleman than any foreigner I have met he is quite young & has brought his Wife two or three times. We are very sorry to find he is going to leave. The Mattresses sent by the society are much too small & we have had them taken to pieces & enlarged – this has much increased our work & made a great litter & though several of the beds are completed it has given D[r] L an excuse for not sending us patients as he said we were not quite ready for them. We have also been very busy in binding the carpets such hard work but now it is all finished & a slip of carpet between the bed. Dr Levin has inspected & pronounces the Wards 'Shöu'[205] We have had constant rumours of patients; but as yet none have arrived. Mes[rs] Wyman & Bluett went to Metz promising to return with 50 french patients but Mr Wyman has returned without – Mr Bluett waits for Capt Blackenbury. I have finished up with a bath the first since I had one at Brussels more than a month ago having worn the same shift night & day for nearly 3 weeks.

20 Nov: (Sunday) As usual unusually busy day. Several reports of coming patients have reached us first 30 then it dwindled down to 12 – we have 35 beds. How shocked the good people of Chasach[206] would be if they peeped in at the window & saw us with needles & thread sewing hard. The Pillows sent are very small & there are no bolsters so we have to put two pillows together & sew some rug or a large Case over them. I was the only one able to go to Church at 10 – when there was high Mass & a Sermon. At 6 went to our lodgings for dinner – leaving S. Ce on guard. Before we had finished a messenger came to say that the

---

[203] Wooden shoes.
[204] Dr Georg Richard Levin (1820–96), the principal medical officer at Épernay. Dr Frank explained that 'our work was performed under strict supervision on the part of the German authorities, the principal medical officer paying daily visits to the ambulance, and inspecting all our cases'. *Report of the operations of the British National Society*, p. 121.
[205] Schön i.e. beautiful.
[206] Champagne – the area of France where Épernay is situated.

patients had arrived so back we hurried & found 36 Germans mostly Bavarians trampling over our carpets & spitting right & left. They had come by an Ambulance Train from near Paris & were very hungry. The bed out of the doctor's room was given up & he slept on the floor. Our Wards were quite full 12 patients in each – when 35 more arrived w[h] we had to decline. None of these are severely wounded – they hope to go on tomorrow as they are on their way home. One, a Bavarian has an iron Cross – he got it for taking 120 Prisoners 6 of whom were Officers at Sedan Captured by 50 Germans – he is wounded in the leg – a most good tempered & amusing fellow. Another talks english & french – was a Student at Munich, is styled 'Count' & has been to London & New York.

21. 6 A M. At the Ambulance to give breakfast to the men who said they were to go by the 7.30 Train – they waited sometime but as no one came to fetch them they set off with knapsack & guns bidding us all adieu – they were wounded about a month ago near Orleans[207] & other places. When we had breakfasted we set to work to clean the place – Mother was ready to cry when she looked at her pattern Wards covered with dirt – the new carpets stained with mud & spittle. We set to work in good earnest & had done something in the way of improvement when we were startled by our friend's returning – They were not to go & though sadly disappointed they bore it very good temperedly. Two had managed to slip away, & we conclude got off by one of the Trains – the Count was one.

25. We have been at the Ambulance daily at 6.30 or soon after – sometimes one or two of us went to Church & then on to the Ambulance at 7. D[r] Frank severely reprimanded the patients for their untidyness telling them they must use the spittoons provided for them & spare the Sisters the trouble of cleaning after them – they have taken it in good part & been more careful. The bedsteads are iron & each has a Locker the top of which is covered with oil cloth. Dr Levin visits us most days as also the Baron Lohu Thos[208] a Johuniter[209] appointed by Prince Plês to superintend the Hospitals. A Russian General & Doctor[210] come occasionally. Count Blücker brought his successor to introduce him – we are very sorry to lose the Count a descendant of the great General's. We have had several other visitors all expressing themselves highly gratified – but we are told we deserve better cases Dr Eberall[211] who selects the patients at the Station for the different Ambulances says he could send us ever so many first rate cases if we had room for them but day after day passes & no more are sent in & these are not sent away. We now have our meals regularly at the Ambulance. Willis one of the

[207] On 9 Nov. 1870 the French defeated a Bavarian army corps and regained Orléans. On 2–4 Dec. 1870, a reinforced Prussian army under Prince Friedrich Charles recaptured the city after heavy fighting.

[208] Baron Sehr-Toss, the principal Johanniter.

[209] Knights of the protestant Order of St John. See note 77.

[210] *The Report of the operations of the British National Society*, p. 35, noted the presence of a Russian Dr Hering at the Épernay ambulance.

[211] Not identified.

Commissionaires helps S. E. in the Kitchen – he was in the Navy before entering the Army & can turn his hand to most things. Our Refectory is a passage leading from the kitchen to the outside beyond the door is piled the dirty linen then a flight of Steps & a small space for a dead house. The Steam from the kitchen boilers occasionally reminds us of a London fog but there is always a Strong rush of air under the door cutting our legs & feet – The passage also serves as Larder & housemaid's ~~Kitchen~~ cupboard. The Table is placed against the wall – we sit on the other side on a School form – it is a long table – we occupy one end. The other part is covered with the cold remains of yesterday – on a beam above crossing the table hangs the uncooked meat requisition – Mutton w^h judging from appearance one would say had died a natural death – making its presence still more evident by occasional drips on the Table cloth. On the partition at our backs hang a variety of brooms & scrubbing brushes. Piled on the Stone floor are uncooked vegetables, pots & pans & crockery.

26 We are told today that some of our men are going but we hardly credit the report, as we are often deceived.

27 Ambulance 5.30. patients breakfast 6.30. Off to meet Train about 7 those who c^d not walk were taken in the Fourgon – They left in high spirits & their thanks & adieus were very hearty some insisting on shaking hands. We almost expected them back again however we went on with our cleaning & were uninterrupted this time – the frenchman is left alone & makes himself useful but as he & our man are engaged in constant conversation he hinders progress. Another patient has arrived a french boy of 18 with 6 Sabre cuts on his head one of the Guard Mobile – he was wounded near Orleans a month ago & was being sent up the country with other prisoners but as he is very feverish he has been brought here instead of going on. Three Prussians conducted him two with fixed bayonets & they would not leave him without a Guard until Mother made herself responsible for him.[212]

Advent Sunday – 7. I went to Church – stayed at the Ambulance in charge of the two prisoners while Mother & the other Sisters went to Church at 10 – then I had my turn in the afternoon & went to Church for Vespers Compline & Salut – It has been quite a day of rest, excepting that an alarm was raised in the afternoon that one of the prisoners had escaped however he was soon found in a house just outside the Ambulance – We had to get up from dinner this evening to receive 7 French prisoners conducted by a Guard – sent from a Hospital nursed by french Sisters at Chateau Thiery, & they had had nothing to eat since the morn^g. They were soon served with hot coffee & bread & meat. Their wounds are slight &

---

[212] The sick and wounded were protected by the Geneva convention. Technically wounded soldiers were 'neutral', and could be kept in ambulances and cared for, whilst nevertheless remaining prisoners. See Bertrand Taithe, 'The Red Cross Flag in the Franco-Prussian war: civilians, humanitarians, and war in the modern age' in *War, medicine and modernity*, ed. R. Cooter, M. Harrison and S. Sturdy (Gloucester, 1998), p. 40.

they were all able to sit at table making a very picturesque group in their various uniforms – a tall irongrey haired man, with two medals – one the Legion of honor, stands prominent – another I picked out as a Breton. Our boy from the Guard mobile has the small pox & has been sent to a small pox hospital. We have a regular sentinel outside now.

29. Ambulance 6.30. Mother very poorly & feverish in bed the Sisters expecting small pox. The Sentinel stopped one of the Carpenters who had been working here during the day as he was going home this evening & would not let him pass until we assured the Sentinel the man was not one of the prisoners in disguise.

S. Andrews Day. Church 6.30. Ambulance 7. Dr Lewis arrived from Metz – Nothing particular through the day. 7.30 P M. 8 more french prisoners. As we have still several vacant beds & the promised wounded do not come in D^r F has consented to take *Sick* & now one Ward is filled with cases of Typhus & Dysentry – this Ward Mother & I have.

5 Decr. I cannot keep my journal & must be content to jot things down from time to time. I used to write when sitting up at night but lately my nights too have been fully employed – We only kept our 'sick' patients a few days. The German Doctors said it was quite a pity to infect the hospital especially as now wounded are coming in daily from Paris, so the poor fellows were carried off on their beds to another Ambulance – & the wounded have since poured in. There was a strong feeling that we ought to have gone to Metz instead of coming here – it was said that 1500 or 2000 sick lay there[213] – Mr Bluett & Mr Wyman have been to enquire into the truth of it – they are satisfied as to the large number of sick & the want of material but it is a question if there be not already plenty of Doctors Sisters there. Dr F. has now sent Dr Webb[214] to inspect & report & he is most anxious that help should be sent there. Capt Blackenbury came on Thursday [Dec 2nd ? in pencil] & pressed something being done for Metz – so D^r F went there & returned on Saturday. He says it is dreadful to see the appearance of distress, evidently the remains of the hardships undergone, still marked on the faces of the patients in the hospitals at Metz. There are no fresh wounded all old wounds since the time of the siege – a good deal of hospital gangreen besides dysentry & fever. Capt B: returned from Versailles on Saturday & urges Mother & S. E's going to Metz & also wishes she sh^d send for more Sisters to come out but this Mother says she cannot do as the Sisters have just been re-called from Saarbrack & Darmstadt unfortunately our Staff has been reduced Mes^{rs} Cane[215] & Watson[216] have gone home, & also Mrs Capel & Miss Veitch who were to have

---

213 Dr Frank estimated that some 20,000 cases needed treatment, *Report of the operations of the British National Society*, p .120. I cannot reconcile these conflicting figures.

214 He left on 27 November 1870.

215 He left on 28 November 1870.

216 W. G. Watson, dresser.

joined us here but as we were so long waiting for work it was thought best they should return to England. If we had gone direct from Chalons to Metz we should have been there at the time of the Capitulation – we have been so often on the point of going & yet have never reached it. Our being here seems a dispensation over w^h we had no controul – none of us wished it – it was arranged for us to go elsewhere – but through mistakes in telegrams & other circumstances we were sent here & so here I suppose we shall remain.

8 Decr. I have not been able to write lately as we are at work from 6.30 A M to 9 P M. & then we sit up every fourth night in turn & go on with our work as usual without any rest on the following day. We are now having fresh wounded from Paris every day – 500 were expected last night & 1200 the night before. We have properly only 36 beds; but we had 46 patients yesterday[217] – those that are pretty well have mattresses on the floor & we evacuate patients as soon as they are able to travel. The Ambulance Trains are beautifully arranged – spring beds & every convenience – so the sick are able to travel much sooner than they could otherwise. Dr Webb telegraphed yesterday to say he had taken an Ambulance at Metz with 150 beds, so Mr Wyman & Mr Crookshanks are gone to join him – our medical Staff therefore is reduced to Dr F. & Mr Bluett. Dr Levin came this mor^g & offered D^r F an Ambulance with 100 beds in exchange for this. Dr F. declined as he & Mr Bluett think it w^d be a pity to give this up after getting it into such good order & now we have 6 more beds in a house across the St: belonging to a french Doctor. I wish however we could accomodate more, as we could undertake 100 patients quite as well as 42. It is sleeting & thawing today – we had a heavy fall of snow followed by frost & the ground has been quite white & very slippery for more than a week. The first morn^g after the fall we set off in the twilight as usual & found deep snow had fallen in the night. Mother said it reminded her of her childhood & stepped along quite rejoiced at this opportunity of renewing her acquaintance with it. We heard yesterday that Garibaldi[218] was close by – but there are so many rumours that we do not know what to believe. It is affirmed that the booming of Canon heard in the night is from the bombardment of Paris.[219] We occasionally hear shots in the early morning & the Prussians are all under arms now. They were called out the other morning; but we do not know for what cause. The german patients bring their guns & other accoutrements with them & it is a great undertaking to stow them away all properly labelled – or numbered. We generally ask if the guns are loaded – but the other day a Dragoon was brought in insensible & his heavy pistol was flung down with

---

[217] Between 1 Dec. 1870 and 12 Jan. 1871, the ambulance received eighty-five gunshot wound cases.

[218] Giuseppe Garibaldi (1807–82), the Italian nationalist. He led a unit of *francs-tireurs* in eastern France, which were effective in harrying the Prussian supply and communication lines, but less effective in open battle.

[219] The direct bombardment of Paris began on the 5 Jan. 1871, but caused more nuisance than damage. See Howard, *Franco-Prussian war*, p. 361.

the other arms a day or two afterwards on taking it up we found it was loaded & it was a great mercy it had not gone off. I got the Sentinal to discharge it. Some men are armed with the new Bavarian gun a most complete & well executed article.[220] It is very interesting to inspect the different arms Saxons, Bavarians, & those of Wirtumberg &c. We have had more than 100 patients & not one death as yet – sometimes we have had most french & at other times more germans. At first I had no preference beyond a drawing to the Bretons. We have had two, one being in the Ward I work in but my partiality for the race is rather diminishing for a more good for nothing boy I never met with & with a few exceptions you may say the same of all the french – they have not the military discipline of the germans – they are more polite but not nearly so obliging. The rough Bavarian snatches a broom out of your hand if you begin to sweep the floor & does it for you while the frenchman looks on. The germans will not lie in their beds longer than they can help but the french are continually getting in & out of bed wrapping up their heads in handkerchiefs or going to bed in their cloth caps & their clothes littering about their untidy beds.

9. Went with Mother to make up the beds in the french Doctor's house – he has given us two room w[h] D[r] F. has supplied with some rough wooden bedsteads when they were made up the rooms looked very inviting with bright wood fires on the hearth. The french Doctor takes charge by night so it will only give us extra day work. We have had some very interesting cases lately. M[r] Crookshank[221] extracted a Chasserpol ball[222] from a man's shoulder a few days ago.

10. D[rs] Lavin & Frank extracted a large piece of lead from a wound over the right eye pronounced to be part of a shell – the poor man is quite insensible & cries out 'auch Gott, auch Gott' most distressingly all day & night.

11. Dec[r]. This morng there seemed less to do than usual & I thought of going to Church at 10 – but D[r] F. came & amputated a finger & then two new patients arrived so we had a busy Sunday after all & in the afternoon Prince Henri of Baden[223] went over the Ambulance & expressed himself highly gratified. It is difficult to mark the days – sitting up confuses one & until today, when I was at Vespers, I had not been inside a Church for 10 days or a fortnight. One of the Doctors sleeps on the premises – throughout the night we hear the Sentinel's

---

220 Henry Rundle, a surgeon, commented that the 'Bavarian bullets made the worst kind of wound, as the bullet exploded when it struck, and usually lodged'. Henry Rundle, *With the Red Cross in the Franco-German war* (London, 1909), p. 30.

221 He departed for Metz on 8 Dec. 1870.

222 The French chassepot rifle had a sighted range of 1600 yards, compared with the Prussian needle rifle's range of 600 yards. 'The Chassepot wound was very clean, the point of entrance not larger than a pea. The ball was long and conical, and propelled with such a force that it seldom lodged.' Rundle, *With the Red Cross*, p. 30.

223 There was no one called Prince Henry of Baden. The reference may be to Prince Henry of Hess (1838–1900), a commander of the guards, who fought at the battle of Gravelotte on 18 Aug. 1870, and was later a general.

heavy tread outside – they are supposed to change every two hours but a few nights ago one was on the whole night – it is cold work, this weather & we supply them with hot Coffee or Soup throughout the night for w^h they are very grateful.

14. The poor man who had the ball extracted died yesterday. Dr F. has told the Sentries they may sit in the Hall if their officers will give permission as the weather is so severe alternative snow & frost we have lived in quite a white world. The Snow was quite deep but being frozen over we did not sink – there has been no snow balling as we should have had in England. Yesterday & today we have had a thaw – the ground is one sheet of ice. Dr Eberarth told me he had written a long letter to the Times about our Ambulance giving due praise to the Sisters. We have had a great many visitors today one was Captain Hinton.[224]

18. (Sunday 1 A M) Yesterday was a very busy day – 14 pat^s evacuated. At 10 – Two amputations of the leg – one a boy of 20. German, Swiss, Prussian, & Norwegian medical men attended as spectators – the latter in their bright new uniforms put the rest in the shade I think all wore swords – one of the Norwegians was a fellow Student of D^r F's & this eveng D^r F brought in Dr Montgomery – with whom he had been associated in work 5 years – partly in Madeira. Our surgery has been rather celebrated lately – The Doctors of the various Nations here had failed to tie the artery of a man wounded in the hand & they could not stop haemorage – then they quarrelled about it – & at last the man was brought to us in a dying state. An incision was made in the arm & the brachial artery tied – this has proved successful – & the case causes quite a sensation. (The man recovered & went home). Baron Seratrous[225] visits the patients most days – he comes in on tip-toes moving about most gingerly with his sword sticking out behind under his mantle like a cat's tail. We had a case of erysipelas[226] from a wound in the jaw. D^r F had him moved to a room in his house the man had to be put through a window on a Stretcher.

4 A M – Lee has just come to say that the poor man is dead. The smallpox boy, who had been reported dead, came to say goodbye as he was going to Germany – he was not marked & looked well.

22 Dec^r. 'O Emannuel' The great Os[227] are passing fast but we have not been once to Vespers to hear them. 2 A M. again sitting up – very cold, the wind moans dismally – the Sentry's heavy tread outside & within patients complainig of pain or asking for drink from time to time. We have a nightman now which is a great help. On Monday Professor Hutor[228] from Berlin came & operated with D^r

---

224 Captain W. L. Hinton, late of the 25th regiment, convoy agent, 27 Sept. 1870 – 13 Apr. 1871.
225 Baron Sehr-Toss, the principal Johanniter.
226 Saint Anthony's fire, an inflammation accompanied by reddened and sore skin, with fever.
227 The O antiphons are sung before and after the Magnificat at vespers on the seven days preceding Christmas eve.
228 Professor Hueter (1838–83), acting consultant at Rheims. The German army made use of eminent civilian surgeon consultants. Dr Frank noted that 'all major operations were performed

F's permission – resection of an elbow[229] in the new way. The faculty came in full force & highly approved – it seemed a most tedious operation & I thought the man would have died under it – the arm was put up in plaister of Paris at once. We had two other operations afterwards. On Tuesday the Professor came punctually at 8.30 A M. He asked me if we had too much to do – I replied we could manage 100 patients if we had room for them – he then said that this is the best Hospital in Epernay & therefore he asked Dr F to exchange two men who were up for two who the Professor wished to operate upon. The men were exchanged & the operations took place immediately – one resection of elbow the other of wrist – I was very sorry to lose one of those who went a tall trouper but his successor seems equally nice – but such an arm poor fellow I fear it will cause his death. I must give up writing now as I no sooner sit down than some one calls for something. Last Tuesday when we were at lunch the Fourgon arrived with seven wounded – our Fourgons meet the Trains & take patients to other Ambulances as well. All were full. We put Mattresses on the floor for these & on Wednesday four more were sent in two Germans & two french – we took the latter out of charity. Some of the french who are too badly wounded to serve again are at large in the town & come here to have their wounds dressed – one very nice lad was wounded at Metz – his thumb was shot off & gangreen has set in. I made up three more beds over the way yesterday – making 9 – Dr F. has gone to Metz – he has had orders from the Society to continue his Ambulance till 15 Jan I am very glad we are not going to leave 31 Dec the time first fixed – but some of us are disappointed. Mr Mansfield went to a rehearsal in Church today as he is to sing at Mass & Salut on Xtmas Day. His being a Protestant seems of no consideration. It was rumoured yesterday morning that there was fighting within 6 miles of us. On Tuesday we had a visit from a lady who had come from America to nurse the sick & wounded. Dr F entertained her at his house – & was as much pleased with her as he is with every person he meets.

Xtmas Eve. 3 A M. Dr F. returned from Metz last night they are getting on well there. The nursing done by two english ladies twelve french Sisters & about two dozen infermieres.

Xtmas Day. 11 P M – I went to Church at 7. & Mother at 10 this morning which was all we did in Ch: going. Mother said Mr Mansfield sung the Agnus Dei beautifully – his was the only solo & only good voice the people in the gallery, even the Sisters, popped their heads over to look at the Singer. Mr Mansfield was to have sung 3 Solos in the afternoon but before Vespers he was sent off in one of the Fourgons with an escourt of Soldiers to take an Officer from one of the neighbouring villages to Chalons. He had fallen out of his carriage &

in his presence after a consultation had been held'. *Report of the operations of the British National Society*, p. 122.
[229] Cutting out or paring down the bone.

broken a collar bone. The place was infested with fronterieures[230] & it is thought
a very dangerous undertaking. The patients dined on roast meat & plum pudding
w[h] they highly appreciated as english. D[r] F went round with Champagne after
they had had their ordinary wine. We were to have had several operations on
Xtmas Eve but D[r] Levin who is said to be a jew wished them postponed until
today & D[r] F never says him nay, so three amputations were arranged for Xtmas
Day, but only one took place, after examination it was decided to defer the
others. We dined late in the Doctors' room where we had had the operations in
the morning our Turkey & Plum Pudding been served on the operating table.

S. John's Day. We had a Xtmas Tree this even[g]. Mother did not wish for it as
we had no time to spare; however S. E. & D[r] F settled it & Willis was dispatched
to a wood of M[me] Fervet's to get one – he brought a Scotch Fir, w[h] he said was
the best he could get as the Prussians had been to the wood & helped themselves.
We began to dress the Tree at 4 & it was lighted at 6 – not much time for preparation but we did the best we could & decorated it with flowers of M[me] F's making
– it was not brilliant but the patients were very well pleased especially when they
got their presents – knives, Pipes, & Purses of Tobacco &c. The Baron, D[r] Levin
& 2 or 3 other gentlemen. Just after lighting the Tree we were horrified to find
among the spectators a man from the house opposite who had had his arm amputated on Monday – he had been brought over in mistake by the man who was sent
for a convalescent patient with one arm. D[r] F. was so annoyed that he went off at
once, however he returned after dinner quite bright. M[r] Mansfield came in the
evening & sang us some songs. D[r] F was so taken with the singing that he told M[r]
M. he might get a Piano.

H. Innocents.[231] M[r] M. has lost no time & the Piano is placed in the middle of
one of the Wards – I wish we had had it with the Tree last night. D[r] F. has taken 2
small rooms in the house of one of our laundresses close by for infectious cases.
We sent two cases of Pierexia there – one died last night & now I have just heard
of the death of the other. A woman was engaged to nurse them & Willis took
things for them so he calls it S. Clements in honor of himself – & the other S.
Catharine as I have the charge of it – I also went to S. Clements occasionally
when I could do so with safety for the other patients. We have kept a french boy
out of charity to help us but he is too idle to work & sits over the stove all day: he
does not look more than 15 & very small but he says he is 19 & is dressed as a
soldier & was taken prisoner. Yesterday Mother tried to make him sweep the yard
& not finding him a very apt pupil took the [broom] herself & swept away in
earnest until turning round she found the grand Chamberlain of all the Russias[232]
behind her looking on highly amused. D[r] F. is so well pleased with the work now,
& the cases several of w[h] he says are much more interesting than any at Sedan,

---

230 *Francs-tireurs.*
231 Feast of the holy innocents, 28 December.
232 Russia sent a number of surgeons to the Red Cross.

that he seems doubtful about returning on the 15 Jan: & the Society are willing to extend the time. Dr Webb is getting on very well at Metz. The American lady went there to offer her services but as they were declined she has gone to join her countrymen at Orleans.[233] The cold is intense – the water freezes so hard in our rooms at night that it is very difficult to break in the morning & then we have to wash with floating ice in the basin but we find a hot water bottle at night a grand thing for supplying us with water in the morning – if we spill any water on the floor it is ice in a few minutes. I tried softening my sponge by taking it to bed – at least placed it under the counterpane but it was no better. Mr Bluett bought some blankets at Metz the other day some he says are for us – hitherto we have only had rugs. Willis says he heard the report of Canon distinctly from Madame Fiervet's wood.

30. Mother is in bed with bronchitis & S. Ce with a bad throat. S E stayed at home to see after them, & Dr F. had gone to visit the invalides at 9 A M when Baron Seratrous arrived with the head of the Johuniters[234] & Baron —[235] another Johaniter with a great Star. – S M A. and I had got the place all straight with the exception of the carpets w^h had not been laid down. We sent for D^r F & the first thing he thought of were the carpets, so I had them put down at once & then he was satisfied. We have had a Lutheran minister officiating in one of the Wards for nearly an hour this afternoon – yesterday several Xtian Brothers came in with the Organist & he & Mr Mansfield played & sung. I have since heard that the gentleman who played the Piano is Professor of Music here & one of the Xtian Brothers is Organist I omitted to mention the presentation of a bouquet to D^r F on Xtmas Day by Willis & the 3 Coachmen. It was composed of evergreens & vegetables, a photograph of themselves in the centre – it had been arranged by the cook at the Station – Carrots & Turnips cut to represent Camilias & slips of Cauliflower, Brussel Sprouts &c. Lee the other Commissionaire has been sent back to England & W Laws & the other Coachmen went straight from Chalons to Brussels.

1 Jan: 1871. 'A happy new year' shouted out in french & german in spite of pain & suffering. We have had a very quiet day for Sunday & I went to Church at 8. & 2.30. however Sunday c^d hardly pass without some sort of stir & during the afternoon the Inspector came & said an Ambulance Train was going today & he hoped we would evacuate as many as possible so we sent off 10. We dined in the surgery as we did on Xtmas Day – the whole of our little party excepting Mother who is still confined to her bed. – We have now a woman to Cook as Mr Bluett insisted on having one & we get our meals more regularly – She roasted a Turkey as well as any english woman but we had Champagne instead of plum pudding & mince pies. Mr Mansfield has been playing on the piano & gave us a song by way

233 Dr T. T. Pratt and the Anglo-American ambulance in Orléans.
234 Count Konigsmarck.
235 Possibly Baron Ludwig Von Ompteda (1828–99), a senior Johanniter in France.

of dessert – the piano is now placed in the Hall. There is but one Church in Epernay but the congregations are miserable even Xtmas Day & today a poor sprinkling of worshippers – The German Soldiers we remarked as the most devout There are no Decorations for Xtmas in the Church. Not even a Créche. S. E. put up some Latin Texts on our walls. We could get no holly but mistletoe is very plentiful growing in abundance on the poplars. The Church clock has struck one. & I must begin to mend my clothes w^h are in rags & my sitting up nights is my only time for mend^g.

4 Jan: Mother is released from prison[236] & came here between 10 & 11. but S. E. has begged D^r F not to stay after the 15th as she knows Mother cannot stand it any longer & S E is most anxious to get her home. The patients are delighted to have Mother again especially her pet '20' who began – directly to show his appreiciation of his 'dear Mother' by tyranizing over her as usual – at present she is sitting behind his pillows forming a bed rest while he sits up. She generally devotes herself especially to the most unprepossessing patients. We have two Bavarian brothers such nice fellows The elder a fine tall man is wounded through the lungs & suffers very much – his little brother has only a scratch on one hand & is only allowed to stay out of consideration of his affection for his brother – he is truly grateful & does everything he can to help us, & is worth a dozen of the french boys who are supposed to be our assistants. The love of these brothers is touching – they eat out of the same Basin & plate each sharing his portion with the other. The well one watches over the other most tenderly – getting up to attend to him in the night instead of leaving it to one of us. The patients we rec^d from the Prussians have paid us dearly they brought in pierexia w^h is now spread^g· Dr F. seems to have taken a panic & says the place is unhealthy though others say there is no Hospital here to be compared to it. Dr F. has 2 patients in his house w^h I call S. Phillips out of compliment to him but it generally goes by the name of pierexia Villa – Mother spends all her time there now in charge of these patients – one is her boy '20' who has had an iron Cross sent him; but how he earned it we are not told, one of his comrades says it is for blacking his Officer's boots – It is said that the iron Cross has been sent out wholesale lately & distributed indiscriminately so the honor attached is small now. We have 2 more pierexia patients at S. Clements w^h with S. Catharine's & Ward I is under my charge.

7th Yesterday was the Epiphany but no notice was taken of it here – it is transferred to Sunday. There was a heavy fall of snow on the evening of the 5th & the following night & morn^g were intensely cold. In the afternoon it began to thaw & has been thawing ever since – it is considerably milder today. We have had some Doctors from Munich, who were passing through with an Ambulance Train, here today. Last night Madame Fiervet's little boy brought us a brioche Cake after

---

[236] I.e. illness.

dinner – he cut it up being the youngest present & after setting 2 pieces aside for the poor the rest was handed round – it is a plain light sort of Cake with a nut in it – who ever gets the nut is to be King or Queen of the Feast & invites the rest to dinner – the nut was found in the portion of the poor. Distant guns were heard again yesterday. We have a man dying who is supposed to have a ball in him but no one can find it. D^r F allowed Professor Hentach[237] to burrow into the poor man's Stomach but it was of no use. A man who was wounded at Sedan died here this week – he was moved here from Dousey a most dreadful object with the most fearful bed sores I ever saw – one leg had been amputated one arm was also wounded it had been saved but was useless – he picked up a good deal at first for he was a complete Skeleton, but at last he succumbed – nothing w^d heal the bed sores & the discharge was very great. Mr Bluett informed us today that the King of Belgium[238] has fled & the people are in a State of Anarchy. Mr Bluett says the news is quite authentic & we shall not be able to get home.

8th Dr Frank has had a letter from Col^l Lt. Linsey with orders for our return – all to leave here on 15th but Dr Webb is to remain with his Staff at Metz. It is D^r F's & S.E's doing & Mr Bluett & I are very sorry but every one else has been crying out for home. We have several empty beds – what with the pierexia panic & the thought of going away D^r F has not cared to have more patients – he sent two away to another ambulance thinking the change w^d do them good – here they had been fed on preserved chicken, port wine & other luxuries – but now they have only boiled beef & carrots & a glass of french wine each in the course of the day – they are in a room by themselves quite alone & if they want anything have to shout until the German Sister hears them through two sets of double doors.

9. Our poor man with a bullet died on Saturday night the little Russian D^r like a true Carrion Crow appeared early the next morning – the bullet was found in the man's back – the Baron demanded the bullet & D^r F let him have it much to Mr Bluett's indignation – the Baron comes & takes possession of everything immediately on the death of a patient but we have no means of ascertaining whether the poor men's relatives receive them. We left here at 8 last night hoping to get early to rest but when we reached Madame Fiervet's we found her table spread & an English woman with her two little girls waiting for us to join in a brioche entertainment. Mother who had come home very tired with a toothache & sick headache sat down & talked away as if she were quite enjoying it all – one of the little girls handed round the Cake & the nut was found in her Sister's, a little girl of about 4. We had a great variety of cakes & sweets – Coffee &

237 Professor Hueter.
238 Leopold II (1835–1909), king from 1865. Both king and country welcomed the Prussian victory. The troubles mention may refer to reports on the domestic power struggle between arch-catholic elements in the government, and the crown. However, these did not spill over into scenes of disorder until Nov. 1871. The issue revolved around the king's desire for a larger army to secure Belgium's security.

Champagne – several toasts were drank touching glasses, & last of all came Orange Salad with Syrup of Blazing rum. Madame has lived abroad since she was 7 years old, a great part of the time in Spain her husband trades there – he is a Cork Cutter – one of the little girls is strikingly pretty. Madame brought her little portable Harmonium & sung some french songs exceedingly well. We did not break up until near eleven. This afternoon there being little to do S. M A. & I went for a walk – we had not gone far before we met a Funeral 2 Coffins borne by soldiers & followed by about 50 more with the Baron, who attends all the Soldiers' Funerals & a Protestant Minister. We followed at a distance to the Cemetery. The Soldiers do not fire over the graves in War time but they presented arms – it was striking to see them uncover their heads simultaneously for the prayers. After the Service each throw a handful of earth on his comrades Coffin. We watched them at a distance from behind some Arbum Vitae.[239] The brother of the old Sedan Case came here this evening hoping to see him, but he died last week. D^r F has given the man bed & board with one of his best Cigars. Now we have blankets Dr F. has recommended our sleeping in them – so I have discarded the sheets I have been using since our arrival & find the blankets most comfortable.

10. This afternoon we heard muffled guns – the men said it was an Officer's Funeral. S M A & I had leave to go & see – we came in sight of the procession entering the Cemetery 4 white Coffins borne & accompanied by Soldiers preceded by a chorister carrying a processional Cross followed by a Priest & 2 others in Surplices – behind the Coffins came the Baron & the Lutheran Minister – the band played the Dead March on entering the Cemetery. The 2 first were Catholics & with a few words & sprinkling of holy water the Priest committed them to the earth – he then retired & the protestant buried the other with some prayers & an exhortation – I was struck by the Soldiers uncovering for the protestant Service & not for the other. Here thre is no distinction made, as at Chalons, but Catholics & protestants, french or germans are buried side by side – instead of crosses they have black sticks with no^s to mark each grave. The Cemetery is nicely planted but at present looks neglected & ill cared for. I brought home a sprig of Arbum Vitae & Rosamary. The Baron is very fond of coming to the Ambulance sniffling a piece of Rosamary – I used to think he brought it as a preservative against infection – but I expect he gathers it in the Cemetery – it is his duty to attend all the Soldiers' Funerals. I am so sleepy having sat up last night that I can hardly keep awake – I heard distant guns yesterday.

13. Yesterday – S M A. & I attended Mother's boy August's (20) Funeral. She w^d not go herself but wanted to know about his Funeral – it was just like the others with the addition of a Soldier's bearing the iron Cross on a black cushion surrounded with a green wreath. After it was over S. M A returned home & I

---

[239] Arbor-vitae; an obsolete botanical term for Thuja orientalis, a variety of cedar.

went for a walk with August Fiervet Thursday being his half holiday. He took me
up one of the vine clad hills until we reached a little wood of his Mother's where
they are in the habit of having picnics in summer. On our way we met men
women & children laden with firewood – they stopped to ask if we had heard the
canon – the reports seem to come from the neighbourhood of Paris – we had
heard it in the town before ascending the hill. The view was lovely looking down
upon Epernay & the Valley of the Marne – the hard frost made the steep road
very slippery but still the people seemed to be able to manage the descent in spite
of their heavy burdens. When we got back it was just time for eveng prayers &
benediction – it was so long since I had been to them that I availed myself of the
opportunity & once more heard my patron Saint invoked with most of the other
Saints in the Calendar – in walking home I was pursued by Madame Fiervet's
little apprentice who said that I was to go with S. E to join Mother at Mme
Dullione's – the girl had hardly finished speaking before a second messenger, a
boy in a smock-frock appeared & desired me to go to Madame D's immediately
as 'ma chére Mère' was expecting me – I sent him to Mme Fiervet's while I went
to the Ambulance in search of S. E. but c^{d} not find her so I went alone though I
was not sure of the house but by good fortune I hit on the right one & was greatly
believed to be met at the door by Madame's maid & little girl – I was ushered
upstairs at once & there I found Mother & S. Ce sitting down with the two
Madames & their children at a round table covered with Cakes & other light
refreshments – most elegant wine glasses of various shapes & sizes were put
round – It seems that Mother had been enticed by Madame to drink a cup of tea
w^{h} w^{d} not detain her more than 10 minutes. She & S Ce arrived at 4 & when I got
there at 5 they seemed to have made little progress having only drank out of one
of the 3 glasses allotted to each & as yet no tea had appeared – the first glass was
a Spanish wine the colour of brown Sherry – next came Champagne – Curaço to
wind up with but before this tea was produced a cold & washy beverage. A large
Sponge Cake was cut & the nut fell to me. Madame sang many songs accompanying herself on her little harmonium. Her Husband is a Spaniard in a large way
of business in cork. Madame took us after tea to the workrooms where we saw
cork in various stages – the parings are sold for under mattresses – we have had
several made for the Ambulance. We did not leave until just 8 o'clock. A few
days ago Madame Fiervêt had a visit from some Prussian Soldiers who went into
our bedrooms wishing to secure them for themselves; but the red Crosses on our
bags protected us & Madame gave them to understand that the rooms were
attached to an Ambulance – She is very much afraid of having soldiers quartered
on her when we leave – she has been to the Prefet but he will not promise her
exemption as the other did – of course she is very grieved about our going, as all
the french people are – one of the women who washed for the Ambulance
brought Mother a present of a hare – at the other Ambulances the washing is
done by requisition we pay for everything excepting a certain allowance of
bread, meat, wine & occasionally vegetables with which we are supplied like all

the other hospitals. The hare has been served twice – yesterday the head & shoulders were dressed & today the hind quarters extended & larded with bacon. Mother & I did not get any dinner yesterday as the sugar plum entertainment served instead but I was too hungry to sleep.

13th 11 P M – Our last night at the Ambulance – tomorrow it is to be turned over to the Russian Doctor. I feel much like part of a decayed body – the Vultures have been pecking at us these last days coming in droves to get all they can out of the Stores. Our Fourgon was sent with some to Meaux & it is to remain there – a fine stove is left for the Russian & the rest have been pretty well dispersed. Dr Levin is the greatest Cormorant – after getting enough to satisfy half a dozen less voracious men he asked Dr F to give him his penknife, a present from Lady Agnes Campbell. Mr St Aubin[240] came from Chalons & has had a large box full of things given him – he missed his Train but seems well pleased to remain & has been playing on the piano this evening. The last few days have been most unsatisfactory – having evacuated all the patients fit to go we have had very little to do & Dr F. proposed our going in turn to Rheims & he actually engaged a carriage to take some of us but Mother wd not consent. Dr Levin has presented Mother & each of the Doctors with a photograph of himself today, & begged her to give 'the Sisters his blessing' as they cd not all understand if he spoke to them himself – he told me he hoped to have the honor of seeing us tomorrow so I anticipate a formal leave taking. It is said the french *have* or are *going to* cut the lines of communication at Epinal in wh case we shall be cut off from Metz.

14th 2 A M A cold frosty morning – the clouds portend another fall of snow. We shall only leave 20 patients. we have had 120 since we came here – 12 deaths.[241] The Germans as well as the french are very sorry to lose us. The Ambulance was to have been handed over to the Russians & Prussians at 2 P M. so we were prepared – our Union Jack has been packed up but our red Cross Banner has not been taken down yet – it droops languidly – everything seems to have an air of melancholy – the day is gloomy the most foggy we have had. About 3 a German Deaconess with a troup of infermiers brought a number of french wounded – I immediately bid a hasty Adiew to the patients & cut off with Madame Fiervet. She had invited us all to dinner but the Doctors were too busy to come. She insisted on buying a fish or her dinner wd not be complete so she took me to a most out of the way Cottage & told Monseur what we required he disappeared but soon returned with 2 small Jack kicking in a handkerchief having chosen one we next proceeded to Madame D's to borrow plate & invite her to dinner – it was fixed for 6.30 & our Cook from the Ambulance was to cook it but

---

[240] Dr Duret Aubin, surgeon at Eulalie hospital, Châlons 11 Aug. 1870 – 31 Jan. 1871.

[241] Dr Frank recorded that overall 162 patients had been treated – 40 French; 62 Bavarian; 14 Saxons; 41 Prussians and 5 from Wurttemburg. The ambulance carried out thirty-one operations, including twelve amputations. Eight had died post-operation. *Report of the operations of the British National Society*, p. 122.

she did not arrive until 6 & it was past 8 before we sat down. We went to Church, packed & did what we c^d to pass the time but it was bitterly cold in our bedrooms & Mother w^d not have a fire as the wood had nearly come to an end. We had Marie our Kitchen girl to wait as Madame Fiervet has engaged her as Mother w^d not take her to England to be one of our Sisters as she wanted – she is a very nice pretty girl. At 10 I begged to be allowed to retire as I was very tired after being up the night before. The Prussians asked our Cook & Marie to remain at the Ambulance but they declined. One of the deaconesses said to Willis dear Cook do not leave us now, he had stayed to help with the patients supper as they seemed so helpless Mr Mansfield stayed until 8 or 9 & the two Prussian Deaconesses questioned him as to what we did for the patients & were quite surprised & not a little shocked to learn that we attended to all their necessities.[242] We had been told before that none of the Prussian Sisters in Epernay ever sat up or attended to the personal wants of the sick – Mr Mansfield was asked by the infermiere for the night where his room was & where he was to sleep. M^r M replied when *our* people stayed to watch the sick they sat up all night & did not sleep.

15th Sunday. 5.30. I was roused by S. E's coming into my room – I got up at 6 & went to Church. 8. Breakfast It was arranged for us to Start at 9.20 but at 8.45 Dr F. came & said it was high time we sh^d be off so we packed up our half made sandwiches & *ran* to the Station – Mother ran accompanied by Gouston a one armed French patient who had been allowed to stay on as his home is at Paris. All our old friends came to see us off, but we had to wait until 10.15. We stood about in the cold on the platform until Dr Levin arrived & took us into a room w^h had a bed made of wooden blocks with dirty blankets in a corner – however there was a fire w^h made it acceptable. Dr Levin made us a little speech in English, the first time I had heard him speak it, He said he C^d not speak English but he wished to tell us how much he felt all we had done for the sick & wounded & to thank us in the name of his country – here his feelings gave way & he turned aside to wipe his tears.[243] He had sent his carriage to take Mother to the Station – but she had run off before. Most of the authorities came to see us off the town Council sent a representative – Ruliu who kept a Resterant where the gentlemen sometimes dined brought presents of Champagne & some of his best Cognac – the Inspector – the Russian Doctor & the Colonel I forget his name, but he is a great man &

---

[242] The German sisters developed a reputation for neglecting the bodily needs of their patients, for their perceived spiritual needs. Charles Gordon, the British deputy inspector of hospitals noted that 'all medical men agreed . . . that the deaconess sister lacked that implicit obedience to her medical chief which any good nurse would be ready and willing to render'. John Hutchinson, *Champions of charity. War and the rise of the Red Cross* (Oxford, 1996), p. 128.

[243] He later wrote that 'it is difficult for one to find words sufficiently expressive of the appreciation due to the medical officers, Dr Frank and Mr Blewitt, and to the Mother and Sisters of All Saints, and to Mr Mansfield for the great care and devotion shown by all and everyone in their noble work.' *Report of the operations of the British National Society*, p. 165.

secured us a Carriage w^h we otherwise w^d not has got on account of the rush of Soldiers – We have a requisition – free pass to Theonville.[244]

Chalons 11.30. Mr St Aubin came to see us with the principal Prussian resident medical officers. We sh^d have reached Fouard[245] at 3.30 in time to catch the Train for Metz but did not get there until 5 so had to go on to Nancy for the night. It has been a most bitterly cold day – Dr F. sat opposite to me smoking. We have a bottle of water in our provision basket – the water froze & had to be broken with a knife before it w^d come out. The country is all one sheet of ice & the trees beautifully frosted. In parts I was reminded of Wales but there were no distant mountains & every here & there were patches of ground planted with vines. At 6.15 arrived at Nancy – walked to the Hotel d'Angleterre but we c^d not be taken in there, so got rooms at another Hotel but there was no place for us to dine in until the other guests had done, so we all turned out for a walk. We saw the Cathedral & Grand Square & returned about 8 found the Sal à manger still occupied but at last they turned out one by one & then we went in to a stifling atmosphere thick with smoke. We retired soon after 10 but only partly undressed as we have to be up at 4.30 so as to start at 5.30 for Metz.

16. 6 A M. Train started arrived Metz 8.15.

12.15. Sitting in a railway Carriage at Metz waiting, to be w^h[246] we ought to have been ¼ of an hour ago. The fortifications here are splendid – I wish we cd have had more time to see this interesting town. On our arrival we went to the Hotel de Metz. & found Dr Webb at breakfast. We had to wait some time before ours was served & Mother & S. E went out for quarter of an hour & made some purchases. We finished breakfast by 9.30 & D^r F went to call on Captain Blackenbury promising to return by 10.45 to take us to Dr Webb's Ambulance – Mother & S. E. went out shopping – I went with S. Ce & M A to the Cathedral & afterwards took a walk in the town alone & visited one or two Churches – We all returned to the Hotel true to our appointment, & waited an hour for D^r F, who returned with Captain B. just in time to take us to the Station – We called at the English Ambulance on our way but had only time to look into one Ward – we saw two or three Sisters of S. Vincent de Paul there – the Ambulance is in the School of the Engineers. Several German boys in Rifle Uniform were being drilled in the Quad. On our way we met Dr Lewis wearing the Uniform of the Glamorganshire Volunteers, he came with Captain B & Mr Wyman to see us off – they put us into a most comfortable 2nd Class Carriage w^h we have to ourselves with the exception of a french lady who has been most persevering in securing our company. We are now moving round Metz in view of the several Forts. The Rifle pits & tumbledown huts mark the part occupied by the Camp – The Moselle is frozen over & men & boys are dibbling for fish through holes in the ice. We

---

[244] Thionville, near the Luxembourg frontier.
[245] Frouard.
[246] 'where'.

have just passed a wall perforated with holes for Canon, also a large Hosp^l &
huts for the sick. Arrived at Theonville about 2 & were put into a fly to drive to
Luxembourgh – 5 Sisters with their luggage inside – the Doctors bundled us in
saying they w^d follow in another – & before we c^d arrange ourselves we were off
– I soon got permission to go outside & enjoyed a five hours drive with a German
Coachman very much – he drove well & the horses kept their ground wonderfully. At first it was frozen snow & then it began to rain making the ground still
more slippery. We met several carts & waggons w^h kept their own place in the
centre of the road making us turn into the sloping sides of deep snow much to our
jeopardy – two or three times I thought we must have gone over & the idea of
being thrown off the box & possibly having to travel inside as one of five with a
broken limb was not inviting. The road was dreary we drove for miles without
seeing a single house – the Churches were few & far between, but all along at
very short distances were Crosses, Crucifixes & tiny Chapels. As the light began
to fade we entered Holland & we were stopped by a Soldier who opened the
Carriage door to see if there were any contraband articles but seeing only Sisters
he was satisfied. We stopped after coming about half way for 10 minutes while
the horses eat some bread – but still no sign of the gentlemen & we had not
arranged what Hotel to go to – the driver said D^r F had told him where to drive
to. It grew darker & darker & the wind howled – I looked out for wolves as
possibly · our next enemies now we were out of the reach of the french
fronteriers.[247] I suggested to I suggested to the man that he should light his lamps
but this he thought unnecessary though he nearly ran into a timber waggon. At
last we came in sight of the lights of Luxembourgh, & the fires of the smelting
pits. The driver pulled up at an Inn the one he said Dr F. had directed him to but it
seemed such a dirty pot-house that we thought the man must have made a
mistake & so S. E. went & secured us rooms in the Hotel de Luxenbourgh; but
this was not until we had sat for more than an hour in a room with the most ordinary people eating & smoking a swathed baby lay at one end of it. We had dinner
at the Hotel de Luxembourg between 8 & 9 & just as we had finished M^r
Goulden from Sedan came in – he is a Lutheran Minister & his Sister worked
with us at Chateau Bazuille & afterwards at Balen Mr G. is now on his way to
England to get aid as he has done before.

17. Jan: Breakfasted 7.45. D^r F came in when we had finished – they had
arrived at 10 last night. I had just time to visit the Cathedral before starting by
Train at 9.30. The Fortifications of this town are wonderful. And now our warlike
scenes are over & were once more in quiet life – it seems so strange to take ones
Ticket & seat as an ordinary passenger & instead of armed soldiers bustling peasants are waiting at the different Stations for the Trains – the few soldiers one sees
are evidently holiday making. Brussels 4 P M & after spending some time over

[247] *Francs-tireurs.*

our luggage had a drive of half an hour to an Hotel near the other Station so as to be ready for an early Start tomorrow. The gentlemen are dining at the Table d'hote but Mother & the other Sisters have gone out to make some purchases. We were looked in upon at one or two places on the road but *our* baggage was untouched – One of the Doctors' boxes was opened & found to contain bones.

18 Left Brussels 6.30 A M. Ostende 9. Boat 9.30

Dover 2.45. London 6 P M.

1871.

Bibliography

Archives

All Saints Sisters of the Poor, Oxford
Bishopgate Institute Library, London
The Church of England Record Centre, London
The Family Record Centre, Islington
Hackney Archive Service: Rose Lipman Library
Lambeth Palace Library and Archives, London
Lloyd's Shipping Registry, London
Public Record Office, Kew
Royal London Hospital Archives, Whitechapel
Wellcome Institute for the History of Medicine, London
West Yorkshire Archive Service: Bradford District Archives

Books, Pamphlets, Articles

A handy guide to Bradford, Bradford, 1873.
A letter to the lord bishop of London, on confession and absolution, with special reference to the case of the Rev. Alfred Poole, London, 1858.
A library of the Fathers of the holy Catholic Church, Psalms of St. Augustine, vol. VI, Oxford, 1857.
Anson, Peter, *Call of the cloister*, revised by A. W. Campbell, SPCK, 1964.
Bennett, Alice Horlock, *Through an anglican sisterhood to Rome*, London, 1914.
Bennett, William J. E., *A farewell letter to his parishioners*, London, 1846.
Bonham, Valerie, *A joyous service*, Windsor, 1989.
Booth, Charles, *Life and labour in London, first series, vol. 5: maps of London poverty*, London, 1901.
Bossart, Louis, *L'industrie et le commerce des Congrégations en Belgique*, Brussels, 1888.
Brown, G. H., ed., *Monks roll – Lives of the fellows of the royal college of physicians of London, 1826–1925*, London, 1955.
Browne, Edward George Kirwan, *Annals of the Tractarian movement, from 1842 to 1860*, London, 1861.
Burgon, John William, *Lives of twelve good men*, 2 vols, London, 1888.
Chittenden, Fred J., ed., *The Royal Horticultural Society dictionary of gardening*, Oxford, 1951.
Clergy List.

Community of St Mary the Virgin, Wantage, *Butler of Wantage: his inheritance and legacy*, London, 1948.

Crockford's Clerical Directory.

De Sales, Francis, *The spiritual conferences*, London, 1906.

Deutschen Biographischen Index, Munich, 1986.

Dictionary of national biography, ed. L. Stephen and S. Lee, 66 vols, London, 1885–1901.

Dix, Morgan, *Harriet Starr Cannon: first mother superior of the Sisterhood of St Mary*, New York, 1896.

Doing the impossible: a short historical sketch of St Margaret's Convent, East Grinstead, 1855–1980, [1984].

[Eley, Charles], *The vicar of Brighton, Mr. Gresley, and the confessional*, Brighton, [1851].

Elwin, Father. *Thirty-nine years in Bombay city*, London, 1913.

Forbes, Archibald, *My experiences of the war between France and Germany*, London, 1871.

Forster, S., and Nagler, J., ed., *On the road to total war. The American Civil War and the German wars of unification, 1861–1871*, Cambridge, 1997.

Foster, Joseph, *Alumni Oxonienses. The members of the University of Oxford, 1715–1886*, 4 vols, Oxford, 1889.

Fry, Herbert, *The royal guide to the London charities 1883–84*, London, 1883.

Furley, John, *In peace and war. Autobiographical sketches*, London, 1905.

Gordon, Charles Alexander, *Lessons on hygiene and surgery from the Franco-Prussian war, 1870–1871*, London, 1871.

Goodman, Margaret, *Experiences of an English Sister of Mercy*, London, 1862.

Grafton, Charles, *A journey Godward*, London, 1910.

Haller, John S., *Farmcarts to Fords. A history of the military ambulance, 1790–1925*, Illinois, 1992.

Harrison, Agnes, 'The under side', *Macmillan's Magazine*, XIX (1869), pp. 331–9.

Harts annual army lists, London, 1870.

Hayden, J. Carleton, 'After the war: the mission and growth of the Episcopal Church among blacks in the South, 1865–1877', *Historical Magazine of the Protestant Episcopal Church*, LXII (1973), 403–428.

Holloway, L., ed., *Medical obituaries – American physicians biographical notices*, New York, 1981.

[Hoskins, Edgar], *The treasury of devotion*, London, 1857.

Howard, Michael, *The Franco-Prussian war. The German invasion of France, 1870–1871*, London, 1961.

Hutchinson, John, *Champions of charity. War and the rise of the Red Cross*, Oxford, 1996.

Instructions in the divine art of systematic meditation, London, [1867].

Kalendar of the English church, and ecclesiastical almanac, London, from 1867.

Kelly's London medical directory, London, 1889.

Lawless, George, *St Augustine of Hippo and his monastic rule*, Oxford, 1990.

Lewis, Harold T., *Yet with a steady beat. The African American struggle for recognition in the Episcopal Church*, Valley Forge, 1996.

Liddon, H. P., *A sister's work: preached at All Saints, Margaret Street . . . and published by the desire of the Mother and Community of All Saints*, London, 1869.

Lives of the fellows of the Royal College of Physicians of London, 1826–1925, London, 1955.

Longmate, Norman, *King cholera*, London, 1966.

Lough, A. G., *The influence of John Mason Neale*, London, 1962.

Luscombe, Edward, *The Scottish episcopal church in the twentieth century*, Edinburgh, 1996.

Mackeson, Charles, ed., *The year book of the Church*, London, 1882.

Mayhew, Peter, *All Saints. Birth and growth of a community*, Oxford, 1987.

McCormac, William, *Notes and recollections of an ambulance surgeon*, London, 1871.

Morris. E. W., *A history of the London Hospital*, London, 1910.

Mumm, S., *Stolen daughters, virgin mothers. Anglican sisterhoods in Victorian Britain*, London, 1999.

Murphy, John Nicolas, *Terra incognita, or the convents of the United Kingdom*, London, 1876.

Nisbet's medical directory, London, 1908.

Nixon, Newton H., *North London or University College Hospital: a history of the hospital*, London, 1882.

[Oakeley, F.], *Devotions commemorative of the most adorable passion of our Lord and Saviour Jesus Christ, translated from Catholic sources*, London, 1842.

Oakeley, F., *Historical notes on the Tractarian movement*, London, 1865.

Palmer, William, *A statement of circumstances connected with the proposal of resolutions at a special general meeting of the Bristol Church Union*, London, 1850.

Pearson, E., and McLaughlin, L., *Our adventures during the war of 1870–71*, London, 1871.

Perry, William Stevens, *The episcopate in America*, New York, 1895.

Phillimore, Walter G. F., *The book of church law*, 10th edn, London, 1905.

Power, D., ed., *Plarr's lives of the fellows of the royal college of surgeons of England*, 2 vols, London, 1930.

Questions on the operations of the British National Society for Aid to the Sick and Wounded in War, and replies, London, 1871.

Redhead, Richard, *Laudes Diurnae. The psalter and canticles in the morning and evening service of the Church of England*, London, 1843.

Reed, John Shelton, *Glorious battle. The cultural politics of anglo-catholicism*, London, 1996.

Report of the operations of the British National Society for Aid to the Sick and Wounded in War during the Franco-German War, 1870–1871, London, 1871.

Rooper, Henrietta P., and Rooper, Wilhelmina L., *An illustrated manual of object lessons*, London, 1883.

Rules of St. Augustine, constitutions and directory for the sisters religious of the Visitation, translated from the French version of 1835, London, 1881.

Rundle, Henry, *With the Red Cross in the Franco-Prussian war*, London, 1909.

[Sayer, Charles L.], *The House of Charity in Soho: a record of work to 1910*, London, n.d.

Select Committee of the House of Commons on conventual and monastic institutions, London, 1870.

Simon, Algernon Barrington, *A short memoir of the Rev. Thomas Chamberlain*, London, 1892.

Summers, Anne, *Angels and citizens. British women as military nurses, 1854–1914*, London, 1988.

Swain, Valentine A. J., 'The Franco-Prussian war, 1870–1871: voluntary aid for the sick and wounded', *British Medical Journal*, III (1970).

Taithe, Betrand, 'The Red Cross flag in the Franco-Prussian war: civilians, humanitarians and war in the modern age', *War, medicine and modernity*, ed. Roger Cooter, Mark Harrison and Steve Sturdy, Gloucester, 1998.

Talbott, John, *A Biographical history of medicine*, New York, 1970.

The little hours of the day, according to the kalendar of the Church of England, London, 1869.

The Medical Directory, London, 1870.

Van Bavel, T. J., *The rule of St Augustine*, London, 1984.

Venn, John, and Venn, J. A., *Alumni Cantabrigienses . . . Part II. From 1752 to 1900*, 6 vols, Cambridge, 1940–54.

Walsh, Walter, *Secret history of the Oxford movement*, London, 1898.

Warem, J. Carne, ed., *Tourist's church guide 1874*, London, 1874.

Weniger, Francis Xavier, *The perfect religious: according to the rule of St Augustine*, Dublin, 1888.

Who was Who, 1897–1915, London, 1920.

Who was Who, 1897–1915, London, 1935.

Who was Who, 1916–1928, London, 1947.

Who was Who, 1929–1940, London, 1947.

Williams, Thomas Jay, and Allan Walter Campbell, *The Park Village Sisterhood*, London, 1965.

Williams, Thomas Jay, *Priscilla Lydia Sellon*, London, 1965.

Williamson, D. G., *Bismarck and Germany, 1862–90*, London, 1998.

Wood, Emily, *The Red Cross story*, London, 1995.

Index

PUBLICATIONS

Forthcoming Publications

Suggestions for publications should be addressed to Dr Stephen Taylor, General Editor, Church of England Record Society, Department of History, University of Reading, Whiteknights, Reading RG6 2AA.